Asian American Poets

A Bio-Bibliographical Critical Sourcebook

Edited by
GUIYOU HUANG

Emmanuel S. Nelson, Advisory Editor

GREENWOOD PRESS
Westport, Connecticut • London

Library of Congress Cataloging-in-Publication Data

Asian American poets : a bio-bibliographical critical sourcebook / edited by Guiyou Huang.
   p.   cm.
  Includes bibliographical references and index.
  ISBN 0–313–31809–3 (alk. paper)
  1. American poetry—Asian American authors—Bio-bibliography—Dictionaries. 2.
American poetry—Asian American authors—Dictionaries. 3. Asian
Americans—Intellectual life—Dictionaries. 4. Asian Americans in literature—Dictionaries.
5. Poets, American—Biography—Dictionaries. I. Huang, Guiyou, 1961–
PS153.A84A826 2002
811'.509895"003—dc21
[B]   2001055629

British Library Cataloguing in Publication Data is available.

Library of Congress Catalog Card Number: 2001055629
ISBN: 0–313–31809–3

First published in 2002

Greenwood Press, 88 Post Road West, Westport, CT 06881
An imprint of Greenwood Publishing Group, Inc.
www.greenwood.com

Printed in the United States of America

The paper used in this book complies with the
Permanent Paper Standard issued by the National
Information Standards Organization (Z39.48–1984).

10 9 8 7 6 5 4 3 2 1

CONTENTS

Acknowledgments   ix

Introduction: The Makers of the Asian American Poetic Landscape   1
    Guiyou Huang

Ai (1947–)   15
    Nikolas Huot

Meena Alexander (1951–)   21
    Purvi Shah

Agha Shahid Ali (1949–2001)   31
    Purvi Shah

Himani Bannerji (1942–)   37
    Chandrima Chakraborty

Mei-Mei Berssenbrugge (1947–)   45
    Xiaoping Yen

Virginia R. Cerenio (1955–)   53
    Melinda L. de Jesús

G.S. Sharat Chandra (1938–2000)   59
    Keith Lawrence

Diana Chang (1934–)   65
    Eduardo de Almeida

Marilyn Mei Ling Chin (1955–   )   71
   Zhou Xiaojing

Eric Chock (1950–   )   83
   Rhoda J. Yen

Rienzi Crusz (1925–   )   89
   Di Gan Blackburn

Chitra Banerjee Divakaruni (1956–   )   93
   Purvi Shah

Jessica Hagedorn (1949–   )   101
   George Uba

Kimiko Hahn (1955–   )   113
   Zhou Xiaojing

Yukihide Maeshima Hartman (1939–   )   121
   Joe Kraus

Sadakichi Hartmann (1867–1944)   125
   Linda Trinh Moser

Garrett Hongo (1951–   )   133
   Roy Osamu Kamada

Lawson Fusao Inada (1938–   )   145
   Gayle K. Sato

Lonny Kaneko (1939–   )   159
   Tamiko Nimura

Myung Mi Kim (1957–   )   165
   James Kyung-Jin Lee

Juliet Sanae Kono (1943–   )   173
   Nikolas Huot

Lydia Kwa (1959–   )   179
   Gaik Cheng Khoo

Alan Chong Lau (1948–   )   185
   Brian Komei Dempster

Carolyn Lau (1946–   )   189
   Rowena Tomaneng Matsunari

Evelyn Lau (1971–   )   195
   Nikolas Huot

Lê Thi Diem Thúy (1972–   )   201
   Melinda L. de Jesús

Li-Young Lee (1957–)   205
  Wenying Xu

Shirley Geok-Lin Lim (1944–)   213
  Nina Morgan

Fatima Lim-Wilson (1961–)   219
  Bill Clem

Wing Tek Lum (1946–)   223
  Lavonne Leong

Pat Matsueda (1952–)   229
  Lavonne Leong

Janice Mirikitani (1941–)   233
  Tamiko Nimura

David Mura (1952–)   243
  Roy Osamu Kamada

Tran Thi Nga (1927–)   255
  Michele Janette

Yone Noguchi (1875–1947)   259
  Edward Marx

Uma Parameswaran (1938–)   267
  Di Gan Blackburn

Albert Saijo (1926–)   271
  Lavonne Leong

Cathy Song (1955–)   275
  Gayle K. Sato

Toyo Suyemoto (1916–)   289
  Robert Hayashi

Arthur Sze (1950–)   293
  Zhou Xiaojing

José Garcia Villa (1908–1997)   305
  Rocío G. Davis

Nanying Stella Wong (1914–)   311
  Shawn Holliday

Nellie Wong (1934–)   313
  Ernest J. Smith

Rita Wong (1968–)   319
  Gaik Cheng Khoo

Merle Woo (1941–   )   323
    Su-ching Huang

Mitsuye (May) Yamada (1923–   )   331
    Di Gan Blackburn

Lois-Ann Yamanaka (1961–   )   337
    Peter E. Morgan

John Yau (1950–   )   343
    Zhou Xiaojing

Selected Bibliography   357

Index   361

About the Editor and Contributors   371

ACKNOWLEDGMENTS

This collection of bio-critical studies owes a great deal to the thirty-two contributors, each of whom made unique contributions. I express special thanks to Dr. George Butler, Senior Editor at Greenwood Publishing, and Professor Emmanuel S. Nelson at the State University of New York College at Cortland, for their support and help in the course of preparing this volume. Mr. David Palmer, Senior Production Editor, and Mr. Charles Eberline, copyeditor, both at Greenwood, deserve kudos for their fine work on the book manuscript. Thanks also to Heather Kendall, my graduate assistant at Kutztown University, for her assistance with this project. Most important, thanks to my wife, Jennifer Y.F. Qian, for unwavering support, and my infant son George Ian, who grew with the book's progress and gives me wonderful delight that keeps me both busy and happy. As always, I alone am responsible for any flaws that may still remain in the final product.

INTRODUCTION: THE MAKERS OF THE ASIAN AMERICAN POETIC LANDSCAPE

Guiyou Huang

Even though Asian American literary writing, especially the longer narrative forms such as the novel and the autobiography, is enjoying an impressive critical popularity, its poetry has been a neglected area of study, despite the proliferation of a large number of poets of Asian descent in the twentieth century. The general lack of criticism is a silent comment on the overall cold reception the Asian American poem has experienced. Poetry as an elite genre has not reached the level of popularity of the novel or the short story partly due to the many difficulties associated with reading and interpreting texts written in verse. In the case of Asian American poetry, the emphasis on political exigencies and ethnographical concerns perhaps also impeded its popularization. As a result of the workings of such cultural and racial factors, Asian American poetry has not harvested the amount of critical attention that it truly deserves. This, on the one hand, explains the subcanonical status in which it has found itself; on the other hand, it speaks to the urgent needs of books—reference works as well as critical studies—in Asian American poetry. *Asian American Poets: A Bio-Bibliographical Critical Sourcebook* is designed to meet such needs and to call attention to an important genre of writing that reflects, perhaps more forcefully than other genres, the intense feelings and emotions that Asian Americans have experienced about themselves, their world, and the interrelations of the two.

As has been frequently debated, with limited consensus reached, the perimeters denoted by the term "Asian America(n)" have been rather unstable because of its totalizing tendency and vague labeling of many heterogeneous Asian groups. In this volume, while the term is used in the title and throughout the entries, its function transcends boundaries delimited by "American": it really means "Asian North American," referring to Asians living and working in the United States and in Canada. But as the reader will undoubtedly notice, a considerable number of Hawaiian poets are also included in this reference book. The Pacific islands, most notably Hawaii, are geographically separate from the mainland United States, and using "Asian American" to encompass Hawaii's Asians has met with resistance from Hawaiian writers. These writers are American by virtue of their nationality and citizenship, but many Hawaiian writers, both native and local, insist on their geographical, cultural, and historical differences from the mainland, which suggests that within the totalizing category "Asian America" Hawaii's Asian writers fit uneasily. Situated in this context, this introduction will look around and beneath the thematic concerns of the works and career paths of Asian American poets, as well as consider the three major components making up this volume—Asian America, Asian Canada, and Hawaii; it will conclude with a discussion of the organization and structure of the book.

This bio-bibliographical critical sourcebook consists of entries on forty-eight poets, most of whom can be conveniently, though not unproblematically, called Asian American poets. The typical Asian American writer is one who lives or has lived in the mainland United States, and whose thematic interests and subject matter are marked by mainland America's historical events and geographical entities. For example, the internment of Japanese Americans during World War II constitutes an enduring theme in the works of many Japanese American poets writing during and after the war, necessitating the use of places as irreplaceable referents to the internment experience, because these places—relocation centers or camps in the deserts of Arizona, Arkansas, Minnesota, South Dakota, Wyoming, and elsewhere—represent the most consciously perpetrated form of institutionalized racism against one group of American citizens.

To better situate the present volume, a look at the current status of Asian American poetry and the trajectory of the development of its criticism is necessary. The recently published *Resource Guide to Asian American Literature* (2001) contains twenty-five chapters, fifteen of which focus on longer narratives—prose works—and of the remaining ten, only two are devoted to discussions of poetry. In the first chapter on poetry in this MLA guide, Sunn Shelley Wong, commenting on the status of poetry, questions the structure of the book to which she was contributing: "The very structure of this resource guide, with its emphasis on prose fiction, already tells us something about the status of poetry today and about the kinds of difficulties that we might encounter in the classroom when we propose to teach it" (285). Wong does not present a survey of Asian American poetry; instead, she attempts to diagnose the problems and difficulties that readers of poetry (including Asian American poetry) often encounter. The title of Wong's chapter, "Sizing Up Asian American Poetry," suggests that even though Asian American studies has successfully made its debut, studies of poetry are still on an inchoate level. The second poetry chapter in the volume, George Uba's "Coordinates of Asian American Poetry: A Survey of the History and a Guide to Teaching," presupposes a similar situation with regard to the status of Asian American poetry and its concomitant criticism: readers and critics are still searching for guide posts in the not-yet-quite-charted terrain of Asian American poetic writing. Uba, however, while recognizing a number of Asian American poets who have established "high-profile reputations," also acknowledges the expansion of the field of poetic production due to the emergence of "the lesser known" poets (326). Wong's and Uba's critiques are among the latest efforts exploring the reading and teaching practice of Asian American poetry.

Asian American poetry took about a century to form what it is today. Yone Noguchi (1875–1947), born in Japan and working in two languages and several poetic forms, published his first collection of poetry, *Seen and Unseen*, in 1897. According to Edward Marx, the author of the entry on Noguchi in this volume, this early Asian American poet anticipated the modernist movement, yet "there has been little rush thus far to claim Noguchi as an Asian American literary ancestor." Sadakichi Hartmann, a half-Japanese, half-German disciple and friend of Walt Whitman, started to produce poems soon after meeting and working with the aging Camden poet and published his own first collection in 1898. Despite the sustained production of poetry by Asian Americans since Noguchi, little notice was taken of it until the 1960s–1970s, when poetry was used as an instrument of political rallies seeking to find voice and celebrate racial pride during the years of the civil rights movement, the audience being more listeners than readers of a racialized poetry charged with political messages. Even so, other than some brief reviews of such activist poetry, hardly any serious studies surfaced, an unsettling reflection not just on the neglected situation of a poetry but also on a numerically—and politically—negligible group of people, Asians in America. In the 1970s, the little attention that was paid to Asian American poetry appeared in prefaces or introductions to poetry anthologies. More serious, academy-based scholarship did not surface until the 1980s, when Asian American literature had put forward a few high-profile writers of fiction, drama, and poetry, though studies of Asian American poetry still remained sparse. Of the limited amount of criticism that existed, much dealt with Asian American poets as a whole, giving relatively little notice to individual poets.

In the 1980s, notably in the last years of that decade, a few articles appeared, including Shirley Geok-lin Lim's "Reconstructing Asian-American Poetry: A Case for Ethnopoetics" (1987); Gayle K. Fujita-Sato's " 'Third World' as Place and Paradigm in Cathy Song's *Picture Bride*" (1988); and Susan Schweik's "The 'Pre-poetics' of Internment: The Example of Toyo Suyemoto" (1989). In the 1990s, though studies of Asian American poetry continued to take totalizing approaches, more articles on individual writers of verse did find their way into scholarly journals and critical collections. These include Patricia Wallace's "Divided Loyalties: Literal and Literary in the Poetry of Lorna Dee Cervantes, Cathy Song, and Rita Dove" in *MELUS* (1993); Priscilla Wald's " 'Chaos Goes Uncourted': John Yau's Dis(-)orienting Poetics" in *Cohesion and Dissent in*

America (1994); and Zhou Xiaojing's "Inheritance and Invention in Li-Young Lee's Poetry" in *MELUS* (1996). On Asian American poetry as a whole, there are Balance Chow's "Asian-American Poetry: An Overview of a Pluralistic Tradition" in *Critical Survey of Poetry: English Language Series* (1992); George Uba's "Versions of Identity in Post-activist Asian American Poetry" in *Reading the Literatures of Asian America* (1992); Uba's "The Representation of Asian American Poetry in *The Heath Anthology of American Literature*" and David Mura's "The Margins at the Center, the Center at the Margins: Acknowledging the Diversity of Asian American Poetry," the last two both appearing in *Reviewing Asian America: Locating Diversity* (1995); Juliana Chang's "Reading Asian American Poetry" in *MELUS* (1996); Stan Yogi's "Yearning for the Past: The Dynamics of Memory in Sansei Internment Poetry" in *Memory and Cultural Politics: New Approaches to American Ethnic Literatures* (1996); and Zhou Xiaojing's "Breaking from Tradition: Experimental Poems by Four Contemporary Asian American Women Poets" in *Revista Canaria de Estudios Ingleses* (1998) and "Rearticulating 'Otherness': Strategies of Cultural and Linguistic Differences in Asian American Women's Poetry" in *Asian American Studies: Identities, Images, Issues Past and Present* (2000).

These titles of studies printed in various venues give the reader a fair sense of what has been done in the past two decades of criticism of Asian American poetry. Even though this is by no means an exhaustive list of scholarship in the field, not many full-length studies or articles can be found beyond this listing, except for some brief notices or reviews of new publications of poetry collections. But the way some titles are phrased—"Overview," "Sizing Up," "Coordinates," "Asian American Poetry," "Asian American Women Poets," and "Internment Poetry"—suggests how tentative and general critical efforts have been over the last two decades of the twentieth century, after decades of virtual silence. Even the best-known poets did not escape this fate. According to Gayle K. Sato in this volume, Lawson Fusao Inada, for example, who has been called "poet laureate of Asian America" and "Japanese America's poet," and whose *Before the War* (1971) is considered the first poetry collection by an Asian American published by a major press, has seen "no books and very few articles about his work." Many of this volume's contributors express similar concerns about the crippling lack of critical attention to Asian American poetry while hoping that with the current flurry of creative activities from Asian American poets (for example, the fruitful and sustained efforts made by the Bamboo Ridge group in Hawaii) and the publication of this sourcebook, studies of Asian American poetry will be reinvigorated.

This reference volume, however, is not an attempt at defining the canon of Asian American poetry; rather, it is an effort to facilitate teaching and research and to showcase major Asian American poets, their literary achievements, and their poetic interpretations of their minoritized experience. In my initial bibliographical research, I located over a hundred poets' names in reference works, anthologies, and bibliographical guides. This book covers the most read and anthologized poets from twentieth-century Asian America. Poets of high profile, including Lawson Fusao Inada, David Mura, Jessica Hagedorn, Cathy Song, Li-Young Lee, Marilyn Chin, Garrett Hongo, Janice Mirikitani, Arthur Sze, John Yau, and others, are widely recognized and easily attracted contributors who are knowledgeable about their work and are willing to write on them. On the other hand, one can only be disappointed to see that some poets, important and well anthologized as they are, were not chosen for representation in this project. Poets who I believe deserve a place in a volume like this—Fred Wah, Cyril Dabydeen, Darrell Lum, and Timothy Liu, among others—were not included here either because prospective contributors did not choose to write on them or because they did not deliver promised contributions for personal or other reasons. By the same token, I would not be surprised if someone thumbs through this book, finds included Nanying Stella Wong, who is by any measure more of a visual artist than a poet of only a few poems, and shakes his/her head wondering why she is kept in while some seemingly more significant poets are left out. When a provisional list of Asian American poets was compiled and presented to would-be contributors, who chose which poet to write on largely depended on the contributors' personal preferences, despite my conscious attempts to persuade them to consider taking up names that would hopefully further improve the coverage of the book's subjects.

Literary and critical anthologies of course involve issues of canon formation and literary authority, and many collections do seek to fulfill the role of helping to define literary canons. Take, for example, Garrett Hongo's *The Open Boat*, a poet's anthology of poetry. Sunn Shelley Wong's reading of Hongo's introduction to his anthology centers on the issue of literary authority: "who controls the formation of canons" (297). *The Norton Anthology of American Literature* (edited by Nina Baym and others) remained for a long time a definitive literature textbook that represented mostly mainstream, white American writers until the two most recent editions which include, among other minority writers, only two Asian American poets, Cathy Song and Li-Young Lee, while the *Heath Anthology* has been much more inclusive from its inception. But does the inclusion of Song and Lee suggest that these two poets are more important than their Asian American peers? Does it mean that they have been accepted by the mainstream audience that is predominantly Caucasian, both the teaching profession and the learning community in higher-education institutions? Why did the editors choose these two younger poets, both born in the late 1950s, and not members of older generations like Lawson Inada (b. 1938) or José Garcia Villa (1908–97)?

A degree of arbitrariness exists in the editorial decisions made by editors of anthologies of belletristic writing as to who should or should not be included; editors can be at once personal and political in their selection of writers. In preparing this volume, I was constantly aware of the attendant dangers of excluding certain writers, while at the same time taking comfort in knowing, and remembering, that the editor is a reader first and a critic second, and that a strictly comprehensive coverage of all poets worthy of a place in a reference like this is impossible. Anthologization of literary writers is a practice that is inevitably vulnerable to subjective manipulation by literary authority—in the form of writer-editors and critic-editors. One may wonder, for example, who knows more about the artistic and aesthetic values of a literary work, the author or the critic? Where does one place those audience members who neither write creative works nor engage in critical analyses but merely read for the sake of pleasure or even just for the sake of killing time? By the same analogy, who is more familiar with the operative functions of an automobile, the maker or the mechanic? What about those who neither make nor repair cars but only drive them? The argument here is that formation of canons may never be free of editors' personal politics and biases, though potentially it could be a more objective, less interventionist process: anyone can dismiss Shakespeare as a great poet on any plausible ground, but he remains firm in his standing in the English canon regardless of any dismissive critical gestures, because his oeuvre has stood the test of time on its merit recognized by a readership large and powerful enough to sustain that standing. However, countless numbers of writers in history have had their names buried in the impenetrably deep recesses of oblivion. In other words, a writer's work must inherently possess vital forces to pass the test of time and reach readers across generations, despite linguistic, cultural, and national boundaries.

The fact that there are critics willing to write on the so-called lesser-known poets suggests that canonization of writers through anthologies is a mutable, fluid, and fallible process. Granted, if an anthology keeps including a writer time and again, chances are that that writer will get taught—and remembered by some. Few write with the intention to be forgotten; writers thus create anthologies as a means of self-preservation and self-canonization, a way of survival, or an attempt at immortality. With ethnic writers, Asian American poets in this case, writing is both a self-preserving strategy and a medium with which to challenge and change the status quo, a way to erase racial inequality and overcome social marginalization, and a tactic to move from the periphery to the center. Nothing can be a more appropriate example to illustrate this observation than a well-known poem by Li-Young Lee, "Persimmons." Zhou Xiaojing in her "Inheritance and Invention in Li-Young Lee's Poetry" views this poem as an example of Lee's reliance on a central image "to show culturally conditioned ways of perception in his poetry" and "his cross-cultural experience in grade school" (117). Wenying Xu in her entry for this volume reads it as a reflection of the difficulties an immigrant student had to face in his childhood. Both readings are text based, and both sound valid. But if we place the poem in the discursive context of postcolonial understanding of center/periphery, ignorance/ knowledge, authority/subjugation, white/colored, teacher/student, we can read the poem as a bristling challenge to presumed authority, a political move to center what has been the marginal. There is no question that Mrs. Walker in "Persimmons" represents authority and the dominant culture, but when it comes to knowledge of ethnic matters, she willy-nilly turns into an ignoramus and an irrelevant outsider, unable to distinguish between a ripe and an unripe persimmon, yet she wields the power to punish an immigrant student for failing to tell "precision" apart from "persimmon," vocabulary the student is learning from a language that is used by Mrs. Walker as a measure of academic success and social acceptability.

The speaker's sly and naughty way of eating the ethnic fruit is intended to demonstrate that he not only understands the conceptual (although not yet the phonetic) differences between the two words, he has practical knowledge of "precision" as he applies it with utmost skill. This demonstration of knowledge—almost dramalike—asserts that knowledge can be taught in school but can also be acquired through hands-on experience; more important, the student's superior knowledge in this matter proves the teacher to be racially biased and intellectually limited. The poem's undeclared purpose seems to be to undermine the teacher's bookish knowledge and presumed, untested authority; ultimately it boils down to an analysis of authority to expose its presumptuous nature. Thus the center is decentered and authority is cast into doubt. In his cogent analysis of power relations of the Occident and the Orient, Edward Said has this to say about authority:

There is nothing mysterious or natural about authority. It is formed, irradiated, disseminated; it is instrumental, it is persuasive; it has status, it establishes canons of taste and value; it is virtually indistinguishable from certain ideas it dignifies as true, and from traditions, perceptions, and judgments it forms, transmits, reproduces. Above all, authority can, indeed must, be analyzed. (19–20)

Asian American poetry, like Lee's "Persimmons," has been written not just to express what Wordsworth calls "the spontaneous overflow of powerful feelings" (243) and emotion "recollected in tranquility" (253); it is used as an instrument by which to share authority that hitherto has been basically monopolized by descendants of the *Mayflower* and members of society with European Caucasian ancestry. *Asian American Poets*, like other references in this series—Emmanuel Nelson's *Asian American Novelists* and Guiyou Huang's *Asian American Autobiographers*—is testimony to one minority group's attempts at analyzing established literary tastes, values, and canons, and a simultaneous presentation of their own. To say that such publishing efforts challenge existing literary canons reduces the value of these works and unnecessarily muddles the debates of canon formation. On the contrary, such scholarly enterprises expand America's literary horizons and enlarge its canons while democratizing the canonizing process, and I am not just alluding to diversity or multiculturalism, but rather the enrichment of American literary and cultural traditions.

But "American" can be a problematical notion considered from a cognitive standpoint because it is a defining term in the full name of the United States of America, as well as an indispensable descriptor of the geographical landmass of North America, though the word takes no part in Canada's national name.

Why Asian Canadian writing has been thus far regarded as an uneasy component of Asian American literature at large has not been effectually explained; a possible reason may be that the linguistic, racial, and cultural boundaries between these two countries seem to be less pronounced than those between, say, the United States and Mexico, though the United States in the middle of the North American continent shares borders with both Canada and Mexico. On the other hand, Canadian Asians have produced an admirable amount of literature—poetry, drama, autobiography, and fiction—but studies do not seem to be as vigorous as those of Asian American literature in the United States. However, there are now clear indications that the designation "Asian Canadian" is gradually picking up currency on both the northern and southern sides of the U.S.-Canadian borders. It seems that increasing numbers of writers, critics, and theorists are building an "Asian Canadian literature" while others are becoming more conscious of it. For example, Uma Parameswaran in the role of a prominent Indian Canadian poet and respected literary critic has developed a well-recognized organization called South Asian Canadian Literature (SACLIT, her own coinage) that promotes writing and publication of literary works produced by South Asians, an active segment of the Asian population in Canada.

Other Asian Canadian poets included in this reference are Himani Bannerji (Indian), Rienzi Crusz (Sri Lankan), Lydia Kwa (Singaporean), Evelyn Lau (Chinese), and Rita Wong (Chinese). The thematic concerns of these poets are as protean as their personal and diasporan experiences. Crusz, for example, writes about "hyphenated identity" and alienation, though he himself feels ambivalent about critics' emphasis on the role of identity in his poetry. Rita Wong, a first-generation Chinese Canadian, has a different reception for her poetry that concerns her sex politics and sexual orientation, as do Evelyn Lau, Merle Woo (Chinese American), and Lê Thi Diem Thúy (Vietnamese American). Sex politics obviously finds expression, in different forms, in many poets gathered in this volume (another example is David Mura, the Japanese American poet who writes about "the internment of desire," echoing the internment of Japanese Americans during World War II). Canadian poets of Asian descent share similar cultural and historical backgrounds with their U.S. counterparts, though their thematic interests and prosodic methods differ in a plethora of ways, as the entries in this volume will show.

The third group of writers that takes up a considerable portion of this reference is Hawaiian poets of Asian descent. These writers—Eric Chock, Garrett Hongo, Juliet Kono, Alan Chong Lau, Wing Tek Lum, Pat Matsueda, Albert Saijo, Cathy Song, and Lois-Ann Yamanaka—are all associated with Hawaii in some way, having grown up local in Hawaii, or having lived there long enough to establish a Hawaiian identity, or having published with Hawaii's now-famous Bamboo Ridge Press and/or the *Bamboo Ridge* literary journal, both of which were founded through the pioneering work of two poets, Eric Chock and Darrell Lum. Bamboo Ridge has made it a focus to publish literature by Hawaii's local writers, as well as work written in Hawaii's Creole English, which serves as a distinguishing marker from Asian American literature produced on the mainland. "[T]he term 'local,' " argues Stephen Sumida, "used by writers of Hawai'i to describe their works and traditions and by the general populace to label a racially mixed and charged, class-conscious polyethnicity championed by some, hated by others, glides with aplomb right against some of the most empowered literary studies in America" (216). Citing examples of the use of place as history, Sumida names Eric Chock, Wing Tek Lum, and Cathy Song in poetry, Susan Nunes and Juliet Kono in fiction, and Darrell Lum in stories and dramas to point out that "these writers within Hawaii's Asian American tradition have a sensibility related to the native Hawaiian sense of place yet learned as well from their Asian American forebears, who themselves generally emigrated from villages, provinces, and families of highly localized identities" (227).

Partly due to Hawaii's geographical remoteness that creates a sense of physical separateness and cultural detachedness, partly due to Hawaii's different history from that of the mainland, partly due to the use of Pidgin in literary writing, and partly due to the island state's higher percentage of residents of color (where the limiting term "minority" is perhaps applicable to no one particular ethnic group), Asian American literature in Hawaii has fared better in its critical reception than its counterpart on the mainland. As Sumida puts it, "Hawaii's literatures and contexts can still be said to have received longer scholarly attention than any other Asian/Pacific American literature and history" (233). Such a conclusion inevitably leads one to wonder why Hawaiian Asians' writing has developed more fully than its mainland counterpart. In one way, a clearly dominant "mainstream" literature does not seem to exist in Hawaii, and in terms of demographics, ethnic Asians—Chinese, Japanese, Koreans, and Filipinos—constitute a big portion of Hawaii's population; thus there is no overshadowing or outshining this literature by a more powerful one, as is the case on the mainland.

Some Asian American writers, both mainland born and foreign born, moved to Hawaii and became identified with local writers there. Pat Matsueda, for example, was born in Japan, immigrated to Hawaii at age seven, and identified herself as Hawaiian. Albert Saijo, on the other hand, was born in Los Angeles in 1926 and moved to Hawaii as recently as 1991, publishing most of his poems through Honolulu's literary venues. Wing Tek Lum was born in Hawaii and published most of his works there as well, but he was educated in Rhode Island and New York and studied in Hong Kong, so a total identification of him as Hawaiian would be less than accurate, if not misleading. Garrett Hongo, born in Hawaii and educated in California, Michigan, and Japan, has a great deal of his writing published by mainland publishers, yet he remains linked to his Hawaiian roots and Hawaiian colleagues. This brief catalogue of Hawaii-based poets' writing careers is meant to illustrate one point: While Hawaii's Asian/Pacific literature retains a visible independent identity deeply rooted in the writers' strong sense of their place and history, as reflected in their poetry and their movements back and forth between the Pacific islands and the mainland, their thematic concerns, career paths, and professional relations all brand them with deep mainland American markers. What has been asserted through such terms as "local," "Pacific," "Hawaiian," "island," and so on registers an insistence on perceived differences from mainland writers, not a completely separate and independent literature and identity.

Besides the geopolitical complexity embodied in Asian Canadian and Hawaii's Asian/Pacific writers, poets represented in this reference are also characterized by varied racial, ethnic, national, and cultural heritages; thus *Asian American Poets* best exemplifies ethnic diversity in its coverage of poets. While most poets are Asian American in the conventional sense of the name, some resist conventionalization about their ethnic or racial heritage. Mei-Mei Berssenbrugge, Diana Chang, Kimiko Hahn, and Sadakichi Hartmann, for example, are Eurasians; John Yau has a Chinese grandfather and an English grandmother; Cathy Song is half Korean and half Chinese, to mention only a few interracial and interethnic cases. It is abundantly clear that Asian American poetry, like its sister genres, has been informed from the very beginning by the poet's personal history, racial identity, and diasporan experience, as well as by political and social issues such as interracial marriages and polyethnic and multicultural heritages. As a result of the dynamics of such cross-border factors and issues, the political/public and the personal/private elements, as well as the communal and individual aspects of Asian American lives, are all inscribed into the poetry. As interviews of poets and analyses of their poetry presented in this volume reveal, the demarcation lines between the personal and the political, if there are any, are at best blurry and easily crossable. The personal and the political are therefore like twins, usually separate but not always separable. Thus any attempt to divide the two is bound to result in disappointment from failure.

The diversity of the poets in this reference can also be seen in the breadth of its gender representation. More than half of the writers collected here are women, which mimics the gender composition of Asian American writers in general: women writers of Asian descent have outnumbered—and outshined—their male counterparts in the field of literary production. Gender and sex issues are articulated by many poets, including lesbian and bisexual poets such as Lydia Kwa, Lê Thi Diem Thúy, Merle Woo, and Rita Wong, all lesbian writers who have not shied away from these very personal and highly politicized issues. Gendered issues such as molestation and prostitution are also not taboos with some poets. Janice Mirikitani, for example, has been very vocal about her own childhood molestation by family members and friends, and as a major voice from the activist period, she has left her marks of influence on Asian American poets after her. There are also poets who write across cultures, literally and figuratively. Tran Thi Nga, for example, collaborated with Wendy Larsen in the writing of *Shallow Graves*. If self-presentation and subject matter determine who is and is not Asian American, this collaborated work problematizes such definition. Nga's stories were recorded on tape, and Larsen transformed them into narrative verse. This retouching—unavoidably a filtering process as well—may have tampered with the authenticity of the narratorial voice of the Vietnamese

American whose stories are being presented. Thus de-collaborating the two, as Uba has done in his article "Friend and Foe," not only illuminates the creative process but also enlightens the reader about two potentially differing views of the Vietnam War.

Atypical but nonetheless noteworthy is the poetic career of Arthur Sze. Understandably, many Asian American poets grow up reading in two or more languages and imbibing intellectual influences from both the mainstream culture and their inherited ethnic culture. This is not exactly true of Sze, however, who did study and translate Chinese poetry—works from his ancestral country—but has also lived with (through marriage) and among Native Americans for three decades, whose cultures have influenced both his prosody and the subject matter of his poetry. In this poet one sees a true convergence of at least three disparate cultural heritages: Chinese, American, and Native American. The conclusion to be drawn from this discussion of the diversity of ethnic representation is a familiar one: no one ethnic culture in an increasingly global, multicultural, and democratic system can remain immutable or unadulterated; the borders between cultures, races, and ethnicities are not dead set and are in fact movable and fluid, like the circulation of blood that keeps the heart beating and enables life to continue. Culture and literature need to be reinvigorated and re-formed for survival, even if survival means a transformation of the old into a new form different from its former shape; Asian American literature, like other ethnic literatures in the United States, has developed into a distinct discipline benefiting from the cross-fertilization of many cultures.

The versatility demonstrated by the poets included in this reference is another gauge of the demographical diversity in representation. David Mura, for example, well known for his collections of poetry and his prose memoir *Turning Japanese* (1991), has also exhibited talents in the dramatic arts and film productions. Jessica Hagedorn, poet, novelist, critic, performer, and editor, is even more illustrative of the versatility of talented Asian American writers. The interdisciplinary, multidimensional nature of her colorful career suggests that poetry is only one venue of personal expression, and that music, like the blues' rhythmic influence on the cadences of Langston Hughes's poetry, "contributed to the further development of her [Hagedorn's] poetry as a type of performance art" (Uba in this volume). Reading about the "less-traveled road" that Robert Frost puzzles over in his "The Road Not Taken," now taken by many American poets of Asian descent, one cannot but be reminded of the recent Oscar-winning Chinese movie *Crouching Tiger, Hidden Dragon*, which appropriates but inverts the word order of the original four-word Chinese expression *cang long wo hu* (hidden dragon crouching tiger), whose figurative meaning alludes to the ubiquitous presence of hidden talents (athletic and intellectual); one just needs to discover them. In the present reference alone, one witnesses the manifest, not hidden, talents of many devoted Asian American poets and artists.

Finally, having discussed the status and criticism of Asian American poetry, its major components, and the diversity of representation, I wish to turn to the structure and organization of this reference volume. Like the three volumes already published in this series, Nelson's *Asian American Novelists*, Huang's *Asian American Autobiographers*, Miles X. Liu's *Asian American Playwrights*, and later to come, Huang's *Asian American Short Story Writers*, each entry in *Asian American Poets* consists of four parts: (1) "Biography," (2) "Major Works and Themes," (3) "Critical Reception," and (4) "Bibliography."

"Biography," the opening section of each entry, provides the reader with a reliable account of the poet's personal life and writing career. With the exceptions of a few poets whose poetry has been widely anthologized, reviewed, and critiqued, most of the poets included are not widely known, and the lack of biographical information often causes difficulty or misunderstanding about a given poet's cultural, racial, and, occasionally, sexual identities, as has sometimes occurred in teaching, book reviews, and critical studies. The authors of the entries either conducted careful, reliable research into the lives of their poets or held personal interviews with poets who are alive and available. Obviously, major events or defining moments in a poet's life that impacted his/her writing are emphasized so as to aid in the reader's reading and understanding of the poet's work.

"Major Works and Themes" refers to major poetical works, excluding works of other genres written by the poet under discussion; though for comparison or contextualizing purposes an author may briefly touch on prose writings by the poet, the focus remains on poetry. Needless to say, some poets have authored numerous volumes of poetry, while others have produced only a few poems. The volume of a poet's production and the amount of criticism (in book reviews and critical articles and books) he/she has garnered determine the amount of space that poet is allocated in this book, which in turn affects the length of discussion of the poet's work in "Major Works and Themes." Clearly, the themes in each poet's work are defined by the author of the entry, but it is easy to see that as minority, immigrant, and marginalized writers (relative to their mainstream counterparts), the poets share many common thematic concerns: family, racism, sexism, identity, loss, language, politics, sex, and history, to name the most obvious. Many of these subject matters are not unique to Asian American writers; writers of other races and ethnicities, including the dominant group, have them as well. These are human experiences and are therefore universal, not just Asian American.

"Critical Reception" either provides a history of the reception of a poet's work or offers contextualized, new readings of the poetry alongside existing criticism and reviews. Most contributors to this volume are specialists in Asian American literature familiar with Asian American issues, and many express a shared disappointment with the generally lukewarm critical attention that has been hitherto paid to Asian American poetry: rarely has an author said that a poet has received "adequate" reception from either Asian American critics or critics at large. Indeed, a great number of authors have stated the very opposite: "scant," "inadequate," "little," and "hardly any" are qualifiers used to describe the paucity of scholarship on a particular poet. Thus many hope that the publication of this reference will create an impetus to a booming of studies of Asian American poetry. For a literature to survive, like any other art form, healthy criticism and audience (both critics and readers) are vitally important.

"Bibliography," the final section of each entry, is no less significant a component of this reference than the others. Because of the paucity of criticism and therefore a shortage of bibliographical items, any work that is available is valuable. This section is usually divided into two parts, "Works by the Poet" and "Studies of the Poet"; often the reader will find the list of "Studies of the Poet" shorter than "Works by the Poet" for reasons I have tried to explain earlier. In some cases, "Studies of the Poet" lists only a few reviews. This very lack of scholarship justifies even more forcefully the need of such a reference work. It is therefore my hope that if a poet has not received deserved attention from the critical profession, the entry on him/her in this volume will serve as a departure point for further exploration. The "Bibliography" will therefore fulfill a reproductive function.

Following the entries, toward the end of the book, I have compiled a general, selected bibliography of Asian American poetry anthologies and of major critical studies (articles and books). This general bibliography provides further sources for the reader's use in studying, teaching, and researching Asian American poets and their works. Ultimately, I hope that this reference volume will not just fill in a blank in Asian American literary studies that is long overdue, but will further promote the writing and study of poetry by talented American poets of Asian descent, old and new.

BIBLIOGRAPHY

Baym, Nina, Gen. Ed. *The Norton Anthology of American Literature*, vol. 2. 5th ed. New York: Norton, 1998.

Frost, Robert. "The Road Not Taken." *Modern Poems: A Norton Introduction*. 2nd ed. Ed. Richard Ellmann and Robert O'Clair. New York: Norton, 1989. 124–25.

Fujita-Sato, Gayle K. " 'Third World' as Place and Paradigm in Cathy Song's *Picture Bride*." *MELUS* 15.1 (1988): 49–72.

Lauter, Paul, Gen. Ed. *The Heath Anthology of American Literature*. 2nd ed. vol. 2. Lexington, MA: Heath, 1994.

Lee, Li-Young. "Persimmons." *Rose*. Rochester: BOA Editions, 1986. 17–19.

Lim, Shirley Geok-lin. "Reconstructing Asian-American Poetry: A Case for Ethnopoetics." *MELUS* 14.2 (1987): 51–63.

Said, Edward. *Orientalism*. New York: Vintage Books, 1979.

Schweik, Susan. "The 'Pre-poetics' of Internment: The Example of Toyo Suyemoto." *American Literary History* 1.1 (1989): 89–109.

Sumida, Stephen H. "Sense of Place, History, and the Concept of the 'Local' in Hawaii's Asian/Pacific American Literatures." *Reading the Literatures of Asian America*. Ed. Shirley Geok-lin Lim and Amy Ling. Philadelphia: Temple University Press, 1992. 215–37.

Uba, George. "Coordinates of Asian American Poetry: A Survey of the History and a Guide to Teaching." *A Resource Guide to Asian American Literature*. Ed. Sau-ling Cynthia Wong and Stephen H. Sumida. New York: MLA, 2001. 309–31.

———. "Friend and Foe: De-collaborating Wendy Wilder Larsen and Tran Thi Nga's *Shallow Graves*." *Journal of American Culture* 16.3 (Fall 1993): 63–70.

Wong, Sunn Shelley. "Sizing Up Asian American Poetry." *A Resource Guide to Asian American Literature*. Ed. Sau-ling Cynthia Wong and Stephen H. Sumida. New York: MLA, 2001. 285–308.

Wordsworth, William. "Preface to *Lyrical Ballads*." *Criticism: Major Statements*. 4th ed. Ed. Charles Kaplan and William Davis Anderson. Boston: Bedford/St. Martin's, 2000. 240–56.

Zhou, Xiaojing. "Inheritance and Invention in Li-Young Lee's Poetry." *MELUS* 21.1 (Spring 1996): 113–32.

AI
(1947–   )

Nikolas Huot

BIOGRAPHY

Florence Ai Ogawa was born on 21 October 1947 in Albany, Texas, of an adulterous affair between her married mother and a Japanese man she met at a bus stop. Raised in Tucson, Arizona, in a strict Catholic household, Ai, following her mother and stepfather, moved to Los Angeles in 1958. Though she stayed in Los Angeles for only three years, this brief period helped her shape her life. When she was twelve years old and attending a Catholic school, a writing assignment changed her life. Pretending to be a martyr about to be fed to the lions, Ai had to write her last letters. Her work was so good that she was asked to read it in front of the class. Although she would not start writing poetry regularly for two more years, Ai's career as a poet began in that class in Los Angeles. She left Los Angeles in 1961 and returned to Tucson to complete high school and attend college. Ai graduated from the University of Arizona in 1969 with a B.A. in English/Oriental studies. Through the poet Galway Kinnell, whom she met while she was an undergraduate and who would become a mentor and friend, Ai pursued her education at the University of California at Irvine, where she earned an M.F.A. in 1971.

Toward her senior year as an undergraduate, Ai changed her surname from Haynes (her second stepfather's name) to Anthony (her first stepfather's name) because she thought it "sounded more poetic" ("Movies" 241). In 1969, she began to adopt the pen name Ai, which means "love" in Japanese. It was only in 1973, when Ai was twenty-six, that she learned of her Japanese ancestry (her mother had kept the story behind Ai's conception a secret). Following this announcement, Ai legally took her biological father's surname and made her pen name her legal middle name; thus was named the poet Florence Ai Ogawa. The same year she learned more about her origins, Ai published her first collection of poetry, *Cruelty* (1973). Her second volume, *Killing Floor* (1979), was the 1978 Lamont Poetry Selection of the Academy of American Poets. Ai's third collection of dramatic monologues, *Sin* (1986), received the Before Columbus Foundation American Book Award in 1987. Ai followed these successful volumes with the publication of *Fate* in 1991 and *Greed* in 1993. Her sixth collection of dramatic monologues, *Vice: New and Selected Poems* (1999), earned Ai the National Book Award for Poetry in 1999. Other than awards, Ai received numerous fellowships over the years, such as the Guggenheim (1975), Bunting (1975), National Endowment for the Arts (1978), Ingram-Merrill (1983), and the St. Botolph Foundation grant (1986).

Currently a professor at Oklahoma State University at Stillwater, Ai has taught and served as visiting poet in such universities as the State University of New York at Binghamton, Wayne State University, George Mason University, Arizona State University, and the University of Colorado at Boulder. She is now preparing the publications of a memoir that deals largely with her Choctaw and Southern Cheyenne ancestors who lived in Oklahoma and of another collection of dramatic monologues.

MAJOR WORKS AND THEMES

Ai's poetry consists exclusively of dramatic monologues. This decision to concentrate on a sole form of poetry arose from Ai's first poetry teacher, who instilled in her the belief that "the first person voice was always the stronger voice to use when writing" (qtd. in Ackerson 8). Ai's dramatic monologues, however, are not vehicles for her own voice. Instead, Ai uses voices of the poor, the rich, the famous, the unknown, and the dead to talk about relationships, sex, violence, love, and death. Using an old poetic style, Ai makes it contemporary not only by the use of her topics but by the personae and the language they use. Far from being old-fashioned, Ai's monologues are hard-hitting, graphic, and violent. As one critic put it, "Imagine a Browning monologue rewritten in the terse manner of Sam Shepard and you have a good idea of what an Ai poem sounds like" (Wojahn 38).

Cruelty, Ai's first collection of short monologues, deals mostly with the plight of anonymous men and women. The lives portrayed in these poems are of those who have no illusions about life and no ways of escaping the many cruelties that befall them. Whether the persona is detached or not from the cruel and depressive weight of life that falls on him or her, disillusion and frustration are found in every poem. In this collection, Ai uses such different voices as an unfulfilled wife ("Why Can't I Leave You?"), a killer ("The Hitchhiker"), a desolate man who must lie to his dying wife ("The Tenant Farmer"), an old prostitute ("Tired Old Whore"), a mother who mercilessly beats her daughter

("Child Beater"), and a disillusioned midwife who wishes a freeing death to a woman ("The Country Midwife: A Day"). Through the desperation and disillusion of these personae, Ai explores relationships between men and women. In her monologues, Ai puts two individuals together in a desperate situation and, without judging or apologizing, discloses the inner thoughts of one character. As her personae are unlikely to lie to themselves, Ai presents the readers with the ugly facts in an unadulterated manner. Whether she is dealing with abortion, child abuse, rape, or domestic abuse, Ai remains unbiased and unburdened with social norms.

If *Cruelty* presents the lives of anonymous people, Ai introduces famous and infamous personae in her second collection, *Killing Floor*. Thus the reader can read the thoughts of such historical figures as Leon Trotsky, Marilyn Monroe, Ira Hayes, Yukio Mishima, and Emiliano Zapata. Using mostly male voices in *Killing Floor* (*Cruelty* used female voices for the most part), Ai examines the same themes as in her previous work but takes on a different approach. Instead of showing her personae as devoid of hope and illusions, Ai portrays them as survivors, as people who learn to adapt to life's cruelties and look past the false hopes. In *Killing Floor*, Ai's personae are able to perceive the pitfalls of their environments and to conceive survival techniques to deal with their treacherous surroundings. Even when they are faced with imminent death, Ai's characters, like Trotsky and Zapata, retain their visions and their fighting spirits. By using known historical characters as her voices, Ai also manages to move the private struggles into a public arena and, in a way, criticizes "a social order which has become somehow anesthetized to human agony" (Forché, qtd. in Field 15).

As the title suggests, *Sin*, Ai's third book of monologues, deals with immoral behavior. For the most part, her characters, known or not, desperately yearn for power; this quest, however, leaves them corrupted and, too often, in a state of "physical and psychological crisis" (Wojahn 38). Whether Ai uses the voice of the Kennedy brothers, of Joseph McCarthy, of the Atlanta child murderer, of a priest, or of an American journalist in her monologues, her characters invariably "offer a kind of stammering, desperate testimony, last-ditch efforts at self-justification before acknowledging their damnation" (Wojahn 38). Most memorable in this collection are "The Priest's Confession," which deals with a clergyman's unrestrained desire for a sixteen-year-old, and "The Journalist," which takes the persona back to the time he took a picture of a self-immolating nun to whom he supplied the necessary matches.

In her following volumes of poetry, Ai relies more and more on her famous personae to explore moral corruption. *Fate* and *Greed* continue to expose the degradation and the vices of the American society. The themes predominantly discussed in the two books are sex, politics, religion, greed (for money, power, and sex), and how people pursue these things with a debasing obsession. In *Fate* and *Greed*, Ai uses the inner voices of Mary Jo Kopechne, J. Edgar Hoover, Jack Ruby, James Dean, Elvis Presley, Alfred Hitchcock, Jimmy Hoffa, and the Virgin Mary, to name but a few. Far from rewriting an accurate history of these people, which Ai does not attempt to do, Ai prefers to write "fictionalized versions of people's lives" (Erb 30): "I always try to be true to character, that's the thing about me. Whatever character, I set up what I like to think are keys to the character at the beginning of the poem, and then I proceed to go back and enlarge, throughout the poem. . . . So I like to think that as long as I'm true to my vision of the character, it's all right" (qtd. in Erb 30). Be that as it may, Ai's monologues expose more the American psyche than the historical figures' states of mind.

In *Vice: New and Selected Poems*, Ai includes eighteen new monologues and fifty-eight previously published in her other collections. Of the eighteen new monologues, the vast majority are taken directly from headlines: "I am . . . getting stuff out of the media and . . . trying to understand what's happening" (qtd. in Erb 29). Ai writes of the police officer who committed suicide four days before receiving a medal of honor for rescuing people after the Oklahoma City bombing ("The Antihero"), of the women caught in a civil war who are raped and murdered ("Rwanda"), of President Clinton's affair ("Blood in the Water"), of a comatose patient raped by an aide ("Sleeping Beauty"), and of JonBenet Ramsey's murder ("False Witness"). In these monologues, Ai zeroes in on the American consciousness and, as in all her previous books, does not worry about social proprieties; after all, as she exposes in her poetry, these conventions and "values" are mainly responsible for the deplorable state of society.

CRITICAL RECEPTION

Despite the many awards Ai has received for her poetry, Ai's monologues have not always been well received by critics. Upon the publication of *Cruelty*, many critics found her choice of subjects appalling, not to mention being too explicit, violent, and pornographic. Some, however, managed to see her poetry beyond the violence and the sex. Eugene Redmond, for example, perceived Ai's poetry as a reflection of the poet's intelligence and her ability in making the reader aware of societal problems. Although deploring her lack of variety and "corny tacked-on endings," Redmond asserts that "the accolades and superlatives attending publication of Ai's poetry are deserved" (167).

Since the publication of her first volume of poetry, however, criticisms have been kinder and often overshadowed by the praises. After *Sin* was published, some critics saw the longer poems as weaker than the short ones, blaming Ai's seeming inability at "keeping the intensity going after two or three pages" (Field 15). Ai has also been accused of using sensationalism to convey her points and criticized for how her "elliptical, expressionistic presentation never allows the [historical figures] to become anything but cartoons" (Wojahn 38). Wojahn believes that Ai is most effective as a poet when she "chooses speakers not based so directly on actual public figures" (38).

For the most part, however, most critics seem to agree that Ai's strengths lie in her ability to "render [the] male experiences as realistically as she does the female ones," in her expertise at "startl[ing] the mind and terrify[ing] the soul," in her "richness of detail and [her] narrative complexity," and in her mastery of the dramatic monologue form (Field 13; "Movies" 240; Wojahn 38). If some critics are uncomfortable with her unadulterated approaches to some controversial issues, none can dismiss Ai and her poetry.

BIBLIOGRAPHY

Works by Ai

Poetry

Cruelty. Boston: Houghton Mifflin, 1973.
Killing Floor. Boston: Houghton Mifflin, 1979.
Sin. Boston: Houghton Mifflin, 1986.
Cruelty/Killing Floor. New York: Thunder's Mouth Press, 1987.
"Interview with a Policeman." *Poetry* (October–November 1987): 2–4.
Fate: New Poems. Boston: Houghton Mifflin, 1991.
Greed. New York: Norton, 1993.
Vice: New and Selected Poems. New York: Norton, 1999.

Essays

"On Being ½ Japanese, ⅛ Choctaw, ¼ Black, and 1/16 Irish." *Ms.* 6 (June 1974): 58.
"Movies, Mom, Poetry, Sex, and Death: A Self-Interview." *Onthebus* 3–4.2–1 (1991): 240–48.

Short Story

"Smoking Gun" (excerpt). *Callaloo* 17.2 (Summer 1994): 405–6.

Studies of Ai

Ackerson, Duane. "Ai." *Contemporary Women Poets*. Ed. Pamela L. Shelton. Detroit: St. James Press, 1998. 8–9.
Becker, Robin. "The Personal Is Political Is Postmodern." *American Poetry Review* 23.6 (November/December 1994): 23–26.
Dooley, Dale A. "Ai." *American Women Writers*. Vol. 5. Ed. Carol Hurd Green and Mary Grimley Mason. New York: Continuum, 1994. 7–9.
Erb, Lisa. "An Interview with Ai: Dancing with the Madness." *Mānoa: A Pacific Journal of International Writing* 2.2 (Fall 1990): 22–40.
Field, C. Renee. "Ai." *Dictionary of Literary Biography*. Vol. 120. Detroit: Gale, 1992. 10–17.
Forché, Carolyn. Foreword. *Cruelty/Killing Floor*. New York: Thunder's Mouth Press, 1987.
Ingram, Claudia. "Writing the Crises: The Deployment of Abjection in Ai's Dramatic Monologues." *Lit: Literature Interpretation Theory* 8.2 (October 1997): 173–91.

Kilcup, Karen L. "Dialogues of the Self: Toward a Theory of (Re)Reading Ai." *Journal of Gender Studies* 7.1 (1998): 5–20.

Leavitt, Michele. "Ai's 'Go.' " *Explicator* 54.2 (Winter 1996): 126–27.

Lee, A. Robert. "Ai." *The Oxford Companion to African American Literature.* Ed. William L. Andrews, Frances Smith Foster, and Trudier Harris. New York: Oxford University Press, 1997. 10.

Moore, Lenard D. Rev. of *Vice. Black Issues Book Review* 2.2 (March/April 2000): 44–45.

Redmond, Eugene. "Five Black Poets: History, Consciousness, Love, and Harshness." *Parnassus: Poetry in Review* 3.2 (1975): 153–72.

Wilson, Rob. "The Will to Transcendence in Contemporary American Poet Ai." *Canadian Review of American Studies* 17.4 (1986): 437–48.

Wojahn, David. "Monologues in Three Tones." Rev. of *Sin. New York Times* 8 June 1986, final ed., sec. 7: 38.

MEENA ALEXANDER
(1951–   )

Purvi Shah

BIOGRAPHY

Born in Allahabad, India, on 17 February 1951, Mary Elizabeth Alexander at the age of fifteen took Meena as her name, a measure that demonstrates the prominence of language and identity in her life and writing. "In an act of defiance against the lingering vestiges of British imperialism, she changed her name to Meena. And it was under the name Meena that she published her first poems," remarks Jeffrey R. Young in "Creating a Life through Literature" (B8). Alexander's poetry of "multiple migrations" reflects the various travels she has made away from her ancestral homes in Kerala, India: to Sudan as a child, to England for graduate study, and to America after marriage (Nair 71).

The first five years of Alexander's life were spent between her grandparents' homes in Kerala. Alexander first crossed the Indian Ocean when her father's job shifted to Khartoum, Sudan. While Alexander still returned to Kerala with her mother and sisters in the summers, it was in Sudan that she began her first experiments with poetry: "In Khartoum, I hid behind the house under a neem tree or by a cool wall. Sometimes I forced myself into the only room where I could close the door, the toilet. I gradually learnt that the toilet was safer, no one would thrust the door open on me" (*The Shock of Arrival* 10). Like other authors who find solace through language, Alexander turned to writing for strength, catharsis, and alternate possibilities.

Alexander learned "to write in snatches," connecting literary efforts with illicit behavior, language with shame, viewing writing as an escape from the conflicts of being female (*The Shock of Arrival* 10). Hema Nair, in "The Poetry of Multiple Migrations," records a conversation with Alexander, stating, "Alexander began writing poetry at age ten. 'I found that I could escape to another world through words,' she remembers. 'Writing freed me from the constraints that would otherwise bind me' " (71). After Alexander showed her early pieces to friends, one of them translated her poems into Arabic for a Khartoum newspaper, constituting—at the age of fifteen—Alexander's first poetry publication. Erika Duncan notes an exchange she had with Alexander: " 'It made a lot of sense to me that my first poems were published in a language that I couldn't read,' Meena says, keeping up somehow the sense of safer invisibility" (26).

Not only did Alexander begin writing at a young age, but she also entered early into scholarly pursuits. At thirteen, she enrolled in the University of Khartoum, beginning graduate studies five years later at the University of Nottingham in England. Alexander's first publication in the field of literary criticism, *The Poetic Self: Towards a Phenomenology of Romanticism* (1979), furthered her doctoral work on conceptions of truth and the self and the body's place in romantic poetry. During her Ph.D. course, immersed in British romantic writing, Alexander began to feel acutely the distress and dislocation of her position as a postcolonial subject, the incongruity of her life and background with the materials she was studying—sensations she would later weave into her work.

Returning to India in 1974, Alexander taught English at various Indian universities, including the University of Delhi and the University of Hyderabad. After marrying an American she met in India, Alexander moved to the United States, where she continues to write and teach. Currently Alexander is a professor of English and women's studies at Hunter College and the Graduate Center at the City University of New York and also serves as a poetry lecturer in Columbia University's Writing Program.

MAJOR WORKS AND THEMES

The title of Alexander's memoir *Fault Lines* offers insight into one of the writer's main preoccupations: self-creation and identity formation in the context of migration. "I have in me these worlds that need to be brought together— very crudely, India and America—and sometimes I feel that I keep treading the edge of the fault line in between," states Alexander in *Yellow Light: The Flowering of Asian American Arts* ("Meena Alexander" 84). This central metaphor of Alexander's work—fault line—draws upon her history of travel in order to showcase the connection between movement and identity. The term highlights the difficulty of maintaining a cohesive self that does not betray the fragile ties of identity and place.

The various terrains Alexander has shifted resonate through her writing, allowing her poems to explore the position of the immigrant, postcolonial, or marginalized subject. "Hotel Alexandria," for example, engages the story of a New York City building's renovation not only to display the forced dispersal of former residents, but also to evoke Alexander's own dislocation and sense of exile. As Ketu Katrak writes, "Her poetic voice seeks an accountability to a history of migration and dislocation as it affects so many ordinary people" ("South Asian American Literature" 206). In "Hotel Alexandria," Alexander combines views of North America with memories of North Africa, juxtaposing the sundry places in which she herself has lived in order to chart a "geography of displacement" that extends to others she observes (Ali and Rasiah 72).

Alexander sees "Hotel Alexandria" as her "first American poem," if not in fact, at least "in spirit" (*The Shock of Arrival* 28). The multitudes of New York City afford Alexander a convergence of ethnicities and traditions where one feels "Manhattan's mixed rivers rising," as she writes in "Art of Pariahs," a poem from the 1996 collection *River and Bridge* (*The Shock of Arrival* 8). New York City, with its cosmopolitan landscape, gives Alexander a location from which to examine the relationship of place to a wide variety of people and cultures. "It is here that I must make up memory, a memory co-equal to the tensions of a city filled with immigrants," she writes. "The scents, the stench of migrancy is everywhere in Manhattan" (*The Shock of Arrival* 137). The urban composition of New York City facilitates Alexander's goal of weaving together the varied experiences of migration and marginalization in order to provide alternative histories.

In Alexander's poetry, belonging and home are created through the excavation and recomposition of the past. In "Migrant Music," the speaker extols "the past: a stringed instrument I must play, inventing what I need" (*The Shock of Arrival* 126). Poems such as "Migrant Music" reflect the poet's desire to investigate how to piece together history. While the image of the fault line showcases the fissures experienced through migration, the framework of music offers a way to conceptualize how to orchestrate life's different fragments.

As a writer, Alexander converts language into her music. In her essay "Piecemeal Shelters," she comments, "The act of writing, it seems to me, makes up a shelter, allows space to what would otherwise be hidden, crossed out, mutilated" (*The Shock of Arrival* 3). Poetry serves as a form for voicing what has been left out of the annals of history, providing Alexander with a chance to place the self in a larger social, national, or historical context. In her migrant narrative, language offers a home.

Language is tied not only to place and memory but also to the body. Alexander herself remarks on the importance of the body to her work, noting in the essay "Language and Shame," "Yet it is only as my body enters into, coasts through, lives in language that I can make sense" (*The Shock of Arrival* 10). The poem "Alphabets of Flesh," part of *Night-Scene, the Garden*, a dramatic poetry piece, puts into play Alexander's sentiment. The speaker appeals to the ferocious alphabets of flesh to "splinter and raze my page" so that she may claim her heritage (*The Shock of Arrival* 15). "Alphabets of Flesh" binds language to the body, suggesting that violent language may yet result in constructing home and tradition. As seen in the title of the poem, the building blocks of belonging come through the body, the flesh that has witnessed pain and dislocation. As Katrak observes, "Often in Alexander's poems, the continuity of history is through the line of the female body, as though memory were ensconced in the cells, muscles, bones" ("South Asian American Literature" 207). For Alexander, language offers a place to record tales told by the body.

Yet language itself is a vexing instrument. Writing in English as a postcolonial immigrant raises complicated questions of power, belonging, and allegiance. Referring to her own use of English as a literary language, Alexander writes, "The process of tearing away, of stripping the language of its canonical burden, of its colonial consolations—by which I also mean the haunting elegiac mask of the Wordsworthian paradigm—is hard indeed. And there were years when I felt I need not dirty my hands with the task of facing up to the violence implicit in the very language I used: English" (*The Shock of Arrival* 4). Alexander speaks of the burdens of using a language brought by colonizers and of transmitting the values, thoughts, and power structures as part of the canon of English literature. In her first novel, *Nampally Road*, published in 1991, the main character, Mira Kannadical, teaches William Wordsworth's poetry only to realize that the ideas do not relate to the social unrest and society present outside the Indian classroom. Mira's plight symbolizes the ruptures in identity implied in the history of British imperialism in India.

Alexander claims a changed English as a force against the perpetuation of imperial power. In her writing, she marks mutated rhythms, the inflections of different histories. She states, "I have never learnt to read or write in Malayalam and turned into a truly postcolonial creature, who had to live in English, though a special sort of English, I must say, for the version of the language I am comfortable with bends and sways to the shores of other territories, other tongues" (*The Shock of Arrival* 11). In her work, Alexander feels the undercurrents of the many languages by which she has been surrounded: Malayalam, Hindi, Arabic, French, and English.

A second way in which Alexander charts a changed tradition of writing in English is by linking various experiences of marginality, and particularly through tying the postcolonial position to women's experiences. Her second project of literary criticism, the 1989 *Women in Romanticism: Mary Wollstonecraft, Dorothy Wordsworth, and Mary Shelley*, grew out of her desire to examine the lesser-heard voices of women writers around the romantic era. In contrast to her previous doctoral work on the self and romantic writing, the experience of "reading and writing about these three women . . . brought me closer to home," says Alexander in the introduction to the text (ix). As she comments on her poem "Her Mother's Words," "It is woman as prisoner of her sex that touched me, a difficult awareness that once led me to a study of Mary Wollstonecraft, writer, revolutionary, radical feminist" (*The Shock of Arrival* 67). Despite recognizing the distinctions made through race and other categories, Alexander links postcolonial and women's writings through the shared experience of marginality. Her critical efforts regarding other female writers have also bled into her own poetry: lines from Dorothy Wordsworth's journal appear in a couple of the pieces from *House of a Thousand Doors*. Alexander attempts to establish another tradition of literary history, making her poetic production a critical, as well as creative, enterprise.

For women, writing allows for new sight—a claim Alexander makes in the early poem "Her Mother's Words," published in her second book, the 1977 *I Root My Name*. Though the speaker of the poem begins by questioning how one can write without a light, she is surprised to see that the street "had such a vision of my woman's soul" (*The Shock of Arrival* 67). The concluding stanza offers the firm response of knowledge through language (*The Shock of Arrival* 67). Through the figure of the mother and the image of the street, Alexander suggests a continuity of knowledge taken from ancestors and the world outside. In light of her use of such images and ideas, Alexander's critical and poetic work fits into the feminist project to establish new traditions and contexts for women writers.

While Alexander claims poetry as her root, her work branches into a variety of fields: she attempts to deal with the "disparate materials" of life and migrancy by writing across genres. Though she started as a poet, she has also published newspaper pieces, essays, criticism, novels, and a memoir. Alexander works across literary modes in order to reflect a variety of experiences, particularly the dislocation and relocation felt through migration. Describing her utilization of multiple forms, Alexander says,

I think of myself as most like a landscape I'm making a palette out of, layering. A palimpsest of self . . . that's how I reach time and the density of experience. I remember how as children we also used to have to shift our clothing when we went from Europe to Sudan to India. I'm used to these changes in the garb. And it's a kind of freedom for me to be able to do that. I would feel terrible if somebody said write only this or only that. Yet I basically think of myself as a poet. (Ali and Rasiah 71)

Writing in different genres enables Alexander to dispute the presence of a cohesive singular experience or identity. Her use of a variety of literary styles aligns with the concept of a fragmented, multistranded self, or, as Ian Gregson explains, "In mainstream poetry, however, there has been a tendency not so much to resist self-reflexive fictiveness as to incorporate it and deploy it as a technique alongside others. The stylistic 'mélange' I referred to, though, is not mere eclecticism—it reflects a genuine concern to oppose single-minded visions of experience with a self-conscious emphasis on diversity and mutability" (5). Though Gregson's discussion focuses on contemporary British poetry, his commentary is particularly apt for understanding Alexander's work since poetry serves as a critical venture for writers who want to "draw attention to their class, gender, nationality or race" (5). By adopting varying literary modes, Alexander explores differing facets of experiences and reaches a range of audiences.

Nonetheless, her experiments with genre are more than an attempt to navigate the American multicultural context. From the outset of her writing career, Al-

exander has been concerned with formal issues in a way that links politics and
creative craft. Her first book, *The Bird's Bright Ring*, published in 1976, demonstrates an attention to experimentation with form: the text is a long poem that
includes elements of prose narrative as well as lyric repetition. *The Bird's Bright
Ring* displays an ambitious attempt to explore the ways in which different forms
can convey alternative views of social, historical, and personal matters. Her
subsequent poetic projects play with form by incorporating prose, narrative, and
dramatic elements: not only has she written a number of prose poems, but pieces
such as *The Storm: A Poem in Five Parts* have been performed on stage. Against
a lyric backdrop, Alexander's writing presents a play of forms.

CRITICAL RECEPTION

As with her ubiquitous presence across literary genres, Alexander is seen not
only within Asian American writing, but also in postcolonial, feminist, women-
of-color, immigrant, and Indian literary contexts. Alexander states that she sees
herself "in many traditions," a versatility that has facilitated the broad dispersal
of her work ("Meena Alexander" 84). Her poems and fiction have appeared in
numerous anthologies, and her critical skills have also been utilized to write
introductions to various collections. Her entry into literary and educational institutions can be seen from the use of an excerpt from her memoir *Fault Lines*
on the Advanced Placement English examination given to assess the college
standing of high school students. As a writer invested in minority experiences,
Alexander has benefited from the current academic and popular interest in ethnicity and identity formation.

Though Alexander's novels have received uneven reviews, her poetry rou-
tinely garners acclaim. "Hers is certainly one of the finest poetic voices among
South Asian American poets," remarks literary critic Katrak ("South Asian
American Literature" 206). In an article for the mainstream feminist magazine
Ms., Nair comments on Alexander's agile use of language. She suggests, "Alexander's writing is imbued with a poetic grace shot through with an inner
violence, like a shimmering piece of two-toned silk" (71). In Nair's description,
Alexander's poems reflect a lyrical beauty alongside renditions of the coarse
brutality of migration, a style that allows for multiple perspectives and points
of appreciation.

While Nair comments on the prominent questions of identity in Alexander's
work, Bruce King marks the importance of two related issues: locale and memory. In his study of Indian poetry in English, King describes the way in which
Alexander (alongside other Indian poets) presents a poetry that demands a new
critical lens: "Such a criticism became necessary when [Jayanta] Mahapatra in
particular, but also such other Indian poets as Alexander, began writing a new,
puzzling, obscure kind of poetry, filled with private symbols, concerned with
other kinds of feelings than those usually felt in social situations. In this poetry
landscape often figures prominently as the poet is concerned with the problem-

atic or fragile nature of the self and its relationship to external reality" (*Modern Indian Poetry* 89). These motifs of landscape, self, and reality not only served as the core terms of Alexander's dissertation work, but also become manifest in her own creative writing. While ontological and physical questions have long engaged writers, Alexander presents a series of contemporary responses from the perspectives of immigrant, feminist, and postcolonial subjects.

The emphasis King places on perception and reflection is also seen in the critical tone of Alexander's projects. In *The Shock of Arrival*, a selected collection of her writings, she not only organizes and reproduces previously published material but also contributes context, commentary, and notes. In this anthology, Alexander provides her own critical annotation and assembly of her work. Her extrapoetic efforts exhibit an attention not only to product, but also process, a concern simultaneously reflected in Alexander's poetry: King adds that Alexander's method of writing draws on an understanding of the poem "as a construction which in its open structure reflects or is part of the act of making poetry" (*Modern Indian Poetry* 90).

BIBLIOGRAPHY

Works by Meena Alexander

Poetry

The Bird's Bright Ring. Calcutta: Writers Workshop, 1976.
I Root My Name. Calcutta: United Writers, 1977.
In the Middle Earth. New Delhi: Enact, 1977.
Without Place. Calcutta: Writers Workshop, 1978.
Stone Roots. New Delhi: Arnold-Heinemann, 1980.
House of a Thousand Doors. Washington, DC: Three Continents Press, 1988.
The Storm: A Poem in Five Parts. New York: Red Dust Press, 1989.
Night-Scene, the Garden. New York: Red Dust Press, 1992.
River and Bridge. Toronto: TSAR, 1996.
Illiterate Heart. Evanston, IL: Triquarterly, 2002.

Criticism

The Poetic Self: Towards a Phenomenology of Romanticism. New Delhi: Arnold-Heinemann, 1979.
Women in Romanticism: Mary Wollstonecraft, Dorothy Wordsworth, and Mary Shelley. Savage, MD: Barnes & Noble Books, 1989.

Novels

Nampally Road. San Francisco: Mercury House, 1991.
Manhattan Music. San Francisco: Mercury House, 1997.

Memoir and Collection

Fault Lines. New York: Feminist Press, 1993.
The Shock of Arrival: Reflections on Postcolonial Experience. Boston: South End Press, 1996.

Studies of Meena Alexander

Ali, Zainab, and Dharini Rasiah. "Interview with Meena Alexander." *Words Matter: Conversations with Asian American Writers*. Ed. King-Kok Cheung. Honolulu: University of Hawai'i Press, 2000. 69–91.

Assisi, Francis. "Humane Feminism Incites Poet Meena Alexander." *India West* 15 February 1991: 1, 44.

Bahri, Deepika, and Mary Vasudeva. "Observing Ourselves among Others: Interview with Meena Alexander." *Between the Lines: South Asians and Postcoloniality*. Ed. Deepika Bahri and Mary Vasudeva. Philadelphia: Temple University Press, 1996. 35–53.

Davé, Shilpa. "The Doors to Home and History: Post-colonial Identities in Meena Alexander and Bharati Mukherjee." *Amerasia Journal* 19.3 (1993): 103–13.

Desai, Anita. "Women Well Set Free." *New York Review of Books* 16 January 1992: 42–45.

Divakaruni, Chitra. "Living in a Pregnant Time: Meena Alexander Discusses Feminism, Literature, Decolonization." *India Currents* May 1991: 19, 58.

Duncan, Erika. "A Portrait of Meena Alexander." *World Literature Today* 73.1 (Winter 1999): 23–28.

Gregson, Ian. *Contemporary Poetry and Postmodernism: Dialogue and Estrangement*. New York: St. Martin's Press, 1996.

Grewal, Inderpal. "Reading and Writing the South Asian Diaspora: Feminism and Nationalism in North America." *Our Feet Walk the Sky: Women of the South Asian Diaspora*. Ed. Women of South Asian Descent Collective. San Francisco: Aunt Lute, 1993. 226–36.

Katrak, Ketu H. "South Asian American Literature." *An Interethnic Companion to Asian American Literature*. Ed. King-Kok Cheung. New York: Cambridge University Press, 1997. 192–218.

———. "South Asian American Writers: Geography and Memory." *Amerasia Journal* 22.3 (1996): 121–38.

King, Bruce. *Modern Indian Poetry in English*. Oxford: Oxford University Press, 1987.

———. Rev. of *House of a Thousand Doors*. *World Literature Written in English* 28.2 (1988): 379–80.

"Meena Alexander: Poet, Novelist, and Memoirist." *Yellow Light: The Flowering of Asian American Arts*. Ed. Amy Ling. Philadelphia: Temple University Press, 1999. 83–91.

Moka-Dias, Brunda. "Meena Alexander." *Asian American Novelists: A Bio-Bibliographical Critical Sourcebook*. Ed. Emmanuel S. Nelson. Westport, CT: Greenwood Press, 2000. 1–7.

Nair, Hema N. "The Poetry of Multiple Migrations." *Ms.* January–February 1994: 71.

Natarajan, Nalini. Rev. of *Fault Lines: A Memoir*. *MELUS* 20 (Spring 1995): 143–45.

Perry, John Oliver. "Contemporary Indian Poetry in English." *World Literature Today* 68.2 (Spring 1994): 261–71.

———. "Exiled by a Woman's Body: Substantial Phenomena in the Poetry of Meena Alexander." *Journal of South Asian Literature* 12 (Winter/Spring 1986): 1–10.

———. Rev. of *River and Bridge*. *World Literature Today* 71.4 (Autumn 1997): 867–68.

Poddar, Prem, and Magdalena Zaborowska. "Migrant 'Markings of Sense and Circumstance.' " *Journal of American Ethnic History* 18.4 (Summer 1999): 176–82.

Ramraj, Rudy S. "Meena Alexander." *Asian American Autobiographers: A Bio-Bibliographical Critical Sourcebook*. Ed. Guiyou Huang. Westport, CT: Greenwood Press, 2001. 17–26.

Rao, Susheela. Rev. of *Fault Lines: A Memoir*. *World Literature Today* 68.4 (Autumn 1994): 883.

Rustomji-Kerns, Roshni. "In a Field of Dreams: Conversations with Meena Alexander." *Weber Studies* 15.1 (Winter 1998): 18–27.

Sen, Sudeep. "New Indian Poetry: The 1990s Perspective." *World Literature Today* 68.2 (Spring 1994): 272–78.

Tharu, Susie. "A Conversation with Meena Alexander." *Chandrabhaga: A Magazine of World Writing* 7 (Summer 1982): 69–74.

Young, Jeffrey R. "Creating a Life through Literature." *Chronicle of Higher Education* 14 March 1997: B8–B9.

AGHA SHAHID ALI
(1949–2001)

Purvi Shah

BIOGRAPHY

Born in New Delhi, India, on 4 February 1949, Agha Shahid Ali located himself as a Kashmiri exile. Ali grew up in a household where poetry could be heard in a wealth of languages—Persian, Urdu, and English. While Ali had translated the work of celebrated Urdu poet Faiz Ahmed Faiz, he himself wrote poetry exclusively in English since the age of ten. This early dedication facilitated the publication of Ali's first poetry book, *Bone-Sculpture*, while he was still in his early twenties.

Although Ali received training at the University of Kashmir, Srinagar, and the University of Delhi, he earned his doctorate in English in the United States from Pennsylvania State University in 1984. Ali's dissertation, which became *T.S. Eliot as Editor*, investigates the celebrated modernist poet's work in editing *The Criterion*. In 1987, Ali's third collection of poetry, *The Half-Inch Himalayas*, was published as part of the respected Wesleyan New Poets series, launching the rise of his U.S. poetry career. Ali received many prestigious awards in the mainstream poetry circuit, including Guggenheim and Ingram-Merrill fellowships as well as grants from the Pennsylvania Council on the Arts and the New York Foundation for the Arts. Ali is an active poet and educator: he has taught at Hamilton College and directed the M.F.A. program in creative writing at the University of Massachusetts at Amherst. After battling a brain tumor for years, Ali died at age 52 on December 8, 2001.

MAJOR WORKS AND THEMES

Much of Ali's poetry evokes the loss of Kashmir as a homeland. "The Country without a Post Office," the title poem in Ali's 1997 collection, examines violence-torn Kashmir through the motif of the impossibility of communication because all post offices are boarded up and delivery of any news is impossible. The speaker of this poem, as in other pieces in this volume, asks how friendships, familial bonds, and human relationships can be maintained in a turbulent environment. As Ketu Katrak observes, Ali's poems "explore and contain the anguish of displacement and exile through memories, history, and the Urdu poetic tradition" ("South Asian American Literature" 203).

The theme of exile can be traced throughout Ali's work. *The Half-Inch Himalayas* is prefaced by an epigraph from Virginia Woolf that ends, "I die in exile." The first poem in the collection, "Postcard from Kashmir," highlights the dislocation felt in receiving reminders (such as a postcard) of one's former homeland. "Postcard from Kashmir" playfully questions the nature of home, particularly when it is represented through the distance implied in correspondence. The transmission of home in miniature across space delves into Ali's concern with "the real and the imagined" (Katrak, "South Asian American Writers" 125). In particular, Katrak comments that Ali's poems present "*simultaneities of geography*, namely, the possibilities of living here, in body, and elsewhere in mind and imagination" (Ibid. 125). Home, for the exile, can be grasped through representations, but only attained partially since physical separation remains.

Ali recalls the landscape of Kashmir alongside his current American context and also evokes a linguistic simultaneity through his knowledge of Urdu and English poems. In addition to publishing his own translations of the famous Urdu poet Faiz Ahmed Faiz, Ali refers to Faiz and Urdu verse in his own poems. While Ali's work draws upon Urdu traditions, it also recalls a rich store of American and British poetry. One of the central poems of *A Nostalgist's Map of America*, "In Search of Evanescence," utilizes the formal features and phrasing of Emily Dickinson's poetry in order to trace the loss of a friend to AIDS. In the ninth section of the poem, Ali begins with an epigraph from Dickinson—"I want to eat Evanescence slowly"—and proceeds with a series of couplets that utilize the Dickinson dash: "I want—Evanescence—slowly. After great pain" (53). In this poem, Ali deploys Dickinson's formal innovation while evoking the ghazal couplet form. Yet Ali shies from offering a series of self-contained couplets, keeping the tension of loss and hope alive.

Though the themes of homeland, loss, and language are central to Ali's work, these ideas are expressed through a deep engagement with the craft of poetry. Ali's investment with form can be seen in his latest editorial project, *Ravishing DisUnities: Real Ghazals in English*, a collection of ghazals written in English by a host of noted poets. In the introduction to the anthology, Ali puts forth his project of advocating "form for form's sake," describing his desire to "take back the gift outright" from poets who have claimed to adopt the ghazal form without maintaining its formal characteristics (1). By speaking of the "gift outright," Ali echoes Robert Frost, evoking American poetic history and establishing the necessity of maintaining a poetic tradition across languages and territories. Ali, who sees himself as a triple exile, finds home in the English language. Unlike many postcolonial poets who profess an alienation from English, the colonizer's language, Ali refuses such distance. Instead, he offers new discoveries within English through the perspective of exile. In Ali's work, the loss of home and life is voiced through poetic tradition, a path that offers an examination of the past without assuring recovery.

CRITICAL RECEPTION

Though Ali's work deals with themes—exile, loss, family history—common to other Asian American poets, his work, which also concentrates on craft and form, has received more critical attention in the mainstream poetry circuit than through the Asian American literary project. *A Nostalgist's Map of America* demonstrates Ali's concern with craft through the use of "intertextual literary effects," comments John Oliver Perry (779). In his review of *A Nostalgist's Map of America*, Perry suggests that though *The Half-Inch Himalayas* was limited by its content of "nostalgia/family narratives of the Indian diaspora," the poems in Ali's subsequent major collection "reach beyond the self-centeredness of nostalgia and of poetry-making" (779). Perry maintains that Ali's earlier work stands too much on intellectual and exile status but that the later pieces develop unique insights.

Lawrence Needham, like Perry, comments on Ali's view of the past, but does not perceive Ali's representations to be self-indulgent. Instead, Needham applauds the poet's ability to refrain from romanticizing a bygone era. Needham refers, as well, to Ali's immersion in craft: tying form and content, Needham postulates that "loss is a basic condition for poetry" (63). Countering Perry's analysis, Needham suggests that Ali has an "ability to look into the heart of loss and not flinch; he resists the temptation to retreat to an idealized 'authentic' past or to lose himself in a continuous present as an antidote to separation and loss" (63).

In *Modern Indian Poetry in English*, Bruce King makes a claim similar to Perry's analysis regarding the progression of Ali's work. While discussing the 1977 anthology *Strangertime*, published in India and edited by Pritish Nandy, King remarks,

Ali is one of those early insights which Nandy often has of promising poets. Although Ali published two books with the Writers Workshop, his early work shows someone with the gift of poetry but who has not assimilated his various influences, which range from traditional Urdu verse to T.S. Eliot. Later, in poems published in American journals,

Ali has started to develop into an interesting writer who might well be considered among the better Indian English poets. (65–66)

Like other critics, King praises Ali for his poetic development and particularly his ability to bring together a variety of forms and influences. Such comprehension of poetic history and agility of language afford Ali recognition by South Asian and American critics and poets alike. In the context of such praise, Ketu Katrak has called Agha Shahid Ali "one of the most significant voices among South Asian poets" ("South Asian American Literature" 203).

BIBLIOGRAPHY

Works by Agha Shahid Ali

Poetry

Bone-Sculpture. Calcutta: Writers Workshop, 1972.
In Memory of Begum Akhtar and Other Poems. Calcutta: Writers Workshop, 1979.
The Half-Inch Himalayas. Middletown, CT: Wesleyan University Press, 1987.
A Walk through the Yellow Pages. Tucson: SUN/gemini Press, 1987.
A Nostalgist's Map of America. New York: W.W. Norton, 1991.
The Belovéd Witness: Selected Poems. New York: Viking Penguin, 1992.
The Country without a Post Office. New York: W.W. Norton, 1997.
Rooms are Never Finished. New York: W.W. Norton, 2001.

Criticism and Collection

T.S. Eliot as Editor. Ann Arbor: UMI Research Press, 1986.
Ravishing DisUnities: Real Ghazals in English. Middletown, CT: Wesleyan University Press, 2000.

Translation

The Rebel's Silhouette: Selected Poems by Faiz Ahmed Faiz. Rev. ed. Amherst: University of Massachusetts Press, 1995.

Studies of Agha Shahid Ali

Hanaway, William L., Jr. Rev. of *The Rebel's Silhouette* by Faiz Ahmed Faiz; trans. Agha Shahid Ali. *World Literature Today* 67.1 (1993): 226.
Katrak, Ketu H. "South Asian American Literature." *An Interethnic Companion to Asian American Literature*. Ed. King-Kok Cheung. New York: Cambridge University Press, 1997. 192–218.
———. "South Asian American Writers: Geography and Memory." *Amerasia Journal* 22.3 (1996): 121–38.
Kennedy, Richard S. "Individual Authors: T.S. Eliot as Editor." *Journal of Modern Literature* 13.3–4 (1986): 461–62.
King, Bruce. *Modern Indian Poetry in English*. Oxford: Oxford University Press, 1987.

————. Rev. of *The Country without a Post Office*. *World Literature Today* 71.3 (1997): 590–91.

Needham, Lawrence. " 'The Sorrows of a Broken Time': Agha Shahid Ali and the Poetry of Loss and Recovery." *Reworlding: The Literature of the Indian Diaspora*. Ed. Emmanuel S. Nelson. Westport, CT: Greenwood Press, 1992. 63–76.

Perry, John Oliver. Rev. of *A Nostalgist's Map of America*. *World Literature Today* 66.4 (1992): 779–80.

See, Dianne. Rev. of *A Nostalgist's Map of America*. *Amerasia Journal* 21.1–2 (1995): 176–78.

HIMANI BANNERJI
(1942–   )

Chandrima Chakraborty

BIOGRAPHY

Himani Bannerji was born in 1942 in what is now Bangladesh. She earned an M.A. in 1965 in Jadavpur University, Calcutta, and was hired as a lecturer in the Department of English in the same year. In 1969, she came to Canada and completed an M.A. in English at the University of Toronto. She dropped out of the Ph.D. program at Toronto in 1976 and began her teaching career in Canada as a part-time instructor in Atkinson College (York University), Toronto. She went back to school in 1980 and completed a Ph.D. at the Ontario Institute of Social Education (OISE). She is currently an associate professor in the Department of Sociology at York University. She is an extremely versatile author and writes poetry, short stories, theory, and reviews of theater and film. Her poems have been published in *CVII, Descant, Landscape, Rikka, Asianadian, Toronto South Asian Review, Fireweed, Borderlines, Canadian Woman Studies, Frank, Setu,* and *Indian Literature.*

MAJOR WORKS AND THEMES

Bannerji's poetry, like many of her theoretical essays, is predominantly concerned with multiculturalism and the locked struggle of unequals. Her first book of poetry, *A Separate Sky*, is an anthology of twenty-five poems and eight translations of selected poems from Bengali writers.

Most critics find Bannerji's poetry "distinctive" for its refusal to fit the binaries promulgated by Canada's official policy on multiculturalism (assimilation equals citizen, visible minority equals other). Bannerji's criticism of Canada's national policy in "terror" and "on a black entertainer" reinstates and reinscribes the otherization of visible minorities as an institutionalized national policy problem rather than a localized issue. The depiction of the majority population wrapped "in transparent plastic" ("terror" 25) implying their apathy and passive endorsement of systemic racism implicates them. The poem also foregrounds the insensitivity and obliviousness of people everywhere outside the geographical boundaries of a nation-state. Bannerji often begins her poems with an individual tragedy and links it to the drama of class struggle. "Canada in winter," for example, begins with a woman dying on the pavement and ends thus: "Millions are dying" (23). Her skillful interspersing of histories and experiences of different cultures in her poems is a response to homogenization and reification of minority communities. Her poetry in general and particularly the translations of Bengali poems in A Separate Sky serve to write in the difference and diversity of multicultural Canada.

Doing Time, Bannerji's second collection of poems, continues her endeavor to question and deconstruct the universalizing of pluralism. In a number of poems, she articulates the need to forge strategic and crucial alliances with other "minority" groups who share a common history of migration (forced or voluntary) and a feeling of alienation and discrimination in the host country. She urges in "upon hearing Beverly Glen Copeland," "revolution in Cuba," and "some kind of weapon" that the time in prison is a time of building solidarities and strategies and reclaiming voices.

Two images are commonly employed in her poetry. The first is that of the prison foreshadowed in the title, Doing Time. The poet speaks of prison structures at various levels of existence—metaphorical, emotional, and physical. She delegitimizes Western liberal theories of freedom and equality by demonstrating in poems such as "Apart-hate" and "freedom" that the nonwhite other still lives in a prison in the metropolis where she insists that the other is "doing time." The symbol of the prison in "doing time" and "to Adrienne Rich: variations on the theme human" indicates the double oppression that women face under patriarchy and imperialism. There are glimpses of the consumerist First World's exploitation of women as means of cheap labor in the poem "in the beginning there was . . ."; "on a black entertainer," on the other hand, demonstrates the nonwhite other "locked in by skin" ("to Adrienne Rich" 15).

The second recurring image in Doing Time is that of the mother-daughter figure. "a birthday," "identity," "arrival," "to Sylvia Plath," and "Mother, do you have a will?" portray the loss of the mother becoming a gain for the progeny. The image of a return to the mother's womb in "to Sylvia Plath" seems to provide a genealogy in the absence of a sense of belonging to a nation space. The stove is presented as the most rational choice for refuge and solace because a return to the mother's womb is no longer possible. The poem " 'Paki Go Home' " exemplifies the existence and popularity of a racialized and monolithic trope in multicultural Canada. The violence and race hatred that this term connotes are eloquently brought out through images such as the exploding grenade and the woman wiping spit off her face (17). The visible minority ironically appears only too visible in the "sunless afternoon" (15).

Bannerji articulates through her poems the frustrations of the immigrant community at large, yet her voice is intensely personal. In spite of her acerbic denunciation of the discriminatory and oppressive world order, there is also hope in her poetry.

CRITICAL RECEPTION

Most critics agree with Coomi S. Vevaina and Barbara Godard that Bannerji is one of the "most outspoken critics of racism in Canada" (34) and that her poetry is very "political." It is no surprise, therefore, that criticisms of Bannerji's poetry are very subjective. Sabi M. Jailall, for example, considers A Separate Sky to be "a work of art that relates to the politics of our times" and "an invaluable source in helping to mold political consciousness so vital to our survival" (25). Michael Thorpe in his review of the same anthology calls Bannerji a "strong-voiced poet," but finds it rather "absurd" that she should celebrate Cuba in comparison to Canada. He argues: "Ms Bannerji's political poetry exemplifies that squinting leftism which obscures real differences between Western crimes and those of the so-called 'socialist' world" (84).

While Thorpe finds fault with the overt socialist content, Vevaina and Godard in their introductory chapter raise questions about the choice of poetry, an "elitist genre within Canadian literature discourse" (33). Kavita A. Sharma expresses her frustration with Bannerji's poetry for the absence of portrayal of "the harsh realities of the majority of Indo-Canadian woman immigrants" (162). She alleges that Bannerji's poetry is elitist because she, like other South Asian writers in Canada, "inhabit[s] a totally different world" from that of her "less fortunate sisters" (158). Both Roshan G. Shahani and Arun Mukherjee applaud the absence in Bannerji's poetry of "the immigrant's sad nostalgia and of the perennial search for roots." Shahani adds that it is "a refreshing change" (181). Marlene Philip is also comfortable with the content but finds fault with her craftsmanship: "Bannerji's craft reflects a poet in control of her material, albeit marred by cliches and abstractions" (34). She notes that Bannerji's prose poems are better compared to the others in the collection Doing Time.

Ioan Davies deems Bannerji's poetry as "expressions of an otherness against a hegemony in which the terms of reference are dictated" by the dominant culture (34). For her, Bannerji's "uniqueness" lies in her representing "a generation of writers in Canada who are not part of the mainstream of our literature" (34). Yet Bannerji's poetry has received very scant critical attention. Bannerji notes this in her interview with Arun Mukherjee in Other Solitudes (150). The reviewers and publication details validate this viewpoint. Most of the reviews of Bannerji's poetry have been either written by South Asians or have appeared in South Asian publications.

BIBLIOGRAPHY

Works by Himani Bannerji

Poetry

A Separate Sky. Toronto: Domestic Bliss, 1982.

Doing Time: Poems. Toronto: Sister Vision Press, 1986.

" 'Paki Go Home.' " Illona Linthwaite, ed. *Ain't I a Woman! Poems of Black and White Women*. London: Virago, 1987. 125–27.

"This is Not a Poem," "Arrival," "The Waters of My Heart." Cyril Dabydeen, ed. *Another Way to Dance: Asian-Canadian Poetry*. Stratford, Ontario: Williams-Wallace, 1990. 13–17.

"On Seeing a Painting of Salome Kissing the Head of St. John," "wife," "upon hearing Beverly Glen Copeland," "doing time," "some kind of weapon," From "Paki Go Home," "in the beginning there was . . . ," "Why do we need a metaphor?" "to Sylvia Plath," "Apart-hate." Diane McGifford and Judith Kearns, ed. *Shakti's Words: An Anthology of South Asian Canadian Women's Poetry*. Toronto: TSAR, 1990. 2–14.

" 'Paki Go Home,' " "death by trivia," "Apart-hate," "letter to Iraq." Smaro Kamboureli, ed. *Making a Difference: Canadian Multicultural Literature*. Toronto: Oxford University Press, 1996. 183–90.

"Voyage," "In This Fugitive Time," "End Notes." Cyril Dabydeen, ed. *Another Way to Dance: Contemporary Asian Poetry from Canada and the United States*. Toronto: TSAR, 1996. 16–20.

Fiction

The Two Sisters. Toronto: Kids Can Press, 1978.

Coloured Pictures. Toronto: Sister Vision Press, 1991.

Short Stories

"The Day It Rained." *Fireweed* 21 (Summer/Fall 1985): 27–31.

"The Other Family." *Other Solitudes: Canadian Multicultural Fictions*. Ed. Linda Hutcheon and Marion Richmond. Toronto: Oxford University Press, 1990. 141–45.

"On a Cold Day." *Her Mother's Ashes, and Other Stories by South Asian Women in Canada and the United States*. Ed. Nurjehan Aziz. Toronto: TSAR, 1994. 26–34.

"The Moon and My Mother." *Contours of the Heart: South Asians Map North America*. Ed. Sunaina Maira and Rajini Srikanth. New York: Asian American Writers' Workshop, 1996. 188–96.

"Colour of Freedom." *West Coast Line* 26–27 (September 1998–February 1999): 177–91.

Critical Works

Himani Bannerji, Linda Carty, Kari Dehli, Susan Heald, and Kate McKenna. *Unsettling Relations: The University as a Site of Feminist Struggles*. Toronto: Women's Press, 1991.

The Writing on the Wall: Essays on Culture and Politics. Toronto: TSAR, 1993.

Thinking Through: Essays on Feminism, Marxism, and Anti-racism. Toronto: Women's Press, 1995.

The Mirror of Class: Essays on Bengali Theatre. Calcutta: Papyrus Publishers, 1998.

The Dark Side of the Nation: Essays on Multiculturalism, Nationalism, and Gender. Toronto: Canadian Scholars' Press, 2000.

Jibanananda, Sudhindranath Ebang (Essays on Modern Bengali Poetry). Calcutta: Dey's Publishing, 2000.

Inventing Subjects: Studies in Hegemony, Patriarchy, and Colonialism. New Delhi: Tulika, 2001.

Books Edited

Returning the Gaze: Essays on Racism, Feminism, and Politics. Toronto: Sister Vision, 1993.

Of Property and Propriety: The Role of Gender and Class in Imperialism and Nationalism. Coedited with S. Mojab and J. Whitehead. Toronto: University of Toronto Press, 2001.

Book Reviews

Rev. of *Still Close to the Island*, by Cyril Dabydeen. *Asianadian* 4.1 (1982): 27–28.

Rev. of *Primitive Offensive*, by Dionne Brand. *Fireweed* 16 (1983): 149–54.

Rev. of *The Age of Light, Soap, and Water: Moral Reform in English Canada, 1885–1925*, by Mariana Valverde. *Resources for Feminist Research* 20.3–4 (Fall–Winter 1991): 157–58.

Rev. of *Women and Social Action in Victorian and Edwardian England*, by Jane Lewis. *Resources for Feminist Research* 21.1–2 (Spring–Summer 1992): 35–36.

Articles

"The Alienated Hero in the Novels of Sunil Gangyopadhyay." *Toronto South Asian Review* 1.3 (1983): 45–56.

"The Story of a Birth." *Fireweed* 16 (1983): 123–33.

"We Appear Silent to People Who Are Deaf to What We Say." *Fireweed* 16 (1983): 8–17.

"Language and Liberation: A Study of Political Theatre in West Bengal." *ARIEL* 15 (October 1984): 131–44.

"Dowry and Commodity." *Man and Development* 7.3 (1985): 106–14.

"One Woman, Two Women, without Women: An Historical Look at Women in Bengali Theatre." *Fuse* (Fall 1985): 23–28.

"Andreij Tarkovsky: A Discourse on Desire and History." *Point/Counterpoint* 2.10 (1986): 57–61.

"Dionne Brand." *Fifty Caribbean Writers: A Bio-Bibliographical Critical Sourcebook.* Ed. Daryl Cumber Dance. Westport, CT: Greenwood Press, 1986. 46–57.

"Popular Images of South Asian Women." *Parallelogram* 2.4 (1986): 17–20.

"Sophie Bissonette and Her Films: Documenting Women in the Workplace." *Fuse* (February/March 1986): 25–27.

"Introducing Racism: Notes towards an Anti-racist Feminism." *Resources for Feminist Research* 16.1 (1987): 10–12.

"Now You See Us/Now You Don't." *Video Guide 40* 8.5 (1987): 7–8.

"That's Not Theoretical: An Interview with Margarethe von Trotta." *Fireweed* 24 (Winter 1987): 76–89.

"Evenings Out: Attending Political Theatre in West Bengal." *Borderlines* 14 (Winter 1988): 25–31.

"The Mirror of Class: Class Subjectivity and Politics in 19th Century Bengal." *Economic and Political Weekly* 24.19 (13 May 1989): 1041–51.

"Reflections on the Hard and Lonely Job of Translating." *Presenting Tagore's Heritage in Canada.* Ed. Joseph T. O'Connell. Toronto: Rabindranath Tagore Lectureship Foundation, 1989. 60–61.

"Class Consciousness, Theatre, and Politics in 19th Century Bengal." *Jadavpur Journal of Comparative Literature* 28 (1989–90): 75–112.

"The Sound Barrier: Translating Ourselves in Language and Experience." *Fireweed* 30 (Summer 1990): 121–34.

Introduction. *Black Markets, White Boyfriends, and Other Acts of Elision.* By Ian Iqbal Rashid. Toronto: TSAR, 1991. ix–xi.

"Fashioning a Self: Educational Proposals for and by Women in Popular Magazines in Colonial Bengal." *Economic and Political Weekly* 26.43 (26 October 1991): 50–62.

"Re: Turning the Gaze: Racism, Sexism, Knowledge, and the Academy." *Resources for Feminist Research* 20.3 (1992): 5–11.

"Mothers and Teachers: Gender and Class in Educational Proposals for and by Women in Colonial Bengal." *Journal of Historical Sociology* 5.1 (March 1992): 1–30.

Introduction. *The 52nd State of Amnesia: Poems.* By Krisantha Sri Bhaggiyadatta. Toronto: TSAR, 1993. vii.

"Writing 'India', Doing Ideology: William Jones' construction of India as an Ideological Category." *Left History* 2.2 (Fall 1994): 5–36.

"Textile Prison: Discourse on Shame (*lajja*) in the Attire of the Gentlewoman (*bhadramahila*) in Colonial Bengal." *Canadian Journal of Sociology* 19.2 (Winter 1994): 169–93.

"Attired in Virtue: Discourse on Shame (*lajja*) and Clothing of the Gentlewoman (*bhadramahila*) in Colonial Bengal." *From the Seams of History: Essays on Indian Women.* Ed. Bharati Ray. New Delhi: Oxford University Press, 1995. 67–106.

"Beyond the Ruling Category to What Actually Happens: Notes on James Mill's Historiography in *The History of British India.*" *Knowledge, Experience, and Ruling Relations: Studies in the Social Organization of Knowledge.* Ed. Marie Campbell and Ann Manicom. Toronto: University of Toronto Press, 1995. 49–64.

"On the Dark Side of the Nation: Politics of Multiculturalism and the State of 'Canada.' " *Journal of Canadian Studies* 31.3 (Fall 1996): 103–28.

"Geography Lessons: On Being an Insider/Outsider to the Canadian Nation." *Dangerous Territories: Struggles for Difference and Equality in Education.* Ed. Leslie G. Roman and Linda Eyre. London: Routledge, 1997. 23–42.

"Mary Wollstonecraft, Feminism, and Humanism: A Spectrum of Reading." *Mary Wollstonecraft and 200 Years of Feminisms.* Ed. Eileen Janes Yeo. London and New York: Rivers Oram Press, 1997. 222–42.

Bannerji, Himani, and Jasodhara Bagchi. "Modernization, Poverty, Gender, and Women's Health in Calcutta's Khidirpur Slum." *Canadian Woman Studies* 17.2 (Spring 1997): 122–28.

"Age of Consent and Hegemonic Social Reform." *Gender and Imperialism*. Ed. Clare Midgeley. Manchester: Manchester University Press, 1998. 21–44.

"Politics and the Writing of History." *Nation, Empire, Colony: Historicizing Gender and Race*. Ed. Ruth Roach Pierson and Nupur Chaudhuri. Bloomington: Indiana University Press, 1998. 287–301.

"A Question of Silence: Reflections on Violence against Women in Communities of Colour." *Scratching the Surface: Canadian Anti-racist Feminist Thought*. Ed. Enakshi Dua and Angela Robertson. Toronto: Women's Press, 1999. 261–77.

"Projects of Hegemony: Towards a Critique of Subaltern Studies' 'Resolution of the Women's Question.' " *Economic and Political Weekly* 35.11 (2000): 902–20.

"The Paradox of Diversity: The Construction of a Multicultural Canada and 'Women of Color.' " *Women's Studies International Forum* 23.5 (September–October 2000): 537–60.

Studies of Himani Bannerji

Bannerji, Himani. "Faculty Voices: Himani Bannerji." Interview with Arun P. Mukherjee. *York Stories: Women in Higher Education*. Ed. York Stories Collective. Toronto: TSAR, 2000. 94–115.

Bannerji, Himani. Interview with Arun P. Mukherjee. *Other Solitudes: Canadian Multicultural Fictions*. Ed. Linda Hutcheon and Marion Richmond. Toronto: Oxford University Press, 1990. 146–52.

Bannerji, Himani. "Women against Religious Fundamentalism." Interview with Fatima Jaffer. *Kinesis* April 1994: 12–13.

Bjerring, Nancy E. "Feminism as Framework for Investigating Canadian Multiculturalism." Rev. of *Returning the Gaze: Essays on Racism, Feminism, and Politics*. *Mosaic* 29 (September 1996): 165–73.

Davies, Ioan. "Senses of Place." Rev. of *A Separate Sky*. *Canadian Forum* 63.727 (April 1983): 33–34.

Henwood, Karen. Rev. of *Unsettling Relations: The University as a Site of Feminist Struggles*. *Feminist Review* 48 (1994): 140–42.

Houle, Karen. Rev. of *Returning the Gaze: Essays on Racism, Feminism, and Politics*. *Left History* 3–4 (Fall–Spring 1995–96): 269–73.

Jacob, Susan. "Breaking the Circle: Recreating the Immigrant Self in Selected Works of Himani Bannerji." *Intersexions: Issues of Race and Gender in Canadian Women's Writing*. Ed. Coomi S. Vevaina and Barbara Godard. New Delhi: Creative, 1996. 189–96.

Jailall, Sabi M. Rev. of *A Separate Sky*. *Asianadian* 4.4 (December 1982): 23–25.

Jenkinson, Dave. Rev. of *Coloured Pictures*. *CM* 19.4 (September 1991): 217–18.

Kudchedkar, Shirin. Rev. of *Returning the Gaze: Essays on Racism, Feminism, and Politics*. *Canadian Woman Studies* 14.2 (Spring 1994): 122–23.

Kumar, Alka. "Voicing the Other: Himani Bannerji's Poetics of Protest." *Central Institute of English and Foreign Languages Bulletin* 9.1 (June 1997): 99–112.

Mukherjee, Arun P. *Towards an Aesthetic of Opposition: Essays on Literature Criticism and Cultural Imperialism*. Stratford, Ontario: Williams-Wallace, 1988. 52–66.

Parameswaran, Uma. Rev. of *Unsettling Relations: The University as a Site of Feminist Struggles*. *Canadian Dimension* 25.7 (October–November 1991): 36–37.

Philip, Marlene. Rev. of *Doing Time. Toronto South Asian Review* 5.3 (Spring 1987): 28–34.

Powell, Barbara. Rev. of *Coloured Pictures. Canadian Children's Literature* 21.1 (Spring 1995): 85–88.

Rev. of *Returning the Gaze: Essays on Racism, Feminism, and Politics. Books in Canada* 22.8 (November 1993): 40–41.

Rev. of *Returning the Gaze: Essays on Racism, Feminism, and Politics. Fuse Magazine* 17.1 (Fall 1993): 39–40.

Rev. of *Unsettling Relations: The University as a Site of Feminist Struggles. Books in Canada* 20.7 (October 1991): 46.

Rev. of *Unsettling Relations: The University as a Site of Feminist Struggles. Paragraph Magazine* 14.1 (1992): 23.

Rev. of *The Writing on the Wall: Essays on Culture and Politics. Books in Canada* 22.8 (November 1993): 40–41.

Rothenberg, Paula. Rev. of *Unsettling Relations: The University as a Site of Feminist Struggles. Signs* 19.2 (Winter 1994): 559–63.

Sanders, Leslie. Rev. of *Doing Time. Canadian Woman Studies* 8.2 (Summer 1987): 129.

Shahani, Roshan G. " 'Some Kind of Weapon': Himani Bannerji and the Praxis of Resistance." *Intersexions: Issues of Race and Gender in Canadian Women's Writing.* Ed. Coomi S. Vevaina and Barbara Godard. New Delhi: Creative, 1996. 179–88.

Sharma, Kavita A. "Indo-Canadian Writers: Double Alienation." Coomi S. Vevaina and Barbara Godard, ed. *Intersexions: Issues of Race and Gender in Canadian Women's Writing.* New Delhi: Creative, 1996.

Thorpe, Michael. Rev. of *A Separate Sky. Toronto South Asian Review* 3.3 (Spring 1985): 83–85.

Vevaina, Coomi S., and Barbara Godard. "Crossings." Vevaina and Godard, ed. *Intersexions: Issues of Race and Gender in Canadian Women's Writing.* New Delhi: Creative, 1996. 1–54.

Weinworth, Michelle. Rev. of *Thinking Through: Essays on Feminism, Marxism, and Anti-racism. Canadian Forum* 75.853 (October 1996): 39–41.

Wyile, Herb. Rev. of *Thinking Through: Essays on Feminism, Marxism, and Anti-racism. Canadian Literature* 152/153 (Spring/Summer 1997): 251–53.

Zuk, Rhoda J. Rev. of *Unsettling Relations: The University as a Site of Feminist Struggles. Dalhousie Review* 72.1 (Spring 1992): 125–28.

MEI-MEI BERSSENBRUGGE
(1947–   )

Xiaoping Yen

BIOGRAPHY

Mei-Mei Berssenbrugge was born in 1947 in Beijing of Chinese and Dutch parents. She grew up in Massachusetts and was educated at Reed College and Columbia University. Since 1974, she has published eight collections of poems and has received numerous awards for her writing, including two National Endowment for the Arts Fellowships, two Before Columbus American Book Awards, a PEN West Award, and book awards from the Asian American Writers' Workshop and the Western States Art Foundation. She has worked as an artist-in-residence with Basement Workshop and Arts Alaska and has taught at Brown University and the Institute of American Indian Arts. She has lived in New Mexico since 1974. Now she also lives in New York City with artist Richard Tuttle and their daughter, Martha.

MAJOR WORKS AND THEMES

Mei-Mei Berssenbrugge is known as an experimental or postmodern poet. According to Paul Hoover, editor of *Postmodern American Poetry: A Norton Anthology* (1994), which includes three of Berssenbrugge's poems, postmodern poetry is "an intellectual and sonic construction." It is not "a means of expressing emotion," and language in the poetry is not "a transparent window onto experience" (xxxv). In other words, a poem "is not 'about' something, a paraphrasable narrative, symbolic nexus, or theme; rather, it is the actuality of words" (xxxvi). Following and expanding the tradition of postmodern poetry,

Berssenbrugge consciously rejects lyricism and narrative structure. Instead, she embraces philosophizing and a poetic structure of seemingly unrelated sentences.

Unlike many Asian American writers, Berssenbrugge does not comment directly on issues such as ethnic identity, the American dream, and social and cultural conflict. Her poetry lacks overt social engagement, comment, or protest. Garrett Hongo, editor of *The Open Boat: Poems from Asian America* (1993), which collects five of Berssenbrugge's poems, considers Berssenbrugge and others like her a new generation of poets "who wish to uphold the notion of a personal subjectivity and poetics *within* the American experience, minority or mainstream" and strive to break away from the old generation of poets "who make their priority the production of a polemicized critique of generalized ideological domination within our culture" (xxxvii).

The collection *Summits Move with the Tide* (1974) contains thirty-two poems of various lengths and a one-act play titled *One, Two Cups*. Poems in this book are "traditional" in the sense that they express the feelings and thoughts of the speakers, which are firmly grounded in narrative events and images. Many of the poems seem to be inspired by the author's travels and stays in places as diverse as Los Sangre de Cristo, New Mexico, Bhauda, Nepal, and New York City. For example, "Written before Easter in New York" describes what the speaker observes in a Young Women's Christian Association (YWCA) cafeteria in New York. A poem titled "Chronicle" is based on stories of childhood in China. The speaker recalls an affluent family, a negligent mother, and a loving grandfather.

The first poem in the collection *Random Possession* (1979), titled "Chronicle" as well, describes with poignancy the death of the speaker's great-grandfather. Another poem, "Rabbit, Hair, Leaf," ponders the ubiquity and randomness of death in nature. Of the seventeen poems in this collection, most depict the speaker(s)' frustration with men who are afraid of love and commitment. They contain many images of a yearning woman reaching out, often unsuccessfully, to an elusive lover, as in "The Reservoir." The language of science and technology starts to be part of Berssenbrugge's poetic diction in this collection. In "Walter Calls It a Dream Screen," the poet uses terms such as "crystallization, matrix, vacuums" and the image of a television screen to portray the speaker's unhappiness with Walter's lack of emotional depth.

The Heat Bird (1983) is composed of four long poems, "Pack Rat Sieve," "Farolita," "Ricochet off Water," and "The Heat Bird." Many of Berssenbrugge's poems are inspired by the landscape of New Mexico, but of all her collections, *The Heat Bird* has the most distinctive presence of a region where the poet has lived since 1974. *The Heat Bird* establishes Berssenbrugge as an experimental poet who abandons the linear mode of development in favor of a nonassociative structure. As a result, images and thoughts in the poems seem to be heaped and superimposed on one another without an obvious connection, and the poems do not seem to have a beginning, middle, or end.

In a later interview about "The Four Year Old Girl," Berssenbrugge explains her objective: "The time of my poems is not a narrative time; I write the beginning of the poem to occur (concurrently) as the end of the poem so that the whole thing rises up at the same time" (Tabios 137). "I'm trying to work with less continuity, to see if I can make a whole without there being easily-followed connections" (Tabios 139). These comments are also applicable to *The Heat Bird*. Very occasionally, Berssenbrugge alludes quite directly to a matter of social significance, as in "The Heat Bird," in which "radiation" may refer to the harmful effects of the atomic tests conducted at deserts in New Mexico.

Empathy (1989) contains eighteen poems, three of which are the product of cooperation between Berssenbrugge and other artists. "Fog" and "Alakanak Break-up" were written in collaboration with the choreography of Theodora Yoshikami for the Morita Dance Company. "Honeymoon" was written in collaboration with the art of Richard Tuttle and was published by the Whitney Museum Library Fellows in a different form as *Hiddenness* in 1987.

"Fog" is another example of Berssenbrugge's use of scientific diction as a poetic medium. Reading the poem is like listening to the voice of a narrator in a PBS *Nature* program. By situating human feelings and impressions in the cosmic universe represented by fog, Berssenbrugge seems to emphasize the subjective nature and the uncertainty of consciousness.

The book contains two poems with Chinese background. "Chinese Space" describes the gates, walls, paving stones, and ponds of Berssenbrugge's ancestral home. However, the focus of the poem is philosophical. Berssenbrugge explores how "seeing" from different perspectives can produce different spatial relationships or realities. The second poem, "Tan Tien," is based on the author's visit to Beijing in the early 1980s. As she does in many of her poems, Berssenbrugge uses images at once original and esoteric. This poem also shows that Berssenbrugge's postmodern poetry is not devoid of expressions of feelings. The speaker feels lonely in the city where she was born, and the loneliness leads to a conceptual discussion of symmetry in human relationships. "Tan Tien," like the title poem "Empathy," provides an example of what Berssenbrugge describes as the "abstract lyricism" of her poetry.

Like "Fog" and "Alakanak Break-up," *Mizu* (1990) was written for performance in collaboration with Theodora Yoshikami (choreography) and Jason Hwang (music), and it was performed at St. Mark's Church-in-the-Bowery. The poem narrates the underwater adventure of a boy who falls into the sea and meets and has meals with people who were thought to be dead. Art, especially visual art, has a significant presence in Berssenbrugge's poetry, and *Mizu*, filled with striking visual images, illustrates her artistic imagination.

The six poems in *Sphericity* (1993), "Ideal," "Size," "Combustion," "Sphericity," "Experience," and "Value," offer many examples of postmodern poetry as defined by Paul Hoover. Much of the poetry is not about feelings or experiences. Rather, it is about "the actuality of words." One way Berssenbrugge achieves this actuality is through placing words in seemingly incongruous context, for example, in the sixth part of "Experience" and in "Value," in which

Berssenbrugge does not answer the questions she asks because these are not questions that can be answered. The poems also contain Berssenbrugge's philosophical reflections. One of the constant themes is the subjectivity of human perception.

According to Eileen Tabios, following an exposure to a pesticide, Berssenbrugge became ill in the early 1990s from immune dysfunction (134). The illness produced some marked changes in her poetic imagination. She turned sharply inward to ponder the role of hormones and genes in life, and the result was *Endocrinology* (1997) and later "Four Year Old Girl," the title poem in her next book. The five-part poem *Endocrinology*, as the title suggests, is about "the lymphic body, secreting hormones, blood, the oozy connectiveness of all life" (Lipman 56). In one part of the poem, the poet reflects on the relationship between hormones and human emotions. The theme is expressed through the juxtaposition of the animal world represented by a bird and the human world by a couple ("The bird watches the man and woman dance" is the first line of the poem). The poet suggests that hormones are the source of human emotions. By stressing that there is a continuum, not an absolute demarcation, between animals and people, Berssenbrugge casts doubt on the myth of romantic love.

The eleven poems in *Four Year Old Girl* (1998) range widely in subject matter and in thematic concerns. Several poems are characterized by abstruse philosophizing. For example, the first poem, "Irises," muses on transcendence, appearance, reality, feelings, and beauty. The poem also shows Berssenbrugge's use of shifting perspectives (from "she" to "you") and non sequiturs ("You place sixteen girls"), two of her trademark techniques in her later poems.

Light and color are the major building blocks of some other poems, and Berssenbrugge enlivens her meditations with refreshing visual images. In "Health," the poet describes a birth in the first part. Continuing the theme of birth, Berssenbrugge discusses the process of artistic creation and the mutable relationship between art and life. In the fourth part of the poem, she presents the discussion in the form of a logical exercise and invites the reader to join her.

The title poem, "Four Year Old Girl," centers on a girl who is suffering from a genetic disease. As poets have done for centuries, Berssenbrugge contemplates the role of fate, which takes the form of genes in her poem, and the related issue of personal guilt. "Feelings of helplessness drove me to fantastic and ridiculous extremes" (51). In an interview about the poem, Berssenbrugge says, "I think a lot about fate and if and how fate can be changed. I've had so much experience with illness that I came to see it as a crisis of being. And I began thinking of how not to pass on illness to my (then) four-year-old daughter, Martha. . . . My poem is the result of being desperately sick and trying to figure out a way spiritually to overcome illness" (Tabios 134). This sheds light on the extent to which personal life serves as an inspiration to her poetry and the process through which it is reflected in the poetry.

CRITICAL RECEPTION

Mei-Mei Berssenbrugge's early poetry attracted little critical notice. However, with the publication of her fourth book, *The Heat Bird*, she started to receive enthusiastic reviews. Kathleen Fraser, an experimental poet, praises Berssenbrugge's success in finding a voice that is true to herself in *The Heat Bird*. "I overhear a poet talking to herself, alone in her most private moments, where the expectation of publicly accessible literary language drops away and the true sorting-out begins" (98). Moreover, Fraser commends Berssenbrugge for doing away with the linear structure of traditional poetry. "Berssenbrugge wants the structure of experience to emerge precisely as the meandering/wandering intelligence delivers it; for her meaning arrives through sensation, the surprised juxtaposition of moment upon moment" (101).

Jed Rasula, in a study of *Empathy*, places Berssenbrugge's writing in the camp of Language poetry in the contemporary American poetic landscape. The distinguishing characteristic of Language poetry, according to Rasula, is "its erosion of the complacent security on which the lyrical ego hoists its banner" (29). In other words, Language poetry is a reaction against poetry that celebrates personal feelings. In *Empathy*, the "delinking of ego from the authoritative center of the compositional matrix" (30) takes the form of discursive abstractions. "[The] course is held through a carefully propositional form, as if a new set of geometric theorems might be the outcome of a poem ('If it is through counting that speech is connected to time, / then crossing an inferred estuary of this conversation is a rest in music')" (35).

Denise Newman's analysis of *Empathy* focuses on the concretion of emotion, fog, seeing, light, and space. Commenting on seeing, Newman stresses Berssenbrugge's fascination with visual perception. "Perception is very much based on interpretation rather than a simple reaction to stimuli. The poet studies light and records its innumerable variations not as a photometer but a painter" (122).

Megan Simpson, in discussing *Empathy* and *Sphericity*, concurs with Newman. "Mei-Mei Berssenbrugge is a poet of perception. Not only is sight more consistently engaged than the other senses in her complexly sensual poetry, but also her vocabulary is concentrated with perceptual and visual terms." Berssenbrugge's language in *Empathy* and *Sphericity* is descriptive, but she does not use description in a traditional way. "Berssenbrugge describes neither the world nor its contents, but the act of perceiving itself" (134). Specifically, the poet is concerned with the subjective nature of perception. Quoting Berssenbrugge's definition of perception as "a camera controlled by the participant," Simpson calls this theory "productive epistemological uncertainty" and "feminine knowing" (144). "She poetically enacts Merleau-Ponty's insight that in perceiving anything, the knowing subject 'can never exhaust its possibilities or empty it of meaning. It always offers more; there is always more to be known' " (144).

W.B. Keckler calls *Endocrinology* a "verbal-visual poem of astonishing originality" for "tracing aesthetics to its somatic origin" (25). The book "engages the senses and intellect in a defamiliarizing way, seeking to chart the numinous areas where perceptions, and particularly aesthetic perceptions, are engendered. This place of genesis is, of course, within the human body, where endocrinal changes and charges are primal forces, heretofore addressed only sporadically and rarely in-depth by contemporary poets" (25).

A number of critics are impressed with Berssenbrugge's collaboration with artists in making her books objects of art in their own right. Robert Phillips, commenting on *Sphericity*, writes, "There is a sense of satisfaction to be derived from handling and reading a fine piece of bookmaking" (84). Susan Smith Nash suggests that the unusual power of *Sphericity* "lies in the juxtaposition of poetry and art in a way that addresses ideas about how one reads poetry and how one derives meaning" (76). W.B. Keckler calls *Endocrinology*'s presentation ingenious. "The combination of poetry and image occasion strange permutations that tease the mind down labyrinthine semantic passageways" (25). Joel Lipman characterizes *Endocrinology*'s "visual totality" as essential to "access its many pleasures as a text and book" (56).

In reviewing *The Four Year Old Girl*, Thomas Fink describes Berssenbrugge as "a master of the long-lined poetic mediation which, dissolving final formulations, uncannily orchestrates the confluence of dense, speculative abstraction, emotional insights, arresting visual details, scientific data, and surreal drifts" (263). A reviewer for *Publishers Weekly* considers it a drawback that Berssenbrugge's poems sometimes resemble logical proofs and are prone to vague generalizations, but on the whole, the reviewer says, her abstract inquiries produce a "radiant" conclusion. "Readers looking to be ravished by the beauty of sound and image—and willing to wrestle with some demanding philosophical conundrums—should look no further" (75).

Leslie Scalapino, a fellow experimental poet, emphasizes the formalistic importance of language in *The Four Year Old Girl*. Language is not a means to convey feelings or emotions, but a "beauty completely devoid of thought." "The lines do not carry over a narrative, from one line to the next; rather, lines are juxtaposed. . . . The lines or images don't build up to something. Pairing of singular beauty is the density" (67). Also commenting on Berssenbrugge's language in *The Four Year Old Girl*, Eileen Tabios, in her book *Black Lightning*, states that Berssenbrugge's "co-optation" of technical language "reflects her long-time interest in feminizing technical jargon which started when she wrote *Random Possession*" (137).

Tabios's book also provides valuable insight into Berssenbrugge's creative process. To research her poem "Four Year Old Girl," Berssenbrugge spent three months reading and annotating books and materials on genetics, philosophy, and art discourse. Then she worked as if she were assembling a collage. She "typed out the passages which caught her attention and printed them out on slips of paper, along with other visual notes—such as xeroxes of illustrations from the genetic books to family photos—on the 10' × 4' surface of a large table. As she perused the notes on the table, sometimes moving them around to form some sort of order, she typed what became the 'First Draft' of the poem" (Tabios 134).

BIBLIOGRAPHY

Works by Mei-Mei Berssenbrugge

Fish Souls. New York: Greenwood Press, 1971.
Summits Move with the Tide. Greenfield Center, NY: Greenfield Review Press, 1974.
Random Possession. New York: I. Reed Books, 1979.
The Heat Bird. Providence, RI: Burning Deck Books, 1983.
Empathy. Barrytown, NY: Station Hill Press, 1989.
Mizu. Tucson, AZ: Chax Press, 1990.
Sphericity. Berkeley, CA: Kelsey St. Press, 1993.
Endocrinology: Poetry, Art. Berkeley, CA: Kelsey St. Press, 1997.
Four Year Old Girl. Berkeley, CA: Kelsey St. Press, 1998.

Studies of Mei-Mei Berssenbrugge

Fink, Thomas. Rev. of *Four Year Old Girl*. *Confrontation* 68/69 (Summer 1999): 263–64.
Fraser, Kathleen. "Overheard." *Poetics Journal* 4 (May 1984): 98–105.
Hongo, Garrett, ed. *The Open Boat: Poems from Asian America*. New York: Anchor Books, 1993.
Hoover, Paul, ed. *Postmodern American Poetry: A Norton Anthology*. New York: Norton, 1994.
Keckler, W.B. Rev. of *Endocrinology*. *American Book Review* 20.1 (November/December 1998): 25.
Lipman, Joel. Rev. of *Endocrinology*. *Independent Publisher* 16.4 (July/August 1998): 56–57.
Nash, Susan Smith. Rev. of *Sphericity*. *Multicultural Review* 2 (December 1993): 76–77.
Newman, Denise. "The Concretion of Emotion: An Analytic Lyric of Mei-Mei Berssenbrugge's *Empathy*." *Talisman* 9 (Fall 1992):119–24.
Phillips, Robert. Rev. of *Sphericity*. *Small Press* 11 (Summer 1993): 84.
Rasula, Jed. "Ten Different Fruits on One Different Tree: Experiment as a Claim of the Book." *Chicago Review* 43.4 (Fall 1997): 28–39.
Rev. of *Four Year Old Girl*. *Publishers Weekly* 2 November 1998: 75.
Scalapino, Leslie. *R-Hu*. Berkeley, CA: Atelos, 2000.
Simpson, Megan. *Poetic Epistemologies: Gender and Knowing in Women's Language-oriented Writing*. Albany: State University of New York Press, 2000.
Tabios, Eileen. *Black Lightning: Poetry-in-Progress*. New York: Asian American Writers' Workshop, 1998.

VIRGINIA R. CERENIO
(1955–   )

Melinda L. de Jesús

BIOGRAPHY

Virginia R. Cerenio was born in California in 1955. A second-generation Filipina American, she grew up in San Francisco and received a B.A. in English
and an M.A. in education from San Francisco State University. Cerenio is a
longtime community activist and advocate for Filipino American elders as well
as a founding member of the Bay Area Pilipino American Writers (BAYPAW)
collective. After eighteen years of managing San Francisco's transit services for
the elderly and disabled, Cerenio is in semiretirement. She currently serves on
the International Hotel Citizen Advisory Committee, a group that has, for the
past thirty years, advocated for the construction of senior housing in San Francisco.

MAJOR WORKS AND THEMES

Virginia Cerenio has published widely and is well represented in Asian Amer-
ican, Filipino American, and multicultural poetry anthologies, including *Break-
ing Silence: An Anthology of Contemporary Asian American Poets* (1983), *The
Forbidden Stitch: An Asian American Women's Anthology* (1989), *Making
Waves: An Anthology of Writings by and about Asian American Women* (1989),
New Worlds of Literature: Writings from America's Many Cultures (1994), *Re-
turning a Borrowed Tongue: An Anthology of Filipino and Filipino American
Poetry* (1995), and *Babaylan: An Anthology of Filipina and Filipina American
Writers* (2000). This entry will focus on her collection of poetry entitled *Tres-*

passing Innocence (1989), which combines the majority of her poems published elsewhere.

Like that of other Filipino/American writers before her, Cerenio's poetry in *Trespassing Innocence* incorporates the themes of identity, history, community and family, cultural legacy, and social justice; it documents and celebrates the lives of those most easily forgotten: immigrants, the poor, the elderly, women of color, children. As such, this collection includes portraits of Filipino immigrant old-timers or *manongs* (elderly Filipino bachelors evicted from the International Hotel). Moreover, it incorporates reflections about contemporary Filipino/American social movements: the People Power movement that ousted Ferdinand Marcos and ended martial law in the Philippines, and San Francisco in the aftermath of the International Hotel protests and the Third World Strikes. Thus *Trespassing Innocence* reflects Cerenio's life as a second-generation Filipina American and community activist: her preoccupation with identity and loss of culture, with local and homeland politics, and with the twist of fate that separates her from family back home. Moreover, Cerenio's poetry is distinctive because of its exploration of Filipina American realities and its Asian American feminist sensibility.

"habits of an asian american woman" opens *Trespassing Innocence* and thus signals Cerenio's Asian American feminist leanings. This poem describes her coming to terms with her terrible habit of agreeing with people. In the second stanza, Cerenio reclaims her explosive anger. The last line tells other Asian American women who struggle in the same way that they would be proud of her.

"we who carry the endless seasons" is Cerenio's most anthologized poem. This taut piece describes how Filipina American daughters feel caught between cultures: burdened with the weight of their mothers' hopes and dreams in America, their sense of responsibility is reinforced by guilt and religion.

The poem "you lovely people" is dedicated to and takes its title from the important novel by celebrated Filipino writer N.V.M. Gonzalez. This short poem deftly describes Filipino immigration and diaspora and its inevitable aftermath: the alienation and dislocation of Filipinos in America. Cerenio notes how easily Filipinos assimilate into American culture but pay a price. The poem ends with the image of the untold stories within the cracks of a manong's "old brown hands" (25). This line can be read as a direct reference to Gonzalez, but also to every Filipino, immigrant and American born, who shares this history.

In the center of this collection are the poems "for a village uncle," "i dance with manong pascual," "manong freddy," and "manong benny," Cerenio's portraits of the old-timers. Similarly, "lunch with manong benny" is a bittersweet celebration of one man's life. The poet captures his cheerful spirit and dignity, contrasting them to his solitary existence: his view of Chinatown laundry flapping the wind, the uneaten pan of *biko*, coconut oil clouding its surface, signaling the relentless passage of time.

In contrast, scattered throughout *Trespassing Innocence* are poems that reflect the poet's concerns about the tumultuous political situation in the Philippines in the mid-1980s. "guerilla children," "revolution," "hail mary," "letter to grandma," "photos from the philippines," "thoughts on pilipinas," and "suicide note" balance the poet's childhood memories of visits to her parents' barrios with the violence and suffering on the nightly news. The strongest of these poems, "letter to grandma," begins disarmingly with a flirtatious greeting. Quickly the poem turns dark as the poet describes what she fears: soldiers attacking nuns and priests, the assassination of opposition leader Benigno Aquino, children describing the torture of their parents, Filipinas forced to work abroad as overseas contract workers. Cerenio finds the nation's beauty in the following: the eyes of hungry beggar children, in Filipinas forced to work as prostitutes, the rich and poor coming together to protest. But the righteous, justifiable anger of the people still scares her. At its heart, the poem explores the poet's guilt at her privileged life in the United States, her fear and cowardice. The poem ends with a prayer that the people will have the courage she will never have. In this way, Cerenio offers her love and hope to the people, reinforcing her view that poetry is one way of contributing to a revolution.

CRITICAL RECEPTION

Cerenio is best known for her association with the Bay Area Pilipino American Writers (BAYPAW), a San Francisco-based coalition of writers and activists, with whom she published *Without Names* (1987). Literary critics Oscar Campomanes and Jean Vengua Gier locate Cerenio as one of the "Flip poets"— American-born and/or raised Filipino writers who came of age during Third World Student and International Hotel protests of the 1960s and 1970s.

In "Filipinos in the United States and Their Literature of Exile" (1992), Campomanes contends that the Flips are writing out of an alienation from both mainstream American and Filipino culture that fuels "their search for kinship with their predecessors in the pioneering generation and their symbolic appropriations of Philippine history and identities from the second, or consciously American, generation" (69). He notes that Cerenio, along with Jeff Tagami and Jaime Jacinto, is among the "few who exhibit tendencies to outgrow the agonized temporizings associated with [the ethnic movements of the 1960s and 1970s]," and includes a brief reading of "you lovely people" in the article (56).

Jean Vengua Gier in " ' . . . To Have Come From Someplace': *October Light, America Is in the Heart*, and 'Flip' Writing after the Third World Strikes" (1995) notes that Cerenio's poetry, like that of her BAYPAW compatriots, is marked by its historical and regional specificity: International Hotel activism and community grassroots organizing anchors their worldview landscape and history. In this way, the Flip poets, while contributing to the genre of American regional literatures, offer important resistance to Campomanes's totalizing diasporic or "exilic" reading of Filipino American literature. She includes favorable readings of "we who carry the endless seasons" and "at city planning" here.

In sum, Virginia Cerenio is one of the most cited and best regarded of the Flip poets and the only Flip woman poet to garner significant critical attention. Cerenio's poetry demonstrates how art and activism feed one another, and how the two enable the celebration and revitalization of communities. Cerenio's socially committed poetry, grounded in historical and regional specificity, documents an important cultural legacy; its lyric power continues to inspire.

Many thanks to Virginia R. Cerenio for providing information for this entry.

BIBLIOGRAPHY

Works by Virginia R. Cerenio

Poetry

"my man is wood" and "dancing with my father." *Liwanag: Literary and Graphic Expressions by Filipinos in America.* Ed. Emily Cachapero. San Francisco: Liwanag Press, 1975.

"habits of an asian-american woman" and "pinay." *Women Talking–Women Listening III.* Dublin, CA: Women Talking–Women Listening Press, 1977. 25, 41.

"guerilla children." *Peace or Perish: A Crisis Anthology.* Ed. Herman Berlandt and Neeli Cherkovski. San Francisco: Poets for Peace, 1983. 25.

"manong benny." *East Wind: Politics and Culture of Asians in the United States* 2.1 (1983): 73.

"you lovely people," "pinay," "pick-up at chef rizal restaurant," "manong benny," and "we who carry the endless seasons." *Breaking Silence: An Anthology of Contemporary Asian American Poets.* Ed. Joseph Bruchac. Greenfield Center, NY: Greenfield Review Press, 1983. 11–15.

"the manong walks." *Bridge* 8.4 (Winter 1983): 36.

"manong freddy." *Gourd Song II: California Poets in the Schools.* San Francisco: San Francisco State University, 1986. 6.

"translating the word." *Gourd Song III: California Poets in the Schools.* San Francisco: San Francisco State University, 1986. 9.

"Untitled." *East Wind: Politics and Culture of Asians in the United States* 5.1 (1986): 18.

"Family Photos: Black and White: 1960." *The Forbidden Stitch: An Asian American Women's Anthology.* Ed. Shirley Lim, Mayumi Tsutakawa, and Margarita Donnelly. Corvallis, OR: Calyx Books, 1989. 77.

Trespassing Innocence. San Francisco: Kearny Street Workshop Press, 1989.

"you lovely people." *Pacific School of Religion Bulletin* 71.3 (Fall 1992): 1.

"the dream." *Parallels: Artists/Poets.* Ed. Oriole Farb Feshbach, Claire Heimarck, and Lucy Rosenfeld. New York: Midmarch Arts Press, 1993. 8.

"why I still write about the philippines." *Asian America: Journal of Culture and the Arts* 2 (1993): 23.

"we who carry the endless seasons." *New Worlds of Literature: Writings from America's Many Cultures.* Ed. Jerome Beatty and J. Paul Hunter. New York: Norton, 1994. 221–22.

"13 June 1994," "July 20, 1994," "my mother," and "23 October 1992." *Returning a*

Borrowed Tongue: An Anthology of Filipino and Filipino American Poetry. Ed.
Nick Carbo. Minneapolis: Coffee House Press, 1995. 55–58.
"translating the world," "revolution," and "letter to grandma." *Without Names: A Collection of Poems.* Ed. Bay Area Pilipino American Writers. San Francisco: Kearny
Street Workshop Press, 1995. 28–31.
"My Annual Haircut," "A Definition of Pain," and "Short Term Memory." *Babaylan:
An Anthology of Filipina and Filipina American Writers.* Ed. Nick Carbo and
Eileen Tabios. San Francisco: Aunt Lute Press, 2000. 203–5.

Fiction

"Dreams of Manong Frankie." *Berkeley Fiction Review* 4 (1983): 34–42.
"Dreams of Manong Frankie." *Making Waves: An Anthology of Writings by and about
Asian American Women.* Ed. Asian Women United of California. Boston: Beacon
Press, 1989. 228–35.
"Dreams of Manong Frankie." *Fiction by Filipinos in America.* Ed. Cecilia Manguerra
Brainard. Quezon City, Philippines: New Day Publishers, 1993. 174–81.

Studies of Virginia R. Cerenio

Athanases, Steven, D. Christiano, and S. Drexler. "Family Gumbo: Urban Students Respond to Contemporary Poets of Color." *English Journal* 81.5 (September 1992):
45–54.
Campomanes, Oscar. "Filipinos in the United States and Their Literature of Exile." *Reading the Literatures of Asian America.* Ed. Shirley Geok-lin Lim and Amy Ling.
Philadelphia: Temple University Press, 1992. 49–78.
Cerenio, Virginia. Interview. *Asian Pacific American Mothers and Daughters: Visions
and Fierce Dreams.* Ed. Organization of Pan Asian American Women. Washington, DC: Organization of Pan Asian American Women, Inc., 1983. 8–17.
Gier, Jean Vengua. " ' . . . To Have Come From Someplace': *October Light, America Is
in the Heart*, and 'Flip' Writing after the Third World Strikes." *Hitting Critical
Mass: A Journal of Asian American Cultural Criticism* 2.2 (Spring 1995): 1–33.
Available: http://socrates.berkeley.edu/critmass/v2n2/gierprint.html (5 January
2001).

G.S. SHARAT CHANDRA
(1938–2000)

Keith Lawrence

BIOGRAPHY

G. S(hankara Chetty) Sharat Chandra was born on 3 May 1938 in Nanjangud, Karnatak, India, to G. Shankara Chetty and Lalithamma Lalitha Chandra. Chandra's father was a prominent criminal lawyer; Chandra was raised in a well-to-do family with Western tastes. As an adult, Chandra expressed two overriding impressions of his childhood: that he grew up in a house filled with good books, and that he had the luxury of time to read them. As a youth, he was especially influenced by the writings of Sartre, Joyce, Lawrence, Pound, and Frost.

From an early age, Chandra was groomed to join his father's legal firm. Pressure to do so intensified when his father was named advocate-general for the state. Acquiescing to his father's will, Chandra enrolled as an undergraduate English major at the University of Mysore, receiving his B.A. degree in 1953. He subsequently received his bachelor of law degree from the same university and in 1958 joined his father's firm as a junior partner. But Chandra spent his spare time writing English poems, which he hid between briefs. Sensing Chandra's ambivalence and desiring to secure his allegiance, Chandra's father tried several times to arrange an appropriate marriage for his son.

In 1962, at age twenty-four, Chandra came to the United States, ostensibly to earn advanced degrees in English and law. But his real purpose, he told Mary Vasudeva and Deepika Bahri, was to "leave the country [India] to pursue a literary life." Accepted at the State University of New York at Oswego, he earned an M.S. degree in English in 1964; in 1966, he graduated with his LL.M. degree from the Osgoode Hall Law School in Toronto, specializing in labor law.

His employment as a law instructor was cut short when he was awarded a fellowship by the Writers' Workshop at the University of Iowa. After receiving his M.F.A. degree in poetry from the University of Iowa in 1968, he joined the faculty of Iowa Wesleyan College.

Previously, on 1 September 1966, he had married Jane Ronnerman, a teacher. He did not tell his parents of his marriage for nearly two years, fearing their reaction when they learned that he had married an American. The couple subsequently had three children: a boy, Bharat, and two girls, Shalini and Anjana.

In 1972 Chandra joined the faculty of Washington State University. He and his family returned to the Midwest in 1983 when he accepted a position with the University of Missouri at Kansas City, where he remained until his death. On 18 April 2000, after a full day on campus, Chandra suffered a sudden brain hemorrhage at his home in Overland Park, Kansas. He died two days later, on the morning of 20 April, without ever having regained consciousness. Colleagues expressed shock and a profound sense of loss. "He was someone who still had so much to write," one of them told John Eberhart of the *Kansas City Star*. Chandra's daughter Shalini suggested that his life had been full and happy, saying simply, "He wanted to be a poet" (B-4). At the time of his death, Chandra left an incomplete novel and an unfinished poetry collection.

MAJOR WORKS AND THEMES

While Chandra's first of seven poetry collections, *Bharata Natyam Dancer and Other Poems*, was very well received in India and thus helped establish Chandra's international reputation, it was never reissued in the United States. Instead, its poems found their way into Chandra's other collections, particularly *April in Nanjangud*, his second and, as it turned out, longest book of poems. Much more insistently than *Bharata Natyam Dancer, April* views and remembers India through an expatriate's heightened awareness, a lonely awareness that separates him from his own country and people. In "Black Pigeon," for example, the speaker worries how long it is "since my pigeon flew," how long since word has come from the speaker's lover. The conclusion of "Matrudesh" espouses a similar despair. "The Doorman," with its simultaneous nods toward Hindu mythology and Freemasonry, metaphorically questions the cost to the immigrant of American cultural entry—or the cost of readmission to the motherland to the Indian expatriate: the speaker asks if the initiate will give up his body to enter. Even supposing an affirmative answer, what is he to do when the doorkeeper responds, "You have outlived your mind"? To the extent that ethnicity is affirmed or celebrated in *April*, there are invariably conditions, qualifications. In "Bronze Men," for instance, the speaker aligns himself with "the bronze men of the sea" who "mould brains of steel"—but such brains are destined only to "rule governments of sand" comprised of "men who rust."

Once or Twice, Chandra's third collection, is physically much slimmer than *April*, but it also contains some of his earliest emphatic indictments of America's stance toward its immigrants. In "Second Journey," the speaker asks the addressee who has come home, "to the color of what"? In "For All Aliens," the speaker warns those who die alien in America that they refuse passage to "those without American clearance," wishing them a good trip.

Chandra's fourth collection, *The Ghost of Meaning*, was published by a small Idaho press and never received a wide audience; and his fifth collection, *Heirloom*, while printed by Oxford University Press, was comprised in large part of poems published earlier in *April* and *Once or Twice*. Still, this latter work deserves notice for its heretofore unpublished "death poems," particularly those like "The Funeral of My Procession" and "Death of the Second-Division Clerk." In these poems, as Ann Struthers explains, is a cynical and "disrespectful attitude" toward death that affords both humor and "a kind of tough strength to his work" (116).

Family of Mirrors, Chandra's sixth collection, is at once his most idiosyncratic and most potentially enduring work—and his only collection currently in print. The volume is divided into five sections; the poems in each section adhere loosely to the respective themes of family, childhood as fable or metaphor, place and displacement, love and lust, and dreams/fantasies, although the final four poems of the book ("If I'm to Answer," "Campus Poet," "Still Kicking in America," and "Swansong") are more aptly described as "poet poems" or "self-reflexive poems" than dream poems. Although the themes of Chandra's earlier collections recur here, themes of separation, otherness, death, and the nature of self, a number of poems in *Mirrors* are characterized by a lightness of tone, a *joie de vivre* mostly missing from the earlier collections, as when the speaker in "The Hamper" remembers hiding in a family hamper as a small boy and then being found by his frantic mother. Too, there is an expansion of earlier "immigrant themes," so that, in effect, Chandra argues that a kind of immigrant status is synonymous with the human condition, especially in a frenetic, fluid, and shrinking world. The speaker of "If I'm to Answer," for example, is at once poet and Everyman when he imagines his life as an endless walking of his front porch, as "pacing the untouched." In "Voyages," death is suggested as a metaphor for the immigrant experience, where we find that existence itself depends on nothing then within our control since most of us have felt nothing "outside of our thoughts."

The universality of displacement and loss and the sharply divisive nature of American social hierarchies are central themes of *Immigrants of Loss*, Chandra's seventh and final poetry collection. Perhaps Chandra's least eclectic and most insistently focused work, *Immigrants* was also critically acclaimed. While *Family of Mirrors* received the lion's share of popular attention, being nominated for the Editors' Choice Pushcart Award (1990) and the Pulitzer Prize in poetry (1993), it was *Immigrants* that earned for Chandra the most prestige, being awarded both the Commonwealth Poetry Prize and the T.S. Eliot Poetry Prize in 1993.

CRITICAL RECEPTION

Critics of Chandra's poetry—and of his story collection, *Sari of the Gods* (1998)—universally praise his "great literary charm," his "clarity and passion," his "acute, philosophical, complicated" purposes, his capacity to "worry as much about inclusion as about exclusion," and his skill in writing the "great variety of the Indian American immigrant experience" (James 119; Struthers 117; Bowers 45; Masello 20). Ann Struthers praises *Heirloom* for its "precise pictures" of India and Indian family life, declaring that in the collection "is illustrated William Carlos Williams' dictum that there is no poetry except in things" (117). Logan Speirs praises the "raw and explicit poetry" (176) of *Immigrants of Loss*; Philip Miller argues that "every sidewalk" in the work "belongs to one of Eliot's unreal cities," and that "as the immigrant's worlds merge, the cycle of immigration is completed" (338). Neil Bowers asserts that *Family of Mirrors* "obliges us to confront difference" as "a region of loneliness and self-doubt," where "inclusion can intensify one's sense of alienation" (42).

Time will, perhaps, bring a more measured response to Chandra's poems. Considered objectively, some of the "light" poems in *Family of Mirrors* are also lightweight; poems like "Raquel Welch Read Tom Wolfe" and "Campus Poet" approach silliness. More crucially, the unapologetic objectification of American women in some of Chandra's "lust poems" is not merely tawdry and offensive but an unfortunate promulgation of sexual stereotypes of the immigrant American male. Still, Chandra's ability to simultaneously reify the Indian American experience and force all readers to confront their own exclusion, their own "immigrant" condition, will insure the continued significance and eminence of his writing.

BIBLIOGRAPHY

Works by G.S. Sharat Chandra

Poetry

Bharata Natyam Dancer and Other Poems. Calcutta: Writers Workshop Publications, 1968.
April in Nanjangud. London: Alan Ross, 1971.
Once or Twice. Sutton, England: Hippopotamus Press, 1974.
The Ghost of Meaning. Lewiston, ID: Confluence Press, 1978.
Heirloom. London and Delhi: Oxford University Press, 1982.
Family of Mirrors. Kansas City, MO: BkMk Press, 1993.
Immigrants of Loss. Sutton, England: Hippopotamus Press, 1993.

Story Collection

Sari of the Gods. Minneapolis: Coffee House, 1998.

Translation

Offsprings of Servagna. Calcutta: Writers Workshop Publications, 1975.

Studies of G.S. Sharat Chandra

Bowers, Neil. "Present Absences: G.S. Sharat Chandra's *Family of Mirrors*." *Poet and Critic* 25.1 (Spring 1994): 42–45.

Contemporary Authors Online. "G. S(hankara Chetty) Sharat Chandra." Gale Literary Database, http://www.galenet.comservlet/GLD. 12 December 2000.

Das, Kamar. "Indian English Poetry by an Expatriate Indian: A Note on G.S. Sharat Chandra's *Heirloom*." *Literary Half-Yearly* 32.1 (January 1991): 34–42.

Eberhart, John Mark. "UMKC Professor, Poet Chandra Dies." *Kansas City Star* 21 April 2000: B-4.

James, Sophie. "India: Home and Away." *London Magazine* 38.7–8 (October/November 1998): 117–19.

Marchant, Fred. Rev. of *Family of Mirrors*. *Weber Studies* 11.2 (Spring/Summer 1994): 148–50.

Masello, David. "Books-in-Brief." Rev. of *Sari of the Gods*. *New York Times Book Review* 3 May 1998: Section 7, 20.

Miller, Philip. "*Immigrants of Loss*: The Pleasures of Mixed Prosodies." *Literary Review* 40.2 (1999): 336–38.

Quinn, Mary Ellen. Rev. of *Sari of the Gods*. *Booklist* 94 (April 1998): 1302.

Rev. of *Sari of the Gods*. *Publishers Weekly* 245.8 (23 February 1998): 50.

Speirs, Logan. "Current Literature 1993: New Writing: 1. Drama and Poetry." *English Studies* 76.2 (1995): 155–84.

Struthers, Ann. Rev. of *Heirloom*. *New Letters* 50.3 (Fall 1983): 116–17.

Vasudeva, Mary, and Deepika Bahri. " 'Swallowing for Twenty Years / The American Mind and Body': An Interview with G.S. Sharat Chandra." *Journal of Commonwealth and Postcolonial Studies* 5.1 (Fall 1997): 9–17.

Williams, Janis. Rev. of *Sari of the Gods*. *Library Journal* 123 (15 April 1998): 117.

DIANA CHANG
(1934–   )

Eduardo de Almeida

BIOGRAPHY

Born in 1934 in New York City to a Eurasian mother and a Chinese father, Diana Chang spent her formative years in China, where she received her training at English-language schools. She returned to the United States after World War II and graduated from Barnard College in 1949. In addition to being a prolific writer—her publications include six novels, four volumes of poetry, and numerous short stories and essays—she has served as an editor for *American Pen*, taught creative writing at Barnard College, and exhibited her paintings. She was awarded the John Hay Whitney Opportunity Fellowship, which helped her to complete her first novel, *The Frontiers of Love*; a grant from the New York State Council on the Arts and a Fulbright Fellowship also rank among the numerous awards she has received. Diana Chang currently lives in Philadelphia.

MAJOR WORKS AND THEMES

Nearly half a century after its original publication, *The Frontiers of Love* remains one of the most anthologized works in Asian American literature, and not surprisingly, critics have focused their attention on thematic markers of racialized subjects whose precarious identities are intermittently constituted in and evacuated from interstitial spaces. The status of agency vis-à-vis reified or easily consumed representations and "authenticity," the reservoir of ethnic markers par excellence, is a central concern for Chang in not only her first novel, but her early poetry as well. What emerges from a consideration of this "hyphenated condition," Chang's term, ostensibly yields the familiar negotiation of superimposed cultures, as the opening lines about being Chinese or American from "Otherness" would suggest. The same refrain appears in "Saying Yes," where answers and qualifications are interspersed with awkward interruptions and ellipses, further resonating with a stanza from "An Appearance of Being Chinese." The acceleration of line breaks, working in tandem with the cascading typographical arrangement, suggests both a deferral of what is "Chinese" and a fragmentation of sorts. However, it is precisely fragmentation of identity that Chang challenges through her dismantling of the infinitive; instead, reflection on the constructedness or "tall tale" of identity is paramount. Here Chang rails against a static and radical particularization of ethnic representation—part and parcel of exoticizing maneuvers—in favor of a modal approach attentive to artistic imperatives within the fluxes of identity. Indeed, Chang has remarked, "I feel I'm my own invention" (qtd. in Ling 71).

Such questions regarding autogenesis also gesture toward existential concerns in "Codes," "The Double," and other poems from *The Horizon Is Definitely Speaking*. Only "Second Nature" and "Once and Future" from this volume and "On Gibson Lane, Sagaponack" from the subsequent volume, *What Matisse Is After*, overtly treat Asian American identity. In fact, the questions that emerge from her later poetry tend to concern such disparate issues as the nature of reality, the relationship between philosophy and art, and the role of landscape in transforming consciousness. *The Mind's Amazement* contemplates the very subjects—namely, painting, poetry, and music—invoked by one of her earliest poems, "Four Views in Praise of Reality." These thematic overtures furnish insight into the tenor of Chang's mind and, in particular, the extent to which she is invested in a "universality" not precluded by ethnicity (Ling 75).

CRITICAL RECEPTION

Diana Chang's resistance to ghettoizing her work prompted its stark vilification by cultural nationalist Frank Chin in the now-infamous 1972 letter to Frank Ching, editor of *Bridge*. In his correspondence, Chin condemns Chang for internalizing "white racist rhetoric about universals of art and being an individual instead of white or yellow" (Ching 32). As Amy Ling astutely notes in her rehabilitation of Chang's work, Chin argues from a politically charged tradition that demands a specific interventionist potential from works by ethnic writers, and as such, the strictures of "responsibility" impair the forging of experiential coalitions.

Perhaps the most striking feature of Chang's poetry is its sparseness and economy of language. There is indeed a certain tonal and lyrical balance never betrayed by the richness of interiority, which, in Shirley Lim's estimation, discloses "a persona so elusive and fragile that we have a sense of endless secrecy, of the utmost eavesdropping when we read her poems" (55). Remarkably, Chang displays yet another dimension of her creativity by including four paintings in her collection *What Matisse Is After*. The profound conceptual interpenetration of painting and writing is manifest in such poems as "Pen and Brush" from *The Mind's Amazement*. The image works as a sensuous complex of metaphors, representing the sister arts of poetry and painting in montaged relation to one another. In his explication of "Plunging into View," Thomas Fink maintains that Chang is paying homage to "action painting" to the extent that she "disrupts the stasis of compositional resolution" by omitting punctuation and exploiting the polyvalence of "painting," read either as act or object (176). While Chang's prose still commands vastly more critical attention than her poetry, scholars would do well to reconsider her poetry in light of its imagistic and experimental inclinations.

BIBLIOGRAPHY

Works by Diana Chang

Poetry

"Four Views of Reality." *American Scholar* 25.1 (1955–56): 67–68.

"Lines for an Anniversary." *American Scholar* 25.1 (1955–56): 66.

"Otherness." *Asian-American Heritage*. Ed. David Hsin-Fu Wand. New York: Washington Square Press, 1974. 135.

"Saying Yes." *Asian-American Heritage*. Ed. David Hsin-Fu Wand. New York: Washington Square Press, 1974. 130.

"Tourist Love." *Asian-American Heritage*. Ed. David Hsin-Fu Wand. New York: Washington Square Press, 1974. 136–37.

"An Appearance of Being Chinese." *New York Quarterly* 17 (1975): 67.

"Artist East and West." *Bridge* 4.4 (1976): 9.

"Still Life." *Bridge* 4.4 (1976): 8.

The Horizon Is Definitely Speaking. Port Jefferson, NY: Backstreet Editions, 1982.

What Matisse Is After. New York: Contact II Publications, 1984.

"Plunging into View." *Long Island Review* 10 (1986): 41.

"On Being in the Midwest." *The Forbidden Stitch: An Asian American Women's Anthology*. Ed. Shirley Lim, Mayumi Tsutakawa, and Margarita Donnelly. Corvallis, OR: Calyx Books, 1989. 123.

"On the Fly." *The Forbidden Stitch: An Asian American Women's Anthology*. Ed. Shirley Lim, Mayumi Tsutakawa, and Margarita Donnelly. Corvallis. OR: Calyx Books, 1989. 124.

"In Two." *Ms.* 1.1 (July–August 1990): 83.

Earth, Water, Light: Landscape Poems Celebrating the East End of Long Island. Northport, NY: Birnham Wood Graphics, 1991.

"Keeping Time." *Chinese American Poetry: An Anthology*. Ed. L. Ling-chi Wang and Henry Yiheng Zhao. Santa Barbara, CA: Asian American Voices, 1991. 20.

"A Persuasion." *Chinese American Poetry: An Anthology*. Ed. L. Ling-chi Wang and Henry Yiheng Zhao. Santa Barbara, CA: Asian American Voices, 1991. 28–29.

"Present Tense." *Chinese American Poetry: An Anthology*. Ed. L. Ling-chi Wang and Henry Yiheng Zhao. Santa Barbara, CA: Asian American Voices, 1991. 26.

"Swimmers." *Chinese American Poetry: An Anthology*. Ed. L. Ling-chi Wang and Henry
    Yiheng Zhao. Santa Barbara, CA: Asian American Voices, 1991. 27.
"A Wall of Their Own." *Chinese American Poetry: An Anthology*. Ed. L. Ling-chi Wang
    and Henry Yiheng Zhao. Santa Barbara, CA: Asian American Voices, 1991. 19.
"At the Window." *Quiet Fire: A Historical Anthology of Asian American Poetry, 1892–*
    1970. Ed. Juliana Chang. New York: Asian American Writers' Workshop, 1996.
    63.
The Mind's Amazement: Poems Inspired by Paintings, Poetry, Music, Dance. Islip, NY:
    Live Poets Society, 1998.

Novels

The Frontiers of Love. New York: Random House, 1956.
A Woman of Thirty. New York: Random House, 1959.
A Passion for Life. New York: Random House, 1961.
The Only Game in Town. New York: Signet, 1963.
Eye to Eye. New York: Harper and Row, 1974.
A Perfect Love. New York: Jove, 1978.

Short Fiction

"Falling Free." *Crosscurrents* 5.3 (1985): 55–72.
"The Story That Swallowed Itself." *Confrontation* 30–31 (1985): 81–86.
"Getting Around." *North American Review* 271.4 (1986): 46–49.
"The Oriental Contingent." *The Forbidden Stitch: An Asian American Women's Anthol-*
    ogy. Ed. Shirley Lim, Mayumi Tsutakawa, and Margarita Donnelly. Corvallis,
    OR: Calyx Books, 1989. 171–77.
"Once Upon a Time." *North American Review* 276.1 (1991): 50–51.

Articles

"Why Do Writers Write?" *American Pen* 1.1 (1969): 1–3.
"Wool Gathering, Ventriloquism, and the Double Life." *American Pen* 3.1 (1970–71):
    1–4.
"Can Writing Be Taught?" *ADE Bulletin* 70 (1981): 35–40.
"Response." *Yellow Light: The Flowering of Asian American Arts*. Ed. Amy Ling. Phil-
    adelphia: Temple University Press, 1999. 37–40.

Edited Volumes

Barkan, Stanley H., and Diana Chang, eds. *Approaching*. Trans. Parker P. Huang. Mer-
    rick, NY: Cross-Cultural Communications, 1989.
Barkan, Stanley H., and Diana Chang, eds. *Saying Yes*. Trans. Parker P. Huang. Merrick,
    NY: Cross-Cultural Communications, 1991.

Studies of Diana Chang

Bishop, Janice. Rev. of *What Matisse Is After*. *The Forbidden Stitch: An Asian American
    Women's Anthology*. Ed. Shirley Lim, Mayumi Tsutakawa, and Margarita Don-
    nelly. Corvallis, OR: Calyx Books, 1989. 242–43.

Ching, Frank, et al. "Who's Afraid of Frank Chin, or Is It Ching?" *Bridge* 2.2 (1972): 29–34.

Fink, Thomas. "Chang's 'Plunging into View.' " *Explicator* 55.3 (1997): 175–77.

———. Rev. of *The Mind's Amazement*. *Confrontation* 66–67 (1998–99): 319–21.

Grow, L.M. "On Diana Chang's 'Four Views in Praise of Reality.' " *Amerasia* 16.1 (1990): 211–15.

Hamalian, Leo. "A MELUS Interview: Diana Chang." *MELUS* 20.4 (1995): 29–43.

Lim, Shirley. Rev. of *The Horizon Is Definitely Speaking*. *Contact II* 7.38–40 (1986): 55–56.

Ling, Amy. "Writer in the Hyphenated Condition: Diana Chang." *MELUS* 7.4 (1980): 69–83.

Wand, David Hsin-Fu. "The Chinese-American Literary Scene: A Galaxy of Poets and a Lone Playwright." *Ethnic Literatures since 1776: The Many Voices of America*. Ed. Wolodymyr T. Zyla and Wendell M. Aycock. Lubbock: Texas Tech University Press, 1978. 121–46.

MARILYN MEI LING CHIN
(1955–   )

Zhou Xiaojing

BIOGRAPHY

Marilyn Chin was born on January 14, 1955, in Hong Kong, and grew up in Portland, Oregon. She received her B.A. in Chinese language and literature from the University of Massachusetts at Amherst in 1977 and her M.F.A. from the University of Iowa in 1981. From 1984 to 1985, she was a Stegner Fellow at Stanford University, where she further pursued her studies in classical Chinese writings. As an immigrant, Chin is keenly aware of her inevitable acculturation, which renders her Chinese heritage more precious to her. She is interested in both Chinese and Japanese poetry, as well as Chinese history and classical writings. Her translations (with the author) of Gozo Yoshimasu's poems, *Devil's Wind: A Thousand Steps and More*, were published in 1980. In the same year, Chin went to Taiwan to study classical Chinese. Modern Chinese poetry also attracted Chin's attention. She translated Ai Qing's poems with Peng Wenlan and Eugene Eoyang. These translations were published in a book, *Selected Poems of Ai Qing*, in 1982. Reading and translating Japanese and Chinese poetry helped Chin develop a unique poetic style and a distinct poetic voice, which have drawn from both Eastern and Western traditions, but which nonetheless remain unmistakably her own.

Chin's first collection of poetry, *Dwarf Bamboo*, published in 1987, won the Bay Area Book Review Award. The same year, Chin won the Centrum Fellowship and the MacDowell Colony Fellowship. Her second volume, *The Phoenix Gone, the Terrace Empty*, published in 1994, won the PEN Josephine Miles Award. Her other honors include three Pushcart Prize awards (1994, 1995, 1997) and inclusion in *The Best American Poetry* (1996). She is also the recipient of a Mary Roberts Rinehart Award (1983), a Virginia Center for the Creative Arts fellowship (1983), two National Endowment for the Arts grants (1985, 1991), and a Senior Fulbright Fellowship to Taiwan (1999–2000), among other awards.

Besides writing and translating poetry, Chin has also done much editing work. Between 1978 and 1982, she worked as the editor of the International Writing Program at the University of Iowa, where she was a teaching fellow from 1980 to 1982. She is the editor of *Writing from the World*, II (1985) and a coeditor of *Dissident Song: A Contemporary Asian American Anthology* (1991) and *The Pushcart Prize XXIII: Best of the Small Presses* (1999). At the same time, Chin has been writing short stories, one of which, entitled "Moon," is published in *Charlie Chan Is Dead: An Anthology of Contemporary Asian American Fiction* (1993). She has been working on a collection of short stories, *Chinese American Revenge Tales*, and her third collection of poetry, *Rhapsody in Plain Yellow*, is forthcoming. While continuing to write poetry and short stories, Chin is translating the work of contemporary Chinese poets. Currently she lives in San Diego, California, and is a professor of creative writing at San Diego State University.

MAJOR WORKS AND THEMES

In the opening poem, "The End of a Beginning," of her first volume, *Dwarf Bamboo*, Chin's persona refers to herself, the poet, as "the beginning of an end, the end of a beginning" in working-class Chinese American history (3). This self that is part of a collective history and identity, a self that is distinctly individual and ethnic, rebellious and creative, occupies center stage in Chin's poems. The complexity of this self and its socially and historically shaped relationships with others create much tension within Chin's poems while generating a sustained investigation of the self in relation to family, to the Chinese American community, to Asian America, and to mainstream America. However, the self in Chin's poems is much more than a mere social construct or a historical product; it retains a basic humanist concept of the individual as the agent of social change, capable of self-reinvention and driven to fulfill its artistic creativity. At the same time, Chin seeks to reclaim and reinvent her Chinese heritage by incorporating and transforming Chinese history, culture, and literary traditions in her poems. She interweaves this process with her exploration of identity politics, constantly relating her persona's identity and experience to that of Chinese Americans in terms of Asian Americans' social status and issues of assimilation and acculturation. Thus the lyric "I" in Chin's poems is radically different from that in traditional European American lyric poetry, which Chin thinks is "dominated by self." As minority American poets, Chin says, "We have to be greater than self" (qtd. in "Marilyn Chin's Feminist Muse" 305). In addition to identities of race, culture, class, and nationality that are intricately constituent of the self in Chin's poems, female gender identity is a predominant aspect of Chin's articulation and investigation of the self through autobiographical poems.

Chin's attempts to reclaim her Chinese cultural heritage are central to her poetics and theme. In her interview with Bill Moyers, Chin reveals her fear of losing her Chinese heritage and the Chinese language. For Chin, this loss "would be like losing a part of myself, losing part of my soul." But she adds, "Poetry seems a way to capture that" ("Marilyn Chin" 70). In her poems, she seeks to inscribe her Chinese cultural identity and to resist European American cultural domination through allusions, subject matter, and experimentation with the lyric form and rhythm by incorporating elements of Chinese aesthetics and poetic structure. The title of her first book, *Dwarf Bamboo*, alludes to Bai Jüyi (Po Chü-yi, 772–846), a great poet of the Tang dynasty (618–907). Chin uses two lines from Bai Jüyi's poem "Planting Bamboo" as the epigraph for her book. This newly planted bamboo with its roots still weak and shade still small, but being resilient, will grow into its full potential. The analogy embodied in this dwarf bamboo is to Chin herself as a young poet, and to the situation of Chinese American poetry itself—an analogy that is echoed in the opening poem of *Dwarf Bamboo* and throughout the book. Chin begins her first book of poetry with the statement "The beginning is always difficult" (*Dwarf Bamboo* 3). This beginning refers to the history both of working-class Chinese Americans and of a Chinese American poetic tradition. But the beginning of the latter signals an end to the long history of manual labor and subservient work to which Chinese American immigrants were confined. Echoing the implications of the dwarf bamboo, the persona in the opening poem assumes the voice of a grandchild, who evokes her grandfather along with Chinese American history while writing poems for the grandfather, an embodiment of an older generation of Chinese American workers. Moreover, this voice, which often speaks with humor and self-mockery, is compelling, ironic, and strident—a unique poetic voice Chin has developed with her theme and style. Drawing from the kind of humor characteristic of Daoist writings, Chin's poetic voice and its mocking tone help her break away from the ponderous, pondering voice of self-importance such as that used in Wordsworth's and Emerson's lyric poems. The irony in her voice is also subversive, for it pluralizes the voice and the viewpoint articulated while undermining it. In fact, the ironic voice in Chin's poems serves multiple functions, creating ambivalence and asserting social critique while rendering her themes complex and multidimensional.

The connections between China and Chinese Americans with respect to cultural heritage are a major theme in Chin's poems. The first section of *Dwarf Bamboo*, subtitled "Parent Node," consists of fourteen poems that allude to various periods of Chinese history, from the first century B.C. to the last dynasty, from the Nationalist movement to the Communist revolution, and from the Japanese invasion to the Great Cultural Revolution. While inscribing Chinese history, Chin incorporates her Chinese heritage into both the content and form of her poems. In "The Cricket," for instance, the culturally distinct content is accompanied by a new composition method. Rather than developing with logical argument or simultaneous movement of observation and contemplation, as is typical of the traditional Western lyric, "The Cricket" depends on a central image to motivate its movement through loose associations, taking historical and conceptual leaps from one stanza to another. The paradox of potentially destructive and creative forces symbolized in the cricket is developed and revealed through a wide range of history and geography outside the borders of European America. Thus Chin's incorporation of Chinese history and culture in her poem is more than a nostalgic gesture or an aesthetic necessity. It has the effect of resisting Eurocentrism and of transforming American poetry.

However, Chin's poems sometimes also convey a sense of Chinese Americans' tenuous connection to their Chinese cultural heritage as a result of the passage of time and of assimilation. Much of this sense and the resulting tensions are dealt with in the second section of her first volume, subtitled "American Soil." The opening poem of this section, "Counting, Recounting," captures Chin's feeling of losing her connection to her ethnic cultural background through reference to the death of her persona's grandmother, who, like the grandfather in the opening poem, has the function of a bridge between China and North America for Chinese Americans. For Chin, capturing her Chinese cultural heritage in poetry involves reinventing the self and what she has inherited. Several of her poems explore the necessity, conditions, and difficulties of this reinvention. For instance, in "Chinaman's Chance," Chin suggests that historical and social conditions for Chinese immigrants have made the survival of Chinese cultural identities difficult. The title of the poem alludes to the racist laws aimed at excluding and disempowering Chinese immigrants economically and politically, making it impossible for them to have a chance to realize their "American dream." As the poem develops, the title begins to reveal another layer of implication: Chinese immigrants' and their children's chase after the materialistic American dream of wealth, which undermines their chance of maintaining and developing Chinese American artistic and intellectual traditions. In a conversation with Maxine Hong Kingston, Chin compares the literary aspirations of Wittman Ah Sing (protagonist in Kingston's *Tripmaster Monkey*) and her own dream of becoming a poet, in contrast to many immigrants' dream of buying a house ("Writing the Other" 1). The conflict between spiritual and material pursuits in the first part of "Chinaman's Chance," though not resolved within the poem, is replaced by another central theme as the speaker's ironic tone gives way to a meditative, defiant, and triumphant voice that proclaims the resilience and indomitable spirit of Chinese Americans who, uprooted, still can reclaim their cultural heritage by reinventing it. As the speaker says, we have arrived small and wooden, and dislocated, but we shall gather what is left to us and "shatter this ancient marble, veined and glorious" (*Dwarf Bamboo* 30).

Despite this proclaimed faith in Chinese Americans' ability to re-create their cultural identity, many of Chin's poems deal with the ambivalence and contradictions involved in Chinese Americans' struggle for survival and material success, on the one hand, and their artistic ambitions, on the other. In "Art Wang Is Alive and Ill and Struggling in Oakland California," Chin dramatizes the difficulties that working-class Chinese Americans have in developing their artistic talents and pursuing their creative ambitions. She employs collage to juxtapose different voices and perspectives within the poem. The first perspective is conveyed through a cynical voice calling Qi Baishi (Chi Pai Shih), a great Chinese painter, a bore (*Dwarf Bamboo* 68). This voice and its viewpoint are juxtaposed with Qi Baishi's voice and perspective on his painting. Chin contrasts this famous painter's life of leisure completely dedicated to the art of painting and his lack of adventurous spirit with the situation of a Chinese American painter, who is at once an individual and an embodiment of a collective condition of Chinese Americans, as his name, Art Wang, suggests. The juxtaposition indicates that for Chinese American artists such as Art Wang, Qi Baishi's artistic credo and practice are impossible to follow. Art Wang works for long hours in his father's chopsuey joint; his "pallette is muddy; his thoughts are mud," and his body is exhausted. As the poem switches the perspective and voice to those of Art Wang's, it reveals to the reader that Art Wang now shares his father's dream of having fast cars and California gold (*Dwarf Bamboo* 68). Still, Chin's persona is in love with this dying, unfulfilled Chinese American painter. This devoted love for Art Wang dramatizes Chin's complex theme of dislocation, assimilation, and cultural identity through intensely personal experience that is resolutely related to a collective history and identity.

Chin often employs gendered and racially marked personal relationships to deal with Chinese Americans' relations with mainstream America. In poems such as "Segments of a Bamboo Screen," "Barbarian Suite," and "Where We Live Now," the interracial relationships between Chinese Americans and white Americans are entangled with Chinese Americans' socially conditioned alienation and problematic assimilation. In "Segments of a Bamboo Screen," the scenes painted on the bamboo screen serve as a Chinese background for the American scene in which the speaker, who refers to herself as a Taiwanese, feels alienated from her half brother, who seems to be identical with the golden-haired and pale-skinned young man sitting in front of the screen. Between herself and this man, the speaker says, there is an ocean of fear and distrust, which she suggests results from the history of racism (*Dwarf Bamboo* 17–19). In fact, both the speaker and the white male are more than individuals; they are embodied relationships between Chinese America and white America.

In "Barbarian Suite," Chin explores the consequences of Chinese Americans' assimilation and conveys a sense of the inevitability of their acculturation. This poem consists of six passages, each articulating a particular aspect of the inevitability of change and the resulting loss and fragmentation in the process of a second-generation Chinese American's acculturation. While asserting her sense of fragmentation, the speaker indicates with irony that assimilation into the American mainstream culture is a process of losing one's ethnic cultural heritage in conformity to the dominant culture. Chin uses the generation gap between the grandchildren and their grandmother to illustrate the distance of younger generations of Chinese Americans from their ethnic culture. However, Chin does not present only one perspective through a single voice on assimilation issues. She uses a series of rhetorical questions to challenge the speaker's sentiment about the loss of her Chinese cultural heritage and to undercut her satisfaction with her American bourgeois lifestyle by switching the first-person pronoun to the second while employing a colloquial and slangy manner of speech to convey a particular attitude. In response to these challenging questions, Chin uses another voice to acknowledge the difficulty of assimilation and the creative, transformative possibilities in the process. In the last passage of this poem, Chin further develops the theme of assimilation by introducing into the poem a new cross-cultural subject who is completely at home with different cultures, and who has a white American boyfriend despite the disapproval of her Chinese ancestors. To a certain extent, this new cross-cultural Chinese American is another example of "the beginning of an end, and the end of a beginning" in Chinese American history. This poem, like most of Chin's poems on the same topics, suggests that historical forces render the transformation of cultural heritage inevitable. Thus reclaiming one's cultural heritage is an ongoing process of renegotiating values and reinventing identities.

In exploring the process and consequences of assimilation, Chin pays particular attention to women's experience. One of the problems of assimilation Chin investigates is the impact of the dominant ideology on Chinese Americans' desires, love relationships, and family structures. Chin feels this impact acutely because of her father's betrayal of her mother in his relationship with a white woman, for whom her father left the family. Transforming this autobiographical experience into a poem, "Where We Live Now," Chin situates the personal life within a larger cultural context, calling the family tragedy "a typical American story" (*Dwarf Bamboo* 41). The white woman in the poem, as in Chin's real-life experience, embodies the dangerous allure of the American dream, in which a white woman is a privileged sign of beauty. In this and other poems, especially those in her second book, Chin seeks to be "a conduit for her mother's voice and the voices of other Asian women" ("Marilyn Chin" 75).

In her second book, *The Phoenix Gone, the Terrace Empty*, Chin further problematizes Asian Americans' assimilation by exposing racial stereotypes of Asian Americans and the perpetual marginalization of their social status. In another autobiographical poem on assimilation, "How I Got That Name," Chin reveals that her father, obsessed with an American white sex icon, changed her name from "Mei Ling" to "Marilyn." However, despite the efforts of immigrants like her father to assimilate, Asian Americans are marked as Other and stereotyped as the "model minority" in the racial hierarchy of the United States. Chin employs self-mockery to expose the naturalized stereotype of Asian Americans. Although the poem is overtly autobiographical, the personal becomes irreducibly social, in part due to Chin's switch of pronouns from the first-person singular to "we" and her contextualization of personal desires, struggles, and failures

through references to Asian Americans' collective history and social conditions—references such as Angel Island and the "paperson," which evokes the
exclusion of Chinese and other Asian immigrants by U.S. racist laws.

As she continues to blur the boundaries between the private and the public
in her poems, Chin begins to focus more on women's experience and their
positions in the social and familial structures and in their relationships with men.
In several poems, she attempts to resolve the "deep pain and guilt" she feels for
her mother as a result of her father's betrayal and her mother's cultural dislocation ("Marilyn Chin" 75). While dealing with her mother's suffering in the
title poem of her second volume, Chin locates it in history and connects it
to other women's experiences. To further her understanding of women's experience and subject positions, Chin reads writings by feminists such as Hélène
Cixous and Adrienne Rich and postcolonial critics such as Edward Said, Homi
Bhabha, and Gayatri Chakravorty Spivak, as well as Asian American feminist
critics such as Amy Ling, Lisa Lowe, and King-Kok Cheung ("Marilyn Chin's
Feminist Muse" 280). In her interview with Eileen Tabios, Chin says that her
feminism grows out of "personal and familial experiences," and that her poem
"The Phoenix Gone, the Terrace Empty" is a "softly-feminist poem" (qtd. in
"Marilyn Chin's Feminist Muse" 280). According to Chin, the poem is in part
inspired by her reading of the excerpts from the notes by an imperial gardener
about one of the imperial consorts of the Ming dynasty (1368–1644), in which
the gardener mentions that "the Royal Consort [is] 'dying of sorrow,' " without
any explanation (qtd. in "Marilyn Chin's Feminist Muse" 280). Although Chin
is intrigued by the abrupt reference, she has no doubt that this royal consort,
like others, is a victim of history.

This title poem is Chin's longest and most ambitious. Artistically, the poem
could be said to be Chin's masterpiece, which took her four years to perfect.
The title of the poem is taken from a line in a poem entitled "Climbing Phoenix
Terrace at Jin Ling" by Li Bai (Li Po, 701–762), a greatly admired poet of the
Tang dynasty. In the Chinese tradition, the phoenix is an auspicious sign, and
Jin Ling used to be the capital of two kingdoms in ancient China. The line in
Li Bai's poem, "The phoenix gone, the terrace empty, the river flows on" (my
translation), alludes to the disappearance of a prosperous dynasty. While the title
of Chin's poem, "The Phoenix Gone, the Terrace Empty," evokes Chinese history and poetic tradition, the images suggest an irretrievable past and historical
changes. However, that past is irreducibly connected to the present with regard
to women's experience. Chin adds an epigram in four Chinese characters, with
translation in English: "The river flows without ceasing." The sense of continuity
implied in the epigraph counterpoises the sense of loss in the title, creating
ambivalence and tension, which help Chin achieve compactness and intensity.
At the same time, the poem's structure and line arrangement are modeled on
the visual aspect of the flowing river, as captured by the three irregular vertical
lines of the Chinese character for rapid, shallow rivers. The poem starts with
the voice of an imperial consort in the royal palace with reference to her pain

caused by her bound feet, thus foregrounding the female body as a subjugated body in the social construction of gender difference. After a brief transition, the poem moves to the speaker's parents and their respective premarital lives in a village and a shantytown in China, then switches to the parents' lives in the United States. As the poem moves through different historical periods and locations, Chin's persona is embarked on a quest for a better understanding of her parents and herself. When the poem shifts to the daughter's life, including her love relationship with an American of whom her family does not approve, it refocuses on women's gender identity and subjugation by alluding to Chinese women's bound feet again, and to a Chinese myth about two star-crossed lovers—the youngest daughter of the Emperor of Heaven and a cowboy on earth—who crossed forbidden boundaries. These allusions not only connect the daughter to her mother's generation and to Chinese women in the past, they also suggest a connection between women's bodies and their gendered subject position, between women's gender identity and their sexuality. Significantly, the closing lines of the poem are spoken in the voice of the mother, who disagrees with her daughter. By ending the poem with the mother's voice and viewpoint, Chin raises questions about her attempt to speak for other women, including her mother.

Chin explores further her right and responsibility to speak for other women in another poem, "The Gilded Cangue," subtitled "(*Phoenix series #2/3*)." Connecting this poem to "The Phoenix Gone, the Terrace Empty," especially to the questions raised in its closing lines, Chin examines the consequences of not speaking for women who have been deprived of a voice. For Chin, these questions also concern the relations between art and life, as the speaker suggests in the poem (*Phoenix Gone* 56). She continues to investigate the possibilities of using her poetry as a conduit for other women's voices in the last poem of her second volume, "A Portrait of the Self as Nation, 1990–1991." As the title indicates, the female speaker in the poem regards her personal identity as part of the collective identities of race, gender, culture, and nationality. Throughout the poem, the female speaker examines her identity and love relationship with a white man in the historical contexts of racism, sexism, and colonialism, exposing "the power of exclusion" exercised against the Other (*Phoenix Gone* 96) and commenting with irony on Eurocentrism. Meshing the personal with the social and political in her poetry, Chin has developed a poetics that collapses the binary opposites between aesthetics and politics.

CRITICAL RECEPTION

Chin's poetry, particularly her second collection, *The Phoenix Gone, the Terrace Empty*, has received glowing reviews. Although there is less critical attention to her first volume, *Dwarf Bamboo*, its reviews are insightful. Almost all reviewers note Chin's in-depth exploration of Chinese Americans' cultural identity in terms of their connections to China and the problems of their assimilation in the United States. Da Zheng observes that Chin's "various allusions to Chinese history and tradition" are a way of dealing with Chinese immigrants' "indissoluble connection with their cultural origin" (Rev. of *Dwarf Bamboo* 174). In her representation of the process of Chinese Americans' assimilation and acculturation, Zheng writes, Chin's satirical remarks often help bring into sharp focus "the conflicting values and hardships" that Chinese Americans confront in their struggles to survive and succeed (175). Zheng also notes Chin's thematic concerns about women's experience of love and betrayal, including Chin's autobiographical poems about her mother's relationship with her father, which are filled with anger, rage, and pain. George Uba also discusses Chin's poems about love in *Dwarf Bamboo*, but he calls the reader's attention to the range and force of Chin's poetic voice, which is "never flat, predictable, or self-indulgent," but invariably "tender, sardonic, jaded, and inspired" (Rev. of *Dwarf Bamboo* 127). Furthermore, Uba points out the effective way in which Chin deals with "that other great love in her life—poetry" through analogues of marriage and meshing desire with anxiety in articulating her artistic aspiration (127). Uba's attention to Chin's articulation about her passion for art, like Zheng's observation of Chin's treatment of women's experience, enriches our reading of Chin's poetry, which cannot be reduced to merely immigrant narratives about assimilation. Dorothy Joan Wang's examination of Chin's use of irony in her poems adds a significant dimension to critical views on sarcasm in Chin's poetic voice. Arguing that irony suggests bifurcation, Wang contends that Chin's employment of irony reproduces the multiple pressures and contradictions in the formation of Asian American subjectivities. Thus sardonic voices in Chin's poems are a means of negotiating identities of race, gender, and culture from multiple subject positions.

In addition to Chin's distinct poetic voice and her major thematic concerns of assimilation, acculturation, and women's oppression by patriarchy, critics also note themes of exile and compassion in Chin's poems, particularly in her second volume. Michael Dennis Browne finds that the "central circumstance" of the many broken lives in Chin's poems is "exile," including linguistic exile—the loss of mother tongue. Even though Chin's own life is characterized by exile, Browne emphasizes, the self that is revealed in the poems is not only vulnerable but also resolute. Browne also notes Chin's sense of "connectedness with others" and her capacity for compassion, which are shown in her portrayal of a range of diverse characters (40). The connectedness to numerous others in a way helps Chin's poems escape self-indulgence and renders personal lives resonant of larger social and historical issues.

Rather than consigning Chin's poetry to the margins, Browne situates it at the center of the American poetic scene. He examines Chin's poetic and cultural hybridity that give rise to a new mode of lyric poetry. Browne's discussion of Chin's literary allusions adds Berryman, Plath, Pound, Williams, Frost, Eliot, Milosz, Keats, and Baudelaire, among others, to the list of her incorporations from Western canons. Identifying as East Asian sources Basho, Du Fu, and

Zhuangzi, Browne further notes that the fact that Chin situates her allusions in specific "social practices" illustrates "the true dimensions of her awareness" (40). Perhaps what is most significant in Chin's incorporation of Japanese and Chinese poetic traditions and her references to Chinese history, including the students' prodemocracy movement in Tiananmen Square, is a counterdiscourse to Orientalism.

Even though critical reception of Chin's work is overwhelmingly positive, some critics—very few—find her subject matter limiting. Charles Altieri, for example, regards Chin's poetry as merely a "content" poetry that employs images "as testimony to typical conditions" of first- and second-generation immigrants' struggles in coming to terms with their social conditions and in negotiating with mainstream American culture (72). The problems with such poems, Altieri contends, lie in the fact that commonplace themes such as assimilation and acculturation in the immigrant experience fail to fully challenge "mainstream values" or to bring "news" to American poetry. Furthermore, Altieri finds that "most poetry devoted to the content of immigrant experience and its aftermath tends to be written in a generic style, very close to dominant American modes of lyric feeling"; therefore, such content poetry also fails to challenge the lyric style of mainstream poetry (73). For Altieri, *The Phoenix Gone, the Terrace Empty* "keeps trying imaginative variations on the standard assimilation story," which eventually reveal "how limited the poetry of self-narration has become" (75). Altieri cites two of Chin's poems, "How I Got That Name" and "A Portrait of the Self as Nation, 1990–1991," to illustrate his contention about the generic constraints of poetry about immigrant experience written in the autobiographical vein of "testimonial lyric" (75). One of the faults Altieri finds with "How I Got That Name" is the fact that Chin's positioning of her persona as one caught between her seduction by American popular culture and the stereotype of the "model minority" impoverishes her poem, because her use of language is restricted to nothing but "the constant verbal revision of what seems a psychic landscape entirely defined by external forces" (76–77). Although Altieri finds that "A Portrait of the Self as Nation" entails a more complex "self-analysis" (77), it fails to "work through any significant mode of self-definition" (79). For Altieri, both the thematic and stylistic limitations of Chin's testimonial poetry render more valuable the radically experimental Asian American poetry such as that by John Yau and Myung Mi Kim. Most Asian American critics will probably disagree with Altieri, whose reading of Chin's poetry does not recognize the full range of Chin's voice, style, and theme. Nevertheless, Altieri's view on contemporary Asian American poetry raises provocative questions about the relations between aesthetics and politics, about the poet's social responsibility and artistic commitment. Chin's poetry provides a site for the exploration of these questions.

BIBLIOGRAPHY

Works by Marilyn Mei Ling Chin

Poetry

Dwarf Bamboo. Greenfield Center, NY: Greenfield Review Press, 1987.
The Phoenix Gone, the Terrace Empty. Minneapolis: Milkweed Editions, 1994.

Short Story

"Moon." *Charlie Chan Is Dead: An Anthology of Contemporary Asian American Fiction.* Ed. and intro. Jessica Hagedorn. New York: Penguin Books, 1993. 87–90.

Interviews

"Writing the Other: A Conversation with Maxine Hong Kingston." *Poetry Flash* 198 (September 1989): 1, 4, 17–18.
"Marilyn Chin." With Bill Moyers. *The Language of Life: A Festival of Poets.* New York: Doubleday, 1995. 67–79.
"Marilyn Chin's Feminist Muse Addresses Women, 'The Grand Victims of History.' " With Eileen Tabios. *Black Lightning: Poetry-in-Progress.* New York: Asian American Writers' Workshop, 1998. 280–312.

Anthologies Edited

Writing from the World, II. Iowa City: University of Iowa Press, 1985.
Dissident Song: A Contemporary Asian American Anthology. With David Wong Louie and Ken Weisner. Santa Cruz, CA: Quarry West, 1991.

Translations

Devil's Wind: A Thousand Steps and More. By Gozo Yoshimasu. Trans. with the author. Oakland: Oakland University, 1980.
Selected Poems of Ai Qing. Trans. with Peng Wenlan and Eugene Eoyang. Ed. Eugene Eoyang. Bloomington: Indiana University Press, 1982.

Studies of Marilyn Mei Ling Chin

Altieri, Charles. "Images of Form vs. Images of Content in Contemporary Asian-American Poetry." *Qui Parle* 9.1 (Fall/Winter 1995): 71–91.
Bensko, John. "A Place of One's Own." Rev. of *The Phoenix Gone, the Terrace Empty. Poet Lore* 89.2 (1995): 73–74.
Browne, Michael Dennis. "Cousin to a Million." Rev. of *The Phoenix Gone, the Terrace Empty. Hungry Mind Review* (Summer 1994): 40.
Hai-Jew, Shalin. Rev. of *Dwarf Bamboo. The Forbidden Stitch: An Asian American Women's Anthology.* Ed. Shirley Geok-lin Lim, Mayumi Tsutakawa, and Margarita Donnelly. Corvallis, OR: Calyx Books, 1989. 262.
Marquart, Lisa. "The Zen of Irony and Wit: Poet Marilyn Chin Strikes a Balance between East and West." *Daily Aztec* 2 March 1994: 9.

Rothschild, Matthew. Rev. of *The Phoenix Gone, the Terrace Empty*. *Progressive* 58.5
    (May 1994): 49–50.
Svoboda, Terese. "Try Bondage." Rev. of *The Phoenix Gone, the Terrace Empty*. *Kenyon
    Review* 17.2 (Spring 1995): 159–60.
Uba, George. Rev. of *Dwarf Bamboo*. *MELUS* 15.1 (Spring 1988): 125–27.
———. "Versions of Identity in Post-activist Asian American Poetry." *Reading the Lit-
    eratures of Asian America*. Ed. Shirley Geok-lin Lim and Amy Ling. Philadelphia:
    Temple University Press, 1992. 33–48.
Walch, Bob. "Poet Marilyn Chin Is Claimed by Two Cultures." Rev. of *The Phoenix
    Gone, the Terrace Empty*. *Monterey County Herald* 4 April 1999: E6.
Wang, Dorothy Joan. "Necessary Figures: Metaphor, Irony, and Parody in the Poetry of
    Li-Young Lee, Marilyn Chin, and John Yau." Diss. University of California,
    Berkeley, 1998.
Zheng, Da. Rev. of *Dwarf Bamboo*. *Amerasia Journal* 21.1–2 (1995): 173–75.
———. Rev. of *The Phoenix Gone, the Terrace Empty*. *Amerasia Journal* 24.2 (Summer
    1998): 186–91.
Zhou, Xiaojing. "Breaking from Tradition: Experimental Poems by Four Contemporary
    Asian American Women Poets." *Revista Canaria de Estudios Ingleses* 37 (No-
    vember 1998; a special issue on twentieth-century American women poets): 199–
    218.
———. "Rearticulating 'Otherness': Strategies of Cultural and Linguistic Differences in
    Asian American Women's Poetry." *Asian American Studies: Identities, Images,
    Issues Past and Present*. Ed. Esther Mikyung Ghymn. New York: Peter Lang,
    2000. 151–77.

ERIC CHOCK
(1950–   )

Rhoda J. Yen

BIOGRAPHY

Eric Chock was born in Hawaii and first became interested in writing as a boy, when he dreamed of becoming a songwriter. Chock recalls listening to folk rock music of the 1960s and 1970s, such as that by Bob Dylan, Paul Simon, and the Beatles, and strumming his guitar while sitting on the beach. He often used the lyrics of his favorite songs to create his own verses. When his lyrics no longer rhymed, he realized that he was writing poetry. Chock later wrote lyrics for a friend who was a musician.

After high school, Chock attended college in Pennsylvania and majored in English. During his undergraduate years, he wrote many letters back home and became involved in activism. Chock soon became a conscientious objector, VISTA worker, and local community organizer. He kept writing in his spare time and then returned home to the University of Hawaii for graduate school. Chock met Phyllis Tompkins, who invited him to apply to the Poets in the Schools program, which was designed to encourage young students in their writing. Chock applied for the job, was accepted, and served as a teacher and coordinator from 1973 to 1995. In 1981, he published *Small Kid Time Hawaii*, a collection of poems written by students in the program.

In 1977, Chock met Stephen Sumida and helped organize the 1978 Talk Story writers conference in Hawaii. He met other local and Asian American writers and realized for the first time that he was considered a Chinese American. In particular, Chock spent time talking with Frank Chin and realized the similarities as well as the differences in growing up Chinese in Hawaii or on the continent.

His discussions with Chin also led him to the conclusion that racism takes many forms, is carried in language and literature, and is perpetuated unconsciously. While preparing for the conference, Chock conceived the idea of creating a literary magazine that would highlight the local literature of the authors attending the conference. Chock recalls: "We wanted it to be both a showcase and a vehicle. In a way, we were riding on the coattails of other ethnic movements around the United States. We were trying to help create a sense of community, at least a sense of literary community" (Burlingame).

Chock and his friend, Darrell Lum, envisioned a racially encompassing body of contributors and invited writers who were teaching at the University of Hawaii as well as individuals who were diametrically opposed to them. Together with Lum, Chock founded the *Bamboo Ridge* literary journal and Bamboo Ridge Press, the company that publishes both the journal and collected works by single authors. Despite having endured criticism, *Bamboo Ridge* has remained on the forefront in publishing local literature, particularly by and about Hawaii's working people, many of them descendants of those who worked on the sugarcane plantations. In upholding that tradition, *Bamboo Ridge* was also one of the first journals to publish work written in Hawaii's Creole English, known as Pidgin, that arose from those same plantations. Writers who have appeared in *Bamboo Ridge* have since become the literary voices of Hawaii: Lois-Ann Yamanaka, Rodney Morales, Gary Pak, Nora Okja Keller, Dana Naone Hall, Wing Tek Lum, Michael McPherson, Mari Kubo, and Cathy Song. In addition, the journal has received numerous awards, including the 1996 Hawaii Award for Literature from the State Foundation on Culture and the Arts and the Hawaii Literary Arts Council.

Chock himself has earned a number of awards and recognitions: the Pushcart Prize XVI, the 1996 Hawaii Award for Literature, the Cades Award for Literature, and the Hawaii Alliance for Arts Education's Arts Educator of the Year Award. Chock was also the University of Hawaii at Manoa Visiting Distinguished Writer in 1995–96. He has served as the president of the board of directors of the Hawaii Literary Arts Council and as a member of the Honolulu City Commission on Culture and the Arts. His own collection of poetry, *Last Days Here*, has been well received, and he is widely known as one of the leading poets using the Pidgin language. His poetry has been published in several anthologies, including *Breaking Silence: An Anthology of Contemporary Asian American Poets* (1983) and *Premonitions: The Kaya Anthology of New Asian North American Poetry* (1995). He currently teaches writing skills and Hawaiian literature at the University of Hawaii's West Oahu campus and continues to write poetry.

MAJOR WORKS AND THEMES

Chock's poetry is, in his own words, "born of the local culture which was developed in Hawaii in the last few decades" (Lew 33). His subjects vary from the personal to the public, and he seeks to combine the two and "capture some sense of the various cultural influences which affect individuals' lives" (Lew 33). He often uses imagery that is particular to the Asian immigrant experience: drinking green tea and savoring a special meal of fish, burning incense to honor an ancestor, working in the sugarcanes, and dreaming of a better life for the new generation to come. The theme of fishing in particular runs throughout Chock's poetry. In *Last Days Here*, Chock devotes an entire section (ten poems altogether) to the "Meaning of Fishing."

One of Chock's most famous poems is "Chinese Fireworks Banned in Hawaii," which offers readers a visual portrait of the winding down of a Chinese family's celebration. The poem depicts the diminishing of Chinese traditions in modern Hawaii as Chock's speaker teaches his children to trace their names in the sky with sparklers, when past celebrations incorporated the use of vibrant fireworks. The poem also evokes a feeling of sadness in the passing of time that often erases the details of joyous family gatherings, depicted in the character Ghislaine filling a Styrofoam cup with red paper confetti to take a piece of the history home with her.

In "Poem for My Father," Chock explores a complicated relationship between father and son. Although the father expresses disapproval over his son's writing ambitions, the son views his father's hopes and opinions as equally puzzling, "just as far and old as the lava chips like flint off his hammer." Chock analogizes the father's efforts to build a wall around the house with his careful endeavors to make the son fulfill his dreams. These dreams are steeped in the father's own memories of fishing and beautiful young women. The poem portrays the generational and cultural conflict common to many Asian American families.

In "The Immigrant," Chock paints a visual picture of an immigrant woman who is the subject of unrelenting stereotypes. Chock uses the phrase "they knew" to distance himself from the attitudes of the natives in their judgments of this laborer. He juxtaposes these judgments with a picture of the woman, who silently and steadily labors in the field, hoping and waiting for the "ship of her dreams" to arrive. The poem presents a stark picture of the immigrant laborer's dreams for a better future and the racist attitudes of the natives who assume that the immigrant is only made for hard labor.

CRITICAL RECEPTION

Chock's poetry has gained critical notice primarily for its use of the modified Pidgin writing system. Pidgin refers to the language variety that is technically called "Hawaii Creole English" or "Hawaii English Creole" by linguists. Traditionally, the language has been viewed with negative and racist attitudes, and it is common for Pidgin speakers (comprised historically of Hawaii's immigrant laborers) to be considered uneducated or coarse. Chock's poetry therefore reinforces and empowers the use of Pidgin among locals and has aided in making Pidgin a means for Hawaiian peoples to form a culture of their own.

Candace Fujikane, for example, interprets Chock's poem "Manoa Cemetery," a reflection on the poet's grandmother, as a statement on the disenfranchisement of Hawaiians (3). In the poem, the narrator relates the story of how a Chinese immigrant is offered land by a Hawaiian king, but takes only enough to bury his ancestors. Despite the history buried on this piece of land, however, the narrator understands that his ownership is uncertain. Fujikane considers Chock's poem to reflect the competing claims to the homeland upon which one's national identity is formed (3). Fujikane concludes, "Unlike Asian American writers . . . who claimed an 'American' identity through a reterritorializing of the American landscape, the narrator of Chock's poem challenges that erection of land as a stable signifier for identity since like his ancestors, he must earn his right to a place on Hawaiian land" (3).

Chock's poetry has also been praised for bringing the local culture of Hawaii into the forefront, given a history of domination in literature by writings from mainland America. Even in the modern popularity of Asian American writing, Chock's poetry stands out as representative of the often-ignored body of work by Pacific Islanders. In a recent speech entitled "On Local Literature," Chock himself explained:

[T]he main underlying point is that we in Hawaii are expected to believe that we are subordinate to the mainland. At best, we are expected to believe that we are really no different here and can even be like the mainland if we try hard enough. We are asked to reject the feeling that Hawaii is special. And when we become numbed and lose the feeling, it then becomes possible to accept mainland history and mainland culture as our own. We are asked to accept mainland literature as the norm. In the process, our own literature loses its cohesiveness, our writings are categorized according to the framework of mainland, mainstream literary history, if at all. (qtd. in Fujikane 2)

BIBLIOGRAPHY

Works by Eric Chock

Poetry

Last Days Here. Honolulu: Bamboo Ridge Press, 1990.
"In the Garden of the Tantalus Museum." *Mid-American Review* 14.1 (Autumn 1993). Available: http://www.bgsu.edu/studentlife/organizations/midamericanreview/14-1.html. Dec., 2000.
"Hawaiian Air." *Tinfish*, No. 2. Ed. Susan M. Schultz. Honolulu: University of Hawaii, 1995. Available: http://wings.buffalo.edu/epc/ezines/tinfish/tinfish02/. Dec., 2000.
"No Evil." *Tinfish*, No. 2. Ed. Susan M. Schultz. Honolulu: University of Hawaii, 1995. Available: http://wings.buffalo.edu/epc/ezines/tinfish/tinfish02/. Dec., 2000.

Anthologies Edited

Talk Story: An Anthology of Hawaii's Local Writers. Honolulu: Petronium Press/Talk Story, 1978.

Ten Thousand Wishes. Honolulu: Bamboo Ridge Press, 1978.
Small Kid Time Hawaii. Honolulu: Bamboo Ridge Press, 1981.
The Best of Bamboo Ridge. With Darrell Lum. Honolulu: Bamboo Ridge Press, 1986.
Paké: Writings by Chinese in Hawaii. With Darrell Lum. Honolulu: Bamboo Ridge Press, 1989.
Growing Up Local: An Anthology of Prose and Poetry from Hawai'i. With James R. Harstad, Darrell Lum, and Bill Teter. Honolulu: Bamboo Ridge Press, 1998.
Best of Honolulu Fiction. With Darrell Lum. Honolulu: Bamboo Ridge Press, 1999.

Studies of Eric Chock

Bruchac, Joseph, ed. *Breaking Silence: An Anthology of Contemporary Asian American Poets*. Greenfield Center, NY: Greenfield Review Press, 1983. 33–38.

Burlingame, Burl. " 'Bamboo' Thriving: 'Bamboo Ridge' Editors Win State Award." *Honolulu Star-Bulletin*. Available: http://starbulletin.com/97/06/23/features/story2.html. Dec., 2000.

Fujikane, Candace. "Between Nationalisms: Hawaii's Local Nation and Its Troubled Racial Paradise." *Hitting Critical Mass: A Journal of Asian American Cultural Criticism* 1.2 (Spring 1994): 1–5. Available: http://istsocrates.berkeley.edu/~critmass/v1n2/fujikane1.html. Dec., 2000.

Leong, Autumn. "Eric Chock: On Writing and Nurturing Writers." Kapi'o Online. Honolulu: Kapi' olani Community College Press, 16 March 1998. Available: http://leahi.kcc.hawaii.edu/news/kapio/3_16_98/intnlfest/chock.html. Dec., 2000.

Lew, Walter K., ed. *Premonitions: The Kaya Anthology of New Asian North American Poetry*. New York: Kaya, 1995.

RIENZI CRUSZ
(1925–   )

Di Gan Blackburn

BIOGRAPHY

Rienzi Crusz was born on 17 October 1925 in Galle, Ceylon (now Sri Lanka). His family moved to Colombo when he was still very young. As a child in a comfortable middle-class burgher family, Crusz received a British-style education and was introduced to the kind of Western literature that would later influence him. He attended high school at St. Joseph's and St. Peter's colleges before majoring in history at the University of Colombo, where he graduated with honors. After a stint as a lecturer at his old high school of St. Joseph's, Crusz went to England in 1951 to study library science as a Colombo Plan Scholar at the University of London. Returning to Ceylon, he took a post as chief research librarian at the Central Bank of Ceylon. He held that position until he emigrated to Canada in 1965 with his three children, partially due to a broken marriage and the political turmoil within Ceylon. In Canada, Crusz earned a B.L.S. from the University of Toronto, where he also worked briefly as a librarian, and an M.A. from the University of Waterloo. He stayed at the University of Waterloo from 1966 to 1993 as a senior reference and collections development librarian (his professional publications are related to this position).

MAJOR WORKS AND THEMES

Crusz began to write poetry for the first time shortly after arriving in Canada and published his poems in a variety of periodicals during the late 1960s and early 1970s. The first volume of his works, *Flesh and Thorn*, appeared in 1974.

It was followed by eight more volumes over the next twenty-five years: *Elephant and Ice, Singing against the Wind, A Time for Loving, Still Close to the Raven, The Rain Doesn't Know Me Anymore, Beatitudes of Ice, Insurgent Rain: Selected Poems, 1974–1996,* and *Lord of the Mountain: The Sardiel Poems.* Crusz's poetry was awarded the Kitchener-Waterloo Prize in 1994.

In many ways, Crusz's often very personal poetry parallels his biography. His first poems were written shortly after his first wife had left him and during his first years as an immigrant in Canada in the late 1960s. Collected in the volume *Flesh and Thorn,* these pieces are very emotional, several of them dealing directly with his wife's betrayal. Although the flame of passion continues to mark Crusz's work, it is especially obvious in poetry of this early period. Crusz's subsequent volumes continue to describe his personal journey in the persona of the "Sun-man," a name emphasizing Crusz's Sri Lankan background (Thorpe 131). As titles such as *Elephant and Ice* suggest ("Elephant" for South Asian, "Ice" for Canada), many of these poems deal with Crusz's experiences as a cross-cultural immigrant.

Though he is best known for his rendering of the emigrant experience, Crusz is also praised for his "unfailing attention to the oral quality of poetry," which might be attributed to his literary education in classic English poetry (Kanaganayakam, "Passionate Dance" 49). Moreover, his extraordinary respect for form has been noticed by several critics, one speculating that he may have been influenced by his father's mathematical background (Parameswaran, "Singing Metaphor" 146). Besides resembling the works of the classic English poets in terms of form, Crusz's poetry also shows the influence of the romantic poets' use of emotion. One critic notes that Crusz's poetry is characterized by a "kind of lyric that gives expression to the power of emotion and sentiment" (Kanaganayakam, "Passionate Dance" 38).

CRITICAL RECEPTION

As one of the first and leading poets in South Asian Canadian Literature (SACLIT), Crusz has been generally well received by South Asian critics but largely neglected by Western scholars. The most extensive study of Crusz is Chelva Kanaganayakam's book *Dark Antonyms and Paradise: The Poetry of Rienzi Crusz.* Another South Asian poet, Uma Parameswaran, has also written several articles on Crusz's poetry. In addition, Crusz's work has been reviewed by a number of literary magazines. Kanaganayakam points out that most of the critical reception has focused largely on Crusz's "hyphenated identity" and his concern with alienation (*Dark Antonyms* 5). The contrasting images in titles such as *Elephant and Ice, Beatitudes of Ice,* and *Singing against the Wind* reinforce this emphasis. Interestingly, Crusz himself is uncomfortable about overemphasizing the role of identity in his poetry and wishes for more attention to its universal themes. As Kanaganayakam laments, many other notable aspects of Crusz's work, such as style, emotion, and relation to other poets, have not been explored to the same depth (*Dark Antonyms* 6).

The most controversial evaluation of Crusz's work centers on the issue of cultural appropriation. Suwanda Sugunasiri in her article " 'Sri Lankan' Canadian Poets: The Bourgeoisie That Fled the Revolution" questions Crusz's status as a "Sri Lankan" poet. Sugunasiri argues that writers like Crusz who voluntarily emigrated to Canada around the time of the Sri Lankan revolution demonstrated a lack of commitment to their motherland. On the other hand, Michael Thorpe calls Crusz "arguably the best living Sri Lankan poet writing in English" (130).

BIBLIOGRAPHY

Works by Rienzi Crusz

Flesh and Thorn. Stratford, Ontario: Pasdeloup Press, 1974.
Elephant and Ice. Erin, Ontario: Porcupine's Quill, 1980.
Singing against the Wind. Erin, Ontario: Porcupine's Quill, 1985.
A Time for Loving. Toronto: TSAR Publications, 1986.
Still Close to the Raven. Toronto: TSAR Publications, 1989.
The Rain Doesn't Know Me Anymore. Toronto: TSAR Publications, 1992.
Beatitudes of Ice. Toronto: TSAR Publications, 1995.
Insurgent Rain: Selected Poems, 1974–1996. Toronto: TSAR Publications, 1997.
Lord of the Mountain: The Sardiel Poems. Toronto: TSAR Publications, 1999.

Studies of Rienzi Crusz

Benson, Eugene, and William Toye, eds. *The Oxford Companion to Canadian Literature*. 2nd ed. New York: Oxford University Press, 1997.
Kanaganayakam, Chelva. *Dark Antonyms and Paradise: The Poetry of Rienzi Crusz*. Toronto: TSAR Publications, 1997.
———. "A Passionate Dance: The Poetry of Rienzi Crusz." *Floating the Borders: New Contexts in Canadian Criticism*. Ed. Nurjehan Aziz. Toronto: TSAR Publications, 1999. 37–50.
Mukherjee, Arun. "Songs of an Immigrant: The Poetry of Rienzi Crusz." *Currents* 4 (1986–87): 19–21.
Parameswaran, Uma. "Rienzi Crusz." *Writers of the Indian Diaspora: A Bio-Bibliographical Critical Sourcebook*. Ed. Emmanuel S. Nelson. Westport, CT: Greenwood Press, 1993. 59–63.
———. "The Singing Metaphor: The Poetry of Rienzi Crusz." *Canadian Literature* 132 (1992): 146–54.
Selvadurai, Shyam. Rev. of *Beatitudes of Ice*. *Books in Canada* 25 (1996): 25.
Sugunasiri, Suwanda H.J. " 'Sri Lankan' Canadian Poets: The Bourgeoisie That Fled the Revolution." *Canadian Literature* 132 (1992): 60–79.
Thorpe, Michael. Rev. of *The Rain Doesn't Know Me Anymore*. *World Literature Today* 68.1 (1994): 130–31.

CHITRA BANERJEE DIVAKARUNI
(1956–   )

Purvi Shah

BIOGRAPHY

Born in July 1956, Chitra Banerjee Divakaruni grew up in Calcutta, India, with the "girlhood ambition . . . to be a teacher" (Lanham 19). After receiving her undergraduate degree in English and Bengali literature from Calcutta University, at the age of nineteen Divakaruni moved to the United States to pursue graduate studies. Her family played a pivotal role in deciding where Divakaruni shifted: she was given permission to go away only if she moved to the city where her elder brother already lived. As a result of this family influence, Divakaruni moved to Dayton, Ohio, in 1976 to obtain a master's degree in English at Wright State University. She left Ohio in 1978 to go to the University of California at Berkeley, where she obtained her Ph.D. in 1984.

Although Divakaruni's scholarly research at Berkeley focused on the role of language in Christopher Marlowe's plays, her creative writing does not echo her academic interest in the Renaissance period but rather broaches topics more closely aligned to her own life and contemporary context. As Divakaruni herself states, "What I write must move me, must satisfy me, must make me feel at once a sense of having discovered—and having uncovered—a truth. If not, it must go no further" (qtd. in "Chitra Banerjee Divakaruni" 137). The kinds of truths Divakaruni's writing explores focus on the familial, social, and national pressures faced by women and immigrants. Her first book of short stories, *Arranged Marriage*, which won the Before Columbus Foundation American Book Award in 1996, exhibits women's turmoil in the absence of decision-making powers. In the earlier poem "The Arranged Marriage," published in her 1991 poetry collection *Black Candle*, Divakaruni depicts the unspoken terror of a hesitant bride whose movements are orchestrated by male relatives.

Divakaruni's investment in women's issues is seen not only in her writing but also in her extraliterary activities—in 1991, the author assisted in the foundation of Maitri, a helpline for South Asian women in the San Francisco Bay Area. In addition to writing and volunteering with Maitri, Divakaruni taught English and creative writing at Foothill College. After working in the Bay Area for twenty years, Divakaruni moved with her husband and two children to Houston, Texas, where she taught creative writing at the University of Houston. But Divakaruni's Texas stint was short: she has moved back to the Bay Area, where she is currently writing full-time and volunteering at Maitri.

MAJOR WORKS AND THEMES

Though she is most widely known for her best-selling 1997 novel *The Mistress of Spices*, Divakaruni first entered the literary world by writing poetry about women and migration, themes that would carry over into her subsequent short stories and novels. The poems in the 1990 collection *The Reason for Nasturtiums* were written around the same time as the pieces in her first influential poetry book, *Black Candle: Poems about Women from India, Pakistan, and Bangladesh. Black Candle*, a text that reviewer Pat Monaghan sees as an "exemplary collection" that is "deeply human, unabashedly feminist," presents a range of South Asian women's experiences (745). In "Burning Bride," Divakaruni tells the tale of a bride whose family cannot pay the full dowry promised to the groom's family. The narrative poem describes the bride's family's poverty as well as the social pressure for the bride to remain married in order to keep the family's name clear and enable the younger sisters to obtain husbands. In this poem, Divakaruni visualizes the impending tragedy concerning "the dark time of my blood" (59). The isolation experienced during menstruation serves as a metonymy for this bride's displacement from the family and South Asian women's general positioning outside social power. As Dharini Rasiah notes, Divakaruni's first three books of poetry "vividly capture her South Asian women subjects' experience with domestic violence, marriage, family, immigration, and death" (140).

Divakaruni couples her interest in women's issues with an examination of migration by imagining the hardships endured by South Asian settlers in America. Drawing upon the history of Indian immigration in the early 1900s, a time when 6,000–15,000 South Asians, mostly Punjabi males, moved to the Pacific Coast of Canada and the United States, Divakaruni re-creates the early struggles in her poems (Yung 425). Due to immigration restrictions that barred these males from bringing their wives and families, bachelor communities formed. As Sucheta Mazumdar writes, "A 1909 Immigration Commission survey of 474 male 'Hindoo' farmworkers found that 215 were married but that all 215 of the wives had remained in India. One such young husband, nurturing memories of his teenage bride, was not able to send for her for forty years. As she got off the plane in San Francisco, in pained bewilderment he gasped, 'But she is such an old woman' " (5). In "The Brides Come to Yuba City," Divakaruni utilizes such historical anecdotes to etch a scene of the first time the Sikh immigrants see their wives. The narrator pitches the tale from the women's point of view. Through exploring ideas of intimacy and consent, "The Brides Come to Yuba City" visualizes the ways in which South Asian women were affected as they entered the northern California bachelor society in Yuba City.

While Divakaruni began by looking at the experiences of Yuba City women, her interest in the history of early Indian immigration grew to extend to the experiences of male settlers. As she tells Rajini Srikanth in an interview for the *Asian Pacific American Journal*, "Initially I was interested in the women's perspective. 'The Brides Come to Yuba City' and 'Yuba City School' grew out of that interest. But as I wrote, I felt that the women's story alone didn't give the entire picture. To explore and tell the complete story, I had to put myself in the place of the men. That's how I wrote 'The Founding of Yuba City' and 'Yuba City Wedding' " (96). In "The Founding of Yuba City," from the 1997 poetry collection *Leaving Yuba City*, Divakaruni charts the thoughts of Punjabi men new to California. The narrator relates the men's first experiences at their farming jobs. In this poem, Divakaruni specifically cites the Alien Land Laws that prevented those unable to obtain U.S. citizenship—nonwhite immigrants—from owning land in America. Akin to the laws that prohibited Asian men from bringing their wives to America until the 1940s, these measures precluded immigrants from possessing any claim to their new world. "The Founding of Yuba City" illustrates the difficulties early South Asian immigrants expected—hard work—and those they did not imagine—racism and legal restrictions.

Though Divakaruni's poems show an overt engagement with history and immigrant experiences, her later work also displays a concern with generic play. Divakaruni describes her first collection of poems, the 1987 *Dark like the River*, by saying, "I was more interested at that point in the emotion of those pieces. Since then, I've become much more concerned about craft—the use of language, the use of imagery, how one says things" (qtd. in Rasiah 151). Divakaruni depicts *Black Candle* as possessing a similar affective aesthetic, a book of poems "remembering" various women with attempts "to give them their special moments through the poems in which they were the center and their pain was the most important element" (qtd. in Rasiah 142).

In *Leaving Yuba City*, this focus on telling particular stories is tied to experimentation with narration and prose formats. In the prose poem "Yuba City Wedding," Divakaruni charts the turmoil faced by a Sikh immigrant as he prepares to marry a local Mexican girl despite opposition from community elders. The use of first-person narration and colloquial language has led Dulcy Brainard to characterize *Leaving Yuba City* as representing early South Asian immigrants' "voices in lush, novelistic prose poems" (68). In a move that shows the proximity of Divakaruni's poetry to prose, editor of *Living in America: Poetry and*

Fiction by South Asian American Writers Roshni Rustomji-Kerns features "Yuba City Wedding" (without the stanza breaks seen in the *Leaving Yuba City* version) in the fiction section of the anthology, saying, "Works such as the following could easily be included in a 'poetry' section" ("Chitra Divakaruni" 95). Rustomji-Kerns justifies the positioning of the piece by claiming a fluidity in South Asian writing:

Poetry, in South Asian traditions of literature—both oral and written—is seldom seen as a specific literary genre existing only in a strictly defined rhythmically patterned literary form. The use of descriptive language, of linguistic ambiguities and nuances, of extensive imagery as well as the presence of *rasa*, the re-creation of emotions, moods, sentiments, have been seen as the essence of poetry (regardless of the literary form) in South Asian art from the earliest times to the present. (95)

Rustomji-Kerns is not alone in presenting Divakaruni's prose poems in such a manner. The version of "Leaving Yuba City" in the anthology *Our Feet Walk the Sky* is also offered with paragraph, not stanza, breaks, a format that leads to its characterization as a "story" in the *Words Matter* bibliography of Divakaruni's works (Rasiah 153). Nonetheless, both of these pieces appear in Divakaruni's latest collection of poems, and the author herself sees "Yuba City Wedding" and "Leaving Yuba City" as "prose poems, charged with poetic language. They depict change and growth of character through dramatic monologue" (qtd. in Srikanth 96–97). Divakaruni's interest is in moving across forms: not only does she infuse her poems with sharp characters and narration, but she conceives of her first novel, *The Mistress of Spices*, as an attempt to "see if the boundaries can be dissolved between poetry and prose" (qtd. in Rasiah 151).

Considering the narrative nature of her poetry, Divakaruni has not found it difficult to move to writing the short stories and novels for which she has become popular. After shifting her creative efforts to prose, Divakaruni explains, "My poetry was becoming more and more narrative, and yet I felt I wasn't able to tell the story just because of the poetic form and the way it focuses on the intense moment" (qtd. in Rasiah 151). Though Divakaruni finds prose to be more suitable for developing characters and expressing stories fully, she maintains that the poet's sense of language, imagery, and craft is still part of her immersion in prose: "Having written poetry, I will always approach language differently than if I hadn't. . . . When I'm revising prose, the poet in me is very careful to see that there's no excess" (qtd. in Srikanth 97).

Divakaruni's work not only mingles poetry and prose but also responds to visual art forms: movies, photographs, and paintings. "At the Sati Temple, Bikaner," printed in *Black Candle* and *Leaving Yuba City*, uses a scene in a Raghubir Singh photo to broach the topic of sati, the Hindu practice of widow self-immolation. The speaker imagines women who have come to pray at a temple memorializing and glorifying sati. Though this poem reflects Divakaruni's interest in gender and power, it does so through responding to "images of India and the Indian experience in America—especially that of women" in "a docu-drama style" (Rev. of *Leaving Yuba City* 64). In *Leaving Yuba City*, Divakaruni extends her response to photos and movies to offer seven poems based on the artist Francesco Clemente's series of Indian miniature paintings. Through these poems, Divakaruni engages "other artists' interpretations of her native land" (Brainard 68).

CRITICAL RECEPTION

Though Divakaruni has received numerous awards for her poetry, including a Pushcart Prize and an Allen Ginsberg Prize, she is more widely known as a fiction writer. Her stories have appeared in mainstream magazines such as *Good Housekeeping*, and her new books routinely receive glowing reviews from American media: the *San Francisco Chronicle* found *Arranged Marriage* to be a book full of "exquisite stories" ("Editors Recommend" 11), and Laura Jamison in *People Weekly* called *Sister of My Heart*, a follow-up to her best-selling *The Mistress of Spices*, "an irresistible novel" (42). South Asian women's groups have called upon Divakaruni's work in their fundraising efforts, and a choreographer has even set some of Divakaruni's writing to movement, fulfilling the author's aim to "open up people's consciousness" (Srikanth 100). Due to Divakaruni's desire for "accessibility," her work has received a tremendous popular response, though it has yet to gain sustained critical attention (Srikanth 100).

Alongside such overwhelming positive feedback for her fiction, critics have given Divakaruni's poetry mixed reviews. While Divakaruni has been praised for the content of her work, she has been taken to task on issues of poetic craft. The *Leaving Yuba City* reviewer in the *Virginia Quarterly Review* suggests, "The enthusiasm of Divakaruni's wide-angled, quickly shifting camera surpasses the skillfulness of her delivery: prosy lines are cut willy-nilly in order to give her verse the casual windblown gust of modernity" (Rev. of *Leaving Yuba City* 64). Lauding Divakaruni's observational powers, such reviewers simultaneously bemoan the collapse of poetry into proselike structures. Yet reviewers for mainstream journals counter such criticism by proclaiming Divakaruni's lyricism, arguing, "What could be the work of a political tract writer is saved from polemicism by the poet's sensuous lines" (Monaghan 745). Others suggest that Divakaruni possesses a "startlingly lyrical voice" (Hoffert 98) and offers poetry that "plunges into the deepest recesses of the heart" (Seaman 1871).

In the context of such mass appeal, Divakaruni has been criticized for promoting exotic and stereotypical images of South Asians in order to be successful in a Western market. But the writer responds to such attacks by saying,

Some time back there was an article, a scathing review of *Black Candle*, and one of the things the critic said was, "Oh, this writer writes for white people," and she meant it as a real put-down. When I read it, I was really angry for a while, and then I thought, Why not? I live in America; America is part of my life; should I not write for white people also? It's a defeatist and hypocritical attitude to say that I will live in America and write only for other Indians. (*Rasiah* 147)

To help all her readers understand the historical and cultural contexts of her poems, Divakaruni regularly provides glossaries and notes. Such a practice demonstrates the poet's concern for inclusion and expressing her community's experiences "as something human and shared" ("Chitra Divakaruni" 47).

BIBLIOGRAPHY

Works by Chitra Banerjee Divakaruni

Poetry

Dark like the River. Calcutta: Writers Workshop, 1987.
The Reason for Nasturtiums. Berkeley, CA: Berkeley Poets Workshop and Press, 1990.
Black Candle: Poems about Women from India, Pakistan, and Bangladesh. Corvallis, OR: Calyx Books, 1991.
"Leaving Yuba City." *Our Feet Walk the Sky: Women of the South Asian Diaspora*. Ed. Women of South Asian Descent Collective. San Francisco: Aunt Lute Books, 1993. 38–40.
Leaving Yuba City: New and Selected Poems. New York: Doubleday, 1997.

Short-Story Collections

Arranged Marriage. New York: Doubleday, 1995.
The Unknown Errors of Our Lives. New York: Doubleday, 2001.

Novels

The Mistress of Spices. New York: Doubleday, 1997.
Sister of My Heart. New York: Doubleday, 1999.
The Vine of Desire. New York: Doubleday, 2002.

Collections Edited

Multitude: Cross-Cultural Readings for Writers. 2nd ed. New York: McGraw-Hill Companies, 1997.
We, Too, Sing America: A Reader for Writers. Boston: McGraw-Hill Companies, 1998.

Studies of Chitra Banerjee Divakaruni

Brainard, Dulcy. Rev. of *Leaving Yuba City*. *Publishers Weekly* 244.35 (25 August 1997): 68.
Bryant, Eric. "Fifty Years of Freedom: 'India: A Celebration of Independence.' " Rev. of *Leaving Yuba City*. *Library Journal* 122.12 (July 1997): 102.
"Chitra Banerjee Divakaruni: Poet and Fiction Writer." *Yellow Light: The Flowering of*

Asian American Arts. Ed. Amy Ling. Philadelphia: Temple University Press, 1999. 136–48.

"Chitra Divakaruni." *Living in America: Poetry and Fiction by South Asian American Writers.* Ed. Roshni Rustomji-Kerns. Boulder, CO: Westview Press, 1995. 47–49, 95–99.

"The Editors Recommend." *San Francisco Chronicle* 13 August 1995: 11.

Hoffert, Barbara. Rev. of *Leaving Yuba City: New and Selected Poems. Library Journal* 123.6 (1 April 1998): 98.

Jamison, Laura. Rev. of *Sister of My Heart. People Weekly* 51.6 (15 February 1999): 42.

Jana, Reena. "The American Dream versus American Reality." Rev. of *Leaving Yuba City. San Francisco Chronicle* 18 January 1998: 5.

Lanham, Fritz. "Magical Mix of Art, Feminism: Houston Gains Fine Novelist, Poet." *Houston Chronicle* 31 January 1999: 19.

Mazumdar, Sucheta. "General Introduction: A Woman-centered Perspective on Asian American History." *Making Waves: An Anthology of Writings by and about Asian American Women.* Ed. Asian Women United of California. Boston: Beacon Press, 1989. 1–21.

Moka-Dias, Brunda. "Chitra Banerjee Divakaruni." *Asian American Novelists: A Bio-Bibliographical Critical Sourcebook.* Ed. Emmanuel S. Nelson. Westport, CT: Greenwood Press, 2000. 87–92.

Monaghan, Pat. "Chitra Banerjee Divakaruni." Rev. of *Black Candle. Booklist* 88.8 (15 December 1991): 745.

Rasiah, Dharini. "Chitra Banerjee Divakaruni." *Words Matter: Conversations with Asian American Writers.* Ed. King-Kok Cheung. Honolulu: University of Hawai'i Press, 2000. 140–53.

Rev. of *Leaving Yuba City. Virginia Quarterly Review* 74.2 (Spring 1998): 64.

Seaman, Donna. "Chitra Banerjee Divakaruni." Rev. of *Leaving Yuba City. Booklist* 93.22 (August 1997): 1871.

Srikanth, Rajini. "Chitra Banerjee Divakaruni: Exploring Human Nature under Fire." *Asian Pacific American Journal* 5.2 (1996): 94–101.

Streuber, Sonja H. "Chitra Banerjee Divakaruni." *Asian American Autobiographers: A Bio-Bibliographical Critical Sourcebook.* Ed. Guiyou Huang. Westport, CT: Greenwood Press, 2001. 67–75.

Yung, Judy. "Appendix: A Chronology of Asian American History." *Making Waves: An Anthology of Writings by and about Asian American Women.* Ed. Asian Women United of California. Boston: Beacon Press, 1989. 423–31.

JESSICA HAGEDORN
(1949–   )

George Uba

BIOGRAPHY

Jessica Hagedorn was born in the Santa Mesa section of Manila in 1949 and attended Assumption Convent, a Catholic school she remembers for its high academic standards and its repressive, rule-driven environment. Her early interest in art and writing stemmed in large measure from her own family—a mother who yearned to be a dancer and eventually devoted herself to painting, and a maternal grandfather who was a teacher, writer, and political cartoonist. Hagedorn's hybridic sensibility as a writer and poet can be attributed in part to her youthful attraction to multiple types of cultural media, including Hollywood movies, Western literary classics, and melodramas and radio serials performed in Tagalog.

Immigration to the United States in the early 1960s played a pivotal role in the development of her artistic sensibility and her anticolonial politicization. She arrived with her mother and brothers at San Francisco in her early teens, after first residing in San Diego. Although she benefited from her academic experience at San Francisco's celebrated Lowell High School, she found that her private isolation and cultural alienation, her geographical movements among and through the city's various neighborhoods, and her heightened sense of freedom helped stimulate her dedication to writing. This freedom also expressed itself in an unfiltered exposure to San Francisco's Beat and post-Beat social and literary scene. Following her high school graduation, she studied theater arts at San Francisco's American Conservatory Theater, which provided multiple instruction in music, acting, martial arts, and mime. Meanwhile, she continued to frequent area bookstores and to immerse herself in the vitality of urban street culture.

Although Hagedorn is versed in canonical Western literature, she nevertheless names specific Filipino literary inspirations, including, among the older generation, writers such as Carlos Bulosan, N.V.M. Gonzalez, and Bienvenido Santos. Also vital to her artistic development was her participation in the Kearny Street Writers' Workshop, which not only drew upon the vitality, idealism, and passionate political engagement of the late 1960s but also introduced her to Asian American history, politics, and literature. Among her numerous literary associates she includes Al Robles, Ishmael Reed, Amiri Baraka, Norman Jayo, Sonia Sanchez, Victor Hernandez Cruz, Janice Mirikitani, Edward Dorn, and Serafin and Lou Syquia. All of her writings exhibit an acute sense of social and cultural contradictions, an unsentimental sympathy for Asian Pacific immigrants, an awareness of and outrage at Western imperialism, and a powerful attraction to minority voices and contemporary urban life.

In 1973, Kenneth Rexroth featured Hagedorn in an anthology entitled *Four Young Women: Poems*. She asserts that around this time she also was in the process of self-discovery as a Filipina American writer. Following a return to the Philippines after a prolonged absence, she explored issues of cultural identity and the tribulations of immigration in the 1975 volume *Dangerous Music*, a collection of poetry and fiction. Also in 1975, having further developed her interest in rock and roll, jazz, and rhythm and blues, as well as in theatrical performance, she formed a band called West Coast Gangster Choir, which included Thulani Davis and Ntozake Shange. Rechristened in 1978 as the Gangster Choir following Hagedorn's move to New York City, the band contributed to the further development of her poetry as a type of performance art, even as her participation in New York's Basement Workshop helped keep her sensibilities aligned with issues of social relevance and political significance. During the 1970s, several of Hagedorn's theatrical works and teleplays were produced. In 1981, her volume *Pet Food and Tropical Apparitions* appeared, again featuring both prose fiction and poetry. These earlier prose and poetry collections, along with newer works placed under the heading "New York Peep Show: 1982–1992," were assembled under one cover in the 1993 volume *Danger and Beauty*.

Between 1988 and 1992, Hagedorn also participated in the performance/theater trio Thought Music. Understanding her performance premises helps clarify Hagedorn's multidimensional idea of poetry and its relationship to theater. In her early band years, she had not fully conceptualized "performance art," even though the band had, in effect, practiced it. She had called the Gangster Choir a "poet's band," which had meant that the musicians would not limit themselves to playing music but would intersperse poetry and other types of "text," along with acting, into the total presentation. Her once-nascent sense of performance art reaches an acme in the production of *Teenytown* (1988), in which she and collaborators Laurie Carlos and Robbie McCauley combine music, acting, poetry, theatrical performances, and television parody within a historically resonant context of the nineteenth-century minstrel show. The effect is a powerful artistic and political statement about racism and individual and cultural integrities. Within the production, poetry functions not merely as an adjunct to a theatrical piece but as a cultural mediation that fully works only within the context of multidimensional—and actual—performance.

In recent years, Hagedorn has devoted increasing attention to prose fiction, theatrical productions, and visual arts. Her sharply satirical, politically engaging, and stylistically daring novel *Dogeaters* (1990) brought her critical acclaim and national renown. The novel was later converted into a successful theatrical production in La Jolla, California. She edited *Charlie Chan Is Dead: An Anthology of Contemporary Asian American Fiction* (1993), a seminal collection of short stories that introduced many new Asian Pacific North American writers to a national reading audience. Almost simultaneously she collaborated with Han Ong on the theatrical production *Airport Music* (1993). Her second novel, *The Gangster of Love* (1996), follows a young woman from the Philippines struggling to establish her musical and artistic career in America amid personal turmoil and among a variety of memorable associates. Always politically informed, Hagedorn served as a commentator for *Crossroads*, a syndicated weekly newsmagazine on public radio. In 1999, *Burning Heart: A Portrait of the Philippines*, a largely pictorial text with photos by Marissa Roth, appeared. Through the 1990s, her poetry appeared in an assortment of anthologies, including *The Heath Anthology of American Literature* and two major Asian American poetry anthologies, *The Open Boat: Poems from Asian America* (1993) and *Premonitions: The Kaya Anthology of New Asian North American Poetry* (1995).

MAJOR WORKS AND THEMES

An interdisciplinary flavor and a refusal to adhere to narrative formulas or conventional lyricism distinguish Hagedorn's poetry. Frequently traversing the borders between music and writing, the poetry projects the energy, immediacy, and often the spontaneity of performance. Thus, while Hagedorn's ideological affiliations tend to be rooted in recognizable cultural politics whose sources date back to the Asian American movement politics of the 1960s and to the anti-bourgeois cultural practices of the Beats of the 1950s, her aesthetics are linked to oral traditions, music, and the kinesthetic properties of theatrical performance and dance. At one moment her poetry may borrow from the auditory registers of music; at another moment the very placement of the words on the page may resemble a linguistic "dance." Throughout her career, her language has tended to be brash and sassy, at times highly elliptical, as if unrestrained by the impulse to make merely rational order out of the highly disordered experience of living in a contemporary urban environment.

The early poems (1968–1972) collected in *Four Young Women* focus on the fragmentation, dislocation, alienation, and insurgency of the Asian Pacific immigrant. Her poem "Autobiography Part One: Manila to San Francisco" offers a series of glimpses of individuals who either adjust to or actively resist the incursions of Western colonialism, which in turn is portrayed as an authoritative but often culturally sterile imperative backed by the gun and resisted through the same militant means. In other poems, such as "The Death of Anna May Wong," Hagedorn testifies to the power of music—especially jazz, funk, and "Latin" sounds—to move her away from the simplified images of the past and to invoke the realities, at once tantalizing and harsh, of inner-city life in America. In "Canto de Nada," she shows that nada (nothing) is what the colonized are left with but that out of that nothing emerges a vigorous, resilient, and procreative self that can even survive excess and overdose.

The poems collected in *Dangerous Music* (1975) were mainly written after Hagedorn's temporary return to the Philippines following the protracted absence resulting from her family's immigration to America. Part of the collection focuses on family members and the profoundly mixed feelings she has about her homeland (at the time still reeling under the Marcos regime). In "Souvenirs," she reflects on how life becomes cheapened under Catholicism and other legacies of Western colonialism but how the Philippines remains sweet and unforgettable at the same time. In "Song for My Father," she finds that despite the contradictions that constitute Filipino culture, she is "trapped" by the lure of her past and the refuge that memories offer against America, "the loneliest of countries" (*Danger and Beauty* 39). She also decries in "Justifiable Homicide" the legacies of American neocolonialism in the form of class violence, mendacity, and cultural schizophrenia left to the yet-unborn generations of Filipino children.

It is also in this collection that she reflects on art itself, one of her enduring themes. In the poem "Canto Negro," she implies that music and dance, especially that which is inflected by a sense of darkness, not only affirms life but ultimately constitutes the spiritual replacement for more traditional modes of worship. She also suggests here and elsewhere that art possesses special conjurative and transformative capacities that create beauty and promote desire and love. Thus in the poem "Sorcery" she maintains that artists—whether musicians, writers, or poets—are self-constructed in beauty, perform feats of magic, and engage in dangerous, invigorating practices. Such artists, as the poem "Listen" suggests, can be as conspiratorial as smiling thieves or as seemingly protective as guardian angels, but in either case they enjoin their audience to engage in a process of interaction. As performance, art never hardens into staid monumentalism. Repeatedly, Hagedorn implies in her poetry that writing by itself—that is, writing that fails to integrate the musical and/or performative element—is caught in the trap of canonical tradition and conformity. But finally, as a form of beauty, art also contains dangers. At times, as in "Something about You," it may be therapeutic, but at other times, it may be the very lure that accompanies the kinds of risky behaviors, including drug and sexual experimentations, that can court self-destruction and premature death ("Latin Music in New York").

Another of Hagedorn's principal themes has involved an ongoing quarrel with empty intellectualism, especially that which privileges the exercise of reason over the less reducible, holistic rhythms of experience. She claims in her offbeat love poem "Solea" that there is real beauty "when I lose my mind" (*Danger and Beauty* 63), suggesting that to explain phenomena merely in a systematic manner is to deprive them of their deeper power and appeal. It is enough to know, for example, that jazz, rhythm and blues, rock and roll, and other forms of musical expression can simultaneously soothe the heart and reexcite the painful memories that require soothing in the first place ("Seeing You Again Makes Me Wanna Wash the Dishes"). To reason beyond such an experiential fact becomes futile. Indeed, it runs the risk of stripping art of its transformative capabilities and reducing it to another sterile museum artifact. Violating traditional categories of genre constitutes a tactic in this effort to defy the imperialism of conventional logic. In "Easter Sunday," Hagedorn at first acknowledges that writing poetry may be therapeutic but then shifts to the position that being "crazy" is better yet. Craziness is a state of nonconformity and antimaterialism; it is therefore something to be cherished and maintained. Behind this position lies her implicit belief that social change and individual integrity are only possible by preserving one's ability to stand outside of and thereby challenge the status quo.

In *Dangerous Music*, Hagedorn courts such personal themes as homecomings and romantic and filial love, and she repeatedly invokes the powers of various types of artistic expression. However, she found her voice hardening and expressing increased dissonance and fierceness in the works comprising the 1981 volume *Pet Food and Tropical Apparitions*. Even when the writings revisit certain themes, arguably there is a sharper urban edge and a more aggressive experimenting with form. For example, "Motown/Smokey Robinson" combines a focus on immigrant life and class divisions with actual lyrics from one of Smokey Robinson and the Miracles' hit tunes in the 1960s. The poem forcibly crosses generic lines by "requiring" the reader (not just the performer) both to read the lines and sing the lyrics. Thematically, it both decries the economic dead ends of barrio life and celebrates the vitality of the urban youth culture associated with the barrio, whether in the Philippines or in the United States. But any sentimentality emerges out of the song, not out of any yearning for actual return. The poem "I Went All the Way Out Here Looking for You, Bob Marley," satirically revises the haves and the have-nots as the "them" and the "they" and worries aloud over the potential dangers of success. Daring to challenge an admired musical talent, the poem suggests that to succeed by exploiting one's cultural roots may result in abandoning one's culture and moving from an association with a humanlike "they" to an impersonal "them." "Chiqui and Terra Nova" is written in paragraph form but with phrases and sentences divided by a series of slash marks, as if the work were intent on dissolving the distinction between poetry and prose. The point seems to be that since Chiqui is a flamboyant street person and Terra Nova an equally flamboyant transsexual, no conventional genre can adequately contain their respective stories.

The poetry in *Pet Food* also increasingly embraces a feminist agenda while further investigating issues of sexuality. For example, "Yolanda Meets the Wild Boys" constitutes an in-your-face declaration of black (minority) feminist power—sexual and otherwise—as Yolanda mesmerizes, then tames, an Amsterdam "punk" culture that despite its exhibitionism and rowdiness is recognized as an unwitting derivative of European history and imperialism. A complex and richly ambiguous poem in its investigation of drugs and sexualities, "The Woman Who Thought She Was More Than a Samba" also can be read as a statement of defiance against the partial representations of women seemingly embodied in the Brazilian dance. Against the apparent stasis and self-repression of this dance, the poem seems to argue for the feminist power it observes in "a sinuous tango" (*Danger and Beauty* 157). Even though the poem does not seem to fully understand the nature of the samba—indeed, the dance in its syncopated rhythms and powerful steps moves as if into the interior of the earth, thereby expressing a kind of inherent "earth power"—the apparent misconception simply lends another translogical register to a poem arguing for women's agency and empowerment.

Over the last dozen years, along with the publication of *Dogeaters, The Gangster of Love*, and *Charlie Chan Is Dead: An Anthology of Contemporary Asian American Fiction*, Hagedorn's poetry has reappeared, most notably in the 1993 volume *Danger and Beauty*, which collected works from her earlier volumes, as well as poetry and prose written afterwards. At times dazzlingly elliptical, her poems continue to defy conventional readings while still yielding recognizable ideas. In "The Mummy," an apparition named "Montana" wears a dress made out of bronze and, enraged over the cultural and religious desecrations produced by Western archaeological expeditions, haunts a locked museum. An important difference in these later poems is the growing self-consciousness over age and time. In the intriguing poem "The Song of Bullets," the speaker, now into middle age and absorbed with the raising of her young daughter, struggles to preserve her rage at the ongoing nightmare of global suffering and injustice and the particular horrors of a homeland wracked by civil unrest, class divisions, and incipient warfare. Similarly, in "All Shook Up," a speaker aware of the connections between exile and exoticism reflects on Western empire and its legacies of racism and an often-dubious pop/pulp culture that at once inspires and sentimentalizes revolution while relentlessly infiltrating the available spaces within colonized countries. The poems "Skull Food" and "Skull Food #2" comment, respectively, on damaged family relations and the damaged city of New York, whose dementia is represented in the relationship of a latter-day flower child turned prostitute named Sunshine with her lover Psycho.

More recently, Hagedorn's poetry has made its online debut. Several of her poems, for example, have appeared on the English Department Web site of the University of Illinois. "Stigmata," for one, retains the brash tone and revisits the cinematic allusions from the past that frequent much of her work while exploring the ambiguous and/or false racializations contained within sets of popular visual imageries. It experiments as well with unmarked dialogue from unnamed speakers. At the same time, the poem projects an increased self-consciousness regarding the ambiguities confronting the artist-provocateur, who in this case takes the form of a woman who is literally crucified but also agentive in the production of various scenes and spectacles. Simultaneously empowered and disempowered, the crucified woman also invokes the dilemma of the artist simultaneously in pursuit of ideological complexity and of general audience accessibility. Thus the poem discovers that it must negotiate between original expression and the common formulas of expression already encoded within a culture. Because of such difficulties, the poem ends by urging itself to begin once again, starting with the image of the woman nailed to the cross. The effort to create satisfactory artistic expression not only never ends but must perpetually renegotiate its own beginning.

CRITICAL RECEPTION

Hagedorn's poetry has received substantially less critical attention than her prose fiction, although this tendency is gradually changing. When Kenneth Rexroth published her early poems in the volume *Four Young Women*, it heralded the start of her public career as a poet, but neither this work nor her two subsequent volumes received the kind of sustained critical attention they merited, notwithstanding the fact that *Dangerous Music* fared well with the reading public and went into three editions.

Hagedorn enhanced her visibility as a poet through her frequent appearances in Asian American poetry anthologies during the 1970s and early 1980s. In her landmark 1982 critical study *Asian American Literature: An Introduction to the Writings and Their Social Context*, Elaine H. Kim examined Hagedorn's poetry for its thematic affiliations. Kim thematized Hagedorn's criticisms of American racism, paranoia, and consumerism. She also demonstrated how Hagedorn's poetry imbues an American landscape of sterility with a minority experience marked by color and vitality, and she declared that the Asian Pacific immigrant, depending on her circumstances, could forge "natural" cultural connections with Latinos in the barrio and African Americans in the ghetto. Additionally, Kim found that Hagedorn, along with other Asian American writers, explores cognate issues of Third World identity and Asian Pacific women's identity.

By the time the comprehensive collection *Danger and Beauty* appeared, Hagedorn had already published *Dogeaters* and edited *Charlie Chan Is Dead*. Not surprisingly, considering the success of these prose fiction publications, the critical reception for *Danger and Beauty* also was more pronounced. Shirley Ancheta's review in *Amerasia Journal* emphasized the aural qualities of Hagedorn's poetry and connected it to Hagedorn's Bay Area performances with her first band. Writing in *Booklist*, Donna Seaman noted that Hagedorn's poems "are like jazzy lyrics or the words to rock-and-roll tunes" and commented on the "colorful beauty and stubborn creativity" of the characters populating her world (1152). Ellen Finnie Duranceau maintained in *Library Journal* that Hagedorn's main theme involves the seduction and subsequent disillusionment of the immigrant. In the earlier work, most of the characters bore the trappings of 1960s-era pop culture and existed in a landscape of isolation and emptiness, exile and violence. Caryn James, writing in the *New York Times Book Review*, observed that Hagedorn's work explores an identity that is mosaiclike through a writing that defies conventional borders of poetry, prose, and song. Hagedorn, contended James, is a blend of poet, shaman, and pop star.

Academic publications, as well, began to concentrate more on the poetry than had been done previously. George Uba's review of *Danger and Beauty* in the winter 1993 issue of *Asian America: Journal of Culture and the Arts* maintained that the book is both a retrospective and a continuing chronicle of a career in change and that Hagedorn is a writer who manages to unite "a collectivist spirit of social activism to a private version of postmodern wit" (187). Uba's entries on Hagedorn in the third and fourth editions of the *Reference Guide to American Literature* (1994; 2000) provided additional analysis of Hagedorn's various writings, and his chapter on Asian American poetry in *A Resource Guide to Asian American Literature* (2001) included specific suggestions on teaching her poetry. Juliana Chang's important work on Asian American poetry includes her 1995 doctoral dissertation, "Word and Flesh: Materiality, Violence, and Asian-American Poetics," which devotes its first chapter to a discussion of the relationship between violence and desire in Hagedorn's poetry. Chang observes that Asian American poets deploy the materiality of language as a response to the materiality of violence. All four of the poets she focuses on problematize language to the point of linguistic violence in order to unsettle complacency and to awaken social response. Hagedorn, according to Chang, particularly thematizes seduction and fantasy in the service of such ends. In her article "On 'Ming the Merciless,' " Chang contends that Hagedorn's poem articulates feminine desire and sexuality by reorganizing interior space not as a feminization of safety signified through the haven of a gendered domestic space but as an embodiment both of female sexuality and the technological "organ" of mass culture that constructs Orientalist images such as Ming the Merciless and seeks to position the Asian as a passive spectator of such constructions. The Asian diasporic female of Hagedorn's poem constitutes that "organ" that at once embodies the technological apparatus of mass culture and intervenes in that space between image and spectator or active giver and passive receiver. Taking a different perspective, the chapter by N.V.M. Gonzalez and Oscar V. Campomanes on "Filipino American Literature" in *An Interethnic Companion to Asian American Literature* (1997) drew attention to the various migrations of language, character, sexuality, music, and violent rebellion between Hagedorn's poetry and her prose construction of Manila society in the novel *Dogeaters*. These migrations help us to understand the dispersals of nationality, the multiple dislocations, and "the portability of Filipino literary identities" (102).

Today, Jessica Hagedorn is widely recognized as a preeminent figure in Asian American literature. Because her poetry is multidimensional and borrows from highly particularized personal histories, it can present a special challenge to many readers. For valuable theoretical perspectives on Asian American poetry in general, which perspectives also can lend context to Hagedorn's poetry, the writings of Juliana Chang, Epifanio San Juan, Jr., and Sunn Shelley Wong are recommended reading.

BIBLIOGRAPHY

Works by Jessica Hagedorn

Poetry

Four Young Women: Poems by Jessica Tarahata Hagedorn, Alice Karle, Barbara Szerlip, and Carol Tinker. Ed. Kenneth Rexroth. New York: McGraw-Hill, 1973.
Dangerous Music. San Francisco: Momo's Press, 1975. (Poetry and prose fiction.)
The Woman Who Thought She Was More Than a Samba. San Francisco: Momo's Press, 1978. (Broadside.)
Pet Food and Tropical Apparitions. San Francisco: Momo's Press, 1981. (Poetry and prose fiction.)
Danger and Beauty. New York: Penguin, 1993. (Poetry and prose fiction.)
Visions of a Daughter, Foretold with Paloma Hagedorn Woo. Milwaukee, WI: Woodland Pattern Book Center, 1994. (Chapbook.)

Prose Fiction

Dogeaters. New York: Pantheon, 1990.
Two Stories: Carnal and Los Gabrieles. Minneapolis: Coffee House Press, 1992.
The Gangster of Love. Boston: Houghton Mifflin, 1996.

Plays, Teleplays, Radio and Screenplays, and Performance Pieces

Chiquita Banana. Third World Women. San Francisco: Third World Communications Group, 1972. 118–27.
Where the Mississippi Meets the Amazon. With Ntozake Shange and Thulani Davis. Staged at Shakespeare Festival Public Theater, New York, 1977.
Mango Tango. Staged at Shakespeare Festival Public Theater, New York, 1978.
Tenement Lover: no palm trees/in new york city. Staged at the Kitchen and the Basement Workshop, New York, 1981.
A Nun's Story. Broadcast on public television's *Alive from Off Center*, 1988.
Holy Food. Broadcast on WNYC's *The Radio Stage*, 1989.
Teenytown. With Laurie Carlos and Robbie McCauley. *Out from Under: Texts by Women Performance Artists*. Ed. Lenora Champagne. New York: Theatre Communications Group, 1990. 89–117.
Airport Music. With Han Ong. Staged at the Public Theatre, New York, and the Berkeley Repertory, Berkeley, CA, 1993.
Fresh Kill. Airwaves Project in Association with Independent Television Service, Channel Four Television, United Kingdom, 1994.
Dogeaters. Staged at La Jolla Playhouse, La Jolla, CA, 1998.

Anthology Edited

Charlie Chan Is Dead: An Anthology of Contemporary Asian American Fiction. New
York: Penguin, 1993.

Nonfiction Prose

Burning Heart: A Portrait of the Philippines. Photos by Marissa Roth. New York: Riz-
zoli, 1999.

Selected Records and Cassettes

A Mouth That Speaks. Berkeley: University of California Extension Media Center, 1974.
Terra Nova. Washington, DC: Watershed Tapes, 1981.
Travels in the Combat Zone. New York: D. Chase, 1982.
A Diamond Hidden in the Mouth of a Corpse. New York: Giorno Poetry Systems Rec-
ords, 1985.
Words in Your Face. St. Paul: Twin Cities Public Television, 1991.
Out of Asia: Asian American Artists Explore Identity in America. Flushing, NY: Asia
Society, 1994.

Studies of Jessica Hagedorn

Aguilar–San Juan, Karin. "The Exile Within/The Question of Identity: Jessica Hagedorn."
Interview in *The State of Asian America: Activism and Resistance in the 1990s*.
Ed. Karin Aguilar–San Juan. Boston: South End Press, 1994. 173–82.
Ancheta, Shirley. Rev. of *Danger and Beauty*. *Amerasia Journal* 20.1 (1994): 197–200.
Campomanes, Oscar V. "About Jessica Hagedorn." *The Oxford Companion to Women's
Writing in the United States*. Ed. Cathy N. Davidson and Linda Wagner-Martin.
New York: Oxford University Press, 1995.
Chang, Juliana. "On 'Ming the Merciless.' " *A Multimedia Companion to Anthology of
Modern American Poetry*. Ed. Cary Nelson. New York: Oxford University Press,
2000. http://www.english.uiuc.edu/maps/poets/g_1/hagedorn/hagedorn.htm.
———. "Reading Asian American Poetry." *MELUS* 21.1 (1996): 81–98.
———. "Word and Flesh: Materiality, Violence, and Asian-American Poetics." Diss.
University of California, Berkeley, 1995.
Damon, Maria. "Kozmic Reappraisals: Revising California Insularity." *Women Poets of
the Americas: Toward a Pan-American Gathering*. Ed. Jacqueline Vaught Brogan
and Cordelia Chavez Candelaria. Notre Dame, IN: University of Notre Dame
Press, 1999.
Duranceau, Ellen Finnie. Rev. of *Danger and Beauty*. *Library Journal* 118 (January
1993): 114.
Evangelista, Susan. "Jessica Hagedorn: Pinay Poet." *Philippine Studies* 35.4 (1987): 475–
87.
Foo, Josephine. "Poetry Chooses Her Listener." *Amerasia Journal* 20.3 (1994): 11–17.
Gonzalez, N.V.M., and Oscar V. Campomanes. "Filipino American Literature." *An In-
terethnic Companion to Asian American Literature*. Ed. King-Kok Cheung. New
York: Cambridge University Press, 1997. 62–124.

Higa, Lori. Rev. of *Pet Food and Tropical Apparitions*. *Contact II* 7.38–40 (1986): 23–24.

James, Caryn. Rev. of *Danger and Beauty*. *New York Times Book Review* 14 March 1993: 12.

"Jessica Hagedorn." Interview in *Listen to Their Voices: Twenty Interviews with Women Who Write*. Ed. Mickey Pearlman. New York: Norton, 1993.

Kim, Elaine H. *Asian American Literature: An Introduction to the Writings and Their Social Context*. Philadelphia: Temple University Press, 1982.

Lawsin, Emily Porcincula. "Jessica Hagedorn: Interview." *Words Matter: Conversations with Asian American Writers*. Ed. King-Kok Cheung. Honolulu: University of Hawai'i Press, 2000.

San Juan, Epifanio, Jr. "Mapping the Boundaries: The Filipino Writer in the U.S.A." *Journal of Ethnic Studies* 19.1 (Spring 1991): 117–31.

Seaman, Donna. Rev. of *Danger and Beauty*. *Booklist* 89 (March 1993): 1152.

Trudeau, Lawrence, ed. *Asian American Literature: Reviews and Criticism of Works of American Writers of Asian Descent*. Detroit: Gale Research, 1999.

Uba, George. "Coordinates of Asian American Poetry: A Survey of the History and a Guide to Teaching." *A Resource Guide to Asian American Literature*. Ed. Sauling Cynthia Wong and Stephen H. Sumida. New York: MLA, 2001. 309–31.

———. "Jessica Tarahata Hagedorn." *Reference Guide to American Literature*. 3rd ed. Ed. Jim Kamp. Detroit and London: St. James Press, 1994. 373–75.

———. "Jessica Tarahata Hagedorn." *Reference Guide to American Literature*. 4th ed. Ed. Thomas Riggs. Detroit: St. James Press, 2000. 357–59.

———. Rev. of *Danger and Beauty*. *Asian America: Journal of Culture and the Arts* 1.2 (Winter 1993): 187–90.

Wong, Sunn Shelley. "Sizing Up Asian American Poetry." *A Resource Guide to Asian American Literature*. Ed. Sau-ling Cynthia Wong and Stephen H. Sumida. New York: MLA, 2001. 285–308.

KIMIKO HAHN
(1955–   )

Zhou Xiaojing

BIOGRAPHY

Kimiko Hahn was born in Mt. Kisco, New York, in 1955, to two artists, Maude Miyako Hamai, from Hawaii, and Walter Hahn, from Wisconsin. She grew up in Pleasantville, New York. During her teenage years, Hahn spent her Saturdays in New York City, trying to participate in the Asian American movement, which was oriented toward community building and a radical identity politics. Being half-white, Hahn was not completely accepted as an insider. However, she would not allow her Eurasian identity to stop her from being part of the movement. Galvanized by the information in the first edition of the movement's journal, *Our Bodies, Our Selves*, which appeared around 1972, Hahn sold copies to girls in her high school in the library parking lot ("Memory, Language, and Desire" 64–65). Since then, activism has been an important part of Hahn's life, and her poetry reflects her political consciousness, particularly her profound understanding of the politics of the body. Being Asian in appearance, she has frequently been asked where she is from—that is, what Asian country she comes from. At school, American children called her Chinese or Japanese, never regarding her as an American like them. Yet when she went to live in Japan while her father studied Japanese art there, her Japanese schoolmates called her American or "gaijin" (outsider, foreigner). Thus Hahn's keen awareness of the body as a site of identity construction, a site of competing ideologies, grew out of her lived experiences, as well as from her encounters with Marxist ideas and her readings of theoretical writings, including psychoanalytical, poststructuralist, and feminist theories.

Apart from political activism, Japanese language and literature were central to Hahn's life and poetry. Hahn majored in English and East Asian studies at the University of Iowa, where she received her B.A. Later she earned an M.A. in Japanese literature from Columbia University. While she was studying at Columbia, Hahn's experience of linguistic confusion enhanced her sense of the materiality of language, the untranslatable aspect of it, and the relations between language and identity. At the same time, she was enchanted and felt empowered by the long tradition of Japanese literature. Her subject matter and poetics are informed by Japanese myths, literature, and language, as well as by feminist and Marxist ideas. With an M.F.A. from Iowa, Hahn is also familiar with Western poetic traditions. T.S. Eliot's use of cross-cultural allusions and untranslated phrases in *The Waste Land* suggested to Hahn exciting possibilities for incorporating both Japanese and American literary traditions into her poetry. William Carlos Williams's capacious mixing of prose with poetry in his book *Paterson* also inspired her. Moreover, theoretical writings, particularly those by feminist writers such as Hélène Cixous, Luce Irigaray, Catherine Clément, Sandra Gilbert, and Adrienne Rich played an important part in Hahn's development as a poet and a feminist. These varied strands of poetic and theoretical discourses find their way into Hahn's poems in terms of style and language, themes and subject matter.

Hahn's earliest poems were published together with pieces by Gale Jackson and Susan Sherman in a book entitled *We Stand Our Ground: Three Women, Their Vision, Their Poems* (1988), along with their discussions of their poems. Hahn's first individual collection, *Air Pocket*, appeared in 1989. Her second book, *Earshot*, published in 1992, won the Theodore Roethke Memorial Poetry Prize and an Association of Asian American Studies Literature Award. Her third volume, *The Unbearable Heart* (1995), received an American Book Award. The year 1999 saw the publication of two collections by Hahn, *Volatile* and *Mosquito and Ant*. In addition to poetry, Hahn also writes personal and autobiographical essays, mostly about gender issues. In 1995, she wrote ten "portraits" of women for a two-hour MTV special, "Ain't Nuthin' But a She-Thing," which was aired in November the same year, and for which she also recorded the voice-overs. Currently Hahn is working on a collection of prose, *The Downpour*.

A recipient of fellowships from the National Endowment for the Arts and the New York Foundation for the Arts, Hahn has also been awarded a Lila Wallace– Reader's Digest Writers' Award. Among her other honors is inclusion of a poem, "Possession," in the 1996 *Best American Poetry*. She is associate professor of English at Queens College, City University of New York. She lives in Manhattan with her husband, Ted Hannan, and their daughters, Miyako Tess and Reiko Lily.

MAJOR WORKS AND THEMES

Hahn's thematic concerns range from the political to the domestic, from desire to jealousy, and from art to language. Central to these themes are women's subjectivity and sexuality, which are interwoven with issues of race, class, and power. Hahn's major themes emerged along with her cross-cultural, interlingual, and intertextual poetics in her first book, *Air Pocket*, and developed in her later works. In poems collected in her first volume, such as "When You Leave," "Dance Instructions for a Young Girl," and "Roost," references to Japanese myth, culture, and language offer refreshing, alternative ways of expression and experience. While seeking to convey intense yet subtle eroticism and to artic-ulate passions of love, Hahn shows equally passionate feelings about social justice. "The Bath: August 6, 1945" is about a rape survivor's experience, which Hahn reconstructs in order to give voice to the survivor's rage and her will to live, and "to *make* history" in spite of her personal history and the history of violence against women (*Air Pocket* 47). In another poem about gendered ex-perience, "Nora," Hahn reimagines and reconstructs the life of a Nicaraguan woman who rebels against her wealthy family and becomes deeply involved in the politics of her country and in the making of national history. These strands of thematic, aesthetic, and cultural concerns converge in the first volume's last and also longest poem, "Resistance," in which fragments from the writings of Stalin and Virginia Woolf are interwoven with those from texts on textiles and anthropology, as well as narratives from Japanese folk tales and classical liter-ature. Employing collage to juxtapose cross-cultural references in a girl's coming-of-age process in a bicultural world, Hahn uses ikat cloth and the resist-dying process as metaphors for female resistance to the oppression of dominant powers.

In her second volume, *Earshot*, Hahn continues to explore the formation of female subjectivity by crossing generic and cultural boundaries. This volume shows Hahn's maturation as a poet and her use of intertextual collage. In several poems, she incorporates Japanese literary texts and Western theoretical dis-courses in her investigation of gendered power relations. These poems illustrate Hahn's development of collage as an organizing principle in her intertextual appropriation and revision from diverse sources, of which *The Tale of Genji* by Murasaki Shikibu becomes the most frequently quoted text in her poems. Her drawing from the Japanese literary traditions also has the function of resisting the primacy of European culture in American literature. In "Revolution," for example, Hahn evokes the classical literary tradition of Japanese women to claim her Japanese cultural heritage, to articulate women's creative power, and to explore "a female culture or aesthetic" ("Three Voices Together" 10). Her per-sona in the poem asserts her desire for the power of words in Japanese women's writings and claims that she connects to "that century" when these women's works occupied a prominent space in Japanese classical literature (*Earshot* 17). By connecting herself to that tradition of women's literature, Hahn empowers herself with female literary models and makes available for her poetry a rich body of literature on women's social conditions and their psychological and emotional experience. Hahn explores women's desire, jealousy, and attachment in their relationships with men and among themselves through intertextual di-alogues and juxtapositions of voices from the texts and from her everyday life, thus creating a dynamic tension and multiple perspectives on the same issues.

Besides women's writings, Hahn also engages in intertextual revisions of and dialogues with writings of male writers from different cultures. Her poem "The Izu Dancer" is modeled on Yasunari Kawabata's short story "The Dancing Girl of Izu" in terms of narrative strategy, which aims to achieve the effect of ambivalence and anticlimax characteristic of Kawabata's writings, particularly "The Dancing Girl of Izu." But Hahn's intertextuality also has a subversive function. She juxtaposes fragments from Kawabata's narrative with autobiographical fragments not only to enact her memories of learning and experiencing the Japanese language, but also to foreground the difference between Kawabata's representation of a Japanese girl's modesty about sexuality and her own intensive sexual desire (*Earshot* 87–93). For Hahn, "real sexual desire for fulfillment and control of this female body" is a "metaphoric desire for political power" ("Memory, Language, and Desire" 69). The politics and aesthetics of desire underlie Hahn's poetics.

As she continues to articulate the autonomy of the female body and female desire in her third book, *The Unbearable Heart*, Hahn finds new ways to locate women's gender identity and sexuality in a larger social, historical context. At the same time, Hahn further develops her intertextual method for exploring ideas and articulating emotions. This third volume contains some of Hahn's most lyrical and moving poems, which are written out of her painful experience of her mother's death after a car accident. In writing about her inconsolable grief over the loss of her mother, Hahn also turns to *The Tale of Genji* to explore its treatment of longing, loss, and bereavement in poems such as "Flooding" and "Wisteria" (*Heart* 15–25). In this volume, Hahn also begins to directly engage theoretical discourses on the formation of subjectivity and sexuality in "Cruising Barthes," juxtaposing Barthes's theory with that of Melanie Klein and challenging both with autobiographical fragments (33–39). In the last poem of this volume, which is an intertextual collage prose poem, "The Hemisphere: Kuchuk Hanem," Hahn juxtaposes fragments from Edward Said's *Orientalism* and Gustave Flaubert's *Flaubert in Egypt* with autobiographical fragments and Kuchuk Hanem's speeches, which she imagines in Hanem's voice. Through these imagined speeches, Hahn gives voice to Hanem, whose articulation about herself and Flaubert resists Flaubert's power to possess her body and to speak for her, thus transforming Hanem from a silent sexual object and an exotic Other in Flaubert's text to an articulate sexual subject. However, Hahn is aware of the risks of speaking in the voice of Hanem from her Western feminist position and in terms of sexuality. As her persona asks, "Will I fall into the trap of writing from the imperialists' point of view?" (*Heart* 51). In response to the questions she poses, Hahn incorporates more fragmentary remarks about Hanem from Flaubert's text to enhance the fundamental difference between her speaking for Hanem and that by the French man.

Hahn's sense of responsibility to give voice to women's experience continues to inform her subject matter in her recent poems collected in *Volatile* and *Mosquito and Ant*. Both of these books show Hahn's persistent passion for social justice and women's history and experience while revealing her more direct assertion about the relations between poetry and social issues. In the opening poem of *Volatile*, "These Current Events," the speaker confronts numerous social problems and the inadequacy of words in providing any solutions, but the poem ends in the speaker's affirmation that even though poetry cannot save any lives, "it fuels the gut that is able" (*Volatile* 12). In poems such as "Found," about a Thai girl who is sold into prostitution, and "If You Speak," about Korean "comfort" women who were sex slaves of the Japanese military during World War II, Hahn's intertextual strategy transforms news reports and history into art to fuel "the gut" that can become an agency of political action. Hahn further illustrates that the art of language and poetic form can be employed to articulate intense personal emotions and to address political and historical issues with passion and poignancy in poems such as "Possession," about her father's grief over her mother's death, and "Blindsided," about Cambodian women's loss of eyesight as a result of witnessing the brutality of the Killing Fields. Both poems are subtitled "zuihitsu" (essay), modeled on *The Pillow Book*, a work by another Japanese woman writer, Sei Shōnagon, that combines observation with reflection and resists any category of literary genres. In "The Volcano's Desire," Hahn interweaves personal lives with national politics and history, meshing sexual desire with political desire while juxtaposing quotes from Marx and Engels's *Communist Manifesto* with narratives from Ernesto Cardenal's *Zero Hour and Other Documentary Poems* and from *Latin American Revolutionary Poetry*, edited by Robert Márquez. In her poem "Mine," she also interweaves excerpts from her interviews with American miners while working on Bill Brand's film *Coalfields* with her own comments to explore social injustice and the sensuality and effectiveness of voices and language.

Hahn's major themes, particularly those concerning women, including womanhood and motherhood, reoccur in *Mosquito and Ant*. Many poems in this collection allude to and reimagine writings of *nü shu*, a thousand-year-old secret script created and used by Chinese women for private correspondence among themselves. Along with her revitalization of this long tradition of women's writing, Hahn continues to draw from Sei Shōnagon's work in poems such as "The Downpour" and "Sewing without Mother," written in the mode of zuihitsu (a genre variously translated into English as "essay," "miscellany," or "random jotting"). Her intertextual dialogue with feminist theories also continues in poems such as "Morning Light" and "Responding to Light." Thus *Mosquito and Ant* has an overarching theme about women's writing that renders the book cohesive and compelling. It testifies to the fact that the power and strength of Hahn's poetry lies in its commitment to the aesthetic and the political with devotion and passion in equal measure.

CRITICAL RECEPTION

Hahn's poetry has received much less critical attention than it deserves. However, almost all the reviews of her poetry are positive and perceptive. In her review of *Earshot*, Juliana Chang notes Hahn's "political and Marxist concerns"

(191) along with her treatment of "troubling and powerful aspects of feminine desire: jealousy, possessiveness and betrayal" (189). Praising Hahn's "poetic range" and "poetic craft," Chang points out that "Hahn provokes us to consider poetic writing *as* theoretical writing" (191–92). The theoretical aspect of Hahn's poetry makes her work poignantly political. Moreover, her engagement with the theoretical never becomes dull or disconnected to everyday reality or loses its emotional intensity. As Elizabeth Millard says in her review of *The Unbearable Heart*, Hahn's poetry is "raw, powerful, utterly radiant." In her elegies for her mother, Millard adds, Hahn is able to produce poems of "absolute, dark beauty" instead of "sentimental broodings" (778). A review of Hahn's two recent volumes asserts that these books, "bold, brave and sharp, are large in the range of their concerns and the intensity of their passions," challenging readers to "confront their political aesthetics via the poetical." The same review also notes Hahn's engagement with Asian women's "literary legacy" (Rev. of *Mosquito and Ant* 76). These critical reviews point to the ways in which Hahn's poetry participates in reinventing the lyric mode and transforming American poetic traditions.

BIBLIOGRAPHY

Works by Kimiko Hahn

Poetry

We Stand Our Ground: Three Women, Their Vision, Their Poems. With Gale Jackson
    and Susan Sherman. New York: Ikon, 1988.
Air Pocket. Brooklyn, NY: Hanging Loose Press, 1989.
Earshot. Brooklyn, NY: Hanging Loose Press, 1992.
The Unbearable Heart. New York: Kaya Productions, 1995.
Mosquito and Ant. New York: Norton, 1999.
Volatile. Brooklyn, NY: Hanging Loose Press, 1999.

Prose

"Three Voices Together: A Collage." With Gale Jackson and Susan Sherman. *We Stand
    Our Ground: Three Women, Their Vision, Their Poems*. New York: Ikon, 1988.
    9–29.
"Memory, Language, and Desire." *Asian Americans: Collages of Identities: Proceedings
    of Cornell Symposium of Asian America, Issues of Identity*. Ed. Lee C. Lee. Ithaca,
    NY: Asian American Studies Program, Cornell University Press, 1992. 64–69.
"Afterbirth." *Charlie Chan Is Dead: An Anthology of Contemporary Asian American
    Fiction*. Ed. and intro. Jessica Hagedorn. New York: Penguin Books, 1993. 132–
    40.

Interview

"Kimiko Hahn: Expressing Self and Desire, Even If One Must Writhe." By Eileen Tabios
    with versions of drafts in progress of two poems by Hahn and Tabios's comments.

Black Lightning: Poetry-in-Progress. New York: Asian American Writers' Workshop, 1998. 24–68.

Studies of Kimiko Hahn

Brouwer, Joel. Rev. of *Mosquito and Ant*. *Progressive* 63.12 (December 1999): 43.

Chang, Juliana. Rev. of *Earshot*. *Amerasia Journal* 21.1–2 (1995): 188–92.

Ethelbert, E. Rev. of *Earshot*. *American Poetry Review* 21.6 (November/December 1992): 33.

Millard, Elizabeth. Rev. of *The Unbearable Heart*. *Booklist* 92.9–10 (January 1996): 778.

Rev. of *Mosquito and Ant*. *Publishers Weekly* 246.17 (26 April 1999): 76.

Zhou, Xiaojing. "Breaking from Tradition: Experimental Poems by Four Contemporary Asian American Women Poets." *Revista Canaria de Estudios Ingleses* 37 (November 1998; a special issue on twentieth-century American women poets): 199–218.

———. "Intercultural Strategies in Asian American Poetry." *Re-placing America: Conversations and Contestations*. Ed. Ruth Hsu, Cynthia Franklin, and Suzanne Kosanke. Honolulu: University of Hawai'i and East-West Center, 2000. 92–108.

YUKIHIDE MAESHIMA HARTMAN
(1939–   )

Joe Kraus

BIOGRAPHY

Yukihide Maeshima Hartman was born on 25 March 1939, in Tokyo. He was raised in Japan in an American-influenced home after his mother, Ito, remarried Albert Eugene Hartman, a civilian attached to the occupying U.S. Army. Hartman has few memories of his father, Hiroji Maeshima, who served in the Japanese air force and was killed during World War II. In 1958, he moved with his mother, stepfather, and siblings to Pearl River, New York. He had an interrupted formal education, attending Fairleigh Dickinson University in 1961, the University of South Carolina in 1962, and the New School for Social Research in 1964 before, during, and after his two-year service in the U.S. Army. He has worked most of his adult life in technical fields, beginning as a television repairman when he first moved to the United States and switching to computer programming in 1982 and subsequently working as a systems analyst. He lives in New York City with his wife, Susan Greene, a painter whose work appears on the covers of *Red Rice*, *Ping*, and *A Coloring Book*.

Hartman reports that he was passionate about writing all his life, deciding as a young man that he would work in English. He was very comfortable in Japanese, but not comfortable enough to write in it. During his time at the New School, he studied with José Garcia Villa and began to write some of the poems that came together in his first chapbook, *A One of Me*, published in 1970. He began attending the St. Mark's Poetry Project in 1977, studying there with Charles North and Lewis Warsh and developing friendships with many fellow poets. Subsequently, he and Michael Slater edited and produced *Fresh Paint:*

An Anthology of Younger Poets in 1977, and he oversaw the Viridian Gallery Series with Vicky Hudspith from 1978 to 1979 and served as the founding editor of *Tamarind* from 1980 to 1990. His work has appeared in many anthologies and magazines, including *Genesis Grasp, New Directions, Broadway, Tamarind, Hanging Loose, The Portable Lower East Side, The World, Out of This World, American Born and Foreign, Quiet Fire: A Historical Anthology of Asian American Poetry 1892–1970*, and *The NuyorAsian Anthology*.

MAJOR WORKS AND THEMES

Perhaps the central theme of Hartman's work is his persistent and gentle exploration of his own interior world. He works through nature, places, and scenarios with which he is familiar, finding in them an immanence and a subtle and persistent beauty. When he writes of love and friendship, for instance, he tends to focus on the comfort and strength he takes from his existing relationships. In "Poem" from *Ping*, he sees a lover off on a short trip, thinking to himself of the ordinary loneliness he will feel in her absence. As such, his interest is characteristically in contentment, something he finds often but knows that he must work to sustain.

He often explores the idea of still-ness, describing motion that stops or celebrating the pauses he discovers in the midst of his daily life. In "Sunset" from *Red Rice*, he recounts a dusky evening at a city park, willing it to remain a landscape even as he reports that there has been a traffic accident nearby. Overlooking the blood of one of the victims, a woman hale enough to exit and investigate the damage to her car, he brings the poem to a close on a note out of his personal scene: "Drama is still in the leaves, greening" (l. 11). "Still" takes on particular weight in the sentence, suggesting both that drama continues in the growth of the leaves even as it passes quickly in the accident, but also implying an oxymoron. "Drama" connotes something in the midst of change, something where an uncertain outcome demands our attention. In the scene, however, as elsewhere, Hartman implies that the greater drama comes in the subtler and distinct moment. He calls our attention to the drama of still-ness, to the insistent beauty of life in its most common and accessible elements.

In a similar vein, when he writes, as he often does, about food and eating, he takes particular joy in the quality of everyday nourishment at several levels. He interests himself in the quiet satisfaction of a good meal with the people he loves. Not quite lapsing into a sensualism of food, he repeatedly explores the atmosphere that comes with such meals, capturing a fleeting and quiet joy. He declares in "The Gold Standard" from *Red Rice*, "To drink or to eat is one way of saying this satisfies me and is beautiful" (l. 22). As he explained in our interview, "Food and love are entrees into a state of being; maybe they are the symbols some people say I can use best."

Hartman occasionally explores his situation as a Japanese American, suggesting the potential for tension in his own circumstances as the child of two cultures that were at war when he was born, but never dwelling on it. Instead, he tends to treat "East" and "West" as symbols that represent separate elements of his own self that complement and strengthen one another, an idea he explores most extensively in his most recent collection, *A Coloring Book*. Acknowledging that he experienced some prejudice in Japan as the stepson of an American and, later, in the United States as an immigrant, he explained that he understands poetry as an important means of forging a balance between two poles.

In his finest poems, Hartman defuses other tensions in comparable ways. His work remains consistently interesting and challenging because he situates himself in the midst of potential conflict and yet almost always turns his attention to the peace he finds at the heart of his experiences. He uses his poetry to redirect the reader's gaze from the busy-ness of the world to quieter and more private concerns. In doing so, he captures the world sufficiently rich and fresh that his work retains an urgency in the midst of its concern for still-ness and quiet.

CRITICAL RECEPTION

The only published critical responses to Hartman's work so far have come in the many warm reviews of his separate collections. No critics have, as yet, considered his work from the perspective of his entire career, nor have any published interviews with him. He has received a number of awards, however, including inclusion in *The Pushcart Prize III: Best of the Small Presses*, 1978–79, and The Fund for Poetry Prize in 1991, and he has been a three-time fellow at the MacDowell Colony. In a context where only a handful of contemporary poets receive much critical attention, Hartman has been fortunate enough to have many able readers.

As early as 1971, Richard Ray's insightful review of *A One of Me* drew out the idea of Hartman's interest in the peacefulness that often escapes notice in the midst of the busy city life. As Ray wrote, "A part of [Hartman's] appeal arises from the consistently gentle speaking voice that can be felt in the poetry and from the way so many individual poems catch and hold for the reader those brief flashes of human experience that cannot be evaluated at the time but which become significant in retrospect." As Ray noted, Hartman already showed a distinctive feel for manipulating syntax, producing a style where he seems to slow down his utterances in accord with his interest in calling our attention to the easily overlooked.

In 1977, Michael Slater called attention to the way Hartman had matured with the publication of his second collection, *Hot Footsteps*. Slater remarked on Hartman's "notion of experience as at every moment unique and elusive, the perception of which can be communicated only by allusion, by vivid but ambiguous imagery which functions as a kind of metaphor, a metaphor that is not a visual analogy but the passion perceived in an object or event" (42). Where Ray had seen the peacefulness at the heart of Hartman's vision, Slater perceived a dynamic tension. He saw Hartman finding passion in the midst of the otherwise-peaceful images of the poems, moving from simple surfaces into personal depths and conflicts.

The reviews of *A Coloring Book* called attention to Hartman's increasingly direct examination of the intersections of the public and the private, of the way in which his personal vocabulary functions in America at large. The tensions at the heart of such poems, more public perhaps than the ones driving his earlier work yet still deeply personal, hint at some of the directions Hartman seems likely to pursue in his coming work. Following the same interest in the story that happens within and around us at all times, Hartman seems prepared to sharpen his explorations of the cultural experiences that can either bind or separate us. Dedicated as he is to the most deeply personal questions, he seems increasingly prepared to answer the difficult questions of how to live in a potentially divided but endlessly stimulating American society.

BIBLIOGRAPHY

Works by Yukihide Maeshima Hartman

Poetry

A One of Me: 27 Poems. New York: Grasp Press, 1970.
Hot Footsteps. New York: Telephone Books, 1976.
Red Rice. Putnam Valley, NY: Swollen Magpie Press, 1980.
Ping. New York: Kulchur Foundation, 1984.
New Poems. Montreal: Empyreal, 1991.
A Coloring Book. Brooklyn, NY: Hanging Loose Press, 1996.
Triangle. New York: Situation Press, 1997.

Anthology Edited

Fresh Paint: An Anthology of Younger Poets (with Michael Slater). New York: Ailanthus Press, 1977.

Studies of Yukihide Maeshima Hartman

Kushner, Bill. Rev. of *A Coloring Book. Poetry Project Newsletter* 162 (October–November 1996).
Ray, Richard. "Slim Volume of Rewarding Poems." Rev. of *A One of Me. Gazette-Mail* [Charleston, WV] 13 June 1971.
Slater, Michael. "Vision Is Dizziness: The Technology of Yuki Hartman." Rev. of *Hot Footsteps. Poetry Project Newsletter* (1 February 1977): 42.

SADAKICHI HARTMANN
(1867–1944)

Linda Trinh Moser

BIOGRAPHY

Carl Sadakichi Hartmann was born on Deshima Island in the harbor of Nagasaki, Japan, in 1867, probably on 8 November. His father, Carl Hermann Oskar Hartmann, was a German merchant. Little is known about his mother, Osada, who was Japanese. After her death in 1868, the infant Sadakichi and his older brother, Taru, were sent to Hamburg, Germany, to be raised by their grandmother and a wealthy uncle, Ernst Hartmann. In his uncle's home, the young Hartmann grew up in luxury. He was educated by private tutors and attended preparatory schools. Most important to his formation were the books on art in both his uncle's and the town's libraries, which he preferred reading over playing. Hartmann later credited his uncle for encouraging what would become a lifelong interest in the arts as a child in the dedication to *A History of American Art* (1902).

After Hartmann's father returned to Germany and remarried a widow with two daughters in 1881, he sent Hartmann, against his will, away to a naval academy in Kiel. Hartmann protested by running away to Paris and refusing his father's orders to return to the academy. In reaction to the rebellion, his father disinherited him and, in 1882, sent him to Philadelphia to live with less prosperous relatives whom Hartmann later depicted as a "plebeian, philistine grand uncle and aunt" (*Conversations* 3).

His uncle's untimely death made it necessary for the fifteen-year-old Hartmann to earn his own living in a customary apprenticeship in the academy of hard knocks. He held a variety of occupations, such as spittoon and window cleaner, press feeder, lithographic stippler, clerk in a tombstone factory, perfume peddler, and negative retoucher. Despite the grueling work, Hartmann managed to continue his self-directed education in the arts, spending nonworking hours at the Philadelphia Mercantile Library and in bookstores where he read literature and examined photographic reproductions of art from around the world.

In November 1884, Hartmann introduced himself to an elderly Walt Whitman, with whom he discussed literature and other arts. Later, he described their talks in *Conversations with Walt Whitman* (1895). Whitman inspired and encouraged Hartmann's earliest poetry. In return, Hartmann acted as the poet's informal secretary, delivering packages and translating German correspondence for him. Although Hartmann later jeopardized their relationship by attributing unflattering comments about other writers to the elderly poet, Whitman retained friendly feelings for his would-be protégé. "I have a soft spot for him—," Whitman wrote, "a liking for him—after all—poor boy!" (Traubel 2:281–82, 321).

In the same years he met with Whitman, Hartmann began a career in journalism, producing essays on literature, art, theater, and even dance as both a free-lancer and staff writer for various publications. He signed his writing with a variety of pseudonyms: Sidney Allan (his best known and most frequently used), Caliban, Chrysanthemum, Hogarth, and Juvenal, among others. In the next twenty-five years, Hartmann traveled throughout Europe and the United States, producing the influential work that would establish him in the art world. Alternating roles as critic, impresario, and artist, Hartmann utilized a variety of genres, writing art criticism, poetry, drama, and novels, as well as biographies. In addition, Hartmann painted in pastels, dabbled in photography, and was reported to be a gifted dancer; he studied dancing in Paris as a young man. He also helped to found *Mother Earth* with Emma Goldman. Later in life, he wrote film reviews and screenplays and appeared as the court magician in Douglas Fairbanks's *Thief of Bagdad* (1923).

In 1891, Hartmann became the McClure Syndicate's foreign correspondent in Europe. In this position, he visited major art exhibits and encountered prominent artists, such as Liszt and Swinburne. He also met Stéphane Mallarmé, with whom he would stay in touch through 1897; this relationship would inspire his own literary forays into symbolism. To promote European artists and poets like Mallarmé in the United States, Hartmann launched *Art Critic* in Boston, one of the nation's first avant-garde publications. Although he worked hard to obtain subscriptions, the journal's European focus failed to interest an American audience. In addition, financial problems brought about by the publication of Hartmann's first play, *Christ*, forced him to stop the magazine after only four issues. Jailed on obscenity charges and forced to pay a $100 fine, Hartmann no longer had funds to publish the journal. The failure of *Art Critic* made it necessary for Hartmann to return to writing. He moved to New York, where he was associated with numerous magazines. Recognizing the value of his insights, Alfred Stieglitz recruited Hartmann as a writer for *Camera Notes* and later for *Camera Work*, for which Hartmann wrote his best and most influential essays on art and photography. These pioneering essays are among the first to discuss photography as an art form.

After 1911, Hartmann left New York and began traveling across the United States, meeting with artists and writers and lecturing on art and photography. During these trips, Hartmann became attracted to the West Coast, where he found relief from the debilitating asthma attacks he later described in *My Crucifixion* (1931). He eventually made California his permanent residence; in 1923, after living in and around San Francisco, he moved permanently to southern California. During these years, Hartmann became part of a Hollywood crowd that included John Barrymore, W.C. Fields, and John Decker. Despite his past accomplishments, "the image he projected to the film-star group was that of an aged, alcoholic jester" (Weaver 11); while the actors enjoyed tales of his earlier bohemian life, they did not believe him. This part of his life is described in Gene Fowler's memoir *Minutes of the Last Meeting* (1954).

Despite excessive drinking and deteriorating health, Hartmann continued to work. Until 1931, he wrote articles describing Hollywood life as a correspondent for *Curtain*, a British theatrical magazine. Between 1923 and 1932, he also struggled to sum up his ideas on art in *Esthetic Verities*, a 278,000-word volume that was never finished or published. In 1938, Hartmann moved to the Morongo Indian Reservation near Banning, California, where he lived in "Catclaw Siding," a shack he built adjoining the home of his daughter Wistaria Linton. From there, he worked on his autobiography and a final collection of his poems; both remained unfinished at the time of his death.

During World War II, the FBI began investigating Hartmann. Although he had become a naturalized citizen in 1894, his German-Japanese ancestry aroused suspicion. Hartmann pleaded with authorities who sought to have him relocated to a Japanese internment camp. Citing his book *A History of American Art* (which was often used as a textbook), he insisted on his commitment to American values. Although the FBI continued to harass him, Hartmann was never interned.

In November 1944, at the age of seventy-seven, Hartmann traveled by bus to visit another daughter, Dorthea Gilliland, in St. Petersburg, Florida. He had intended to gather materials for his autobiography, which would remain unfinished. Only a few hours after arriving in his daughter's home, Hartmann died suddenly.

MAJOR WORKS AND THEMES

Hartmann's earliest attempts at poetry reveal the influence of Walt Whitman. In a prose-poem, "To Walt Whitman" (1887), Hartmann's narrator describes Whitman's poetry as "the grandest lessons of my life." Whitman's exclamatory tone and thematic interest in democracy are evident in Hartmann's tribute; however, despite the narrator's claim of being "bound" to the poet "forever," Hartmann abandoned Whitman's style just three years later in *Poems*, a broadside of seven short prose poems written from 1886 to 1889. This collection reveals the influence of French symbolist poets with whom Hartmann had associated during his frequent trips to Europe. In *Poems*, Van Deusen perceives echoes of symbolism in "their melancholy tendency toward *le rêve*, their faint synaesthetic effects, and the Baudelairean vision of the city" (158).

Hartmann's professional interest in symbolism went beyond writing poetry. He became one of the first American critics to describe and defend the European movement. He "apparently suggested," for example, the title of poet Stuart Merrill's groundbreaking 1890 translations of French symbolist poetry *Pastels in Prose* (Van Deusen 158). More important are his essays that introduced symbolism to American audiences. In 1892–93, Hartmann discussed Arthur Rimbaud's use of tone color in a series of articles for the *Weekly Review*. In an 1893 issue of *Art Critic*, Hartmann also introduced Mallarmé by describing his famous Tuesday literary soirées. He promoted symbolism as an editor as well. In that year, the *Art Critic* also included the poetry of Paul Verlaine. In 1900, his article on Henri de Régnier, a disciple of Mallarmé, appeared in *New Yorker Staats Zeitung*, a German-language paper. In addition, Hartmann was associated with American symbolists. His prose-poem "Leitmotif" appears as the introduction to *Whisperings of a Wind Harp* (1897) by American symbolist Anne Throop.

Hartmann's debt to French symbolism is especially apparent in the 1898 edition of *Naked Ghosts*, which he dedicated to Mallarmé "with every sentiment of regard and respect." Representative of the style Hartmann uses throughout his first collection of poems are the first lines from "Cyanogen Seas," in which he creates a haunting, dreamlike atmosphere by using words that combine the different senses. Hartmann expresses the symbolist interest in subjective experience in other poems as well. "To Stéphane Mallarmé: A Strain in Red" utilizes religious and sensual imagery as Hartmann describes the poet's work as a chalice from which he drinks "the blood of roses."

In the 1903 revised edition of *Naked Ghosts*, Hartmann includes two poems, both written much earlier in 1887, that pay homage to his first mentor, Whitman. Van Deusen notes that Hartmann's "Oh, to Create!" echoes the first lines of Whitman's "Song of the Exposition" (158). He would again find inspiration from Whitman in "To the 'Flat-Iron' " (1903), a tribute to that famous building located at Twenty-third Street and Broadway in New York. This poem, however, resembles Whitman less in style than in theme. Hartmann's interest in the building as an "Emblem staunch of common sense" (*Sadakichi Hartmann* 146) and his description of it as "typically American" (*Sadakichi Hartmann* 140) mirror Whitman's interest in finding democratic and American poetic forms.

While Hartmann continued to find inspiration in Whitman's work in 1903, by the time *Drifting Flowers of the Sea and Other Poems* appeared in 1904, "the older poet's influence on Hartmann's poetic practice ha[d] disappeared completely" (Van Deusen 158). The collection includes six adaptations of the five-line Japanese tanka to which Hartmann adds rhyme. Describing Hartmann's language in *Drifting Flowers* as "much less flamboyant" than it had been in earlier collections, Van Deusen notes that "formally the verse is much more closely patterned, though thematically Hartmann is still concerned with lost love and lost innocence" (158).

Hartmann's interest in Japanese poetic forms continued in his subsequent work. His 1904 essay "The Japanese Conception of Poetry" appeared in *Reader Magazine*, predating the interest in haiku by American imagists. In 1913, Hartmann published *My Rubaiyat*, a collection of unrhymed poems written in quatrains. In these poems, Hartmann reveals a stronger interest in social issues; he protests a growing military, the inequality of women, and attitudes toward the elderly and calls for reform to uplift the poor. The collection was republished twice in 1916, first as one of the *Bruno Chap Books*, then in a revised San Francisco edition that added more than seventy six-line stanzas and rhyme.

Hartmann continued to revise and edit previously published examples of his Japanese-inspired poems in 1916, 1920, 1926, and 1933. Both the 1926 and 1933 editions are called *Japanese Rhythms*; in addition to haiku and tanka, they include poems in the four-line dodoitsu form. The 1933 edition also contains adaptations of haiku by Basho, who had, by that time, become well known to Americans. In the last years of his life, Hartmann began preparing a collection of his poems; the earliest one is dated 1892 and the latest 1942. They had previously appeared in collections and in a variety of little magazines and journals. This final collection, however, was never finished.

Hartmann's poetry represents only one of the genres he worked in. His best-known works are concerned with art. In addition, Hartmann wrote short stories, collected in *Schopenhauer in the Air* (1899), and a novella, *The Last Thirty Days of Christ* (1920). Of all his creative efforts, Hartmann seemed most interested in drama. In 1896, he published *A Tragedy in a New York Flat*, a realist play; however, most of Hartmann's dramatic efforts are best described as symbolist. *Christ* (1893) is the first in a cycle of plays including *Buddha* (1897) and *Confucius* (1923). Other plays, *Mohammed, Moses, Ossada's Revenge*, and *Baker Eddy*, followed but were neither published nor produced.

CRITICAL RECEPTION

Little attention has been paid to the analysis of Hartmann's poetry; however, during his lifetime, he and his work were highly praised by other writers. Gertrude Stein remarked that "Sadakichi is singular, never plural," and Ezra Pound wrote, "If one had not been oneself, it wd. have been worthwhile being Sadakichi" (*White Chrysanthemums* vi).

Much of what has been written on Hartmann focuses on biographical details. His enigmatic personality and flamboyant antics inspired *Greenwich Village* to devote its November 1915 issue to articles describing Hartmann as "the King of Bohemia"; a year later, "The Most Mysterious Personality in American Letters" (1916) did likewise. Emma Goldman described him in *Living My Life*

(1931), as did Gene Fowler in *Minutes of the Last Meeting* (1954); the latter immortalized Hartmann as an aging bohemian relic.

More recent biographical studies of Hartmann, most notably by George Knox and Harry Lawton, have corrected Fowler's depiction of him as a "magnificent charlatan." Their efforts (aided by Hartmann's librarian daughter, Wistaria Linton) have inspired a recuperation of Hartmann's works. In June 1958 and May 1970, they helped organize an exhibit of Hartmann's manuscripts, books, and artwork at the library of the University of California at Riverside. They also founded the *Sadakichi Hartmann Newsletter*.

The initial recuperation inspired some attention to Hartmann's poetry. In his foreword to *White Chrysanthemums*, Kenneth Rexroth describes Hartmann's poetic works "as decadent, influenced by Verlaine, Baudelaire, Germain Nouveau, Renée Vivien; in other words, pretty corny by contemporary taste" (x). Marshall Van Deusen describes Hartmann's poetry with more objectivity, finding both positive and negative attributes. He admires, for example, Hartmann's tanka and haiku because "[t]heir concentration succeeds admirably in controlling the sentimentality that often threatens to invade his longer poems" (159). Van Deusen's 1987 entry offers the only broad overview of Hartmann's oeuvre while tracing the influences of Whitman, French symbolism, and Japanese poetic forms.

In "Walt Whitman and Asian American Writers" (1993), Xilao Li moves studies of Hartmann in another direction. In addition to exploring connections between Hartmann and Whitman, Li presents Hartmann as a link between Whitman and modernist poets. Li's article furthermore follows in the footsteps of scholars trying to present Hartmann in the context of Asian American letters. Hartmann's poems are included in several important anthologies such as *Asian-American Heritage: An Anthology of Prose and Poetry* (1974) and *Quiet Fire: A Historical Anthology of Asian American Poetry, 1892–1970* (1996). Cheung and Yogi list his works and studies of him in *Asian American Literature: An Annotated Bibliography* (1988). Although Elaine Kim does not extensively analyze Hartmann's work, she quotes one of his essays to suggest his acute awareness of racism and colonialism: "Anyone familiar with colonization . . . should feel ashamed to belong to the white race" (*White Chrysanthemums* 117).

Despite the interest in Hartmann's poetry by scholars of Asian American literature, much more work needs to be done. Moving beyond biographical details, critics need to begin to analyze specific poems as well as Hartmann's contributions and connections to American literature.

BIBLIOGRAPHY

Works by Sadakichi Hartmann

Poetry

Poems. New York: privately published, 1889.
"Drifting Flowers of the Sea" and Other Poems to Elizabeth Blanche Walsh. N.p.: n.p., 1904.

My Rubaiyat. St. Louis: Mangan, 1913; New York: G. Bruno, 1916.
Tanka and Haiku: 14 Japanese Rhythms. New York: G. Bruno, 1915.
Naked Ghosts: Four Poems. South Pasadena, CA: Fantasia, 1925.
Japanese Rhythms, Tanka, Haik(ai) and Other Forms Translated, Adapted, or Imitated
    by Sadakichi Hartmann. N.p.: n.p., 1926.

Collections Including Hartmann's Poetry

Asian-American Heritage: An Anthology of Prose and Poetry. Ed. David Hsin-Fu Wand.
    New York: Washington Square, 1974.
CALAFIA: The California Poetry. Ed. Ishmael Reed. Berkeley: Y'Bird, 1979.

Drama

A Tragedy in a New York Flat: A Dramatic Episode in Two Scenes. [New York]: pri-
    vately printed, 1896.
Moses: A Drama in Six Episodes. N.p.: n.p., 1934.
Buddha, Confucius, Christ: Three Prophetic Plays. Ed. Harry Lawton and George Knox.
    New York: Herder & Herder, 1971.

Fiction

Schopenhauer in the Air: Seven Stories. New York: privately printed, 1899.
Schopenhauer in the Air: Twelve Stories. Rochester, NY: Stylus, 1908.
The Last Thirty Days of Christ. New York: privately printed, 1920.

Art Criticism

Shakespeare in Art. Boston: L.C. Page, 1901; London: Jarrold, 1901.
A History of American Art. 2 vols. Boston: L.C. Page, 1902; revised, Boston: L.C. Page,
    1932.
Japanese Art. Boston: L.C. Page, 1904.
Composition in Portraiture. New York: E.L. Wilson, 1909.
Landscape and Figure Composition. New York: Baker & Taylor, 1910.
The Whistler Book. Boston: L.C. Page, 1910.
The Valiant Knights of Daguerre: Selected Critical Essays on Photography and Profiles
    of Photographic Pioneers. Ed. Harry Lawton and George Knox. Berkeley: Uni-
    versity of California Press, 1978.
Sadakichi Hartmann: Critical Modernist. Ed. Jean Calhoun Weaver. Berkeley: University
    of California Press, 1991.

Other Nonfiction

Conversations with Walt Whitman. 1895. New York: Haskell House, 1973.
My Theory of Soul-Atoms. New York: Stylus, 1910.
Passport to Immortality. Beaumont, CA: privately printed, 1927.
My Crucifixion: Asthma for 40 Years. Tujunga, CA: Cloister Press of Hollywood, 1931.
White Chrysanthemums: Literary Fragments and Pronouncements. Ed. George Knox and
    Harry Lawton. New York: Herder & Herder, 1971.
The Whitman-Hartmann Controversy, Including "Conversations with Walt Whitman"
    and Other Essays. Ed. George Knox and Harry Lawton. Bern: Herbert Lang;
    Frankfurt and Munich: Peter Lang, 1976.

Studies of Sadakichi Hartmann

Boswell, Peyton. "Peyton Boswell Comments; King of Bohemia." *Art Digest* 19.5 (1944): 3.

Bruno, Guido, et al. "Notes on Hartmann." *Greenwich Village* 3 (November 1915): 7–10+.

Cheung, King-Kok, and Stan Yogi. *Asian American Literature: An Annotated Bibliography*. New York: MLA, 1988.

Fowler, Gene. *Minutes of the Last Meeting*. New York: Viking, 1954.

Goldman, Emma. *Living My Life*. New York: Knopf, 1931.

Hansen, Helga. "Requiem (in Memory of Sadakichi Hartmann)." *Art Digest* 19.6 (1944): 24.

Haslam, Gerald W. "The Exotics: Yone Noguchi, Shiesei Tsuneishi, and Sadakichi Hartmann." *CLA Journal* 19.3 (1976): 362–73.

Hill, Richard. "The First Hippie." *Swank International* 16 (April 1969): 16–18.

Kim, Elaine. *Asian American Literature: An Introduction to the Writings and Their Social Context*. Philadelphia: Temple University Press, 1982. 283–84 n. 14.

Knox, George, and Harry W. Lawton. *The Life and Times of Sadakichi Hartmann*, 1867–1944. Riverside, CA: UC Riverside Library and Riverside Press-Enterprise, 1970.

Li, Xilao. "Walt Whitman and Asian American Writers." *Walt Whitman Quarterly Review* 10.4 (Spring 1993): 179–94.

"The Most Mysterious Personality in American Letters." *Current Opinion* 61 (August 1916): 124–25.

Traubel, Horace. *With Walt Whitman in Camden*. New York: Mitchell Kennerley, 1915.

Van Deusen, Marshall. "Sadakichi Hartmann." *Dictionary of Literary Biography*. Vol. 54. Ed. Peter Quartermain. Detroit: Gale, 1987. 154–63.

Weaver, Jean Calhoun. Introduction to *Sadakichi Hartmann: Critical Modernist*. Berkeley: University of California Press, 1991. 1–44.

GARRETT HONGO
(1951–   )

Roy Osamu Kamada

BIOGRAPHY

Garrett Kaoru Hongo was born on 30 May 1951 in the village of Volcano on the island of Hawaii. At the time of his birth, his parents were working at the Hongo Store, a family-owned general store in Volcano. Three months before his birth, his grandfather passed away, and a family dispute erupted. As a result of this dispute, his family left the island of Hawaii and moved to the island of Oahu, where they lived for the next five years on the north shore working the plantations. In 1957, Hongo's father, Albert, moved the family to Los Angeles and began attending trade school, where he studied electronics. In an interview with Alice Evans, Hongo remarks, "When I moved from Hawaii to Los Angeles there was no *aloha* in Los Angeles. Man, there was a lot of brutality. But it's good that I learned about that too, because you have to ward things off" (39). Hongo writes about this brutality in his memoir *Volcano* and suggests that after the idyllic early years spent in Hawaii, this new world taught him hard lessons about racism, poverty, and social injustice. He remarks on the strict and unspoken guidelines that governed behavior, the rigid lines of racial division, and the prohibitions against speaking out. However, he also recalls receiving a powerful injunction from his maternal grandfather, Kubota, to tell the stories of racial injustice, to speak eloquently and beautifully about the history and legacy of Japanese American internment during World War II, to uncover and thereby heal the shame of the earlier generations of Japanese Americans.

In many ways this injunction from his grandfather has guided much of Hongo's artistic and intellectual development. While Hongo was initially interested in photography, his interest in writing developed early, in a high school class. But it was when he got to college that he began his literary studies in earnest and began to demonstrate what would become a lifelong commitment to social justice.

Hongo graduated with honors from Pomona College in 1973 with a B.A. in English. While studying at an affiliated school, Pitzer College, Hongo came in contact with Burt Meyers, a poet whose fiercely independent authority immediately appealed to Hongo. Meyers represented a complex figure of the poet, politically conscious yet unswervingly devoted to the craft of poetry, the kind of poet that Hongo himself would become. In his memoir *Volcano*, Hongo writes of Meyers, "He could look into my eyes and see into the history I was not myself ready to address, to live by. He knew part of my story, the part no one else knew or seemed to want to know, and he said he would help me with it" (191). As his studies on literature continued, Hongo began to educate himself in multiple traditions, becoming as acquainted with the Eastern traditions of Chinese and Japanese poetry as he was with European modernism. Additionally, Hongo became involved in political and social causes, though not without some censure from his white professors. In the introduction to *The Open Boat: Poems from Asian America*, Hongo writes about how when he joined "with other Asian American students to form an association and sponsor cultural events, my professors, though kindly, twitted me for 'Asian Americking' and 'going ethnic on them.' My new commitments to ethnic awareness and cultural activism seemed threatening. I wondered if my bright, eupeptic, and pipe-smoking white male professors from Yale and Berkeley worried that I might go the route of radicalism and Angela Davis" (xxi–xxii).

After graduating from Pomona, Hongo moved to Japan with the help of a Thomas J. Watson Fellowship. He spent most of his year in Japan living and studying at Kyoto Temple. After returning to the United States in 1974, Hongo enrolled in the master's program in Japanese language and literature at the University of Michigan. However, after a year of study he dropped out and eventually ended up living in Seattle. During this period after his departure from Pomona, Hongo met Wakako Yamauchi, Alan Chong Lau, and Lawson Inada, all of whom would have a great impact and influence upon his life and poetry.

While living in Seattle, Hongo founded the Asian Exclusion Act, a theater group that staged productions of Frank Chin's *The Year of the Dragon*, Wakako Yamauchi's *And Your Soul Shall Dance*, and Hongo's own *Nisei Bar and Grill*. Based upon the success of *Nisei Bar and Grill*, Hongo got a job in Hollywood as a writer for a sit-com. After a brief stint in Hollywood, he returned to Seattle and, in 1978, became poet-in-residence at the Seattle Arts Commission. Using the money saved from his time in Hollywood, Hongo bought himself several months to devote to his studies. In *Volcano*, he writes, "I worried over nothing for a few months. I read poetry and I wrote poetry. In translation I studied Greek poetry, I studied Chinese poetry, I studied the South Americans" (207). The following fall, Hongo left Seattle to attend the creative writing program at the University of California at Irvine.

At Irvine, Hongo studied with Charles Wright and C.K. Williams. Of Wright, Hongo has remarked that he taught him "to believe in my poetry, to let my poetry lead me into my life, not the other way around" (Evans 46). In *Volcano* and elsewhere, Hongo credits Williams's demanding standards for enabling his own breakthroughs, for his finding the courage to write the kind of poetry that had true feeling. After he received his M.F.A. in 1980, Hongo remained at Irvine and did two years of postgraduate work in English and critical theory.

In 1982, Wesleyan University Press published *Yellow Light*. In the fall of that year, Hongo began teaching as an assistant professor at the University of Southern California. After his father's death in 1984, he began making a series of visits to Hawaii. In part, his father's death gave Hongo the desire to return to Hawaii and reconnect himself as his father had never been able to. Knowing the tragedy of his father's inability to make the journey home made Hongo's own desire to make that journey much more powerful. In 1988, Knopf published his second collection of poetry, *The River of Heaven*, a collection of poems that came largely out of his experiences in returning and reestablishing his connection with what he had thought had been lost: a homeland. *The River of Heaven* was the Lamont Poetry Selection of the Academy of American Poets and a finalist for the Pulitzer Prize in Poetry in 1989.

In 1995, Knopf published *Volcano: A Memoir of Hawai'i*. In addition to his own work as a writer, Hongo has also been a prolific and influential editor. He has edited three major volumes: *The Open Boat: Poems from Asian America* (1993), *Songs My Mother Taught Me: Stories, Plays, and Memoir* by Wakako Yamauchi (1994), and *Under Western Eyes: Personal Essays from Asian America* (1995). He has been an active participant in the literary community, serving as a judge for the National Poetry Series, the William Carlos Williams Prize, the Kingsley-Tufts Poetry Prize, the National Book Award, the *Los Angeles Times* Book Award, and the Pulitzer Prize. Among the many places at which Hongo has spoken are the Japanese American National Museum, the University of Houston, Vanderbilt University, the Bread Loaf Writers' Conference, the University of Chicago, and the University of California at Berkeley. Hongo has also participated in the opening panel discussions at the annual meetings of the Modern Language Association and participated in a panel discussion at the 1996 Democratic National Convention that was moderated by Senator Bill Bradley. Among his many awards, he has received the Oregon Book Award in Non-Fiction, the Rockefeller Foundation Residency Fellowship, the John Simon Guggenheim Memorial Foundation Fellowship, two National Endowment for the Arts fellowships, the Lamont Prize, the Discovery/*The Nation* award, and the Hopwood Prize. Hongo has taught at the University of Washington, the University of California at Irvine, the University of Missouri at Columbia, the University of Houston, and the University of Oregon, where he is currently Distinguished Professor of Arts and Sciences.

MAJOR WORKS AND THEMES

Garrett Hongo's poetry, much like his prose, is frequently concerned with giving voice to those whom history, racism, and culture have made silent. In particular, Hongo has focused on the problems of Asian Americans, their history, and their great courage. In an interview with Alice Evans, Hongo remarks, "I'm talking about those that the literature has forgotten, those that the culture has forgotten. It's important to me that we be remembered, that there be a literature for us, that we be sung about, that there be songs for the lives that my people have lived" (44). In practice, Hongo has balanced a highly sophisticated aesthetic with his own powerful vision of compassion. He has sought to uncover the splendor in the lives of the oppressed without ever mitigating or romanticizing their state.

Hongo opens his first collection of poetry, *Yellow Light*, with a series of portraits of his family and community. Here, as throughout the whole collection, he portrays his subjects with an almost desolate tenderness. In the first poem, "Yellow Light," Hongo employs a filmic aesthetic: the unnamed woman walks home from the bus stop carrying her groceries, and as she reaches her door, the moon rises from behind some eucalyptus trees and covers everything in a heavy yellow light. With an almost Homeric sensibility, Hongo catalogues the details of this world, bathing them over in this heavy light that is sensuous yet bitter. He avoids any hint of sentimentality, instead choosing to end his poem on this ambiguous, yet distinctly forgiving image.

This is a trope that Hongo uses again at the end of "Stepchild," a long poem that attempts to chronicle the history of Asians in America. In this poem, Hongo speaks out against the social forces that have worked to deprive Asian Americans of their identity. It is a poem full of rage and seeks to chronicle not only a history of racism, but also a history of internalized racism. At the end of the poem, after cataloguing everything from the Asian Exclusion Acts of the nineteenth century to the legacies of silence and shame in the Japanese American community after World War II and internment, the poet seeks repose and meditation. The poem ends with the image of the sun ripening yellow melons on the window sill, "the yellow ones we call bitter" (63). Here, as at the end of "Yellow Light," Hongo ends the poem with a sensuous yet caustic image. This kind of method, here and throughout his body of work, enables Hongo to avoid sentimentality; he figures history through the lens of these images, sensuous, lush, organic, and yet laden with an acrimony that gives voice to generations of frustrations and denials.

Yet even as Hongo develops his almost Wordsworthian themes, he also demonstrates his own storytelling impulse, a method he uses to great advantage as he portrays the lives of the forgotten. In a poem like "Off from Swing Shift," one of several written about his father, Hongo portrays a man waiting for his one real win, his one moment of grace, of beating the odds stacked up against him. Here we see clearly, as the father drops his grinning facade, the pathos and sadness of his waiting. For at the end his waiting is in vain, the radio does not call the names of the horses he has bet on, "No one speaks a word" (14).

In contrast to these daily and mundane tragedies, Hongo counters with moments of unexpected grace and tenderness. In the poem "Stay with Me," a young white woman breaks down in tears and is comforted by a young black man who happens to be riding the same bus. Regarding this poem, Hongo writes that it "was a poem about something I *hadn't* seen happen in Los Angeles, but that I wished could've happened. The poem emerged from my own wish to found an intimate village out of the chance, strangely merciful meeting of two people, one filled with need and one stumbling forward, impelled by his own mysterious compassion" (*Volcano* 255). Even as he expresses his longing for this kind of mercy and compassion in the outside world, so too does he express his desire for this kind of mercy in his own, private world. In "What For," the speaker recalls how, at age six, he longed for the magical power to heal wounds, in particular his father's chronic pains, his deafness, and his sense of deprivation.

In *Yellow Light*, Hongo begins developing the same themes that will preoccupy all of his work: the homelessness of the diasporic experience and the relentless attempts by the children of diaspora to connect to some kind of inheritance, to develop some sense of belonging, of home. Even in this early work, Hongo's focus is clear: to link the individual's private experience with a larger cultural whole, to situate that individual within history, and to give the voiceless voice.

In his second collection of poetry, *The River of Heaven*, Hongo expands upon the themes initially developed in *Yellow Light*. However, there is a melancholic overtone to this collection, in part due to the deaths of his father and grandfather (the book is, in fact, dedicated to both of them). *The River of Heaven* is divided into two sections. Part one deals primarily with characters (both real and partially imagined) situated in Hawaii; part two is more focused on Hongo's experiences on the mainland. The collection is infused with a poignant sense of nostalgia throughout; many of the poems in part one evince Hongo's own preoccupation with his attempts to stitch together a coherent sense of identity that is situated in Hawaii.

Hongo begins *The River of Heaven* with an elegy for his dead father, "Mendocino Rose." In the poem, he recalls listening to Gabby Pahinui's version of a nineteenth-century Hawaiian lyric, a dirge written by Queen Kapiolani as she mourned her husband, King David Kalakaua, who had died far from home. Hongo notes, "The song is about the dying of a loved one who is far away from home, in a kind of exile" (*Volcano* 321). The next three poems, "Nostalgic Catalogue," "Village: Kahuku-*mura*," and "Ancestral Graves, Kahuku," memorialize elements of the past as Hongo recalls it, a past that is very nearly vanished. In "Village: Kahuku-*mura*," he describes how the plantation village that he lived in as a child has fallen into disrepair. In "Ancestral Graves, Kahuku," Hongo recounts the history of this gravesite and articulates something of the impulse driving his own poetics. He recalls the story of his grandfather's sister, who was beaten to death for having a sexual relationship with a Scotsman. Here, as throughout his body of work, Hongo seeks to reclaim and rearticulate the stories of the forgotten. He makes the argument that shame does not lie in any deed, but rather shame ought only to lie in our forgetting the past.

In "O-Bon: *Dance for the Dead*," Hongo uses language to re-create what he has never had, a full record of the past, a full sense of his own heritage. He repeats throughout the poem what he lacks: "I have no memories or photograph of my father" (14). Yet even as he proceeds through this catalogue of lack, he provides, in language, exactly what he is mourning. For while he has no photo or memory of his father returning from war, he describes him nonetheless. Similarly, while he lacks a photo of his grandfather the day the Japanese bombed Pearl Harbor, he describes him vividly. Hongo uses his great facility with language to summon his lost dead. Indeed, that is what happens over the remainder of part one of *The River of Heaven*; Hongo summons his dead and gives them voice through a series of dramatic monologues.

In "The Unreal Dwelling: My Years in Volcano," Hongo takes on the voice of his grandfather, Torau Hongo, and details his history without sentimentalizing or excusing any of his actions. Even as he expresses his desire in "O-Bon: *Dance for the Dead*" for the dead to dance beside him, to become a part of his song, Hongo evokes the presence of his grandfather, summoning him in language as powerful as it is beautiful. "The Unreal Dwelling" tells the story of a man who has lied, cheated, and gambled his way through life; he has left behind children and an adulterous wife. Yet this character is sympathetic not only because of his panache, but also because of the gesture he makes at the end of his life. Hongo imagines his grandfather searching for forgiveness and thereby indicates his own absolution for his grandfather; in envisioning his grandfather's quest for mercy, Hongo forgives the man who abandoned his father.

In part two of *The River of Heaven*, Hongo returns to the mainland, but does not depart from his method of cataloguing and recording the plights of those whom society has attempted to forget. In "Metered Onramp," Hongo chronicles "the bums and ragpickers, the shopping bag people sifting through the loose dirt and refuse piles for whatever treasure they could find" (43). He ends this poem watching one of the homeless, a woman named Sally, throwing herself down a long slope. Hongo avoids any sentimental characterization; instead, Sally is powerfully mysterious to the speaker of the poem, unknown and unknowable. Her mystery is not something to be mocked or even comprehended; she is utterly and completely other from the speaker, and all he and the rest of the commuters can do is marvel and crouch in their cars. This kind of gesture is very typical of Hongo's aesthetic: he seeks to chronicle lives that would otherwise remain invisible, and yet he acknowledges his own distance from the very ones he seeks to give voice to.

In the last poem of *The River of Heaven*, "The Legend," Hongo makes this point even more forcefully. In this poem, he tells of a random act of street violence: an Asian man leaving the laundry, walking to his car, is shot and killed by a young boy running down the icy sidewalk. In this poem, the speaker confronts his own distance from this violence; he confronts his own shame at how far away he is from this scene. For even while he might imagine, as he does in the poem "Stay with Me" in *Yellow Light*, a scene of compassion and comfort, in "The Legend," there is no one to comfort this dying man. There are echoes of Hongo's father in this description. In *Volcano*, Hongo writes of his father that since he was "hard of hearing since child-hood, language and speech came with difficulty to him" (29). If anything, these similarities between the unnamed victim and Hongo's father make all the more poignant and powerful the speaker's distance.

At the end of this poem, Hongo confesses his shame at feeling distinct from the wounded man. The power of this confession lies at the heart of Hongo's work; it is, in many ways, an articulation of his own crisis as an intellectual and as a poet. For while he might want to chronicle the lives of the downtrodden, give voice to the voiceless, he must also acknowledge that by his very position as a poet, as an academic, as a professor and teacher, he is also distinct from them; he is distinct from his own past, from his own self. What he can do, what he has done throughout his work, is make a plea for the redemptive potential of language and story. Referring to a Japanese legend about mercy and love, Hongo does not attempt to mitigate the tragedy of the man's death or the savagery of the world in which it happened; rather, "the poem functions to bestow dignity and intimacy upon a story of anonymous street violence, providing, through legend, an afterlife consolation for unexplainable suffering" (Filipelli 46). It is this form of consolation, this attempt to compensate (however inadequately) for a history of trauma and deprivation through the lyric beauty of language, that has stood and continues to stand at the heart of Hongo's work.

CRITICAL RECEPTION

Hongo has received a great deal of critical acclaim over the course of his career. Diane Wakoski, in an early review of *Yellow Light*, compares Hongo to Galway Kinnell, Denise Levertov, and Federico García Lorca. She says, "Not to slight those poets, favorites of mine, but Hongo is astonishing" (4). She calls "Off from Swing Shift" "the best poem I have seen on the American treatment of native Japanese during the Second World War because it is not really written about that subject" (4). Here Wakoski refers to the clear yet oblique fashion in which Hongo exposes the costs of historical traumas. George Uba in a 1985 review of *Yellow Light* notes that Hongo does not "merely trumpet the familiar tune of ethnic pride. Rather, he excels at balancing a passionate interest in ordinary working-class people performing ordinary activities, with a deep-felt concern over what they are often the unknowing victims of" (123). Uba notes that Hongo's project in *Yellow Light* concerns "the quest for a personal identity and the desire to build and retrieve a collective identity by sifting through the past" (123).

Phoebe Pettingell, in a 1988 review of *The River of Heaven*, remarks that "Hongo's verses become an elaborate ritual of atonement for leaving behind his culturally ambiguous background" (16). While she perhaps overstates things a bit in claiming that Hongo leaves behind his background, she does point to his themes of homelessness in the diasporic experience. Robert Schultz writes that "Hongo's book is carefully structured to make explicit the way music and story can mitigate suffering" (151). He points to Hongo's use of a Whitmanic sense of rhythm, his effective use of the catalogue as a technique to build and sustain rhythm within language. It is not only Hongo's technique, but also the ends to which he directs that technique that have caught the eyes of critics. For while Hongo might employ the Homeric catalogue within his Whitmanic rhythms, he bends these techniques to his own obsessions, to his own endeavors to reclaim a lost past.

Laurie Filipelli's monograph on Hongo was published in 1997 and remains, thus far, the only extended critique of his work. She provides a nicely detailed biography and some extended analysis and commentary on Hongo's work. In her monograph, she notes, "Traditional in his Euro-American Romantic leanings, yet eclectic in his openness to other influences, both literary and non-literary, Hongo is at once conservative and modern" (6). She goes on to cite "Hongo's increasing homage to the Romantics" (7), particularly in his use of landscape as a primary thematic in his work. She notes how Los Angeles and Hawaii stand at opposing ends of the spectrum in Hongo's work:

Los Angeles becomes, in a sense, the failed dream, a city as inhumane as it is diverse. Functioning as a redemptive counterpoint to L.A., Hawaii is where Hongo wants to belong[; however,] the enchanting beauty of the rural setting of his birthplace is realistically balanced against the oppressive history of immigrant workers on the sugar plantations. Hawaii and L.A. become paradoxically linked by the common thread of his own identity, producing in him a need to infuse his Los Angeles experience with missing elements of mystery and beauty. (8)

Filipelli ends her monograph by remarking that Hongo complicates our ideas of the West, particularly in terms of expansion and opportunity. She notes that Hongo "unearths identity not by surging forward into the unknown, but by moving back toward the landscape and culture of his origins" (51).

As a whole, critics have responded positively to Hongo's work; they have cited his poetic technique, his musical ear, his deep and abiding compassion for those whose stories he tells, and his ambitiously mythic sensibilities. Mark Jarman, commenting on *Volcano*, Hongo's prose memoir, says that "in his writing, both poetry and prose, Hongo has attempted to embody what he calls the world of feeling and specificities among the vast and monolithic Other of race in America. If he has succeeded, as I think he has time and again, then his experience must become part of our experience" (343).

BIBLIOGRAPHY

Works by Garrett Hongo

Poetry

The Buddha Bandits down Highway 99. By Garrett Hongo, Alan Chong Lau, and Lawson
  Fusao Inada. Mountain View, CA: Buddhahead, 1978.
Yellow Light: Poems. Middletown, CT: Wesleyan University Press, 1982.
The River of Heaven: Poems. New York: Knopf, 1988.

Uncollected Poems

"Ass Why Hard." *The Best of Bamboo Ridge: The Hawaii Writers' Quarterly.* Ed. Eric
  Chock and Darrell H.Y. Lum. Honolulu: Bamboo Ridge, 1986. 35–36.
"Stomping with Pettit on the Battenkill." *Poems for a Small Planet: Contemporary Amer-
  ican Nature Poetry.* Ed. Robert Pack and Jay Parini. Hanover, NH: University
  Press of New England, 1993. 104–5.
"Looking at Kilauea." *Ploughshares* 19.4 (Winter 1993): 183–87.
"Under the Oaks at Holmes Hall, Overtaken by Rain." *Southern Review* 35.3 (Summer
  1999): 460.

Prose

Volcano: A Memoir of Hawai'i. New York: Knopf, 1995.

Anthologies Edited

The Open Boat: Poems from Asian America. New York: Anchor Books, 1993.
Under Western Eyes: Personal Essays from Asian America. New York: Anchor/Double-
  day, 1995.

Book Introduction

Yamauchi, Wakako. *Songs My Mother Taught Me: Stories, Plays, and Memoir.* New
  York: Feminist Press at the City University of New York, 1994.

Play Production

Nisei Bar and Grill. Seattle: Ethnic Cultural Center, 1976.

Essays and Articles

"Sea and Scholarship: Confessional Narrative in Charles Olson's 'Maximus, to Him-
  self.' " *New England Review and Bread Loaf Quarterly* 8.1 (1985): 118–29.
"In the Bamboo Grove: Some Notes on the Poetic Line." *The Line in Postmodern Poetry.*
  Ed. Robert Frank and Henry Sayre. Urbana: University of Illinois Press, 1988.
  83–96.
"The Activity of the Poet." *Ohio Review* 41 (Summer 1988): 75–92.
" 'Kubota.' " *Ploughshares* 16.2–3 (1990): 107–18.
"America Singing—An Address to the Newly Arrived Peoples." *Parnassus: Poetry in
  Review* 17.1 (1992): 9–20.

"Asian American Literature, Questions of Identity—The Academy of American Poets
    Symposium." UCLA Asian American Studies Center, 23 April 1992. *Amerasia
    Journal* 20.3 (1994): 1–8.
"Garrett Hongo: A Poet's Notebook." *The Poet's Notebook*. Ed. Stephen Kuusisto, Deb-
    orah Tall, and David Weiss. New York: Norton, 1995. 102–9.
"Sojourning." *The Writing Path*. Ed. Michael Pettit. Iowa City: University of Iowa Press,
    1995. 243–47.
"Sunbird." *Into the Fire*. Ed. Sylvia Watanabe and Carol Bruchac. Greenfield Center,
    NY: Greenfield Review Press, 1996. 139–46.
"Lost in Place: Longing for the Brave New World of L.A." *LA Weekly* 16–22 August
    1996: 30–32.
"Hope Alive: Writers at the Unconvention." *LA Weekly* 6–13 September 1996: 9–10.
"Gardens We Have Left: Against Nationalisms in Literature." *Profession* (1997): 18–22.
"HR 442: Redress." *Outside the Law: Narratives on Justice in America*. Ed. Susan Rich-
    ards Shreve and Porter Shreve. Boston: Beacon Press, 1997. 82–92.
"Prix de Claremont (The Confessions of a Literary Prize Judge)." *LA Weekly Literary
    Supplement* 1997: 14–15.
"A Man on a Child's Swing: Contemporary Japanese Poetry." *The Poetry of Our World:
    An International Anthology of Contemporary Poetry*. Ed. Jeffry Paine. New York:
    HarperCollins, 2000. 453–57.

Introductions, Interviews, Reviews, and Notes

"A Conversation with Sandra M. Gilbert." Interview. *Missouri Review* 9.1 (1985–86):
    89–109.
"A Redress of Grievances." *Los Angeles Times* Op-Ed 17 September 1987, sec. 2: 5.
"Gretel Ehrlich's 'Heart Mountain.' " *New York Times Book Review* 6 November 1988:
    31.
"Poetry Feature: Mark Jarman." *Boston Review* July 1989: 8.
"The Used World." *Agni* 28 (Winter 1989): 304–6.
"Poetry as Democracy: A Letter to AWP." *AWP Chronicle* 23.3 (1990): 4.
"R.S. Thomas." *Poetry Pilot* February 1990: 2–5.
"Eulogy: Homage to Spark Matsunaga." *Hawaii Herald* 20 April 1990: 2+.
"Turning Japanese: Memoirs of a Sansei by David Mura." *Mānoa: A Pacific Journal of
    International Writing* 3.2 (1991): 227–29.
"On Walt Whitman's 'Leaves of Grass.' " *Massachusetts Review* 33.1 (1992): 81–84.
"Ministry: Looking at Kilauea." Introduction. *Hot Spots: America's Volcanic Land-
    scapes*. By Diane Cook and Len Jenshel. Boston: Little, Brown, 1996. i–v.
"Thinking in Public: A Forum." *American Literary History* 10.1 (1998): 1–83.

Studies of Garrett Hongo

Childress, Boyd. Rev. *of Volcano: A Memoir of Hawai'i. Library Journal* 120.9 (15 May
    1995): 70.
Colley, Sharon. "An Interview with Garrett Hongo." *Forkroads: A Journal of Ethnic
    American Literature* 4 (Summer 1996): 47–63.
Drake, Barbara. "Garrett Kaoru Hongo." *Dictionary of Literary Biography: American
    Poets since World War Two*. Vol. 120. Detroit: Gale, 1992. 133–36.

Evans, Alice. "A Vicious Kind of Tenderness: An Interview with Garrett Hongo." *Poets and Writers Magazine* 20.5 (September/October 1992): 36–46.

Filipelli, Laurie. *Garrett Hongo.* Boise, ID: Boise State University Press, 1997.

Galef, David. Rev. of *Volcano. New York Times Book Review* 16 July 1995: 20.

"Garrett Hongo, Poet." Interview. *Yellow Light: The Flowering of Asian American Arts.* Ed. Amy Ling. Philadelphia: Temple University Press, 1999. 103–10.

Hai-Jew, Shalin. Rev. of *Volcano. Northwest Asian Weekly* 14.23 (9 June 1995): 15.

"Hongo, Garrett Kaoru." *Contemporary Authors.* Ed. Susan Trosky. Vol. 133. Detroit: Gale, 1991. 183–84.

Ikeda, Stewart David. "The Open Boat: Poems from Asian America." *Ploughshares* 20.1 (Spring 1994): 202.

Jalon, Allan. "A Visit to His Mentor." *Los Angeles Times Book Review* 17 September 1995: 14.

Jarman, Mark. "The Volcano Inside." *Southern Review* 32.2 (1996): 337–43.

Kaganoff, Penny. Rev. of *The River of Heaven. Publishers Weekly* 12 February 1988: 81.

Kamada, Roy. "Heterogeneity, Hybridity, and Multiplicity in *Volcano*: Garrett Hongo's Interventionist Poetics and the Intersectionality of Asian-American Identity." *The Diasporic Imagination: Identifying Asian-American Representations in America.* 2 vols. Ed. Somdatta Mandal. New Delhi: Prestige Books, 2000. 182–97.

Kaufman, Ellen. Rev. of *The Open Boat: Poems from Asian America. Library Journal* 118.2 (1 February 1993): 84.

Kessler, J. "A Letter to Garrett Hongo." *Amerasia Journal* 20.3 (1994): 19–24.

Kingston, M.H. "A Letter to Garrett Hongo, upon the Publication of the 'Open Boat.' " *Amerasia Journal* 20.3 (1994): 25–26.

Lee, A. Robert. "Ethnicities: The American Self-Tellings of Leslie Marmon Silko, Richard Rodriguez, Darryl Pickney, and Garrett Hongo." *Writing Lives: American Biography and Autobiography.* Ed. Hans Bak and Hans Krabbendam. Amsterdam, Netherlands: VU University Press, 1998. 122–35.

Moffett, Penelope. "Verses Chronicle Tales of Asian-Americans." *Los Angeles Times* 19 March 1987: V1, V19.

Monaghan, Peter. "How a Small, Nondescript Writing Program Achieved Distinction." *Chronicle of Higher Education* 24 April 1998: A13.

Moyers, Bill D. "Garrett Kaoru Hongo." *The Language of Life: A Festival of Poets.* New York: Doubleday, 1995. 201–15.

Moyers, Bill D. *The Power of the Word.* Vol. 3. Videocassette. PBS Video distributor, 1989.

Moyers, Bill D., et al. *Ancestral Voices.* PBS Video, 1989.

Muratori, Fred. Rev. of *The River of Heaven. Library Journal* 113.8 (1 May 1988): 81.

Oyama, Richard. "You Can Go Home Again: Writer and Poet Garrett Hongo Reclaims His Birthplace and Heritage in *Volcano: A Memoir of Hawai'i." Asianweek* 17.3 (8 September 1995): 13.

Pettingell, Phoebe. "Writers and Writing: Voices of Democracy." *New Leader* 13 June 1988: 15–16.

Rev. of *Yellow Light. Los Angeles Times Book Review* 16 May 1982: 9.

Rev. of *Yellow Light. Virginia Quarterly Review* 59.1 (Winter 1983): 26.

St. John, David. "Raised Voices in the Choir: A Review of 1982 Poetry Selections." *Antioch Review* 41.2 (Spring 1983): 231–44.

Sato, Dan. "*Volcano*: A Poet's Record of His Search for His Roots." *International Examiner* 22.10 (6 June 1995): 13.

Schultz, Robert. Rev. of *The River of Heaven*. *Hudson Review* (Spring 1989): 151.

Tabios, Eileen. "Garrett Hongo: *Feeling* Knowing, Knowing *Feeling*." *Asian Pacific American Journal* 5.1 (1996): 139–71.

Tillinghast, Richard. Rev. of *Yellow Light*. *Sewanee Review* 91.3 (Summer 1983): 478.

Uba, George. Rev. of *Yellow Light*. *Journal of Ethnic Studies* 12.4 (Winter 1985): 123–25.

Wakoski, Diane. Rev. of *Yellow Light*. *American Book Review* 6.2 (January/February 1984): 4–5.

LAWSON FUSAO INADA
(1938–)

Gayle K. Sato

BIOGRAPHY

Ancestry and geography are key to understanding the poetry of Lawson Inada, a sansei (third-generation) Japanese American born on 26 May 1938 in Fresno, California. Before and after the "evacuation" and "relocation" of Japanese Americans to concentration camps during World War II, which occurred when Inada was four, he lived in Fresno's West Side, a racially mixed, working-class community in which his multicultural poetics and politics took root and found their expressive beginnings through jazz. Inada's poems are forever emerging from and returning to the places called "Camp" and "Fresno."

Inada's maternal grandparents immigrated from Wakayama in 1907 and founded the Fresno Fish Market in 1912, a landmark institution until its closure in 1982. Inada's mother, Masako Saito, was born in Fresno the year the Fish Market opened for business. Fusaji Inada, the poet's father, was born in Watsonville in 1910, the son of farmers who immigrated from Kumamoto in 1896 and 1901 and labored on a sugarcane plantation in Hawaii before settling in the San Jose region as sharecroppers. Like most issei who endured a host of legislated and unofficial forms of racial discrimination, the Saitos and Inadas banked their hopes for a future in America on their nisei offspring. On the eve of World War II, they had achieved a measure of success through the accomplishments of two of their children—Masako had become a teacher, Fusaji was a dentist, and a four-year-old grandson was soon to enter school.

But from 1942 until the war's end, they were sent to three different concentration camps—Fresno Assembly Center, a temporary holding station, Jerome,

Arkansas, and Amache, Colorado. Fortunately, there was something to come back to when the war ended, since the Fresno Fish Market escaped the fate of many other issei businesses and properties that were lost through forced liquidation prior to internment or through vandalism, theft, and broken promises while the owners were interned. Inada lived in Fresno for the next fifteen years, helping out at the store and growing up among Asian, black, and Chicano friends—the "ABCs," as he calls it, of a West Side education. This was a listening education in particular, for the jazz music and multicultural accents absorbed from home life, jukebox, and street culture laid the foundation for Inada's vision and craft as a poet. In 1959, he graduated from what is now California State University at Fresno, where poet Philip Levine was one of his mentors. A scholarship funded two years of graduate study at the University of Iowa from 1960 to 1962, which were followed by a teaching appointment at the University of New Hampshire at Durham from 1962 to 1965. During this period, Inada met and married Janet Francis, and they decided to head west again after the appointment at Durham ended. Inada earned an M.F.A. from the University of Oregon in 1966 and started teaching in the English Department at Southern Oregon State College (now Southern Oregon University [SOU]), a position he still holds. The Inadas raised two sons in Ashland, Oregon—Miles Fusao and Lowell Masao, named for Miles Davis and Robert Lowell (Endo 16). The elder son Miles, a digital and multimedia artist also on the faculty of SOU, is creating a three-dimensional computer animation about the internment based on *Legends from Camp*.

Inada's poetic practice is embedded in a multifaceted career as artist and educator. From his early years at Southern Oregon State, when he served, for example, as director of a "Students of Other Cultures" project, to the establishment of Portland's Japanese American Historical Plaza in 1990, where his poems are engraved in stone alongside the Willamette River, Inada has worked in every imaginable capacity as an artist and educator. He has lectured abroad and throughout the United States, organized and performed in cultural festivals and writers' conferences, edited and written groundbreaking books and essays on Asian American writers, penned columns for community newspapers, and collaborated with musicians, singers, dancers, playwrights, and filmmakers.

MAJOR WORKS AND THEMES

Inada's major works are *Before the War: Poems As They Happened* (1971), *Legends from Camp* (1992), *Drawing the Line* (1997), and two coauthored poetry collections, *3 Northwest Poets: Drake, Inada, Lawder* (1970) and *The Buddha Bandits down Highway 99* (1978). *Before the War* is considered the first poetry collection by an Asian American to be published by a major press. *Legends from Camp* won a 1994 American Book Award, and *Drawing the Line* received the Hazel Hill Award for Poetry as part of the Oregon Book Awards for 2000. Inada has also published widely in journals, magazines, and anthologies, many of them special editions and collections with a regional, multicultural, or Asian American focus. Some of the more important of these are *Down at the Santa Fe Depot: Twenty Fresno Poets* (1970), *Yardbird Reader* (1974), *Settling America* (1974), *Counterpoint* (1976), *Greenfield Review* (1977), *Leaving the Bough* (1982), and *Turning Shadows into Light* (1982).

This journal/anthology archive is important because many individually published poems have not been reprinted in Inada's books, and for the few that have been, historical recontextualization illuminates their contribution to Inada's development. "West Side Songs," for example, originally published in a book that most readers today have never seen (*Down at the Santa Fe Depot*), became an example of Inada's signature style through recirculation in three of the earliest and most influential books about Asian American literature: Kai-yu Hsu and Helen Palubinskas's *Asian-American Authors* (1972), Frank Chin, Jeffery Paul Chan, Inada, and Shawn Wong's *Aiiieeeee!* (1974), and Elaine Kim's *Asian American Literature* (1982). The speaker in "West Side Songs" resembles the narrator of Ralph Ellison's novel *Invisible Man*, exposing and simultaneously repudiating his internalization of racial stereotypes that have fostered feelings of cultural inferiority and hostility toward other minority groups. "West Side Songs" explodes the myth that it should conform to a stereotyped idea of quaint Oriental writing, critiques romantic notions of Third World solidarity, and breaks Japanese cultural taboos against airing critical, controversial opinions in public. Its confrontational themes and style characterized the activist poetry of the 1960s and 1970s and may seem irrelevant to today's cultural politics, but as George Uba's "Versions of Identity in Post-activist Asian American Poetry" and the republication of "West Side Songs" in *Quiet Fire: A Historical Anthology of Asian American Poetry, 1892–1970* attest, Inada's earliest poems not only continue to inform his own later work but helped to open up the space in which today's Asian American poets practice their craft.

During the 1970s, Inada experimented in a different direction, producing long poems that were as recklessly expansive as "West Side Songs" was ironically understated. "Asian Brother, Asian Sister" (*Settling America*, 1976) and "Pumice, and Obsidian" (*Counterpoint*, 1976) are ten and thirteen pages long, respectively; "I Told You So" is an eighteen-page poem concluding *The Buddha Bandits down Highway 99* (1978); "Japanese Geometry" is a whopping fifty-two pages in *Yardbird Reader* (1974). These poems may be seen as efforts to unstitch the terse lines of "West Side Songs" and unpack an incompletely told experience of racism and its impact on personal development, yielding a new style that is illustrated by "The Discovery of Tradition," a different kind of long poem published in *Leaving the Bough* (1982). "The Discovery of Tradition" effectively mingles the major innovations of the 1970s—looser lines, playful line arrangements, repetition, use of "stage directions" or parenthetical "asides" to insert the rhythmic time of dance, music, conversation, and improvisation into the poem, a voice more openly searching and willing to express tenderness. Most important, Inada discovered the right blend of narrative and poetry.

Whereas "Japanese Geometry," "Pumice, and Obsidian," and "I Told You So" give the impression that the stories they are trying to tell (about internment, self-denial, the struggle for a new cultural and political consciousness) are being rewritten as sequences of images in order to keep the poems "poetic," "The Discovery of Tradition" is unafraid to narrate, and this comfortable indulgence in narration bespeaks the emergence of a speaker who is unafraid to "tell" on himself and speak as a Japanese American.

As the examples of "West Side Songs" and "The Discovery of Tradition" show, the anthology/journal archive must be sifted for a complete picture of Inada's development. However, the major works do reveal patterns of development that the scattered poems cannot, and chief among these is the relationship between Inada's poetic practice and the Japanese American internment.

Before the War defines a process of cultural "disintern"ment by transforming the meaning of "exposure" and "exile." In their original, disabling senses, these conditions are represented through objects that are characteristic of the desert locales where concentration camps were built and that were collected and crafted by internees to pass the time—objects such as weathered stones, bleached wood, and bone fossils. This craftwork was showcased as an example of spiritual triumph in Allen Eaton's *Beauty behind Barbed Wire: The Arts of the Japanese in Our War Relocation Camps* (1952), a view of camp life interrogated by Inada's use of the same objects to portray brutal living conditions. For example, the poem "Shells" juxtaposes the image of tortoise shells decorating an internee's garden with a living animal randomly bludgeoned by a soldier assigned to "guard" dangerous issei who grow gardens in the wasteland. But vulnerability and victimization are most clearly represented in the figure of a disguised, buried, and therefore doubly silenced Japanese American musician who (dis)appears in the first poem of *Before the War* when a surreal snowstorm blows into his room and covers everything in sight.

In counterpoint to an official representation of concentration camps as civilized settings where artistic urges and the need for beauty were satisfied, *Before the War* redefines exposure and exile to show that they can only be productive as self-determined, self-imposed displacement. This new kind of voluntary "relocation" is a conscious excavation of silenced history and repressed experience so that the Japanese American subject can speak its way back toward a wholeness that Alice Walker has called "racial health" (85). In *Before the War*, two sequences of love poems addressed to "Janet" encapsulate the transformation of inclement weather as a condition of victimization and enforced survival into weathering as a process of self-imposed regeneration. The first sequence, which traces the development of a love relationship, coincides with the speaker's departure from the West Coast in a section of the book entitled "Into the Open." The second sequence, which expresses the speaker's desire for a child and celebrates a pregnancy, marks the speaker's return to the West Coast as a father in a section of the book entitled "Coming into Oregon." Together, these poems for "Janet" mark the key points of departure and return in Inada's poetics of relocation. Leaving and returning to the West Coast map a process of consciously rejecting a racist definition of Japanese Americans as persons to be "relocated" because they are inherently alien to "American" society, and consciously reformulating Japanese American identity as a distinctive, embodied, empowered presence. The persona through which the journey away from and back to the West Coast is rendered, that of a man willing to expose his inner self and cast off protective disguises, and the imagery of a magical, energizing snowstorm and tender, damp greenery through which love and pregnancy are represented clearly reformulate the earlier representations of camp through imagery of life-threatening erosion, ironic sustenance, and disappearance.

Legends from Camp is organized around places and aesthetic traditions rather than a journey narrative, as indicated by its five section titles, "Camp," "Fresno," "Jazz," "Oregon," and "Performance." As these titles indicate, the recuperation of Japanese American subjectivity initiated in *Before the War* has progressed to the point where the subject of "home"—past and present hometowns, aesthetic traditions of Japanese folk art and American jazz in which Inada feels at home—now accounts for 90 percent of the poems in *Legends from Camp*. Rhythms and rhetoric have mellowed but at the same time have become more clarified, intense, and integrated. Family members, jazz musicians, and other individuals are now treated explicitly and extensively; poems are openly autobiographical and forthright about identifying artistic and spiritual mentors. For good measure, prose introductions to each section of the book contextualize the poems in the author's life history and memory of the past. In short, the "ABCs" of a West Side education now become manifest in poems that redefine a life of "cultural deprivation" as they do "relocation," commanding readers to understand an issei family business through the international working class of Fresno's "Chinatown," Japanese American voices through jazz and Navajo song, living in Oregon through remembering Fresno. Progressing beyond the difficult work of initiating "disintern"ment, the speaker of *Legends from Camp* now experiences cultural recuperation as a work-in-progress, which reveals itself to be an increasingly multicultural project since "relocation" and "disintern"ment belong to a much larger history of racism and antiracism in the United States.

Whereas *Legends from Camp* marked significant changes in Inada's formal techniques and treatment of themes compared to the first book, *Drawing the Line* continues in the mode established by *Legends from Camp*. Inada's third book underscores the continuing centrality of internment and its inseparability from other dominant domains of experience, notably "performance" poetry and Oregon's geographies. In the introduction to *Legends from Camp*, Inada imagines his great-grandchildren in the next century asking their Japanese American peers, "What camp were they in?" as a routine method of introducing themselves and getting acquainted. The imagining of such a use for the question signifies the healing distance traveled since the war, but it also indicates that far from being an overwritten story, the narrative of internment must go on being a work-in-progress. *Drawing the Line* insists that there are reasons for continuing to speak about camp and demonstrates ways of doing it without silencing or marginalizing other histories and issues.

The book's cover features a drawing of Heart Mountain by Yosh Kuromiya, to whom the poem "Drawing the Line" is dedicated. "Yosh" in Inada's poem is a young nisei interned at Heart Mountain, Wyoming, a budding artist working patiently every day to perfect a drawing of the majestic landmark for which his camp is named, who finds that he must also "draw the line" by refusing to be drafted when the freedom to exercise this particular duty as an American citizen is "restored" to interned nisei men in 1943. (Heart Mountain was the site of organized, nonviolent resistance by a group of nisei called the Fair Play Committee. See Frank Emi's "Draft Resistance at the Heart Mountain Concentration Camp and the Fair Play Committee.") Many years after the war, Inada's Yosh returns to Heart Mountain to locate the spot where he produced his original drawing and to recuperate, if possible, the perspective on life that enabled him to respond to beauty while he was behind barbed wire and to respect the depths of his own heart. In *Before the War*, Inada repudiated an official interpretation and manipulation of artwork produced "behind barbed wire," and Yosh's drawing is likewise informed by a politics of resistance. The beauty it expresses is not created within or through the materials and existence of camp life but originates and remains inviolate beyond the barbed-wire enclosure of Heart Mountain Relocation Center. The poem "ends" in transit, in celebration of Yosh's successful "relocation" as he beholds the mountain in his old age and remembers his idealism, moral courage, and artistic ambition. By closing with an affirmation of Yosh's future, "Drawing the Line" looks back to the poem that opens Inada's first book, for the return to Heart Mountain and resumption of drawing "rewrite" the fate of the musician who (dis)appeared in the act of plucking out a rhythm. Yosh is a successful example of the process of "disintern"ment undertaken in order to recuperate racial health. "Drawing the line" and "plucking out a rhythm" are creative acts that define a practice of "relocation" that is at once political, poetic, and performative.

CRITICAL RECEPTION

Although Inada has been called "poet laureate of Asian America" and "Japanese America's poet," there are no books and very few articles about his work, and except for scattered references to *Before the War* in Elaine Kim's *Asian American Literature*, no discussions of Inada's poetry in scholarly studies of Asian American writing. The timing of Inada's first two books may account for some of this neglect, since *Before the War* was out of print when Asian American literature began to penetrate the educational establishment in the 1980s and *Legends from Camp* (1992) appeared too late for inclusion in new anthologies like *The Heath Anthology of American Literature* (1990) or *The Open Boat* (1993) that responded to inroads made by multicultural literatures and the explosion of new Asian American writing in the late 1980s. However, inclusion of Inada's work in newer anthologies like *Premonitions: The Kaya Anthology of New Asian North American Poetry* (1995) and *Oxford's Modern American Poets* (2000) should stimulate a rapid rise in critical studies over the next decade.

Inada's readers have long recognized that his use of jazz is unparalleled among Asian American writers, but only recently has literary criticism begun to engage this subject. Juliana Chang's "Time, Jazz, and the Racial Subject: Lawson Inada's Jazz Poetics" is perhaps the first substantial study of this aspect of Inada's art and one of the few articles devoted wholly to Inada's writing. Chang analyzes Inada's response to jazz as a learned and earned "affiliation," a type of relationship with several important implications (154). First, it is a relationship to jazz that respects differences between African American and Japanese American histories and avoids compensatory substitution of sansei subjectivity with black consciousness and experience. Second, it enables the use of jazz as an "alternative code of legitimation" that repudiates dominant constructions of Japanese American subjectivity and decenters the binary opposition of "white vs. colored" in dominant paradigms of race relations in the United States (153–54). Third, affiliation with the jazz tradition means reciprocation rather than exploitation or consumption: by "bringing the signature style of various African American musicians into poetic language," Inada's poetry "returns to jazz this very articulation of a Japanese American culture and poetics" (154).

Other articles on Inada's poetry center on its relationship to internment. Vern Rutsala's "The Unfinished House: Notes on Poetry and Memory" (1982) places Inada's camp poems from *Before the War* within an international poetics of memory. Discussing Inada alongside various figures including Villon, Wordsworth, Philip Larkin, Robert Penn Warren, and Pao Chao (an ancient Chinese poet) foregrounds the specific historical and political meanings of Inada's memory work. Stan Yogi's "Yearning for the Past: The Dynamics of Memory in Sansei Internment Poetry" (1996) also analyzes the camp poems from *Before the War* in terms of memory's therapeutic and political functions, but places Inada's work within a specifically Japanese American poetics of remembering. Inada is compared to Janice Mirikitani and David Mura as sansei poets who interrogate nisei silence about the camps. Whereas Yogi's and Rutsala's articles focus only on the one section in *Before the War* that deals directly with camp, Gayle Sato's "Lawson Inada's Poetics of Relocation: Weathering, Nesting, Leaving the Bough" (2000–2001) examines the meaning of internment within the total structure of *Before the War* and the relationship of *Before the War* to subsequent representations of internment in "The Discovery of Tradition," *Legends from Camp*, and *Drawing the Line*. Sato reads Inada's entire oeuvre as a practice of "writing relocation," which is defined as a literary correlative to the redress movement of the 1980s, a new development in narrative patterns of Asian American "mobility" identified by Sau-ling Wong in *Reading Asian American Literature* (1993), and an example of the self-imposed, enabling dislocation discussed in Caren Kaplan's "Deterritorializations: The Rewriting of Home and Exile in Western Feminist Discourse" (1987).

Inada's poetry also receives brief treatment in several articles on Asian American or Japanese American literature. In each case, his poems are discussed either in the article's introduction or conclusion, an indication that regardless of differences in the critics' analytical approaches or the historical moments from which they write, Inada is consistently seen as an exemplary poet. Shirley Lim's "Reconstructing Asian-American Poetry: A Case for Ethnopoetics" (1987) is an early attempt to insert theories of reading and textuality into discussions of Asian American writing centered on its ethnocultural content. Lim uses "Chinks" (a section of "West Side Songs") to illustrate the interpretive challenges faced by readers of Asian American literature, who must educate themselves in order to understand the poem's use of pidgin, allusions to Asian American cultures and histories, and strategic silence.

More recently, James Lu's "Enacting Asian American Transformations: An Inter-ethnic Perspective" (1998) also situates a brief comment on one poem by Inada within a call for new approaches to reading Asian American writers. Lu's article reviews the debate over "fake" and "real" cultural representations and places Inada's "Since When As Ever More" (1983) within this debate as an example of shifting and conflicting subjectivities to make the point that the *Aiiieeeee!* editors, who led the attack against Maxine Hong Kingston's method of using Chinese mythology, themselves endorse the very process of transformation for which they have criticized other writers. Another article that calls attention to the linguistic and cultural hybridity of Inada's poetry is Benzi Zhang's "Mapping Carnivalistic Discourse in Japanese-American Writing" (1999), which cites *Before the War* as a pioneering example of writing that pluralizes the representation of "American" experience. Zhang reads "Into the Open," the second section of *Before the War*, as a declaration of independence from the totalizing effects of both submissive "Oriental" and assimilationist "American" versions of Japanese American identity. Juliana Chang's "Reading Asian American Poetry" (1996) cites Inada's "Kicking the Habit"—which compares white cultural hegemony to an "addiction" to the English language—as an example of "critical" as opposed to "liberal multiculturalism." Chang reads the "Angloholic" speaker/poet's imagined abdication of English, which is the language of his profession and his native tongue, as an act that "counters the misperception of the Asian American as foreign to English and denaturalizes his and the reader's relation to English" (92).

Poets whose careers intersect with Inada's have written some of the most perceptive appraisals of his work. Garrett Hongo, for example, in his introduction to *The Open Boat* (1993), recalls the impact of "the Sansei poet Lawson Fusao Inada" (xxi) during his formative years as a writer and speaks also of Inada's continuing importance as a role model through the 1990s. Appealing for an end to clashes between Asian American critics and writers who bring different priorities to the evaluation of literature—"personal subjectivity and

poetics" versus "polemicized critique of generalized ideological domination"—
Hongo reminds us of Inada's "reverence for power, precision, and beauty in
language" (xxxvi), without which no amount of commitment to political and
social change can produce the verbal art called poetry. Lonny Kaneko writes
from the perspective of an older sansei who understands Inada as a peer rather
than a forerunner. His warm, witty review of *The Buddha Bandits down Highway 99* for *Amerasia Journal* (1979) captures the style of early Inada and his
influence on other writers: "Anyone who's good enough to be imitated's gotta
have style. Lawson's got style. I mean, the first time I met Lawson he was
wearing a knit navy watch cap over a head that may or may not have been
shaved" (92–93). Kaneko's review of *Legends from Camp* for *Amerasia Journal*
(1993) again reveals his extraordinary responsiveness to Inada's writing. One
of Kaneko's most important observations is that Inada's mature poetry is deceptively simple: "The danger in reading these poems is that they can be read
easily and quickly, so that the temptation may be to let them go by without
letting the words, the rhymes, the subtle ironies, the refrains, the chant, begin
to work their work on the subconscious" (167). Kaneko's ability to penetrate
the depths of Inada's writing and describe it with perfect simplicity evokes
Inada's comparable response to Toshio Mori, a likewise deceptively simple Japanese American writer.

In contrast to Kaneko's assessment, and a rare example of a writer/critic
expressing dissatisfaction with Inada's art and status, is David Mura's "The
Margins at the Center, the Center at the Margins: Acknowledging the Diversity
of Asian American Poetry" (1995). Mura's appeal for a radical expansion of
criteria to acknowledge and value differences among Asian American poets instead of maintaining hierarchies of "important" and "marginal" writers echoes
the arguments found in Hongo's introduction and Lu's article. However, Mura
does not praise Inada's poetry, instead faulting it (in a collective assessment of
Inada, Wing Tek Lum, Eric Chock, and Juliet Kono) for sticking to "a unified
lyrical 'I' " and "straight declamatory syntax," avoiding "traditional forms of
the Anglo-American tradition" and "words that might be deemed too Latinate
or intellectual," and using narratives uncritically, without attempting to "question
their premises or their ability to capture experience" (173). What are worth
emphasizing here are the contradictions of Mura's stance, for although he is
generally perceived and perceives himself to be at odds politically and aesthetically with "the poet laureate of Asian America," he and Inada both write lin-
guistically and culturally hybrid poems that are thoroughly autobiographical,
reflect with a special intensity the cultural and political milieu of particular
moments in the history of Asian American literary production, and are intensely
concerned with the effect of internment, minority status, and Japanese culture
on the sexuality and formation of Japanese American men. Thus, although
Mura's personal essays, autobiography, and poetry cannot be counted as literary
criticism in any explicit or formal sense, this writing is a provocative, productive
site from which to review Inada's poetry.

Inada says that he wrote his first poem in 1957 ("A Letter to the Editor"), and now that his writing career is midway through a fifth decade, critics are beginning to take stock of his achievements and investigate the particular relationships of his poetry to the cultural domains in which they are grounded, domains usefully defined by the poet himself as "Camp," "Fresno," "Jazz," "Oregon," and "Performance," the sections of *Legends from Camp*. A reliable biography is needed as an aid to reading the pervasive autobiographical element of Inada's poetry, including his relationship to the *Aiiieeeee!* editorial group. This in turn would facilitate a comparison of the views expressed in the *Aiiieeeee!* introductions with critical stances articulated in essays authored by Inada alone. Drawing on biographical data, feminist and psychological investigations could initiate a much-needed assessment of the centrality of men and masculinity to every phase of Inada's writing. Such criticism could illuminate the particular and combined influences of figures like Philip Levine, Michael Harper, Ishmael Reed, Jeffery Paul Chan, Frank Chin, Shawn Wong, Garrett Hongo, Alan Lau, Miles Horiuchi, John Okada, Toshio Mori, Fusaji Inada, Busuke Saito, Miles and Lowell Inada, and others whom Inada frequently writes for and about. In short, there is a tremendous amount of scholarly and interpretive work to be done on this writer whose appeal to lay audiences, critics, students, musicians, and poets alike is truly borderless.

BIBLIOGRAPHY

Works by Lawson Fusao Inada

Poetry

3 Northwest Poets. With Albert Drake and Douglas Lawder. Madison, WI: Quixote Press, 1970.

"West Side Songs." *Down at the Santa Fe Depot: 20 Fresno Poets*. Ed. David Kherdian and James Baloian. Fresno, CA: Giligia Press, 1970. 46–53. Rpt. in *Asian-American Authors*. Ed. Kai-yu Hsu and Helen Palubinskas. Boston: Houghton Mifflin, 1972. 111–12.

Before the War: Poems As They Happened. New York: Morrow, 1971.

"Four Songs for Asian America." *Bridge* 2 (August 1973): 23–25.

"Asian Brother, Asian Sister." *Settling America: The Ethnic Expression of 14 Contemporary Poets*. Ed. David Kherdian. New York: Macmillan, 1974. 48–58.

"Japanese Geometry." *Yardbird Reader*. Vol. 3. Ed. Shawn Wong and Frank Chin. Berkeley: Yardbird, 1974. 130–82.

"Nightsong in Asian America." *Yardbird Reader*. Vol. 3. Ed. Shawn Wong and Frank Chin. Berkeley: Yardbird, 1974. xv.

"My Name Is Rice Field." *Rafu Shimpo Supplement* 21 December 1974: N.p.

"Amache Gate." *Time to Greez! Incantations from the Third World*. Ed. Janice Mirikitani. San Francisco: Glide/Third World Communications, 1975. 73–77.

"Pumice, and Obsidian." *Counterpoint: Perspectives on Asian America*. Ed. Emma Gee. Los Angeles: UCLA Asian American Studies Center, 1976. 543–55.

"From Left to Right." *Greenfield Review* 6.1–2 (Spring 1977): 110.
"The Island, the People, and the River." *Greenfield Review* 6.1–2 (Spring 1977): 105–8.
"Kap-pa Song." *Greenfield Review* 6.1–2 (Spring 1977): 101–4.
"Making Miso." *Greenfield Review* 6.1–2 (Spring 1977): 99–100.
"My Father and Myself Facing the Sun." *Greenfield Review* 6.1–2 (Spring 1977): 108–9.
The Buddha Bandits down Highway 99. With Garrett Hongo and Alan Chong Lau. Mountain View, CA: Buddhahead Press, 1978.
"Something for Yardbird." *Yardbird Lives!* Ed. Ishmael Reed and Al Young. New York: Grove Press, 1978. 23–24.
"The Discovery of Tradition." *Leaving the Bough: 50 American Poets of the 80s*. Ed. Roger Gaess. New York: International Publishers, 1982. 80–88.
"Songs in the Ancient Tradition." *Turning Shadows into Light*. Ed. Mayumi Tsutakawa and Alan Chong Lau. Seattle: Young Pine Press, 1982. 91–94.
"Since When As Ever More." *Breaking Silence: An Anthology of Contemporary Asian American Poets*. Ed. Joseph Bruchac. Greenfield Center, NY: Greenfield Review Press, 1983. 84–88.
"Blue Monk." *International Examiner Literary Supplement* 19 July 1989: 4–5.
"Reflections on War." *Amerasia* 17.1 (1991): 39–41.
Legends from Camp. Minneapolis: Coffee House Press, 1992.
Drawing the Line. Minneapolis: Coffee House Press, 1997.

Prose and Criticism

"The Vision of America in John Okada's *No-No Boy*." *Proceedings of the Comparative Literature Symposium* 9 (1978): 275–87.
"Tribute to Toshio." *Ayumi: A Japanese American Anthology*. Ed. Janice Mirikitani. San Francisco: Japanese American Anthology Committee, 1980. 189–90.
Introduction. *No-No Boy*. By John Okada. Seattle: University of Washington Press, 1981. iii–vi.
"Of Place and Displacement: The Range of Japanese American Literature." *Three American Literatures: Essays in Chicano, Native American, and Asian-American Literature for Teachers of American Literature*. Ed. Houston A. Baker, Jr. Intro. Walter J. Ong. New York: MLA, 1982. 254–65.
"Standing on Seventh Street." New introduction to *Yokohama, California*. By Toshio Mori. Intro. William Saroyan. Seattle: University of Washington Press, 1985. v–xxvii.
In This Great Land of Freedom: The Japanese Pioneers of Oregon. Ed. Lawson Fusao Inada, Akemi Kikumura, Mary Worthington, and Eiichiro Azuma. Los Angeles: Japanese American National Museum, 1993.
"A Letter to the Editor, July 28, 1993." *Amerasia Journal* 20.3 (1994): 27–30.
Only What We Could Carry: The Japanese American Internment Experience. Ed. with intro. Lawson Fusao Inada. Preface by Patricia Wakida. Berkeley, CA: Heyday Press, 2000.
Unfinished Message: Selected Works of Toshio Mori. Intro. Lawson Fusao Inada. Berkeley: Heyday Press, 2000.
" 'Ghostly Camps, Alien Nation'—An Essay Review by Lawson Fusao Inada." Rev. of *Democracy on Trial: The Japanese-American Evacuation and Relocation in*

World War II, by Page Smith. *Modern American Poetry* 11 February 2001. Available: http://www.english.uiuc.edu/maps/poets/g_l/inada/ghostly.htm. Accessed in April 2001.

Studies of Lawson Fusao Inada

Chan, Jeffery Paul, Frank Chin, Lawson Fusao Inada, and Shawn Wong, eds. *The Big Aiiieeeee!: An Anthology of Chinese American and Japanese American Literature.* New York: Meridian, 1991.

Chang, Juliana. "Time, Jazz, and the Racial Subject: Lawson Inada's Jazz Poetics." *Racing and (E)Racing Language: Living with the Color of Our Words.* Ed. Ellen J. Goldner and Safiya Henderson-Holmes. Syracuse: Syracuse University Press, 2001. 134–54.

———, ed. *Quiet Fire: A Historical Anthology of Asian American Poetry, 1892–1970.* New York: Asian American Writers' Workshop, 1996.

———. "Reading Asian American Poetry." *MELUS* 21.1 (Spring 1996): 81–98.

Chin, Frank, Jeffery Paul Chan, Lawson Fusao Inada, and Shawn Hsu Wong, eds. *Aiiieeeee! An Anthology of Asian American Writers.* 1974. Washington, DC: Howard University Press, 1983.

Dong, Arthur, dir. *Claiming a Voice: The Visual Communications Story.* Videocassette. DeepFocus Productions and Visual Communications, 1990. [Lawson Inada is included in this documentary of Visual Communications' twenty-year history as one example of Asian American artists claiming a voice in media.]

Eaton, Allen Hendershott. *Beauty behind Barbed Wire: The Arts of the Japanese in Our War Relocation Camps.* New York: Harper, 1952.

Emi, Frank Seishi. "Draft Resistance at the Heart Mountain Concentration Camp and the Fair Play Committee." *Frontiers of Asian American Studies: Writing, Research, and Commentary.* Ed. Gail M. Nomura. Pullman: Washington State University Press, 1989. 41–69.

Endo, Ellen. "Is Anyone Out There Really Listening? An Interview with Lawson Inada, Poet." *Rafu Shimpo Supplement* 21 December 1974. 16.

Hongo, Garrett. Introduction. *The Open Boat: Poems from Asian America.* Ed. Garrett Hongo. New York: Anchor, 1993. xvii–xlii.

Hsu, Kai-yu, and Helen Palubinskas, eds. *Asian-American Authors.* Boston: Houghton Mifflin, 1972.

"Inada, Lawson Fusao 1938–   ." *Contemporary Authors: A Bio-Bibliographical Guide to Current Authors and Their Works.* Vols. 33–36. Ed. Ann Evory. Detroit: Gale Research Co., 1973. 432–33.

Kaneko, Lonny. "A Journey into Place, Race, and Spirit." Rev. of *The Buddha Bandits down Highway 99. Amerasia Journal* 6.2 (1979): 91–95.

———. Rev. of *Legends from Camp: Poems by Lawson Inada. Amerasia Journal* 19.1 (1993): 167–70.

Kaplan, Caren. "Deterritorializations: The Rewriting of Home and Exile in Western Feminist Discourse." *Cultural Critique* 6 (1987): 187–98.

Kim, Elaine H. *Asian American Literature: An Introduction to the Writings and Their Social Context.* Philadelphia: Temple University Press, 1982.

Kondo, Alan, dir. *I Told You So.* Perf. Lawson Inada. Videocassette. Visual Communications, 1974. [Documentary portrait of Inada that weaves downtown scenes of Fresno with words from his poems.]

Lauter, Paul, Gen. Ed. *The Heath Anthology of American Literature*. 1990. 2nd ed. 2 vols. Lexington, MA: Heath, 1994.

Lim, Shirley. "Reconstructing Asian-American Poetry: A Case for Ethnopoetics." *MELUS* 14.2 (Summer 1987): 51–63.

Lu, James. "Enacting Asian American Transformations: An Inter-ethnic Perspective." *MELUS* 23.4 (Winter 1998): 85–99.

Mura, David. "The Margins at the Center, the Center at the Margins: Acknowledging the Diversity of Asian American Poetry." *Reviewing Asian America: Locating Diversity*. Ed. Wendy L. Ng, Soo-Young Chin, James S. Moy, and Gary Y. Okihiro. Pullman: Washington State University Press, 1995. 171–83.

Rutsala, Vern. "The Unfinished House: Notes on Poetry and Memory." *American Poetry Review* 11.2 (March/April 1982): 30+.

Salisbury, Ralph. "Dialogue with Lawson Fusao Inada." *Northwest Review* 20.2–3 (1982): 60–75.

Sato, Gayle K. "Lawson F. Inada." *Reading Japanese American Literature: The Legacy of Three Generations* [*Nikkei Amerika Bungaku: Sansedai No Kiseki O Yomu*]. Ed. Teruyo Ueki and Gayle K. Sato. 1997. Osaka: Sogensha, 1999. 168–75.

———. "Lawson Inada's Poetics of Relocation: Weathering, Nesting, Leaving the Bough." *Amerasia Journal* 26.3 (2000–2001): 139–60.

Uba, George. "The Representation of Asian American Poetry in *The Heath Anthology of American Literature*." *Reviewing Asian America: Locating Diversity*. Ed. Wendy L. Ng, Soo-Young Chin, James S. Moy, and Gary Y. Okihiro. Pullman: Washington State University Press, 1995. 185–93.

———. "Versions of Identity in Post-activist Asian American Poetry." *Reading the Literatures of Asian America*. Ed. Shirley Geok-lin Lim and Amy Ling. Philadelphia: Temple University Press, 1992. 33–48.

Walker, Alice. "Zora Neale Hurston: A Cautionary Tale and a Partisan Review." *In Search of Our Mothers' Gardens*. New York: Harcourt, 1983. 83–92.

Wong, Sau-ling Cynthia. "The Politics of Mobility." *Reading Asian American Literature: From Necessity to Extravagance*. Princeton, NJ: Princeton University Press, 1993. 118–65.

Yogi, Stan. "Yearning for the Past: The Dynamics of Memory in Sansei Internment Poetry." *Memory and Cultural Politics: New Approaches to American Ethnic Literatures*. Ed. Amritjit Singh, Joseph T. Skerrett, Jr., and Robert E. Hogan. Boston: Northeastern University Press, 1996. 245–65.

Zhang, Benzi. "Mapping Carnivalistic Discourse in Japanese-American Writing." *MELUS* 24.4 (Winter 1999): 19–40.

LONNY KANEKO
(1939–   )

Tamiko Nimura

BIOGRAPHY

Sansei (third-generation Japanese American) writer Lonny Minoru Kaneko was born on 15 November 1939 to his nisei parents Lois and Sanetomo ("Sanny") Kaneko. During World War II, the U.S. government "relocated" Kaneko's family to Camp Harmony in Puyallup, Washington. Shortly thereafter, Kaneko's family was incarcerated in Minidoka, Idaho, where he spent his preschool years. His chapbook of poetry *Coming Home from Camp* (1986) reflects his family's experiences during and after the wartime internment. Kaneko began writing poetry in 1960 with Theodore Roethke's advanced writing classes, despite Roethke's advice to the contrary (e-mail); "Roethke is probably the strongest influence [on my writing]," Kaneko observes, "since I still like to write in form or often have a 'formal' response" (e-mail). A playwright and fiction writer as well as a poet, Kaneko has won several awards for his writing, including the Coeur d'Alene Festival of Arts poetry contest (1973), *Amerasia Journal*'s short-story contest (1975), the Pacific Northwest Writers Conference award (1977), and a National Endowment for the Arts fellowship (1981). He currently teaches creative writing in the English Department at Highline Community College and lives on Vashon Island, Washington.

MAJOR WORKS AND THEMES

Kaneko has published poems in various magazines and anthologies; however, his major collection is the thirteen-poem chapbook *Coming Home from Camp* (hereafter *Coming Home*). Like the works of other sansei poets (Lawson Fusao Inada, Janice Mirikitani), a significant number of Kaneko's poems elaborate on the internment and its psychological aftermath. In a review of another Asian American poetry book, Kaneko describes his philosophy of what a poem should be:

Something that's your very own. Later it becomes a record of the traveling you do both outside and inside yourself, the calculation of where you've been, where it's bringing you. . . .

We are all of us trying to trace the trails we've uncovered or fill in the blank places on the map. As poets we look for our own voices, the shape and sound of our vowels and consonants. These make us human; the trails make us alive. (Rev. of *Buddha Bandits* 92)

As Kaneko's book implicitly argues, the internment shattered the idea of "home" for Japanese Americans. Kaneko's parents, in particular, were never able to buy a house, and Kaneko himself acknowledges that home for him was elusive during the writing of *Coming Home*: "I don't know that the title poem admits to there being any real home, for at that time of my life I was living and working part of the year in California and part of the year in Seattle" (e-mail). In light of this quest for home, *Coming Home* can be read as a poetic cycle that struggles to integrate creatively the past and the present, the expressed and the repressed, the conscious and the unconscious, and the decay and the renewal of landscapes and bodies.

Kaneko establishes many of these contrasts in the two opening poems, "On Ordinary Days" and "Beast from the Heart." The former poem describes camp life: the stark roads inside the campgrounds and "an ache that gnaws deep" (*Coming Home* n.p.). The latter poem takes place in a postcamp present; it portrays the nightmares that haunt Kaneko and "those who love [him]" (*Coming Home* n.p.). Juxtaposed, these poems interweave physical details of Kaneko's past (camp life) with his intangible and unconscious present (nightmares). The next poem, "Butcher," describes a father who butchers his daughter's pet chicken in camp. Kaneko uses the situation to play on the irony of the "yellow" imprisoned, reenacting imprisonment and slow death ("ten thousand hens" [*Coming Home* n.p.]). Years later, this incident from camp life continues to imprison father and daughter.

Other poems in the book deal with the decay and renewal of landscapes and bodies. "Bad Knees Harry: Japanese Gardener" is a playful tribute to a gardener who "was perpetual motion without effect" (*Coming Home* n.p.). "Rooms" reveals a conflict between complacent surfaces and inner turmoil. In this poem, "home" is a space that repeats the stifling conditions of camp life; decaying houses are prominent images in *Coming Home*.

Coming Home concludes with several poems of rebirth that confront the camp experience. Unlike "Ordinary Days," where the reader must look for clues about camp ("homes beyond the fence" and "single rooms"), the final four poems name the camp experience with terms like "Camp Harmony" and "Minidoka." In "Family Album," a series of verbal snapshots that linger on the internment years (1942, 1943, and 1944), the speaker acknowledges his anger about the internment. He lingers on the bitter irony that his family was incarcerated in the desert of Minidoka, a name that means "water. Something we choke on" (*Coming Home* n.p.). "Earthquake Country" illustrates the fissures among family members: distances, divorces, diseases. Yet here Kaneko redefines stability through flexibility. Kaneko uses his own poetic voice to reclaim the voices of his nisei parents, most notably in the title (and final) poem of *Coming Home*. Divided into three sections, "Her Words to No One," "His Words after Work," and "Son's Words to His Teenage Children," the poem integrates his mother's, his father's, and his own voice, addressing the reader along with his teenage children.

CRITICAL RECEPTION

Kaneko's finely crafted poetry deserves critical attention; however, it has received almost none to date. This fact may be partially due to the limited availability of *Coming Home from Camp*. The chapbook had a limited press run of 300 copies, though it is included in the book arts collections of several university libraries. In her foundational study *Asian American Literature*, Elaine Kim provides a brief gloss on "Family Album," but does not analyze it in detail (261). The difficulty in locating *Coming Home*, coupled with a general focus on novels in Asian American literary criticism, may have deterred literary critics from writing about his poetry thus far. The book was also never reviewed for popular newspapers.

In Asian American literary studies, Kaneko is more widely known for his short story "The Shoyu Kid," perhaps because it is included in the seminal anthology *The Big Aiiieeeee!* (1991). (With the exception of Elaine Kim's book, the critical studies listed here deal solely with "The Shoyu Kid.") A dark and haunting tale of adolescent internment life, "The Shoyu Kid" has won critical attention from several Asian American literary critics (Sau-ling Wong, David Eng, and David Palumbo-Liu).

Whether Kaneko's work will receive its deserved critical attention remains to be seen. Concerning the relatively recent explosion of Japanese American (and Asian American) writing, Kaneko wrote in 1983, "I was consciously writing about my camp memories in 1961, but could never get those poems published. . . . [S]everal other poems I've since had published were begun in the mid-60's. I wonder if [Asian American writers] seemed quiet only because there was no one around to hear" (Bruchac xiv).

BIBLIOGRAPHY

Works by Lonny Kaneko

Poetry

"Family Album for Charlotte Davis." *Amerasia Journal* 2.2 (Summer 1975): 134.
"Issei." *Greenfield Review* 6.1–2 (1977): 20.
"Lee Siu Long: Little Dragon Lee." *Greenfield Review* 6.1–2 (1977): 22–24.
"Renewal: Algona, Washington." *Greenfield Review* 6.1–2 (1977): 21.
"Violets for Mother." *Greenfield Review* 8.3–4 (1979): 178.
"What We Can Lose in San Francisco." *Greenfield Review* 8.3–4 (1979): 179.
"Renewal: Algona, Washington." *Ayumi: A Japanese American Anthology*. Ed. Janice
    Mirikitani and the Japanese American Anthology Committee. San Francisco: Jap-
    anese American Anthology Committee, 1980. 192.
"Requiem for John Kazuo Yamamoto, Sr." *Amerasia Journal* 9.2 (1982): 117–20.
"Coming Home from Camp." *Breaking Silence: An Anthology of Contemporary Asian
    American Poets*. Ed. Joseph Bruchac. Greenfield Center, NY: Greenfield Review
    Press, 1983. 104–6.
"The Secret." Bruchac, 106–7.
Coming Home from Camp. Waldron Island, WA: Brooding Heron Press, 1986.
"Bailey Getzert: The First Grade, 1945." *An Ear to the Ground: An Anthology of Con-
    temporary American Poetry*. Ed. Marie Harris and Kathleen Aguero. Athens: Uni-
    versity of Georgia Press, 1989. 142–43.
"Beasts from the Heart." Harris and Aguero, 143–44.
"Wild Light." Harris and Aguero, 141–42.
"Song for Lovers." *On a Bed of Rice: An Asian American Erotic Feast*. Ed. Geraldine
    Kudaka. New York: Anchor, 1995. 274–75.

Short Stories

"The Shoyu Kid." *The Big Aiiieeeee!* Ed. Jeffery Paul Chan, Frank Chin, Lawson Fusao
    Inada, and Shawn Wong. New York: Meridian, 1991. 304–14.
"Nobody's Hero." *Asian American Literature: A Brief Introduction and Anthology*. Ed.
    Shawn Wong. New York: HarperCollins, 1996. 147–56.
"Old Lady." *Seattle Review* 21.1 (1999): 66–72.

Criticism

Rev. of *The Buddha Bandits down Highway 99*, by Garrett Hongo, Alan Chong Lau,
    and Lawson Fusao Inada. *Amerasia Journal* 6.2 (1979): 91–95.

Drama

With Amy Sanbo. *Lady Is Dying*. Asian American Theater Company, San Francisco. 21
    October 1977.

Biography

Kaneko, Lonny. E-mail to the author. 23 January 2001.

Studies of Lonny Kaneko

Bruchac, Joseph. Introduction. *Breaking Silence: An Anthology of Contemporary Asian American Poets*. Greenfield Center, NY: Greenfield Review Press, 1983. xii–xv.

Eng, David L. "Primal Glances: Race and Psychoanalysis in Lonny Kaneko's 'The Shoyu Kid.' " *Critical Mass: A Journal of Asian American Cultural Criticism* 1.2 (1994): 65–83.

Kim, Elaine. "Multiple Mirrors and Many Images: New Directions in Asian American Literature." *Asian American Literature: An Introduction to the Writings and Their Social Context*. Philadelphia: Temple University Press, 1982. 214–79.

Palumbo-Liu, David. "Transacting Culture: Bodies at the Seam of the Social." *Asian/ American: Historical Crossings of a Racial Frontier*. Stanford, CA: Stanford University Press, 1999. 116–46.

Wong, Sau-ling Cynthia. "Big Eaters, Treat Lovers, Food Prostitutes, Food Pornographers, and Doughnut Makers." *Reading Asian American Literature: From Necessity to Extravagance*. Princeton, NJ: Princeton University Press, 1993. 18–76.

———. "Encounters with the Racial Shadow." *Reading Asian American Literature*, 77–117.

MYUNG MI KIM
(1957–   )

James Kyung-Jin Lee

BIOGRAPHY

Myung Mi Kim was born on 6 December 1957 in Seoul, South Korea. At the age of nine, her family immigrated to the United States. Because her father, a surgeon retooling himself to become a psychiatrist, held a foreign visa and required sponsorship from hospitals, Kim spent her early teenage years moving from town to town across the country, first to Oklahoma, then to South Dakota, finally settling in Ohio during her junior and senior high school years. Living in predominantly white communities in the Midwest compelled Kim to learn and excel at English quickly. Although she knew little when she first arrived, Kim completed high school a year early. Kim's initial foray into writing coincided with her father's sudden death. She wrote her first poem (in English) when she was fourteen, and her English teacher was so impressed by it that the poem soon found its way into a small literary magazine. Still, Kim did not consider herself a writer by profession until well after high school: she attended Oberlin College and planned to double-major in music and chemistry, fully intending to become a doctor. Instead, she received a graduate degree in creative writing from the Johns Hopkins University at the age of twenty-one, entered the New York University clinical social work program, taught as a high school teacher in New York's Stuyvesant High School, and also worked as an ESL instructor. Kim moved back to the Midwest to enter the Iowa Writers Workshop and in 1986 received an M.F.A. in creative writing. It was during this time in Iowa that Kim began a correspondence with poet Kathleen Fraser, from which resulted some important publications in the avant-garde journal *How(ever)*; she also coedited the journal in the early 1990s.

Almost two decades since she wrote her first poem and five years after graduating from Iowa would pass before Kelsey St. Press approached Kim to publish what became her first book of poetry, *Under Flag* (1991). Met with critical acclaim in the literary and academic communities, *Under Flag* garnered the Multicultural Publishers Exchange Award of Merit in 1992. In 1996, Kim published *The Bounty* through Minneapolis-based Chax Press; *The Bounty* was soon followed by Sun & Moon Press's publication of *Dura* in 1998. Throughout the 1990s, Kim's poetry enjoyed what she calls the "anthologizing phenomenon" endemic to innovative writers, both in Asian American and avant-garde collections. She has received a steady string of accolades, including two Fund for Poetry Awards, two Gertrude Stein Awards for Innovative North American Poetry from Sun & Moon Press, and a prestigious writing residency at the Djerassi Resident Artists Program. Kim also has served as the Edelstein-Keller Writer in Residence at the University of Minnesota and an artist in residence at her alma mater, Oberlin College and is currently a Distinguished Writer in Residence at St. Mary's College in California. Kim is also on the faculty of the Creative Writing Program at San Francisco State University, where she has taught since 1991. In 2002, the University of California Press published her fourth book of poetry, entitled *Commons*. Kim plans in the near future to publish a collection of talks and readings that she has given over the past ten years, as it is in these live negotiations with her audience that new artistic spaces are opened to explore the connections between creative and critical work.

MAJOR WORKS AND THEMES

Kim's work has often been compared to the creative inquiries launched by the Language poets, a loose network of writers emerging from the 1960s and 1970s that sought to explore how the structures of language encode relations of power. Yet such a direct correlation is misleading. While Kim's poetry participates in an ongoing investigation of the interdependence of language and power, ideology and representation, she does not look to using material that might appear naïve and colloquial with the same kind of strident skepticism as the early Language poets. At least part of Kim's ongoing project revolves around the provisional creation of a "third language" informed by the collision, at its most basic level, of Korean and English and how both languages are subject to a host of political forces that helped shape their cultural domain. But Kim's work does not simply interrogate and denaturalize codified language; rather, her poems are a constant process of folding in more of the world. Kim's poetry, therefore, acts as both world map and microscope, continually probing global relations through time and space by focusing, conversely, on the fundamental units of meaning in language.

Kim frequently casts herself as a "perpetual foreigner," not simply because of her identity as an immigrant woman poet of Korean descent, but because her poetry refuses easy acknowledgment of its purpose. It is this very demand to make any presentation of language recognizable that for Kim requires a vigilant refusal to accede to conventional forms, to plumb ever more deeply the conditions that make any utterance—understood or not—possible. The final words to *The Bounty* serve as an example of this exploration. For Kim, any entry into a sustained meditation on language is, on its most visceral level, an admission that poetry can be seen as nothing more than the inchoate firing and misfiring of one's neurons. Such a physiological depiction of the poetic process at once undermines the sentimentality ascribed to poetry but also gives liberating permission to explore the synapse of language without being fettered by given rules and conventions. Often, Kim makes central what is regarded as marginal in traditional poetry. Her meditation on the "anacrusis," a poetic term that describes the preliminary syllable considered as not part of a given metrical pattern of a poem, becomes a thematic arena from which to explore what she considers a poetics attentive to the prosody of life itself.

What appears at first an unregulated arrangement of phrases and words in Kim's poetry is her attempt to find deeper patterns of affiliation, and by doing so to unveil the geopolitical, economic, and ideological forces at work in "easy" language. In both *The Bounty* and *Dura*, Kim interrogates, thematizes, and formalizes the processes of translation and instruction. If the book is primarily a tool to "instruct," to perhaps translate Korean and English, Kim suggests that the reader consider the ideological imperatives embedded in the politics of translation and consider such instructive efforts as laconic rather than transparent moments. *The Bounty* begins by suggesting that it is a "study book," presumably of the Korean alphabet (*hangul*), but the opening section's consideration of the fourteen consonants in *hangul* organizes a series of words and phrases that bear little resemblance to conventional lines of poetry or even of traditional syntax in either Korean or English. In *Dura* (conceived as one long poem in seven parts), Kim "mistranslates" four Korean words into English and later demands, "Translate: 38th parallel." In each of these examples, Kim exemplifies that easy acquisition of knowledge has more to do with our acquiescence to language structures in which the historical forces of political oppression and geopolitical division are already embedded, that the project of translation and instruction is never an innocent one. Kim's own "mistranslations" and unruly attempts at "instruction" compel the reader to create different patterns of understanding and perhaps different ways of arranging the world. To this extent, the misrecognition and restructuring of language serve as gestures to point to the freedom possible in the transformation of political arrangements, if only we might refuse to mitigate the rules that produce historical atrocity.

From the "cracking open" of received structures and ideas into a new poetics that gives voice to the provisionally liberating possibilities of the word unfettered, Kim's literary vista forces a reconsideration of historical moments and refigures them through the perception and experiences of those who have suffered from the disasters of war, violence, and imperialism. In *Under Flag*, Kim employs the voice of authority, the "master's voice" responsible for determining and defining the boundaries of identity that compel people to remain subject to regimes of regulation and often repression: these are people "under flag." Whether it is the interlocutor at a citizenship hearing, a litany of military ordnance and equipment, or the figures of soldiers in Korea raping young women, Kim dons these voices to demonstrate that each of them is intimately connected, as each exemplifies the language of authority. Interestingly, these are the voices that seem the most familiar to the reader, suggesting in their accessibility that we as readers are implicated in such violence because we know this language so well. Yet if the violence that inheres in such knowable language is where we begin by way of implication and complicity, Kim's poems invite her readers to imagine the recombination of language and the world through the experience uttered at the margins—unregulated, unruly, contingent, poetry that establishes unfamiliar patterns of new human agency, demanding attention.

CRITICAL RECEPTION

Kim's work has received the most sustained critical attention from scholars of Asian American literature and culture, yet even this academic community has only begun to give Kim's poetry the sustained treatment it deserves. Literary and cultural critic Elaine Kim asserts that Kim's work exemplifies the hybrid and multiple identities that Korean American women must occupy in their immigrant experience from gender oppression in Korea to the added layer of racism in the United States. Hyun Yi Kang provides the most engaged and rigorous interrogation, focusing particularly on how Kim's poems critique the formation of Korean American identity and the ways in which a "body politic" is constructed and configured through the abstraction of the actual bodies of women. Both assessments point out that Kim's poems bear resonance and resemblance to Theresa Hak Kyung Cha's seminal work *Dictée* (1982), a multimedia narrative work whose interrogation of nationalist historiography, immigrant and gendered identity, and narrative indeterminacy seems to place Kim's work as a direct Asian American literary descendant of *Dictée*. Indeed, Kim herself acknowledges her delight when she discovered Cha's work in a New York bookstore in 1982 and the indebtedness she feels toward *Dictée* in enabling a creative space for the kind of poems she writes.

Reviews of Kim's three books of poetry have also attempted to engage with her treatment of cultural identity, to much less success. Edgar Knowlton erroneously assumes that Kim's poems in *Dura* are examples of a writer struggling with the English language, his condescending praise barely hiding a disdain for Kim's larger poetic project: "One can only be favorably impressed by the eagerness with which this poet must have learned to control the mighty riches contained in English dictionaries" (389). Other reviewers are more sensitive, linking Kim's work with that of other avant-garde writers such as Kathleen

Fraser, George Oppen, and Susan Howe. But again, Asian American reviewers remain the most attentive to the larger political and creative project at work in Kim's poetry. Vikas Menon in *Ten Magazine* (the journal published by the New York–based Asian American Writers' Workshop) describes *Dura* as "consistently 'outside' as in the music of Ornette Coleman or John Coltrane, shimmering in startling resonance as she strips words from their contexts, flummoxing denotation and imbuing them with a spectral tenor" (18).

By far the most exciting critical work done on Kim has yet to be published, in student papers and longer projects and in poetry classrooms. One example is a senior thesis written by Jane Chi Yun Park, entitled "Remembering Memory: An Analysis of Myung Mi Kim's *Under Flag*." Then a senior at Brown University, Park interviewed Kim for her project and weaved this conversation with extensive close readings of several poems in *Under Flag*. Attuned to both Kim's concern with Korean, Korean American, immigrant, and women's identities and the poet's negotiations with Language poetry and critical theory, Park argues that Kim's work demands that the reader "fill in the gaps" and blank space left intentionally in the work; these poetic silences invite the reader to write his or her own experience into the poem. Poet/critics such as Harryette Mullen have been regularly teaching Kim's work in their poetry classes as she and other writers of color in the academy struggle to construct course syllabi of U.S. writers of color who do not fit well into received forms and themes of "minority" literature. For Mullen, Kim's work remains vitally important in the ongoing and often-specious "canon" debates, for it is Kim's refusal to play into the terms of what Henry Louis Gates, Jr., has called the "anthropological fallacy" to which writers of color are often relegated that make Kim's poems so useful in showing others how it is possible to write with thematic and formal innovation and political responsibility.

BIBLIOGRAPHY

Works by Myung Mi Kim

Poetry

Under Flag. Berkeley, CA: Kelsey St. Press, 1991.
The Bounty. Minneapolis, MN: Chax Press, 1996.
Dura. Los Angeles: Sun & Moon Press, 1998.
Spelt. With Susan Gevirtz. San Francisco: A+bend Press, 1999.
Commons. Berkeley and Los Angeles: University of California Press, 2002.

Works in Anthologies

"Into Such Assembly" and "Rose of Sharon." *The Forbidden Stitch: An Asian American Women's Anthology*. Corvallis, OR: Calyx Books, 1989. 18–20.
From *DURA*. *Writing Away Here: A Korean/American Anthology*. Oakland: Korean American Arts Festival, 1994. 138–40.

"Anna O Addendum." *Premonitions: The Kaya Anthology of New Asian North American Poetry*. Ed. Walter K. Lew. New York: Kaya Productions, 1995. 360–70.

"Primer." *The Gertrude Stein Awards in Innovative American Poetry, 1993–1994*. Los Angeles: Sun & Moon Press, 1995. 265–75.

From *The Bounty*. *The Gertrude Stein Awards in Innovative American Poetry 1994–1995*. Los Angeles: Sun & Moon Press, 1996.

From *The Bounty*. *Primary Trouble: An Anthology of Contemporary American Poetry*. Ed. Leonard Schwartz, Joseph Donahue, and Edward Foster. Jersey City, NJ: Talisman House, 1996. 187–91.

"Into Such Assembly" and "Rose of Sharon." *Asian American Literature: A Brief Introduction and Anthology*. Ed. Shawn Wong. New York: HarperCollins, 1996.

From "Thirty and Five Books" in *Dura*. *Making More Waves: New Writing by Asian American Women*. Ed. Elaine H. Kim, Lilia V. Villaneuva, and Asian Women United of California. Boston: Beacon Press, 1997. 202–3.

From *The Bounty*. *Moving Borders: Three Decades of Innovative Writing by Women*. Ed. Mary Margaret Sloan. Jersey City, NJ: Talisman House, 1998.

"Into Such Assembly." *Asian-American Literature: An Anthology*. Ed. Shirley Geok-lin Lim. Lincolnwood, IL: NTC Publishing Group, 2000. 517–20.

Works in Literary Journals

"Arrival Which Is Not an Arrival." *Pavement* 7 (1986): 56–59.

"Pleasure as Steadfast" and "The Days She Came To." *Antioch Review* 44 (1986): 112–15.

"Father Hat." *Ironwood* 29 (1987): 145.

"And Sing We" and "These Fishing Two." *Ironwood* 30 (1987): 178–80.

"Body as One as History." *f.(lip)*. Vancouver, Canada (Fall 1989).

"From the Sea on to the Land." *How(ever)* 3.2 (1990).

"Food, Shelter, Clothing." *Zyzzyva* 7 (1991): 111–15.

"From a Far: Reading Theresa Hak Kyung Cha's DICTEE." *How(ever)* 4.4 (1991): 11.

"Under Flag" and "Demarcation." *Sulfur* 28–29 (1991): 132–37.

"The Site of the Capital." *International Examiner* March 1992: 17.

From *The Bounty*. *Black Bread* (Spring 1992): 44–47.

From *The Bounty*. *lyric &* (Spring 1992).

From *The Bounty*. *Notus* (Fall 1992): 90–93.

From *The Bounty*. *Avec* 6 (1993): 133–35.

"Primer." *Conjunctions* 21 (1993): 52–60.

"Field of Inquiry." *Writing from the New Coast: Technique*. o bleck Editions (Fall 1993): 175–77.

From "Anna O Addendum." *Writing from the New Coast: Presentation*. o blek Editions (Fall 1993): 154–56.

From *DURA*. *Avec* 7 (January 1994): 89–93.

From *The Bounty*. *Hambone* 11 (Spring 1994): 64–68.

From *DURA*. *Positions: East Asia Cultures Critique* (Winter 1994): 538–41.

From *DURA*. *Conjunctions* 24 (1995): 153–58.

From *DURA*. *Sulfur* 36 (Spring 1995): 72–80.

From *DURA*. *Exact Change Yearbook 1995* September 1995: 389–91.

"Exordium." *Positions: East Asia Cultures Critique* (Winter 1996): 417–19.

"Generosity as Method: An Interview with Myung Mi Kim." *Tripwire: A Journal of Poetics* (Spring 1998): 75–85.

From *Commons. Chain* 5 (Summer 1998): 109–10.

From *Commons. Five Fingers Review* 18 (1999): 91–92.

From *Commons. Proliferation* 5 (1999).

From *Commons. Conjunctions* (Spring 1999): 299–306.

"Spelt." *Chain* 6 (Summer 1999): 88–96.

"Anacrusis," text of a talk given at "Page Mothers Conference," University of California, San Diego. *how2*. Available: http://www.departments.bucknell.edu/stadler_center/how2. January, 2001.

Studies of Myung Mi Kim

Kang, Hyun Yi. "Compositional Subjects: Enfiguring Asian/American Women." Diss. University of California, Santa Cruz, 1995.

———. "Re-membering Home." *Dangerous Women: Gender and Korean Nationalism*. Ed. Elaine H. Kim and Chungmoo Choi. New York: Routledge, 1998. 249–90.

Kim, Elaine H. "Korean American Literature." *An Interethnic Companion to Asian American Literature*. Ed. King-Kok Cheung. New York: Cambridge University Press, 1997. 156–91.

Knowlton, Edgar C., Jr. Rev. of *Dura. World Literature Today* 73.2 (1999): 389.

Lee, James Kyung-Jin. Interview with Myung Mi Kim. *Words Matter: Conversations with Asian American Writers*. Ed. King-Kok Cheung. Honolulu: University of Hawai'i Press, 2000. 92–104.

———. " 'What was given, given over?': Competing Subjectivities in Myung Mi Kim's 'Into Such Assembly.' " Thesis. University of California, Los Angeles, 1995.

Menon, Vikas. Rev. of *Dura. Ten Magazine* 5.1 (Spring 1999): 18.

Park, Jane. "Remembering Memory: An Analysis of Myung Mi Kim's *Under Flag*." Diss. Brown University, 1995.

Rev. of *DURA. Publishers Weekly* 245.35 (31 August 1998): 69.

JULIET SANAE KONO
(1943–   )

Nikolas Huot

BIOGRAPHY

Juliet Sanae Kono was born in 1943 in Hilo, Hawaii. She grew up in this small town during the last years of the territory with her parents and grandparents. After moving to Honolulu and raising her children, Kono returned to school and applied herself to writing poetry. While majoring in English at the University of Hawaii at Manoa, Kono published her first book of poems, *Hilo Rains* (1988). After the completion of her baccalaureate, Kono earned her M.A. and started teaching at Leeward Community College. Since attending the University of Hawaii, Kono has worked with the Bamboo Ridge study group, which encourages local Hawaiian writers to pursue their crafts, and Bamboo Ridge Press, which gives Hawaiian writers an outlet for publication. With the help of Bamboo Ridge, Kono published her second volume of poetry, *Tsunami Years*, in 1995. A year later, Kono's writings were brought to life by Jackie Pualani Johnson, a University of Hawaii at Hilo drama professor, as an outreach program for the Pacific Tsunami Museum.

In 1998, Kono was awarded one of five national fellowships by the Japan–United States Friendship Commission, an independent federal agency dedicated to promoting mutual understanding and cooperation between these two countries. Through this highly competitive fellowship, Kono traveled and studied in Japan for six months. Other than teaching, Kono has conducted workshops at such colleges as Wellesley and the Massachusetts Institute of Technology and has lectured on the use of Hawaiian Creole English in literature. Juliet Kono lives, writes, and teaches in Honolulu.

MAJOR WORKS AND THEMES

Juliet Kono examines in her poetry the events in her life that have touched and affected her. Through her poems, Kono explores her childhood memories, the many tragedies that befell Japanese immigrants in Hawaii (tsunamis, World War II, death, illnesses), the lives of those she loves, and her personal pains and struggles. Mostly autobiographical, Kono's volumes of poetry are carefully structured into separate chronological clusters that introduce the reader to significant periods in her life. From *Hilo Rains* to *Tsunami Years*, Kono brings the reader from the dawning of World War II, when Japanese immigrants like her grandparents tried to make a life for themselves, to the present day, when Kono tries to accept the death of her son.

Hilo Rains starts Kono's retrospection by describing her life as a child growing up with her grandparents on a sugarcane plantation. Intertwining poems from a child's viewpoint with poems from a historical perspective, Kono discusses the difficult and harsh lives of Japanese plantation workers who, hoping for better lives, must content themselves with the little they have. Curfews, blackouts, threats of internment camps, tsunamis, poverty, cancer from sulfur used on plantations, and the constant struggle to keep one's Japanese culture and identity are central parts of the Japanese experience in Hawaii and of Kono's poetry. In her poems, Kono brings this general experience of Japanese Americans to life by showing how her family has been living on the island since her grandparents' arrival. As each part of the volume discusses a different generation of Japanese Americans, Kono explores their different struggles and emphasizes past events that are meaningful to her. In *Hilo Rains*, such significant personal experiences include the loss of her grandfather to cancer ("Sulfur," "The Wake," "Ojichan"), the poverty that follows her family ("Smoke," "Coupons"), the relationship she has with her parents ("Sonless," "Reconciliation"), and the attempt to keep Japanese traditions alive for another generation ("Sashimi," "Yonsei").

As times change in different parts of the volume, so do the voices used by Kono to express significant memories. Whereas a child's voice talks about her grandparents at the beginning of the collection, the second part of *Hilo Rains* finds a teenager and a young adult discussing the lives of her parents. As the book progresses, the speaker continues to grow older as the reader can definitely hear Kono's voice as a wife and mother in the third and final part of *Hilo Rains*. This constant growing of the speaker does not end with Kono's first volume of poetry, however. *Tsunami Years* introduces the reader to a woman in her fifties who has been living with her mother-in-law for some time, who reflects on the devastation caused by tsunamis, and who is trying to come to terms with the death of her older son. Perhaps because the poet has grown herself between the publication of her two books, the voice emerging from *Tsunami Years* is more confident and more candid.

Separated into three clusters as well, the second volume of poetry also explores certain events that have deeply impacted Kono's life; in this collection, however, the events discussed deal mostly with death. Whether it is the deteriorating process of Alzheimer's disease, the sudden and unexpected tsunami, or the downward spiraling of mental illness, *Tsunami Years* reflects on death and its many faces. The first part, "The Elizabeth Poems," discusses Kono's life as the main caregiver for her mother-in-law, who is suffering from Alzheimer's disease. Although some poems show the devastating effects of the illness on the person living with Alzheimer's disease, most poems are concerned with how it affects those who must care for the ill. In the majority of the poems, Kono depicts her thankless job and the insults of the mother-in-law who takes her for hired help. Far from being accepting of the situation, Kono quite openly displays the strains the illness caused in her marriage and her frustrations toward her mother-in-law. Although she learns about herself in the process, Kono still finds the situation very difficult and unrewarding.

"Tsunami Years," the second section of the book, illustrates the material and psychological devastation created by the 1946 and 1960 tsunamis that hit Hawaii. In a multitude of voices, Kono recounts the last breath of those who perished in the water and the ordeal of the survivors, who must somehow rebuild their lives. Powerlessness and dejection are in every poem as Kono tells of those who lost their houses, their livelihoods, their loved ones, and even their religion. Her poetry brings to life the stories of those who experienced the waves firsthand, from the "School Boy from Up Mauka" who picks up the colorful fish at Laupahoehoe Point and then turns to see the wave to the mother in "Lost Birds" who cries quietly and puts her daughter to sleep among water-salvaged books and toys. The horror of the situation is especially palpable in "Joji and the Iceman," which tells of a boy who, after storing the dead bodies on ice blocks overnight to keep them from decaying, must separate the bodies with a pickaxe.

Death continues to be the major theme in "Painter," the third section of *Tsunami Years*. In "Painter," however, Kono talks about the death of those she loved and of the traditional Japanese way of life. Through her poems, Kono remembers her grandfather's kindness, her father's stubbornness, and an old friend's affection. Looking back, Kono also discusses how the traditional Japanese ways that her mother is so attached to are slowly disappearing. Most eloquent in this section, however, are the poems dedicated to the memories of her son. As her son is sinking deeper into mental illness, Kono reveals in her poems a mother's pains as she must watch helplessly his suicide attempts and his painful struggles with sanity.

CRITICAL RECEPTION

Following the tradition of prominent Hawaiian writers such as Milton Murayama, Edward Sakamoto, Lois-Ann Yamanaka, and Darrell H.Y. Lum, Juliet Kono freely uses Hawaiian Creole English in her poetry. Her frequent use of the dialect, as well as some Japanese words, provides credibility for her dialogues and roots her poetry deeply into the local identity of Hawaii. Unfortunately, as is too often the case for Hawaiian writers, Juliet Kono has received very little attention from mainland critics. Indeed, Kono's poetry has gone unnoticed by critics and reviewers despite being presented with the 1991 Elliot Cades Award for Literature, the James Clavell Award in 1991, and the Ka Palapala Po'okela Award for Excellence in Writing Literature in 1996. This disregard may be readily explained, however, by her lack of exposure, since Kono has mostly published her poems in small journals or in local publications such as the *Hawai'i Herald, Makali'i, Hapa,* and *Hawaii Review.*

Even though most critics have not read Juliet Kono's work, those who have are quite adamant about her talent. Colleague and friend Cathy Song believes that the themes in Kono's poems are "explored with language that shimmers with multiple luminescent layers of meaning, each poem a pearl of truth wrested out of the heart of living" (*Tsunami Years* back cover). Stan Yogi agrees with Song's assessment as he commends Kono's "spare and dignified style" (144). Kono's most enthusiastic critic, however, is Lynn Emanuel. The prizewinning poet greatly praises Kono's "wonderful work" and calls it "courageous, timely, and written with images that stop the breath." She continues to acclaim Kono's poetry by calling it "extremely smart and extremely sensuous" (*Tsunami Years* back cover). One can only hope that Juliet Kono's talent will soon be acclaimed and recognized by more people and that her poetry will make its way to the mainland.

BIBLIOGRAPHY

Works by Juliet Sanae Kono

Poetry

Hilo Rains. Honolulu: Bamboo Ridge Press, 1988.
Tsunami Years. Honolulu: Bamboo Ridge Press, 1995.

Drama and Anthology Edited

Sister Stew: Fiction and Poetry by Women. Ed. with Cathy Song. Honolulu: Bamboo Ridge Press, 1991.
Tsunami Years. Dir. Jackie Pualani Johnson. Hilo Tsunami Museum and University of Hawaii at Hilo Theater, 1996.

Studies of Juliet Sanae Kono

Oi, Cynthia. "Chick Chat: A Four-Way Conversation with Hawaii's Foremost Writing Women." *Honolulu Star-Bulletin* 5 Feb. 2001. Available: http://starbulletin.com/ 2001/02/05/features/story1.html.
Roddy, Kevin M. Rev. of *Sister Stew. Library Journal* 117.12 (July 1992): 85.

Usui, Masami. "A Conflict with Tsunami in Juliet S. Kono's Poetry." *Studies in American Literature* 35 (February 1999): 157–74.

Yogi, Stan. "Japanese American Literature." *An Interethnic Companion to Asian American Literature.* Ed. King-Kok Cheung. New York: Cambridge University Press, 1997. 125–55.

LYDIA KWA
(1959–)

Gaik Cheng Khoo

BIOGRAPHY

Singaporean-born Lydia Kwa came to Canada in 1980 to attend university. She trained as a psychologist at the University of Toronto and Queen's University in Ontario. Her informal training in creative writing came from regularly attending a writers' group workshop while she was at Queen's. Coincidentally, Kwa also came out as a lesbian when she began to take writing seriously, and an early poem, "Orchid Riddles," hints at this. Winning a few prizes in poetry contests for her submissions to student publications then gave her more confidence to get published in journals like *Contemporary Verse 2*. Kwa's other foundational moment in her life came earlier when her secondary school English teacher in Singapore asked to borrow her composition book to show to future students.

After graduating, Kwa moved to Calgary to work as a clinical psychologist before ending up in Vancouver in 1993, where she currently resides and works. Both Kwa's books feature distinct elements of Vancouver, citing detailed locales of the downtown area and grittier East Vancouver. She is currently working on a second novel set in seventh-century A.D. China during the reign of Empress Wu, who was the first and only woman to usurp the throne from the "rightful" heirs, her sons. Kwa is interested in exploring the interconnectedness of cruelty and power, of how talented and powerful women who subscribe to patriarchy justify their cruelty. This interest stems from her involvement with Direct Action against Refugee Exploitation, an ad hoc group of women formed to support the Fujianese boat migrants who landed on the shores of British Columbia in the summer of 1999 and were consequently incarcerated. Prison visits with the Fujianese women gave Kwa an up-close look at the cruelty of institutions toward those dependent upon them.

MAJOR WORKS AND THEMES

The relationship between parents and children is a theme that pervades Kwa's own research as a psychologist as well as both her poetry collection *The Colours of Heroines* and her novel *This Place Called Absence*. In fact, Kwa's doctoral thesis dealt with perceptions of parents, teachers, and adolescents of competence and depressive behaviors. Consciousness about the hierarchy or abuse of power within relationships—familial and between lovers or between psychologist and client—is a consistent thread. Poems like "Travelling Time," "Scooter," "Who Is She Beyond?" and "Hard Hats and Safety Boots Must Be Worn" convey the clinging memory and power of impossible but faraway parents just as the ghost of the father who committed suicide haunts his family in her novel. Using the apt metaphor of vampirism in "A Taste for Blood," she addresses the cyclical nature of the abuse of power in continuous victimization: "I write another life past this fear, to break the tyranny of other" (*Colours* 70).

Kwa evokes the vivid images and smells of her childhood in Singapore of street hawkers, night markets, and pungent fruit. Yet her poetry and novel do not dwell nostalgically in the past but instead bridge time and space, contemporary Vancouver and the Singapore of the past. "Bugis Street," for example, is a poem about the famous street in Singapore that transvestites and prostitutes used to frequent and a similar street in Vancouver.

While the processing of pain via memory is a major theme, playfulness abounds as well in the eccentric feminist musings of women and lingerie. Here Kwa displays her ability for sensual and subtle humorous imagery. The integration of emotional psychic reality and social reality is something that preoccupies the poet. In an interview with writer Larissa Lai about *This Place Called Absence*, Kwa expresses her hopes that her novel would reach those "who are interested in the life of the psyche and how that reality converses with outer realities. I hope it will inspire people not only in the sense of thinking, but also to enact social change." When I interviewed Kwa, she explained that language for her is not used to define or identify reality as much as to show it up. Indeed, her latest group of poems in process, "Suite of Hands," blurs the lines between internal and external reality. It is surrealist dreamscape, hallucinatory, expanding our ability to imagine less inhibited associations. In this set of poems, there is a visceral interest in the language of the body as a site of disassociations and new associations.

CRITICAL RECEPTION

Aside from reviews, not much has been written about Kwa's poetic work in Canada or the United States despite the fact that *The Colours of Heroines* appeared in 1994 and some of the poems in that book had been published in Canadian journals and small magazines such as *West Coast Line, Secrets from the Orange Couch, Descant, absinthe, Grain, New Quarterly*, and *Contemporary Verse 2* throughout the 1990s. Poems like "Hard Hats and Safety Boots Must Be Worn on This Project," "Still Life with Frangipani," and "Orchid Riddles" were included in the first Chinese Canadian anthology, *Many-mouthed Birds: Contemporary Writing by Chinese Canadians*, edited by Bennett Lee and Jim Wong-Chu in 1991.

In his final poetry column before he passed away, George Woodcock praises Kwa as a "memory writer of almost Proustian intensity, who has lived variously and remembered astonishingly" (41). Other well-known Canadian poets such as Daphne Marlatt, Fred Wah, and Dionne Brand have also recognized her contribution to a broadening canon of Canadian writing. On the back cover of *Colours*, Marlatt writes, "Equally at home in a finely cadenced erotic lyric or candid and multi-layered prose, [Kwa's] writing resonates well beyond the edge of the page." Perhaps the lack of attention to her work, as Karlyn Koh suggests, is due to the fact that her poetry does not yield easy answers to the complexities of identity. Discussing the work of several Asian Canadian women writers, Koh speculates that "work that cannot be immediately understood as 'telling the story and making it plain' somehow fall into the wayside of literary multiculturalism" (22). Referring to Kwa's book of poetry and prose, she asks, "Is it possible that [*Colours*] offers no cure for (mis)understanding the 'native informant,' a possibility violently inscribed in and by the Western episteme?" To elaborate, Koh states that Kwa's poetry "traces the positioning of 'Asian', and in particular 'Chinese' in the diaspora, and disavows the persistent reliance on 'authenticity' by white readers of 'ethnic' texts" (22). Perhaps as the study and understanding of Asian Canadian or Southeast Asian North American writing broaden in scope to include all the complexities of subjectivity, Kwa's work will then be given its due recognition.

BIBLIOGRAPHY

Works by Lydia Kwa

Poetry

"Cats in the House." *Contemporary Verse 2* 12.1 (Spring 1989): 35–36.
"Hanging Out." *Contemporary Verse 2* 12.1 (Spring 1989): 37–38.
"First Lessons." *More Garden Varieties Two*. Stratford, Ontario: Mercury Press, 1990.
"Locating the Legend." *Matrix* 30 (Winter 1990): 40.
"Signs." *Contemporary Verse 2* 12.4 (Winter 1990): 31.
"Two Dreams." *Antigonish Review* 80 (Winter 1990): 12.
"I Want to Name the Other She." *Secrets from the Orange Couch* 4.1 (April 1991): 43.
The Colours of Heroines. Toronto: Women's Press, 1994.
"Excerpts from 'Suite of Hands.' " *Swallowing Clouds: An Anthology of Chinese-*

Canadian Poetry. Ed. Andy Quan and Jim Wong-Chu. Vancouver: Arsenal Pulp Press, 1999.

"Lost." *Alter Vox* 1 (Spring 1999): 26.

"To Sit with You." *Alter Vox* 1 (Spring 1999): 26.

"Powell Street Wars." *Rice Paper* 5.3 (Summer 1999): 33.

"Last Summer." *West Coast Line* 33.2 (Fall 1999): 50.

"Mango Re-visited." *West Coast Line* 33.2 (Fall 1999): 52.

"Nocturne." *West Coast Line* 33.2 (Fall 1999): 51.

"What Is a Love Poem?" *West Coast Line* 33.2 (Fall 1999): 49.

Novel

This Place Called Absence. Winnipeg, Manitoba: Turnstone Press, 1999.

Short Story

"Eczema." *absinthe* 8.1/2 (Fall 1995): 8–12.

Studies of Lydia Kwa

Studies of The Colours of Heroines

"The Colours of Heroines." *Books in Canada* 24 (May 1995): 46.

"Fall Announcements List of English-Language Books Published between July and December 1994." *Quill & Quire* 60.9 (September 1994): 26–57.

Khoo, Gaik Cheng. "*The Colours of Heroines* by Lydia Kwa." *Calyx* 17.3 (1998): 117–18.

Koh, Karlyn. "Speculations and (Dis)identification: Notes on Asian Canadian Women Writers." *New Scholars–New Visions in Canadian Studies* 1.1 (Summer 1996): 1–30.

Kong, Sook. "Literary Treats: Asian Canadian Women Writers-Performers at the Go-for-Broke Revue." *Kinesis* November 1995: 23–24.

Lu, T. "*The Colours of Heroines.*" *Fireweed* 48 (Summer 1995): 68–69.

Symons, Ellen. "Truths, under the Surface of Things." *Capital Xtra!* 24 March 1995: 18.

Woodcock, George. "Clearly a Wobbly." *BC BookWorld* Summer 1995: 41.

Studies of This Place Called Absence

Bartley, Jim. "First Fiction: Two Writers to Watch." *Globe and Mail* 10 June 2000: D15.

D'anna, Lynette. "Debut Novel's Impeccable Prose Is Breathtaking." *Winnipeg Free Press* 25 June 2000, D4.

D'Souza, Irene. "Running Away from This Place Called Absence." *Prairie Books Now* 23 (Summer 2000): 9.

Fong Bates, Judy. "*This Place Called Absence.*" *Quill & Quire* 66.6 (July 2000): 49–50.

Godolphin, Helen. "*This Place Called Absence.*" *Geist* 37 (Summer 2000).

Khoo, Gaik Cheng. Interview with Lydia Kwa. The Continental Cafe, Vancouver. 4 January, 2001.

Lai, Larissa. Rev. of *This Place Called Absence. Rice Paper* 6.2 (2000): n.p.

"*This Place Called Absence.*" *Open Letter* 10.7 (2000): 99–104.
"*This Place Called Absence.*" *Vancouver Magazine* 33.5 (June 2000): 22.
Wall, Karolle L. "*This Place Called Absence.*" *Herizons* 14.4 (Spring 2001): 30.
Younka, Reina. "*This Place Called Absence.*" *Prairie Fire* 22.2 (2001): 118–19.

ALAN CHONG LAU
(1948–   )

Brian Komei Dempster

BIOGRAPHY

Alan Chong Lau was born on 11 July 1948 in Oroville, California. He received a B.A. in art from the University of California at Santa Cruz in 1976. He is coauthor of *The Buddha Bandits down Highway 99* (with Garrett Hongo and Lawson Inada, 1978) and the author of *Songs for Jadina*, which received the 1981 American Book Award. His most recent collection of poetry, *Blues and Greens: A Produce Worker's Journal*, appeared in 2000.

MAJOR WORKS AND THEMES

The Buddha Bandits down Highway 99 contains the themes found in much of Lau's work: family history, cultural heritage, and place. In a series of prose poems, he vividly portrays the experience of growing up Chinese American in the small town of Paradise, California. Isolation from other Chinese Americans, limited exposure to his ancestors' traditions, and the challenges his family faces when they open up the only Chinese restaurant in Paradise all inform Lau's poetic vision. *Songs for Jadina* centers on Lau's epic quest to excavate his familial and cultural history. Stretching across time and not rooted in any one setting, these interconnected poems leave out most punctuation, relying upon short lines packed with images. The opening section, in which Lau explores his Hakka ancestral origins in China, is a prelude to his characterization of the various generations of his family. Although Lau paints many characters, the poet's father is the central figure around whom his search for identity revolves.

Separated by geography and the passing years, Lau and his father have inevitably grown apart, yet their love and respect for one another remain, and they both find ways to express these feelings: the father sends birthday letters to his son; the son writes poems about his father's artistry as a chef.

Lau's poems about his family's struggle to survive in America resonate with the book's historical concerns, namely, the injustices that Chinese immigrants like his grandfather suffered while they attempted to enter the United States through Angel Island Immigration Station from 1910 to 1940. In "the promise," Lau blends his own details with Immigration Authority questions, the speech of former detainees, and the text of poems carved into the Angel Island walls to create a polyphonic structure that is a metaphor for the chaotic nature of the immigration experience.

While Lau's earlier work is grounded in family and history, *Blues and Greens* draws upon his everyday observations as a produce worker in an Asian grocery store. The narrator, who is often implied, writes homages to vegetables and fruits and descriptions of customers who populate the produce section. Woven into these subtle and evocative portraits, which draw upon elements of classical Chinese and Japanese poetry, are aphorisms from what Lau calls the "Ten Commandments of Good Business" as well as intercom announcements and dialogues between customers.

CRITICAL RECEPTION

Although Lau's poetry is well known in Asian American literary circles, the body of criticism about his work is modest. The underappreciation of Lau's work is only underscored by the fact that his poetry has been well received by those who are respected in the field. Sam Hamill praises Lau's poems for their disarming honesty, dignity, and subtle politics (32). Genny Lim calls *Songs for Jadina* "a single moving tribute to his Chinese ancestry" and Lau "a skilled poet with a positive political awareness of his ethnic identity and history" (9). Like Hamill and Lim, Seattle poet Judith Roche compliments Lau for his ability to write effectively about his ancestry, culture, and history (23).

While the majority of reviews of Lau's work are favorable, certain critics have taken issue with his use of language. According to Barry Wallenstein, Lau "presents a sentence structure so collapsed that it often sounds unlike any real speaking person" (17). Lonny Kaneko asserts, however, that Lau "has a marvelous ear for Chinese America. . . . His language and his journey makes Alan's poetry distinctive, personal and Asian American" (94). Hamill echoes Kaneko when he states that Lau has "an educated ear for the sounds and rhythms of utterance" (32).

Perhaps the relative dearth of criticism about Lau is due to the small press runs of his earlier books, which are both now out of print. More likely is that Lau, who is a dedicated and successful visual artist, the literary editor of an Asian American newspaper in Seattle, and a produce worker, has struggled to find the time to write poetry, instead avidly promoting the careers of other Asian American artists. As a result, there was a twenty-year gap between the publication of *Songs for Jadina* and his most recent book, *Blues and Greens*. Hopefully this momentous event will promote more widespread discussion of Lau's work and bring him the critical attention he deserves.

BIBLIOGRAPHY

Works by Alan Chong Lau

With Garrett Kaoru Hongo and Lawson Fusao Inada. *The Buddha Bandits down Highway 99*. Mountain View, CA: Buddhahead Press, 1978.

Songs for Jadina. Greenfield Center, NY: Greenfield Review Press, 1980.

Blues and Greens: A Produce Worker's Journal. Honolulu: University of Hawai'i Press, 2000.

Studies of Alan Chong Lau

Desoto, Hisaye Yamamoto. Rev. of *Songs for Jadina*. *MELUS* 10.4 (Winter 1983): 78–83.

Hamill, Sam. "Alan Lau and Colleen McElroy: Local Poets against the Grain." Rev. of *Songs for Jadina*. *Weekly* 7 October 1981: 32.

Kaneko, Lonny. "A Journey into Place, Race, and Spirit." Rev. of *The Buddha Bandits down Highway 99*. *Amerasia Journal* 6.2 (1979): 91–95.

Lim, Genny. Rev. of *Songs for Jadina*. *East/West* 20 May 1981: 9.

Rev. of *The Buddha Bandits down Highway 99*. *Bridge: An Asian American Perspective* Spring/Summer 1980: 46.

Roche, Judith. Rev. of *Songs for Jadina*. *Seattle Voice* June 1981: 23.

Wallenstein, Barry. Rev. of *Songs for Jadina*. *American Book Review* 4.6 (September/October 1982): 17.

Yee, Cordell. Rev. of *The Buddha Bandits down Highway 99*. *East/West* 22 August 1979: 11.

CAROLYN LAU
(1946–   )

Rowena Tomaneng Matsunari

BIOGRAPHY

Carolyn Lau was born in 1946 in Hawaii. She was educated in California and attended San Francisco State University. She also actively studied Chinese philosophy. She is an educator who teaches poetry and movement to bilingual Chinese and Southeast Asian immigrant children. She has received an American Book Award in 1988 for *Wode Shuofa: My Way of Speaking* and a California Arts Council Fellowship.

MAJOR WORKS AND THEMES

Although Lau's poetry has appeared in several anthologies and literary periodicals, *Wode Shuofa: My Way of Speaking*, published in 1988, is her only collection of poetry. Lau's writings, foremost, reflect her study of Chinese philosophy—Confucianism, Taoism, and Buddhism. Many of her poems explore the ideas behind these traditions as well as how these principles affect individual behaviors and desires. Other poems present Lau's attitudes about gender, sexuality, and the craft of writing. Female speakers dominate her poems, and narrative content highlights the experiences of women, especially in relation to societal/cultural expectations of womanhood.

To maintain order and harmony among the hierarchy of state, society, and family, Confucius (551–479 B.C.) advocated restoration of the imperial government, social and family organizations, and the rules of propriety prescribed in the classical literature of the early Zhou dynasty. The most important element in his system was the individual. Confucius taught that each human being must cultivate such values as honesty, love, and filial piety through study of models provided in ancient literature. However, Confucius did not focus on issues pertaining to phenomenology, metaphysics, and human rights against tyranny. Fouth- and third-century B.C. disciples Mencius and Xunzi (Hsun-tzu) clarified these issues. Mencius asserted that human nature was basically good and that it could only be developed by study, but also by a process of inner self-cultivation. He also placed greater responsibilities on the ruler for the welfare of the people. Mencius pointed out that the Mandate of Heaven could be withdrawn if people disposed of a tyrant. Xunzi asserted that rebellion was fundamentally evil. He taught that through a study of the classics and rules of propriety, virtue could be acquired and order could be reestablished in society ("Chinese Philosophy" http://encarta.msn.com).

Lau's poetry critiques the philosophical tradition left by Confucius and his disciples, a tradition that supported the lower-class and subservient position of women within the hierarchy of state, society, and family. In the poem "WHEN WIDOW LAU TOOK A LOVER" in *Wode Shuofa*, the female speaker paints a picture of gender oppression. The repetition of the sexual abuse and the hope that it will stop are emphasized with the modifying phrase "Over and Over," which points to both the sex and the mental thoughts of the speaker. "The Meaning of 'Bondsmaid' in Chinese" conveys the lack of intimacy between a Chinese wife and husband. The female speaker identifies with the figure of a "bondsmaid" who is obligated to work. Also, the allusion to Mencius in line 2 signifies the wife's rejection of Confucianism and its principles of conduct. Despite Mencius's questioning of tyranny, gender oppression was never addressed.

The poem "TWENTY-EIGHT NATURES OF GUANYIN" in *Wode Shuofa* turns our attention to Lau's familiarity with Taoism and Buddhism. Taoism is based on the writings of Laozi (fifth century B.C., the author of the *Daodejing* [Classic of the Way and Its Power] and Zhuangzi (third century B.C.). In "Taoism, or the Way," Judith A. Berling points out that Taoism provided an alternative to Confucianism in that it argued that the order and harmony of nature were more stable than any institution constructed by human learning (9). Taoism also inspired "an intense affirmation of life: physical life—health, wellbeing, vitality" (10). Buddhism, in contrast, arose from the teachings of Gautama Buddha, who lived in northern India in the sixth century B.C. Buddhism holds four noble truths: there is suffering, suffering has a cause, suffering has an end, and there is a path that leads to the end of suffering. Buddhism encourages freedom from self and earthly desires because it is human beings' attachment to notions of self that causes suffering. Freeing the heart from greed, hatred, and delusion opens the mind to wisdom and the heart to compassion and kindness ("About Buddhism" http://www.ncf.carleton.ca 1).

Guanyin—the goddess of mercy—is an allusion to the popular deity Bodhisattva of compassion, kindness, joy, and giving. A Bodhisattva is one who has attained enlightenment, but chooses to help others achieve it. Worshipped in China as Guanyin or Guanshiyin, the name Guanyin means "contemplating the world of sounds" ("Guanyin, Guanyin, Guanshiyin" http://www.jps.net 1996 1–7). Lau's poem "TWENTY-EIGHT NATURES OF GUANYIN" is a celebration of Guanyin's presence in everyday life, from relationships between parent and child and between man and woman to children playing games. It is in this sense that the poem synthesizes Taoism and Buddhism. The first stanza, for example, illustrates human harmony with and reverence for nature. Although "sun" and "rain" denote opposite natural phenomena, the words also connote life and renewal. The boy "bathing" in sun and rain emphasizes his recognition of complementary elements in the natural environment. That the poem is about "contemplation of the world's sounds" is further evidenced by Lau's depiction of human beings and inanimate objects talking, muttering, and listening.

Lau's poetry is imagistic and emotionally compelling. Imagistic poetry has its roots in Japanese haiku, a lyric form that represents the poet's impression of a natural object or scene, viewed at a particular season or month. Imagist poetry also relies on free verse, using the natural rhythms of language and natural pauses. The writer's degree of concentration in rendering a precise response to a visual object or scene is crucial to the success of the poem.

The poem "Zhoukoudian Bride's Harvest" exemplifies Lau's use of the imagistic style. In lines 1–5 the female speaker presents a romantic scene in springtime, a time of birth and renewal of nature, through personification of the speaker's heart leaping. Lau's lush visual and kinesthetic imagery continues in lines 25–29. The images of winter's mist and floating suggest the speaker's haziness of memory and distance from the object of her love. Yet even with the distance of time and space, the speaker emphasizes a constancy in her feelings for her Beijing Man as "earth requiring water."

Another aspect of Lau's poetry focuses on the personal in her explorations of gender and sexual identity in Chinese culture. The poem "BEING CHINESE IN ENGLISH" in *Wode Shuofa* explores the repression of sexuality/desire in Chinese culture. The couple interested in orgasm is compared to crickets because they are making noise and are anxious about being discovered. It is also evident that the female speaker is the more nervous because of her gender, and she fears the judgment of the men near. In the final stanza, the speaker conveys a tone of frustration that she cannot freely express sexual desire. In contrast, the poem "Not for Sale" expresses defiance on the part of the female speaker. Her body is "not for sale," an object to be disposed of or bought. Because the female body becomes a sacred object to revere, the speaker undermines how women are devalued in traditional Chinese society.

Like many other writers, Lau, too, reflects upon the relationship between the poet and the writing process. In the poem "The Way Somatology Knows Poetry," Lau realizes the ways in which European and Chinese literature have influenced her poetry. This dual heritage is not a source of conflict: In line 12, Lau says, "gleaning words is a way to live" (82). The poem "A Definition of

Eurydice" contrasts female and male writers. Lau appropriates the tragic myth of Orpheus and Eurydice as a means to redefine Eurydice's character as a creator of ideas. Despite society's admiration for Orpheus, the musician and poet who could charm wild beasts, it is Eurydice with whom the speaker identifies.

Taken as a whole, Lau's writings reflect a distinctly "Asian American" sensibility or double consciousness. Lau's poems explore the continued influence of ancient Chinese philosophy in contemporary society, yet she also incorporates a Western perspective, especially in relation to gender and sexuality.

CRITICAL RECEPTION

Lau's writings, like those of many other contemporary Asian American poets, have received little or no critical attention. The previous discussion expounds on these few sentences that have been written in reference to her work.

BIBLIOGRAPHY

Works by Carolyn Lau

Wode Shuofa: My Way of Speaking. Santa Fe: Tooth of Time Books, 1988.
"Zhoukoudian Bride's Harvest." *The Forbidden Stitch: An Asian American Women's Anthology.* Ed. Shirley Geok-lin Lim, Mayumi Tsutakawa, and Margarita Donnelly. Corvallis, OR: Calyx Books, 1989. 126–27.
"As If Neurophilosophy Might Respond." *Journal of Ethnic Studies* 18.1 (Spring 1990): 91–92.
"A Brand of North American Dialectic." *Journal of Ethnic Studies* 18.1 (Spring 1990): 88.
"Easter's Oakland, 1989." *Journal of Ethnic Studies* 18.1 (Spring 1990): 87.
"Footloose among Fourth Century Sophists or Discovering Ah Q in Ourselves." *Journal of Ethnic Studies* 18.1 (Spring 1990): 80.
"Gethsemane: Opus 42." *Journal of Ethnic Studies* 18.1 (Spring 1990): 84.
"How Real Men Sit on the Toilet Mantra: A Distinction between Minimalism and Nominalism or Textures in California Buddhism." *Journal of Ethnic Studies* 18.1 (Spring 1990): 84.
"A Kind of Neo-Daoism circa 220–420." *Journal of Ethnic Studies* 18.1 (Spring 1990): 89.
"The Meaning of 'Bondsmaid' in Chinese." *Journal of Ethnic Studies* 18.1 (Spring 1990): 81.
"Not for Sale." *Journal of Ethnic Studies* 18.1 (Spring 1990): 86.
"On 'Excess and Privation.' " *Journal of Ethnic Studies* 18.1 (Spring 1990): 90.
"On the Train from Beijing to Hohhot." *Journal of Ethnic Studies* 18.1 (Spring 1990): 79–80.
"Options in Semiotics." *Journal of Ethnic Studies* 18.1 (Spring 1990): 85.
"R & R." *Journal of Ethnic Studies* 18.1 (Spring 1990): 83.
"The Way Somatology Knows Poetry." *Journal of Ethnic Studies* 18.1 (Spring 1990): 82.

Chinese American Poetry: An Anthology. Ed. L. Ling-Chi Wang and Henry Yiheng Zhao. Santa Barbara, CA: Asian American Voices, 1991.

"A Definition of Eurydice." *Parnassus: Poetry in Review* 17.1 (Spring 1991): 166.

"Porter Bras." *Parnassus: Poetry in Review* 17.1 (Spring 1991): 166.

"On the Fifth Anniversary of My Father's Death." *More Light: Father and Daughter Poems.* Ed. Jason Shinder. Fort Worth, TX: Harcourt Brace, 1993.

"Ha'ina 'ia mai ana ka puana" (Let the story be told). *Chicago Review* 39.3–4 (Summer–Fall 1993): 168–75.

The Body Electric: America's Best Poetry from the American Review. Ed. Stephen Berg, David Bonanno, and Arthur Vogelsang. Intro. Harold Bloom. New York: Norton, 2000.

Studies Relating to Carolyn Lau

"About Buddhism." Available: http://www.ncf.carleton.ca (February 2001).

Berling, Judith A. "Taoism, or the Way." *Focus on Asian Studies* 2.1 (Fall 1982): 9–11.

"Chinese Philosophy." Available: http://encarta.msn.com (February 2001).

"Guanyin, Guanyin, Guanshiyin." Available: http://www.jps.net/namofo/BTTS/Guanyin.html. Accessed on 2/15/01.

EVELYN LAU
(1971–   )

Nikolas Huot

BIOGRAPHY

Evelyn Yee-Fun Lau was born on 2 July 1971 in Vancouver, British Columbia, to Chinese immigrants. From the time she was six years old, Lau wanted to become a writer. At the age of thirteen, she began to publish poems and short stories in magazines; she even won an essay contest sponsored by the *Vancouver Sun* to meet the pope. Unfortunately, the repressive constraints of her parents, who obsessively pushed her to become a doctor and denied her any creative outlet, led her to take her life to the streets at the age of fourteen. Spiraling down into a life of drug abuse and prostitution, Lau tried to commit suicide twice before she was seventeen. Putting her thoughts on paper was the only thing that helped her get through psychologically. She chronicled her life on the streets in a diary, which was published in 1989 when she was barely eighteen. *Runaway: Diary of a Street Kid* made it to the Canadian best-seller list and stayed there for thirty weeks. In 1994, her autobiography was made into a ninety-seven-minute television movie entitled *The Diary of Evelyn Lau*.

One year after the publication of *Runaway*, Lau published her first collection of poetry, *You Are Not Who You Claim* (1990). Since then, Lau has written two other volumes of poetry, *Oedipal Dreams* (1992) and *In the House of Slaves* (1994); two collections of short stories, *Fresh Girls and Other Stories* (1993) and *Choose Me* (1999); one novel, *Other Women* (1995); and one collection of essays, *Inside Out: Reflections on a Life So Far* (2001). Over the years, she also contributed some reviews and articles to *Vancouver Magazine* and to the *Globe and Mail*. Her poetry has appeared in numerous literary magazines such as

Kenyon Review, Southern Review, Antigonish Review, and *Prairie Fire* and has been anthologized in such works as *Best American Poetry 1992* (edited by Charles Simic), *Premonitions* (1995, edited by Walter K. Lew), and *Lit from Within* (1995), a compact disc featuring songs and poetry by Canadian artists that benefits women's crisis centers in Canada.

MAJOR WORKS AND THEMES

"I tend to explore the darker, more perverse regions of sexuality in my work. I am not interested in writing pornography or even erotica; I am more interested in the psychology behind sexual behavior, and the issues of power and abuse," writes Evelyn Lau in her biographical note for *Left Bank: Sex, Family, Tribe,* to which she contributed "Mercy," a short story later republished in *Fresh Girls.* This interest in sexual behavior and power is evident not only in her fiction writing but in her poetry as well.

In her first volume of poetry, *You Are Not Who You Claim,* Lau writes of a bleak world of drugs and prostitution. Her poems express the death of innocence and the cruel reality that follows those who live on the streets. Whether Lau is writing about child abuse ("Talking Back"), pedophilia ("First Experiences"), prostitution ("Rm. 809, Delta Place"), unfulfilled relationships ("I Am Sure This Is"), or drug abuse ("Tambourine Man"), she uses the voice of the abused and powerless. Lau's poetry depicts sex and drugs not as recreational experiences, but as tools one must (ab)use to survive. In her poems, the reader cannot help but feel the loss and the devastation the speaker is going through; at the same time, however, there is a certain sense of emotional detachment in her poetry that does not let the speaker suffer a second time when recalling a past experience. Overall, Lau's poetry is full of detachment and bleakness, a strategy she learned in order to survive: "I don't think I've ever admired compassion in writing. I've admired detachment instead—a hardness and a merciless perspective" (qtd. in Yanofsky "Writer" J3).

Oedipal Dreams, Lau's second volume of poetry, continues this depiction of the brutal underworld with a detached attitude. Many poems in this collection deal with the same topics introduced in her first volume; however, this time, the speaker seems to be more concerned with the aftermath and psychological effects following a life of violence, prostitution, and drug abuse. In her second book, Lau groups her poems in unmarked categories, leaving only a blank page between sections. The first and longest section of the book deals with the speaker's recollections of her former life and its pervasive physical and psychological violence. The short second section of the volume ties in the first and subsequent divisions of the book. The six poems present lost speakers in search of something more substantial (love, security, honesty, or stability) in their bleak lives that would help them deal with the harsh reality. Unfortunately, as in most poems by Lau, the speakers only find more disappointments, heartaches, and more lost people like them who are also searching for something they are never able to reach. The third section of *Oedipal Dreams* is concerned with depression and disillusion in the world, which ushers in the fourth section about suicide. The fifth and last section reintroduces the subject of sex and prostitution. This time, however, Lau approaches sex solely as a power relationship between two individuals that often includes violence. In this section, Lau writes of sadomasochism and group sex for the first time and, besides the violence, depicts the dullness and apathy associated with it ("Monkey on the Ceiling").

In the House of Slaves, Lau's third and most recent volume of poetry, pursues the theme of sadomasochism introduced in the last part of *Oedipal Dreams*. If the dominatrix felt pleasure in *Oedipal Dreams* ("you are making me happy" ["Afternoon #1"]), she wants something more in Lau's third book of poetry. In the first part of the book, the dominatrix soon realizes that despite being called mistress, she is still the slave in the relationship because she does what she is told and does not reap any pleasure or satisfaction from the relation. She starts to recognize and repulse her role in the degrading acts. This realization comes to a height as she dreams of a reawakening in "Where Did You Learn?" In the second part of the book, she does find someone to wait for her. The reader witnesses their lives together, but never manages to get too close. The relationship is doomed from the start, however, and she, once again, is left alone to "resume the process of making myself perfect" ("Solipsism"). The question of whether she will succeed in achieving this degree of perfection (or at least wholeness) is unanswered in Lau's final poem. Perhaps her fourth volume of poetry will answer this question and discuss her journey to fulfillment.

CRITICAL RECEPTION

Lau's three volumes of poetry have been relatively well received by the critics, although most do not know exactly what to make of the overt preoccupation with sex and violence. As a way of approaching her work, critics too often choose the easy way out and explain Lau's poetry in the context of her former life as a teenage prostitute. Many of these critics have categorized the author into "the hooker who can write" and perceived her poetry as merely autobiographical or, worse yet, as a sociological document. Gerry Shikatani expresses that trend in his review of *You Are Not Who You Claim* when he asks how we should read Lau's poetry. "As that 'runaway' or maybe teenaged talent? I hope not" is his answer as he discusses Lau's frequent originality and subtlety in her first published volume of poetry (G13). Shikatani mentions Lau's "lack of restraint [that occasionally leads her poetry] into melodramatic excess or dreary statement," which he sees as "characteristic of a writer's early efforts," but also commends how her "images and language flow seemingly freely" (G13). Overall positive, Shikatani believes that the publication of *You Are Not Who You Claim* "signals the emergence of a potentially impressive artist" (G13). Shikatani was right in his assessment of Lau's first volume of poetry; in 1990, Lau won the Air Canada/Canadian Authors' Association's Award for Most Promising Writer under 30, and the following year she was awarded the Milton Acorn People's Poetry Award for a work that sustained the tradition of a people's literature in Canada and internationally.

Her second volume of poetry, *Oedipal Dreams*, was even more successful. At the age of twenty-one, Lau became the youngest poet ever to be nominated for the Governor General's Award, the most prestigious award in Canadian literature. Although she did not win the award, she did win praises from critics all over the country. Her poetry was called powerful and "too good to miss" by fellow poet Marilyn Bowering and "loaded with intelligence and jeweled with unexpected moments of insight" by writer Brian Fawcett (*Oedipal Dreams* back cover). For its originality and nonconformity, *Oedipal Dreams* is considered a landmark in Canadian poetry and, as such, has been published in more than ten countries.

Although not as critically acclaimed as *Oedipal Dreams, In the House of Slaves* has nonetheless been relatively well received by critics. In no other works reviewed, however, has the critics' discomfort at the portrayal of sadomasochism and the uselessness of love been so evident. In her review for the *Gazette*, Anne Cimon acknowledges her uneasiness with such sexual encounters and deplores how Lau portrays love as "an aberration" (14). Cimon admits "a certain finesse" to Lau's poetry, but, somewhat equivocally, ends her review by writing that "dotted with Oriental touches of beauty," her poetry is like "the emptiness of a Zen rock garden" (14). E. Russell Smith's review is empty of such ambiguity. His review clearly denotes his admiration for Lau's poetry and her literary achievements. In his estimation, *In the House of Slaves* is the best volume of poetry Lau has produced so far, "adding structure and maturity to the subtle lyricism of the earlier volumes" (B3). Although she has been stigmatized as the "hooker who writes," this collection of poetry, Smith declares, proves Lau's "right to write and be heard in any company" (B3). Indeed, her numerous awards and accolades, as well as her prolific career, prove that the talented Evelyn Lau is, and will be for years to come, a powerful presence in literary circles as a poet and writer.

BIBLIOGRAPHY

Works by Evelyn Lau

Poetry

You Are Not Who You Claim. Victoria, British Columbia: Porcépic Books, 1990.
Oedipal Dreams. Victoria, British Columbia: Beach Holme, 1992.
In the House of Slaves. Toronto: Coach House Press, 1994.

Autobiography

Runaway: Diary of a Street Kid. Toronto: HarperCollins, 1989.

Novel

Other Women. Toronto: Random House, 1995.

Short Stories

Fresh Girls and Other Stories. Toronto: HarperCollins, 1993.
"California." *Canadian Forum* 73.829 (May 1994): 30–34.
"If Wishes Were Horses." *Capilano Review* 2.14 (Fall 1994): 5–11.
Choose Me: Stories. Toronto: Doubleday, 1999.

Essays

"Global Exchange." Rev. of *Gold by the Inch*, by Lawrence Chua. *Voice Literary Supplement* 7 April 1998, 13.
"Father Figures." *Desire in Seven Voices.* Ed. Lorna Crozier. Vancouver: Douglas and McIntyre, 1999. 43–61.
Inside Out: Reflections on a Life So Far. Toronto: Doubleday, 2001.

Studies of Evelyn Lau

Alexis, Andre. "Longing for Love—or Is It Status?" Rev. of *Other Women. Toronto Star* 23 September 1995, final ed.: J16.
Asimakopulos, Anna. "Dark Eroticism with Ring of Truth." Rev. of *Fresh Girls. Gazette* [Montreal] 2 October 1993, final ed.: J2.
Bendall, Molly. Rev. of *In the House of Slaves. Antioch Review* 53.4 (Fall 1995): 502.
Boothroyd, Jim. "Evelyn Lau Spins a Novel in Brief." Rev. of *Other Women. Gazette* [Montreal] 2 September 1995, final ed.: G2.
Chang, Elaine. "Run through the Borders: Feminism, Postmodernism, and Runaway Subjectivity." *Border Theory: The Limits of Cultural Politics.* Ed. Scott Michaelsen and David E. Johnson. Minneapolis: University of Minnesota Press, 1997. 169–94.
Cimon, Anne. Rev. of *In the House of Slaves. Gazette* [Montreal] 18 June 1994, final ed., Books: 14.
Condé, Mary. "An Interview with Evelyn Lau." *Etudes Canadiennes/Canadian Studies* 21.38 (June 1995): 105–11.
Dean, Misao. "Reading Evelyn Right." *Canadian Forum* 73.837 (1995): 22–26.
Halim, Nadia. "Beyond Prurience." Rev. of *In the House of Slaves. Canadian Forum* 73.833 (1994): 41–42.
Hluchy, Patricia, and Rob Howatson. "The Pen Is Mightier Than the Sordid." *Maclean's* 106.41 (1993): 72–73.
Hunnewell, Susannah. Rev. of *Other Women. New York Times* 7 July 1996, final ed., sec. 7: 15.
James-French, Davy. "A Curiously Lifeless Story about Desire; Evelyn Lau's First Novel Leaves the Reader Feeling Lonely." Rev. of *Other Women. Ottawa Citizen* 17 September 1995, final ed.: C3.
Mallick, Heather. "Evelyn Lau Exploits Real Life." *Jam! Books* 18 April 1999. Available: http://www.canoe.ca/JamBooksReviewsC/choose_lau.html. Dec. 2000.

Nickson, Keith. "The Dark Side of Desire." Rev. of *Fresh Girls. Toronto Star* 16 October 1993, final ed.: J17.

Richards, Linda. "*January Magazine* Interviews Evelyn Lau." *January Magazine* October 1999. Available: http://januarymagazine.com/profiles/lau.html. Dec. 2000.

Shikatani, Gerry. "A Significant Account." Rev. of *You Are Not Who You Claim. Toronto Star* 24 November 1990, Saturday ed.: G13.

Smith, E. Russell. Rev. of *In the House of Slaves. Ottawa Citizen* 21 August 1994, final ed.: B3.

Stoberock, Johanna. Rev. of *Other Women. Seattle Times* 7 July 1996, final ed.: M2.

Taylor, Erika. Rev. of *Fresh Girls. Los Angeles Times* 3 September 1995, home ed., Book Reviews: 6.

———. Rev. of *Runaway. Los Angeles Times* 8 October 1995, home ed., Book Reviews: 6.

von Flotow, Luise. "Women and Eroticism." Rev. of *In the House of Slaves. Canadian Literature* 154 (Autumn 1997): 150–52.

Wanner, Irene. "*Fresh Girls* Wiser Than It Appears." *Seattle Times* 23 April 1995, final ed.: M2.

Yanofsky, Joel. "From Hooking to Three-Book Deal; Evelyn Lau Has Seen It All and Writes to Tell about It." *Gazette* [Montreal] 9 October 1993, final ed.: J2.

———. "A Writer Too Much in Spotlight: Evelyn Lau's Misadventures Make Her Object of Fascination in Media." *Gazette* [Montreal] 15 May 1999, final ed.: J3+.

LÊ THI DIEM THÚY
(1972–)

Melinda L. de Jesús

BIOGRAPHY

Lê Thi Diem Thúy (Thúy Lê) was born in Phan Thiet, South Vietnam, in 1972. She left Vietnam by boat in 1978, was relocated to a Singapore refugee camp, and eventually settled in southern California. Lê graduated from Hampshire College and currently resides in Northampton, Massachusetts. A versatile and prolific writer, Lê is also known for her solo performances, *Red Fiery Summer/ Mua He Do Lua* and *the bodies between us*. Her memoir, *The Gangster We Are All Looking For*, is forthcoming from Knopf (2002). Lê is currently working on a novel entitled *The Bodies between Us*.

MAJOR WORKS AND THEMES

Currently Thúy Lê has four poems in print: "shrapnel shards on blue water" and "Foresee" in *The Very Inside: An Anthology of Writing by Asian and Pacific Islander Lesbian and Bisexual Women* (1994) ("Foresee" also in *The Arc of Love: An Anthology of Lesbian Love Poems* ([1996]); and "untitled" and "Big Sister, Little Sister" in *Watermark: Vietnamese American Poetry and Prose* (1998). That Lê's poetry has been published in two separate anthologies of lesbian poetry as well as an anthology of Vietnamese American writing signals the centrality of both sexual and racial identity as important themes in her work. Critic Monique Tru'o'ng maintains that "Vietnamese American literature speaks of death and other irreconcilable losses and longs always for peace—peace of mind" (219). Certainly these same themes permeate Lê's poetry, as do the themes of memory, family, and history. Furthermore, Lê's work is notable for its distinctive use of water/ocean imagery.

"shrapnel shards on blue water," which is dedicated to the poet's sister, Lê Thi Diem Trinh, describes Lê's desperate need to break the silence about her family's dislocation and alienation in the United States. Lê alludes to this up-rooting through different memories of her family's life next to the sea: she recalls first her mother's daily trips to Saigon along the South China Sea, then her father's futile attempts to fish in the Pacific Ocean from an inflatable raft. Lê underscores the sense of powerlessness that transcribes the refugee experi-ence (51–52), insisting that remembering the past enables the future; that sur-vival depends on remembering one's roots and what one has lost (56–62). These forceful lines are a fierce declaration to her sister and family, but can also be read as a healing mantra for all Vietnamese Americans today.

The themes of death, loss, and memory also permeate "untitled" and "Big Sister, Little Sister." In "untitled," Lê describes the negative of her sister in her coffin and what she remembers of that moment: fleeting images of her sister's face and hair, her body wrapped in pink cloth. She describes the inadequacy of the negative, of memory, to encompass this memory and its significance: her sister's journey into the unknown.

"Big Sister, Little Sister" focuses once again on Lê's memories of her sister and her sense of responsibility as the eldest girl in her family (1–2). The poet describes finding her dead sister's dress hidden in the attic and how putting it on connects them, even as it emphasizes the space between them. Soaked in the ocean (it is implied that the sister has drowned), the wet dress symbolizes the family's hidden grief as well as its aftermath: the accumulation of pain via silence and denial, their unshed tears. Thus the speaker takes on the "biggest-girl" role: by wearing the dress, she remembers her sister and her loss and can lead her family in grieving and remembering (16).

As in "shrapnel shards," Lê uses water imagery here to signal the divide between her life in Vietnam and America, in having a sister and then losing her. At the end of the poem, the poet imagines that each drop of her own sweat in her sister's dress pushes back the ocean and time itself, enabling the sisters to bridge the distance between them. In this way, they are united beyond life and death.

The poem "Foresee" differs radically from those previously discussed in terms of its subject matter and form. This love poem is an elliptical, sensuous, sug-gestive description of the electric beginnings of a romance. The poem begins with the lover wishing for nightfall and the speaker's imagining what night may bring. The image of the lottery signifies the hoped-for relationship—their house—but the poet emphasizes its inherent fragility and instability, underscor-ing love as both thrilling and dangerous. Moreover, their union is an engulfing within the sea, suggestive of sex, orgasm, and surrender (42–49). In the final stanzas, the poet returns to the present and the opening of the poem: the lovers' anticipation of nightfall. Here the poem turns back on itself, back to the point of foretelling: what she has just imagined is about to happen like she always knew "it could be" (53–55).

CRITICAL RECEPTION

Lê Thi Diem Thúy is at the beginning of her career as a writer and performer, yet her work has already garnered significant critical attention. Her short piece "The Gangster We Are All Looking For" was included in *The Best American Essays of 1997* and was also awarded a Pushcart Prize "Special Mention." Lê has received grants from the Bridge Residency at the Headlands Center for the Arts as well as a New Works for a New World grant from New WORLD Theater at the University of Massachusetts at Amherst and the New England Foundation for the Arts. Finally, Hugh Garvey in the *Voice Literary Supplement*, in a 1998 article spotlighting emerging new writers, heralded Lê as a "writer on the verge" of a breakthrough. Through her previous work, together with the forthcoming publications of her novel and memoir, Lê Thi Diem Thúy has established herself as a Vietnamese American and lesbian-of-color poet of great promise—and one to keep an eye on.

BIBLIOGRAPHY

Works by Lê Thi Diem Thúy

Poetry

"Foresee." *The Very Inside: An Anthology of Writing by Asian and Pacific Islander Lesbian and Bisexual Women*. Ed. Sharon Lim-Hing. Toronto: Sister Vision Press, 1994. 212–14.
"shrapnel shards on blue water." *The Very Inside: An Anthology of Writing by Asian and Pacific Islander Lesbian and Bisexual Women*. Ed. Sharon Lim-Hing. Toronto: Sister Vision Press, 1994. 2–5.
"Foresee." *The Arc of Love: An Anthology of Lesbian Love Poems*. Ed. Clare Coss. New York: Scribner, 1996. 73–74.
"Big Sister, Little Sister." *Watermark: Vietnamese American Poetry and Prose*. Ed. Barbara Tran, Monique T.D. Tru'o'ng, and Luu Truong Khoi. New York: Asian American Writers' Workshop, 1998. 85–86.
"untitled." *Watermark: Vietnamese American Poetry and Prose*. Ed. Barbara Tran, Monique T.D. Tru'o'ng, and Luu Truong Khoi. New York: Asian American Writers' Workshop, 1998. 83–84.

Drama

Red Fiery Summer/Mua He Do Lua. Bold Worlds: A Century of Asian American Writing. Ed. Rajini Srikanth and Esther Iwanaga. New Brunswick, NJ: Rutgers University Press, 2001.
the bodies between us. The Color of Theater: Race, Ethnicity and Contemporary Per-

formance. Ed. Roberta Uno and Lucy Mae San Pablo Burns. New York: Continuum, 2002.

Fiction

The Bodies between Us. Forthcoming.

Nonfiction

"The Gangster We Are All Looking For." *Massachusetts Review* 36.4 (Winter 1995): 511–13.
"Ma and Ba." Excerpt from "The Gangster We Are All Looking For." *Harper's Magazine* 292 (April 1996): 15–19.
"The Gangster We Are All Looking For." *The Best American Essays of 1997*. Ed. Ian Frazier. Boston: Houghton Mifflin, 1997. 190–202.
"California Palms." *Half and Half: Writers on Growing Up Biracial and Bicultural*. Ed. Claudine Chiawei O'Hearn. New York: Pantheon, 1998. 38–48.
The Gangster We Are All Looking For. New York: Alfred Knopf, 2001.

Studies of Lê Thi Diem Thúy

Garvey, Hugh. "Lê Thi Diem Thúy." In "Writers on the Verge." Ed. Joy Press. *Voice Literary Supplement* 22 (2 June 1998): 78–80.
Trotter, Mary. "Performance Review: The Fourth International Women Playwrights Conference." Rev. of "red fiery summer." *Theatre Journal* 49.4 (December 1997): 523.
Tru'o'ng, Monique T.D. "Vietnamese American Literature." *An Interethnic Companion to Asian American Literature*. Ed. King-Kok Cheung. New York: Cambridge University Press, 1997. 219–46.

LI-YOUNG LEE
(1957–   )

Wenying Xu

BIOGRAPHY

Li-Young Lee was born in 1957 in Indonesia of Chinese parents who had left China during its Anti-Rightist movement of the early 1950s. His mother's grandfather was the notorious Yuan Shi-kai, a warlord who became the first president of the Republic of China after the revolution led by Sun Zhongshan (Sun Yat-sen) that abolished China's monarchy and founded the first republic in 1911. Lee's father was the son of a gangster and entrepreneur. He studied Western medicine and was Mao Zedong's personal physician until he and his family left China for Indonesia. Lee's father taught medicine and philosophy at Gamaliel University in Jakarta and became a medical advisor to Sukarno. When Lee was eighteen months old, his father was arrested by the Sukarno government and was held as a political prisoner because of his love for Western culture—Shakespeare, opera, Kierkegaard, and the Bible. Lee was three years old when the entire family escaped to Hong Kong. After a few years of wandering in Asia, they immigrated to the United States. For a time they lived in Pittsburgh, Pennsylvania, where his father studied at Pittsburgh Theological Seminary. After his father completed his studies, they moved to East Vandergrift, a small mill town in western Pennsylvania, where his father became the minister for an all-white Presbyterian congregation, which called him "their heathen minister" (*The Winged Seed* 82). As a child, Lee accompanied his father as he delivered food and comfort to the homes of the poor and invalid. He witnessed the indignity of human suffering and the immense compassion of his father. During these early years, Lee also learned from his father to recite classical Chinese poetry and to love the *Song of Songs*, both of which had a shaping power in Lee's poetry.

In 1975, Lee went to the University of Pittsburgh and majored in biochemistry but fell in love with poetry. It was at Pittsburgh that Lee met the poet Gerald Stern, whose *Lucky Life* sparked Lee's fascination with poetry. Stern played a significant part in Lee's development as a poet and wrote the foreword to Lee's first book of poetry, *Rose*. Lee went on to study in the M.F.A. programs at the University of Arizona and the State University of New York at Brockport. Although he never finished his master's degree, the State University of New York at Brockport awarded him an honorary doctorate. For several years, Lee worked at a warehouse in Chicago, stacking boxes of books from nine to five and reading and writing poetry late at night. He, his wife, Donna, and their two sons lived in a poorly heated two-room apartment where all four of them slept in the living room on a pullout couch. In order to care for their sons during the day, Donna Lee worked on call as a CAT-scan technologist, available for night emergencies. After the children were put to bed, Lee retreated into the other room, crowded with books and paper, to be absorbed in the poems of Emily Dickinson, Pablo Neruda, John Donne, John Keats, Rainer Maria Rilke, Walt Whitman, T.S. Eliot, and others. It was also in this crowded room and in the small hours that Lee worked, against the exhaustion of his body, to put down on the page his songs of love for his father, mother, wife, sons, mankind, and all.

Lee still lives in Chicago and makes his living from poetry readings and teaching appointments at colleges around the country. With two published books of poetry, *Rose* (1986) and *The City in Which I Love You* (1990), and a memoir, *The Winged Seed* (1995), Lee has emerged as one of America's most prominent young poets. He has received some of the most prestigious literary honors, including funding from the National Endowment for the Arts, the Writer's Award from the Mrs. Giles Whiting Foundation, and a fellowship from the John Simon Guggenheim Memorial Foundation. In 1987, *Rose* won the Delmore Schwartz Memorial Poetry Award from New York University. *The City in Which I Love You* won the 1990 Lamont Poetry Selection of the Academy of American Poets.

MAJOR WORKS AND THEMES

Lee's poetry portrays two stages of his life—a lonely child who was tenderly loved by his father and a searching young man whose memory of his father intensifies his love for his wife and sons. *Rose* is a book of poetry about himself as a child, and the father's tenderness is a dominant theme. *The City in Which I Love You* is about Lee the young man and his search for a larger history on whose cusp he places himself. As a small child, Lee followed his family, crossing seas and passing cities in search of safety—Jakarta, Hong Kong, Macao, Japan, Singapore, Seattle, and Pittsburgh. When they did settle down in western Pennsylvania, they were the only Asians in a white town where people made little effort to understand someone so different from them. In his memoir *The Winged Seed*, Lee recalls a childhood made lonely by things other children said of him: "They say you keep snakes and grasshoppers in a bushel on your back porch and eat them. They say you don't have manners, you lift your plates to your mouths and push the food in with sticks. . . . Is it true you all sleep in one bed together? And that you have cousins hiding in the basement? That you got kicked out of your country because they didn't want you so now you're here? . . . They say you don't believe in God, but you worship the Devil" (86).

In "Persimmons," Lee writes about a sixth grade teacher, Mrs. Walker. The reader understands that the immigrant child was humiliated for mispronunciations and that the sixth grader understood perfectly the meanings of the two words *persimmon* and *precision*. Lee goes on to describe his precise knowledge of persimmons in order to expose the monolingual, racist culture that Mrs. Walker represents. Mrs. Walker brought a green persimmon to class and mistakenly called it a *"Chinese apple"* (*Rose* 18). She cut it up with a knife and divided it among the children. Lee declined his share because of his knowledge of the sour and astringent taste of an unripe persimmon, but he was not spared when the other children scrunched up their faces, silently accusing the Chinese boy of belonging to a foolish people who eat such terrible-tasting "apples." Other words also caused Lee trouble, such as *fight* and *fright*. In these small examples of misusing English words, Lee vividly pictures the difficulties of his early childhood, but his loneliness and pain at school are balanced by love and tenderness at home.

In Lee's poetry and memoir, the figure of the father is larger than life—a man who lived multiple lives and who raised his children with both unbending discipline and infinite love. In "The Gift," Lee paints the picture of his father's tender love as he removed a splinter from the hand of his seven-year-old son. Taking a spatial and temporal leap, the poet juxtaposes this event with a moment of affection between him and his wife.

One of the recurrent themes in Lee's poetry is that love begets love. His father's love for his family has bestowed on the poet the capacity to be a devoted husband and a loving father. The poet's love for his father, made powerful and sad by the latter's passing, transposes and grows in his love for his own son. "The Life" begins with the scene of a young, tired father putting his infant son to sleep. The weight of the infant son, which was his own weight in his father's arms, transformed into the weight of an earthen jar holding the ashes of his father.

Such deft poetic movement, melting and welding of time and space, and memories bleeding into memories make Lee's poetry an immense delight. His most prominent device for achieving such fluidity is the use of a unifying object, be it a persimmon or hair. "Dreaming of Hair" is an excellent example to demonstrate how one small object links the different landmarks of Lee's journey of the heart. After evoking the analogy between his wife's hair and the willow he climbed in childhood, Lee leaps into a dream. Then he moves to his father in the grave. His father's hair is the thread of memory that "stitches" the broken heart and infuses love.

The father's death preoccupies the poet in his search for home and for heaven, which are linked in the poet's mind, for a sense of belonging that can shore up against the "feeling of disconnection and dislocation" (Moyers 258). Often this search assumes the language of supplication laced with Christian allusions. The opening poem of *The City in Which I Love You*, "Furious Versions," presents a poet torn between an imaginary future and an emotional past entangled with his father. Lee casts his father in the figure of Solomon and himself in that of his father who took his wife and children to embark on a perilous journey to safety. It is significant for the poet to relive the past of his father. "He must first merge himself through memory and imagination with his father before he can emerge as a strong presence and lover, just as the biblical Son must merge with his heavenly Father before he achieves figural Bridegroom status" (Hesford 43).

To revive his memory of the past is to humanize his father, who was God-like in life. To love his father leads the poet to embrace his ethnic identity. This inward journey takes place in "Cleaving," in which he reads/eats the food, the culture, and the people of Chinatown, New York. With the metaphor of eating, he establishes an affinity with his people—all the diasporic Chinese—and defends them against racism, such as Emerson's remark about the Chinese managing to preserve *"the ugliest features in the world"* for four thousand years (*The City* 83).

Lee's poetry is passionate. He writes because he cannot forget. He told Bill Moyers, "I can't *not* write" (269).

CRITICAL RECEPTION

Lee's poetry, like that of most living poets, has not been given the scholarly attention it deserves, but two major articles have offered good explications of his work. Walter Hesford opens up the religious dimension of Lee's poetry, particularly *The City in Which I Love You*. He argues that "motifs, images, and verses from the *Song of Songs* serve to unify the collection of poetry" and that Lee has offered a "distinctively Chinese-American rendition of the biblical Song" (37). Hesford points out the major themes of the five parts in *The City*. Parts I and II present the poet wrestling with his father, his traumatic experience as a refugee, and his religious inheritance. Part III focuses on the poet's love for his wife. Part IV presents his wife, the mother of his sons, and himself as a father. Part V "celebrates the Chinese Immigrant self" (42). *The City* traces the poet's "wandering through a sacred and profane and somewhat bewildering city" (42). Hesford argues that this city is Rome, which "has figured as the world city, or the city as *world*; hence its suitability as a site of the search for love" (42). Hesford goes on to perform careful readings of a large number of the poems in *The City* and unveils Lee's various allusions to the New Testament and his celebration of both divine and erotic love. Hesford concludes that "Lee's rendition of the biblical Song does not constitute a critique but a resinging of it, one that restores its erotic, soulful, tribal qualities often lost or ignored in orthodox appropriations" (56).

The other article is written by Zhou Xiaojing, who argues against the tendency to interpret Lee's poetry by emphasizing Lee's Chinese ethnicity, as is done by people like Gerald Stern, L. Ling-chi Wang, and Henry Yiheng Zhao. By reducing Lee's art to expressions of his ethnicity, Zhou points out, these critics minimize "the rich cross-cultural sources of influence on Lee's work and of the creative experiment in his poetry" (114). On the strength of Hans-Georg Gadamer's notion of "horizon," Zhou argues that "one's heritage is not possessed once for all, nor is it necessarily inherited through ethnic lineage. Rather, it is changed and renewed with the changing conditions of human life and human consciousness" (115). Zhou takes a quick inventory of Lee's cultural heritages, which include classical Chinese poetry, the King James Bible, especially the Psalms and the Book of Exodus, and his exposure to various Asian cultures and America. She concludes that Lee's "position of straddling different cultures and histories leads to an expansion of his conceptual and perceptual horizon," a position that, according to Mikhail Bakhtin, promises creativity (116). This creativity is evident in Lee's poetic technique of using a "central image as the organizing principle for both the subject matter and structure of the poem" (117). This technique allows Lee freedom to collage memories and experiences, present and past, and different cultural motifs. After carefully reading some of Lee's exemplary poems, Zhou concludes that Lee's poetry shows that Chinese American poets "can remake themselves in images of their own invention," and "the invention of new Chinese-American images in Lee's poems is rooted in the reality of Chinese-Americans' lives," yet his art transcends "the boundaries of any single cultural heritage or ethnic identity" (131).

Other critical responses mainly consist of interviews and reviews. Bill Moyers's interview offers interesting biographical information and Lee's early assessment of his poetic project. James Lee's interview focuses on the writing of *The Winged Seed*. In this interview, Lee articulates his experience in his experiment with prose and admits that the "things that are closest to me and dearest to me defy language" (11). Tod Marshall's interview is interesting in that Lee for the first time states in print that his poetry is an attempt to have a dialogue with the universe, which is the poet's "highest nature, his true self" (131). In response to Marshall's question whether Lee has gone beyond the cultural phase of being an Asian American poet, Lee answers, "I have no dialogue with cultural existence. Culture made that up—Asian-American, African-American, whatever. I have no interest in that. I have an interest in spiritual lineage connected to poetry. . . . an artist has to discover a dialogue that is so essential to his being, to his self, that it is no longer cultural or canonical, but a dialogue with his truest self. His most naked spirit" (132).

Roger Mitchell points out in his review of *Rose*, "Lee has committed himself to tenderness the way other poets commit themselves to reality, the imagination, nature" (136). However, Mitchell believes that tenderness compromises truth and that "tenderness is not an aesthetic matter" (136). Judith Kitchen, in her review of *The City in Which I Love You*, identifies Lee as a poet offering his "viewpoint of the émigré." Lee's voice is unique in that he positions himself "as father and son, Chinese and American, exile and citizen" (160). Yibing Huang's review of *The Winged Seed* emphasizes the tension between father and son. The "I" in the memoir "can never become a singular and independent self, free from the parasitic presence of the father" (190). Huang sees the book of prose as "the drive to remember and recall" so that Lee could exercise "spiritual self-therapy or exorcism" (191).

BIBLIOGRAPHY

Works by Li-Young Lee

Poetry

Rose. Rochester, NY: BOA Editions, 1986.
"The Cleaving." *TriQuarterly* 77 (Winter 1989/90): 258–66.
"The Waiting." *TriQuarterly* 77 (Winter 1989/90): 254–57.
The City in Which I Love You. Rochester, NY: BOA Editions, 1990.
"This Room and Everything in It." *American Poetry Review* 19 (May/June 1990): 38.
"The Sacrifice." *Ploughshares* 16 (Winter 1990/91): 60–61.
"This Hour and What Is Dead." *Ploughshares* 16 (Winter 1990/91): 62–63.
"The Hammock." *Kenyon Review* 22.1 (Winter 2000): 125.
"Hurry toward Beginning." *Kenyon Review* 22.1 (Winter 2000): 126–27.
"The Moon from Any Window." *Kenyon Review* 22.1 (Winter 2000): 127–28.
"One Heart." *Kenyon Review* 22.1 (Winter 2000): 127.

Prose

The Winged Seed: A Remembrance. New York: Simon and Schuster, 1995.

Studies of Li-Young Lee

Engles, Tim. "Lee's Persimmons." *Explicator* 54.3 (Spring 1996): 191–92.
Hesford, Walter A. "*The City in Which I Love You*: Li-Young Lee's Excellent Song." *Christianity and Literature* 46.1 (Autumn 1996): 37–60.
Huang, Yibing. "*The Winged Seed*." *Amerasia Journal* 24.2 (Summer 1998): 189–91.
Kitchen, Judith. "*The City in Which I Love You*." *Georgia Review* 45.1 (Spring 1991): 160–63.
———. "*Rose*." *Georgia Review* 42.2 (Summer 1988): 419–22.
Lee, James. "Li-Young Lee." *Bomb* 51 (Spring 1995): 10–13.
Marshall, Tod. "To Witness the Invisible: A Talk with Li-Young Lee." *Kenyon Review* 22.1 (Winter 2000): 129–47.
McGovern, Martin. "*Rose*." *Kenyon Review* 9.4 (Fall 1987): 134–35.

Mitchell, Roger. "*Rose.*" *Prairie Schooner* 63 (Fall 1989): 129–39.

Moyers, Bill. "Li-Young Lee." *The Language of Life: A Festival of Poets.* New York: Doubleday, 1995. 257–69.

Nelson, Marilyn. "*The City in Which I Love You.*" *Kenyon Review* 13 (Fall 1991): 214–26.

Nobles, Edward. "*Rose.*" *Southern Humanities Review* 22 (Spring 1988): 200–1.

Pinsker, Sanford. "*Rose.*" *Literary Review* 32 (Winter 1989): 256–62.

Rector, Liam. "*Rose.*" *Hudson Review* 41 (Summer 1988): 399–400.

Shefler, Laura. "Strength of the Spirit." *Pitt Magazine* 13.5 (December 1998): 30–35.

Zhou, Xiaojing. "Inheritance and Invention in Li-Young Lee's Poetry." *MELUS* 21.1 (Spring 1996): 113–32.

SHIRLEY GEOK-LIN LIM
(1944–   )

Nina Morgan

BIOGRAPHY

Shirley Geok-lin Lim, born on 27 December 1944 in Malacca, Malaysia, published her first poem in the *Malacca Times* at the tender age of ten; by eleven, she already knew that she would be a poet. Born the only daughter to parents whose middle-class lifestyle and marriage contained many disappointments that resulted in social displacement and a dissolution of the marriage, Lim was exposed early to the rough conjunction of different cultures and desires in a household of many voices and languages in which English and the trappings of Western culture dominated her younger years at home and a strong sense of isolation led her to her studies. Abandoned by their mother when they were children, Shirley (named by her father after Shirley Temple) and her brothers encountered years of desperation. In a childhood poised on the verge of starvation, physical as well as emotional, Lim discovered in literature a site beyond the confines of society, poverty, and chauvinism where she might create and assert her own identity, her own world.

Lim's colonial education continually challenged her sense of identity. As a child in a Catholic convent school, at the same time as she was severely and sometimes secretly punished, she was simultaneously often admired for her intelligence and vocality; thus she became, ironically, an outcast and a social leader. Her academic achievement was driven at least in part by a desire to escape her hunger, but excelling under the cultural imperialism of her British colonial education came at the price of losing a piece of the potential Malaysian intellectual within her. The first person ever to win the highest honors bestowed by the British to a student in English at the University of Malaya—a "First Class Honors"—Lim, moving to the United States on scholarships she won, earned her M.A. (1971) and Ph.D. (1973) from Brandeis University.

Crossing all genres, Lim is known for her prolific writing: she has over 100 scholarly articles and chapters published; her short stories and poems appear in over 65 anthologies and in as many journals worldwide. A much-sought-after speaker, Lim has given the keynote address or has been an invited lecturer to over 120 symposia or conferences. Likewise, she has given at least 150 readings of her work internationally, from Harvard, Princeton, the Massachusetts Institute of Technology, Wellesley, and the University of California to the University of Hong Kong, the National University of Singapore, the University of Århus, Denmark, the University of Munich, and the University of Malaya. In addition to her autobiography *Among the White Moon Faces: An Asian-American Memoir of Homelands* (1996; also published in Singapore in 1996 as *Among the White Moon Faces: Memoirs of a Nonya Feminist*), Lim has published numerous volumes of creative writing: *Crossing the Peninsula and Other Poems* (1980); *Another Country and Other Stories* (1982); *No Man's Grove and Other Poems* (1985); *Modern Secrets: New and Selected Poems* (1989); *Monsoon History: Selected Poems* (1994); *Life's Mysteries: The Best of Shirley Lim* (1995); *Two Dreams* (1997); and *What the Fortune Teller Didn't Say* (1998). Her books on literary criticism include *Nationalism and Literature: Literature in English from the Philippines and Singapore* (1993) and *Writing Southeast/Asia in English: Against the Grain* (1994). Among the nine texts that Lim has produced and that have shaped the field of Asian American studies are volumes of which she has either been the editor or coeditor: *The Forbidden Stitch: An Asian American Women's Anthology* (1989), *Approaches to Teaching Kingston's* The Woman Warrior (1991), and *Asian-American Literature: An Anthology* (2000). Her commitment to creative writing and also to the academy can be seen in three recent collections: *South-east Asian American Writing: Tilting the Continent* (1999), *Transnational Asia Pacific: Gender, Culture, and the Public Sphere* (1999), and *Power, Race, and Gender in Academe: Strangers in the Tower?* (2000).

The winner of numerous prestigious awards and prizes—the Commonwealth Poetry Prize in 1980 for her first book of poetry, *Crossing the Peninsula*, the American Book Award/Before Columbus Award in 1990, the American Book Award in 1997, National Endowment for the Humanities fellowships (1978, 1987), Mellon Fellowship (1983, 1987), Fulbright Scholar (1996), to list a few—Lim has also been the chair of Women's Studies at the University of California at Santa Barbara (1997–99). Her work in women's studies includes her service on the editorial boards of *Feminist Studies* and *Women's Studies Quarterly*, though these are not the only journals with which Lim (who also was the founding editor of *Asian America: Journal of Culture and the Arts*) is involved, as she maintains an advisory position on at least ten other journals. Currently a Chair Professor at the University of Hong Kong, Lim has just published her first novel, *Joss and Gold* (2001), and she is writing a second novel in addition to another critical study, *Informing the American Nation: Asia, Genre, and Gender*. Her many interviews worldwide (at least thirty, including *Asiaweek, South China Morning Post*, and in *The Diasporic Imagination: Identifying Asian-American Representations in America*) include radio and television interviews, most recently "Fooling with Words," a Public Broadcasting System (PBS) special with Bill Moyers (21 September 1999). A growing number of Web sites containing biographical information, short articles, and interviews with Lim indicates that her work is increasingly popular, accessible, and relevant.

MAJOR WORKS AND THEMES

Lim's is a poetry of precision. Tight lines, concrete yet lyrical images, and raw emotion characterize Lim's confrontations with the past and the places she has occupied in relation to her parents, her Asian heritage, and her Western world. With a hard-won feminist perspective, Lim's poetry indicts political and cultural forms of oppression while simultaneously maintaining a personal voice that nevertheless effects a transnational, transcultural perspective.

In *What the Fortune Teller Didn't Say* (1998), Lim offers a collection of new and some previously published poems but focuses her work thematically under the titles of three important poems: "What the Fortune Teller Didn't Say," "Lost Name Woman," and "Learning to Love America." The transition evident in this collection—from a child wrapped in the contradictions of tradition to a woman learning to live in the oftentimes empty spaces of an American life—yields emotions of nostalgia and loss, of compensation, acceptance, and self-understanding. In the final poem, "Self-Portrait," that self-understanding is always fragmented, always compromised, and always ambitious for more self. The fight for a sense of self, so often shaped in and against class, ethnic, racial, and gender-biased forces, is confronted in many of Lim's poems, where she often portrays the lives of other women whose stories are rarely given expression. Because of this constant move outward, Lim's work is not solipsistic; in an interview in *ARIEL* with Kirpal Singh, Lim expresses her wish to explore the complexities, contradictions, and ambivalences concerning all relationships.

In "Pantoun for Chinese Women," a poem that is among her better-known works, Lim portrays the horrible moment of female infanticide and shows us that culture not only defines much of our identity, its traditions and values can rob us of that same self as well. The constrained poetic form of the pantoun (alternately spelled "pantun" or "pantoum") is a rare genre of poem requiring strict adherence to line patterns and repetition. This distinct Malayan verse form demands great poetic skill and is consequently unusual and powerful; it is especially meaningful in this context of an indictment of a misogyny that repeats itself through the ages.

Issues of migration—from the spaces of home, country, and self—echo in all of Lim's five books of poetry. Whether leaving or returning, journeys are always ambivalent, fraught with contradiction, yet are the central metaphors of her work. The attempt to find the aesthetic in the postcolonial experience makes Lim's language and symbolism as confrontational with politics as it is inquisitive of the personal spaces we negotiate for ourselves.

The question of labor—of the work that one produces—is important in all of Lim's writing, for the labor of the writer creates a life space, a home: "Listening, and telling my own stories," she indicates at the end of her memoir *Among the White Moon Faces* that she is moving home. Locating the self in and through writing means creating and re-creating history, family, identity, power, and love against the losses of memory and its attendant absences.

CRITICAL RECEPTION

Attention to Lim's writing is increasingly international; not surprisingly, it is difficult to categorize her writing according to a national space. Laurel Means has argued that Lim's work has earned its "rightful place" in postcolonial Malaysian writing, yet Lim is clearly seen as an Asian American writer by many critics and students of literature. At the same time, she has been heralded as the "voice of the Commonwealth" and a representative poet of the Southeast Asian diaspora. Her creative writing has been the subject of many scholarly articles, book chapters, and conference papers. Her work is addressed in numerous dissertations as well. Placing her work within the Asian American canon, Zhou Xiaojing suggests that Lim's "characters' emotional and psychological state of being in-between two worlds is characteristic of the Asian-American experience. . . . [Her writing] is reminiscent of Diana Chang and Hisaye Yamamoto. . . . [In] her sensitivity to issues of colonialism, nationalism, race, ethnicity, gender, and class, Lim's writings are closely linked to the work of Theresa Hak Kyung Cha." In discussing *Monsoon History*, Brinda Bose observes that Lim "poignantly expresses . . . the complexities of diasporic identity" (1033), while Eddie Tay suggests that this same collection shows us how the "exile exists in a liminal state, neither here nor there," but, he adds, it is due to the "conditions of exile" that Lim reveals the processes through which one might "forge a new identity." Bernard Gadd argues that in *Modern Secrets* Lim is "at her best when she is most subjective" (533). In terms of literary theory, Laurel Means has offered a Bakhtinian analysis of Lim's poetry, and Nina Morgan has read Lim through Jacques Derrida's approaches to presence and absence. Since Lim won the Commonwealth Poetry Award for her first book of poetry, *Crossing the Peninsula* (1980), her five books of poetry have crossed into many countries and have been greeted with acclaim and welcome.

BIBLIOGRAPHY

Works by Shirley Geok-lin Lim

Poetry

Crossing the Peninsula and Other Poems. Kuala Lumpur: Heinemann Writing in Asia
    Series, 1980.
No Man's Grove and Other Poems. Singapore: National University of Singapore English
    Department Press, 1985.
Modern Secrets: New and Selected Poems. Sydney: Dangaroo Press, 1989.
Monsoon History: Selected Poems. London: Skoob Pacifica, 1994.
What the Fortune Teller Didn't Say. Albuquerque, NM: West End Press, 1998.

Autobiography

Among the White Moon Faces: An Asian-American Memoir of Homelands. New York:
    Feminist Press, 1996.
Among the White Moon Faces: Memoirs of a Nonya Feminist. Singapore: Times Books
    International, 1996.

Short Stories

Another Country and Other Stories. Singapore: Times Books International, 1982.
Life's Mysteries: The Best of Shirley Lim. Singapore: Times Books International, 1995.
Two Dreams. New York: Feminist Press, 1997.

Novel

Joss and Gold. New York: Feminist Press, 2001.

Studies of Shirley Geok-lin Lim

Bose, Brinda. Rev. of *Monsoon History*. *World Literature Today* 70.4 (Autumn 1996):
    1033.
Brewster, Anne. "Singaporean and Malaysian Women Poets, Local and Expatriate." *The
    Writer's Sense of the Contemporary: Papers in Southeast Asian and Australian
    Literature*. Ed. Bruce Bennett, Ee Tiang Hong, and Ron Shepherd. Nedlands:
    Centre for Studies in Australian Literature, University of Western Australia, 1982.
Eng, Ooi Boo. "Singapore/Malaysian Poetry: At Least Something and Less and More."
    Southeast Asian Review of English 2 (August 1981): 44–62.
Gadd, Bernard. Rev. of *Modern Secrets*. *World Literature Today* 64.3 (Summer 1990):
    533.
Means, Laurel. Introduction. *Monsoon History*. By Shirley Geok-lin Lim. London:
    Skoob, 1994.
———. "The 'Orient-ation' of Eden: Christian/Buddhist Dialogics in the Poetry of Shir-
    ley Geok-lin Lim." *Christianity and Literature* 43.2 (Winter 1994): 189–203.
Morgan, Nina. "Locating Shirley Geok-lin Lim, an Interview." *The Diasporic Imagina-
    tion: Identifying Asian-American Representations in America*. Ed. Somdatta Man-
    dal. New Delhi: Prestige Press, 2000.

————. "Locating the Space of Fiction: The Revenance of History in Chinese American Literature." *Remapping Chinese America: An International Conference on Chinese American Literature*. 11–12 June 1999. Taiwan: Academia Sinica, 1999.

Patke, Rajeev S. "Poetry and the Immigrant Experience." *Crossing Cultures: Essays on Literature and Culture of the Asia-Pacific*. London: Skoob, 1996.

Singh, Kirpal. "An Interview with Shirley Geok-lin Lim." *ARIEL: A Review of International English Literature* 30.4 (October 1999): 135–41.

Tay, Eddie. "An Orphanage of Mind." *The Poetry Billboard*. Available: http://poetry.s-one.net.sg/esyorphan.htm. Dec. 2000.

Tee, Kim Tong. "The Exile Writes Back: Reading Shirley Geok-lin Lim." *Remapping Chinese America: An International Conference on Chinese American Literature*. 11–12 June 1999. Taiwan: Academia Sinica, 1999.

Whitlock, Gillian. *The Intimate Empire: Reading Women's Autobiography*. London: Cassell Academic, 2000.

Zhou, Xiaojing. Introduction. *Two Dreams*. By Shirley Geok-lin Lim. New York: Feminist Press, 1997.

FATIMA LIM-WILSON
(1961–   )

Bill Clem

BIOGRAPHY

Fatima Lim-Wilson was born in Manila in 1961. After growing up and attending primary and secondary schools in the capital of the Philippines, Lim-Wilson went on to study English literature at the Ateneo de Manila University, from which she graduated with a bachelor of arts cum laude in 1982. Upon graduation, she traveled to Japan, where, as a scholar, she studied Japanese literature and language for one academic year. Continuing to travel and to pursue education, she moved to the United States, where, in 1985, she earned an M.A. in English literature with an emphasis in creative writing from the State University of New York at Buffalo. Lim-Wilson then moved back to the Philippines and from 1986 to 1987 worked as the confidential assistant to Rene Saguisag, the spokesperson for the Corazon Aquino administration. When Saguisag won a senate seat, Lim-Wilson served as his confidential assistant from 1987 to 1989. Finishing her time in the direct politics of her homeland, she traveled back to the United States to continue graduate education; she completed a Ph.D. in creative writing from the University of Denver in 1992. Just before finishing the doctorate, Lim-Wilson published her first collection, *Wandering Roots/From the Hothouse*, which won both the Philippine National Book Award and the Colorado Book Award.

As a notable success in the world of creative writing, Lim-Wilson has received numerous awards, scholarships, and grants worldwide, which include Palanca Awards (Philippines) and scholarships from the Universities of Vienna and Oslo, Oxford University, Uppsala University in Sweden, and University

College, Dublin. She has received writing scholarships and grants from Bread Loaf Writers' Conference, Duke University Writers' Workshop, the Seattle Arts Commission, the King County Arts Commission, Hedgebrook Residence (a writers' retreat for women), and the University of the Philippines Writers' Workshop. Her second book, *Crossing the Snow Bridge* (1995), won the Ohio State University Press/*The Journal* Award in Poetry. A former instructor in English at Shoreline Community College who has neither written nor published since her second book, Lim-Wilson lives in Seattle with her husband and children.

MAJOR WORKS AND THEMES

As an international traveler and well-educated woman, Fatima Lim-Wilson uses the world and its multifarious machinations as well as her personal life and experiences to create her poetry. She can be understood as a poet who finds no division between the personal and the political; in fact, she eschews such an arbitrary distinction and fashions poems that speak on all subjects: politics, revolutions, imperialism, colonialism, love, family, the body, and sex. While writing on all these issues, Lim-Wilson uses poetic forms from the English tradition as well as free-verse lines and wholly organic forms to produce her art.

Wandering Roots/From the Hothouse, Lim-Wilson's first collection, contains poems written from 1978 to 1989 and displays the poet's growing talent: here the reader first reads and hears Lim-Wilson's commitment to personal exploration and her concern with international problems and situations. "Upon My Father's Calligraphy" and "Father, in Old Town, Stockholm," open the collection; as free-verse lyrics, they explore the young speaker's thoughts on what she and her siblings might have understood had they known that their father, too, wrote poetry; his distance from them, through both time and space, disconcerts the poet at first glance but brings her eventually to an understanding that gender constructions and silence can cause great conflict and misunderstanding.

Relations between men and women, physically brutal or passionately intimate, constitute the bulk of Lim-Wilson's lines in this first collection. The moving poem "Slave Woman of Tarlac, Tarlac" brings to life the horror of a woman returning to the Philippines from Kuwait after enduring rape and torture at the hands of a soldier. Although the speaker attempts to console and protect the woman, she is unable to do so because the woman retreats into herself, unable to think of anything other than the brutality inflicted upon her. While "Minister's Wife" is concerned with the emotions of the minister, it tells of the ways in which the minister cannot bear to live after the death of his wife, a woman who functioned as a soul mate to her husband and whom all the fishermen desired.

Tackling the directly political to expose the machinations of evil, Lim-Wilson often writes of the consequences produced by greed and war. In "Another Coup," the poet plays with the sonnet, using only thirteen lines and refusing strict meter, to present to the reader the poet's inability to make sense of the happenings of war. The poem opens with "A few dead and a few missing," a

line designed to stun the reader. The casual line, no doubt spoken condescend-
ingly by someone unaffected by the conflict, is refuted throughout the poem; it
is never rhymed in any way, while other lines are given offhand feminine
rhymed statuses. These lines countermand the flippancy of the first line as they
display the many horrible casualties war forces upon its innocent victims. The
reader is presented with such images so that she or he is shocked: each horrific
image comes in a little package (one or two to a line) of disorder and freakish-
ness: fish with great bones, the president speaking French, gunfire surrounding
nationalism, and music made from murder. The speaker of the first line is re-
fused his right to speak, and the images aggregate to overwhelm his assertion.
Using the sonnet in this masterful way refuses to sing and glorify violence; it
refuses to accept the incredulity imperialism serves.

Lim-Wilson's second collection, *Crossing the Snow Bridge*, continues the
themes and concerns present in the first collection, but its poems show the reader
a more mature and sophisticated poet. The poet seems to work with greater ease
in both traditional forms and free-verse/organic writing in this collection. A
notable example of her ability to work in form is "Rice and Fish Sonnet."
Although she breaks the rules of strict prosody, Lim-Wilson uses the form and
rhyme of an English or Shakespearean sonnet to speak to her love; the content
of the poem, however, subverts the intention of the form as it is traditionally
understood. This poem is not from a man to his ladylove; rather, a woman
speaks to her love, presumably her husband. As she speaks to him, she critiques
American—read here capitalist and Anglo-American—values of eating, everyday life, community, and child rearing.

The poem opens as the poet addresses her love and recalls a memory, one of
an enjoyable meal spent together before lovemaking. The atmosphere changes
immediately in the first line as she recalls that the room is lamplit. Although
they are eating "authentic" food, they eat it in a restaurant in the United States,
the location the reader presumes from the second stanza, in which the persona
laments the drudgery of capitalist machinery, machinery that makes life more
easily manageable. In such a place, bones are thrown away—an ominous sign
of the waste produced by such economics.

The third quatrain offers a direct comparison of two cultures, the Filipino
culture from which the poet comes and the American culture from which her
love comes. Filipino culture is communal, natural, healthy, and preferred here,
while American culture is lonely, unnatural, unhealthy, and ultimately disap-
pointing with its "lukewarm surprise." In the couplet, the poet takes all this into
consideration and decides that love might help to mollify the situation. This
little song creates a brilliant exposé on tradition and innovation as it maps the
terrain of an immigrant's thoughts on culture, politics, and love.

Other poems in this award-winning collection also sing of the poet's concerns
and anxieties: "Alphabet Soup, or Mimicry as a Second Language" and "Upon
Overhearing Tagalog" seek to understand the necessity and dangers of imperialism and language; "Playing Mahjong with My Father's Ghost" and "Sisters"

explore family and personal issues; and "Dreaming Magellan" and "Luzviminda, or Filipinas Make Such Good Maids" decry the ignorance of history and the subjugation of women under patriarchy, respectively.

CRITICAL RECEPTION

Aside from a couple of reviews and advance praise notices from publishers, Fatima Lim-Wilson's poetry has not received the attention it deserves. Even though many of the poems originally appeared in well-known and respected journals such as *Asian American Pacific Journal*, the *Kenyon Review*, the *Massachusetts Review*, and *Poetry*, the only studies of her work come from the introduction to her first collection and from reviews in smaller journals.

In the introduction to *Wandering Roots/From the Hothouse*, Isagani R. Cruz hails Lim-Wilson as "the most accomplished young Filipino poet of our time" because "[s]he has the ability to catch the exact nuance, the precise word, even the perfect sound, in her attempts to depict her personal, but always universal, experience" (viii). The only two reviews of Lim-Wilson's second book, *Crossing the Snow Bridge*, find merit in the collection. Angela Sorby in the *Chicago Review* believes that Lim-Wilson's poems "are dangerous, moving, living things . . . poems that arise from truly intense and fascinating encounters with the forces of imperialism and cultural dislocation—not to mention weddings, grandparents, and ghosts" (89). Paul Guest, writing for the *Crab Orchard Review*, finds that "the disjuncture of experience and language creates poems that seek to arrive at moments of magic, souls flaming, voices of broken glass that are filigreed in sweeps of violent lyricism" (268). Readers must hope that, upon the publication of this reference volume, critics will take notice of this fine poet and her work and begin to explore it.

BIBLIOGRAPHY

Works by Fatima Lim-Wilson

Wandering Roots/From the Hothouse. Manila: Anvil Publishing, 1991.
Crossing the Snow Bridge. Columbus: Ohio State University Press, 1995.

Studies of Fatima Lim-Wilson

Cruz, Isagani R. Introduction. *Wandering Roots/From the Hothouse*. Manila: Anvil Publishing, 1991. viii–x.
Guest, Paul. Rev. of *Crossing the Snow Bridge*. *Crab Orchard Review* 3.2 (1998): 267–68.
Sorby, Angela. Rev. of *Crossing the Snow Bridge*. *Chicago Review* 42.1 (1996): 88–89.

WING TEK LUM
(1946–)

Lavonne Leong

BIOGRAPHY

The youngest of three sons, Wing Tek Lum was born in Honolulu, Hawaii, on 11 November 1946 to second-generation Chinese American parents. His mother's early death while Lum was still in high school is the subject of some of his most emotionally challenging poetry. Lum continued on to Brown University in Providence, Rhode Island, where he majored in engineering. His first attempts at poetry writing led him to creative-writing courses at Brown and, eventually, the editorship of the university's literary magazine. He received his bachelor's degree in 1969 and moved from Providence to New York City.

One year later, Lum received the prestigious Poetry Center Award (now known as the Discovery/The Nation Award), given every year to four promising poets who have not yet published a collection. Lum spent three years in New York, where he studied at the Union Theological Seminary, eventually taking a master's degree in divinity in 1973. During this time, he also worked for the Chinese Youth Council in Manhattan's Chinatown as a social worker. Lum's years in New York brought him into contact with Frank Chin, an Asian American writer whose outspoken opinions on Asian American literature would influence Lum's literary work profoundly.

Although Lum's parents had spoken some Cantonese at home, he had never learned it; this, in turn, limited both his work and his cultural interactions. In 1973, Lum moved from New York to Hong Kong to learn Cantonese. He also continued his community work, this time for the Hong Kong Society for the Deaf. In Hong Kong, Lum found new perspectives on old themes: language, authenticity, and cultural boundaries. In Hong Kong's English-language book-shops, he discovered the work of the late-fourth-century poet T'ao Ch'ien (Tao Yuanming), to whom, along with Frank Chin, *Expounding the Doubtful Points* (1987) is dedicated. The book received a 1988 American Book Award from the Before Columbus Foundation and an Outstanding Book Award from the Association for Asian American Studies (AAAS). Although *Expounding the Doubtful Points* is Lum's only solo collection to date, he has continued to publish in literary venues.

Lum married in Hong Kong and in 1976 returned to Honolulu to join his family's real-estate firm, where he lives with his wife and daughter. He is closely involved with Hawaii's literary community and has been called "one of the mainstays of Hawaii's East-West culture" (Garcia 36). Wing Tek Lum is presently at work upon a series of poems inspired by photographic and documentary records of the Rape of Nanking.

MAJOR WORKS AND THEMES

Lum's best-known work is "Minority Poem," in which the speaker comments bitterly on the phrase "American as apple pie" and suggests that minorities in America can only fit into that perky simile as the discarded parts of the apple—the peelings. It is easy, as anthologies have done, to portray Lum as a poet whose simple advocacy of separatism takes precedence over all other concerns.

Lum's approaches, however, are considerably more varied. Bitterness at the pressure to become "assimilated" (which he describes, in another well-known poem, "Terms of Assimilation" [*Expounding* 68] as becoming "an ass," "or worse, a sterile" hybrid, neither one thing nor the other) characterizes some of Lum's early work, but he also presents a "dream of America" in "Chinese Hot Pot," the poem that concludes *Expounding the Doubtful Points*, as a celebration of both separate identity and shared experience. The tension in Lum's work often stems from his exploration of the profound complications of identity faced by successive generations of Asian Americans. The problem Lum constructs is less often how to keep one's identity pure and separate than how to define, and make fertile, one's already-hybrid social and cultural self.

The Chinese American speaker in "Taking Her to the Open Market" (*Expounding* 81) is anxious to prove his authentic Chineseness to his Chinese companion. He denigrates American values and shows his respect for the old ways, in this case his appreciation of the freshness of the fish at the market. His friend is not impressed; the fish is dead, and no matter how recently it was killed, it is not fresh to her "Hong Kong eyes." "Discovering That You Speak Cantonese" (*Expounding* 82) is another work poised between disdain for the inauthentic and the fear of being inauthentic oneself. This poem illustrates the constant double vision of the hybrid identity and the difficulty of guarding that which the speaker is never sure is really his. The poem's speaker, who learned Cantonese as a second language, pities the linguistic limitations of the poem's much less skilled addressee. At the same time, the speaker is aware that this must be how his wife, a native Cantonese speaker, feels while speaking Chinese to him.

Lum's poetry is as often about empathy as it is about irreconcilable difference, from the wife's voice in "A Wife Reminisces" to the sobering reminder in "Chinese New Year," written during the Vietnam War, that "for others this is Tet." "Discovering That You Speak Cantonese" creates a complex double empathy with both the inadequate "you" and the speaker's fluently speaking wife. Lum's work is family and community oriented and evolves with the events in his life: the lives and deaths of his parents, his marriage, the birth of his daughter. Several of his poems have been occasioned by other Asian poetry, notably "Urban Love Songs," inspired by Tzu Yeh, and "Poems after Wang Wei." He has also published *What the Kite Thinks*, a work written with three other poets, based on the Japanese verse form *renshi*, in which a cycle of poems is written, each poem using the last line of the previous poem as the first line of the next poem.

CRITICAL RECEPTION

When Chinese American writers are discussed in print, Wing Tek Lum is frequently mentioned. His poems have been widely anthologized and are taught in universities across America. However, Lum's work has received comparatively little critical and scholarly attention, perhaps for the same reason that makes his poems so readily teachable: his immediate accessibility.

Critics sometimes seem disappointed with the dearth of verbal pyrotechnics in Lum's approach. His work has been called "flat and didactic" (Heckathorn 138), a charge Lum makes against himself—and humorously refutes—in "Expounding the Doubtful Points." The poem's speaker becomes depressed at the thought of the "razzle dazzle" in other poets' work, but remembers a friend's basketball metaphor: some people pay so much attention to "fancy dribbling" that they forget to shoot the ball into the basket.

Academic evaluations of Lum's work tend to focus on the relationship of his cultural heritage to his poetry. Gary Balfantz and John Wat have examined the relationship of Lum's "Urban Love Songs" (subtitled "After Tzu Yeh") to Tzu Yeh's original work, written during the fourth century and employing the Chinese *wu-yen shih* form, whose quatrains are composed of five-syllable lines. Wat and Balfantz enumerate some of the more complicated aspects of Lum's interaction with the form and content of Tzu Yeh's work: Tzu Yeh's uncertain, possibly even plural, identity and Lum's reading of Tzu Yeh through an English translation.

Gayle K. Fujita-Sato's "The Island Influence on Chinese American Writers: Wing Tek Lum, Darrell H.Y. Lum, and Eric Chock" locates Lum in an even more precise cultural nexus, the intersection of Lum's Chinese American identity with his identity as a resident of Hawaii. Whereas Sato considers these as separate issues of identity, Pat Matsueda melds them together in her review of

Expounding the Doubtful Points: "Lum's culture is that of China and his society that of America" (6). Matsueda explores the effects of Lum's cultural identity on his poetic praxis, finding that his cultural "separatism" is not so much political as "linguistic, cultural, psychological—a separatism that requires constant vigilance of the heart and mind, which are where identity resides and is vulnerable" (7).

BIBLIOGRAPHY

Works by Wing Tek Lum

Poetry

Expounding the Doubtful Points. Honolulu: Bamboo Ridge Press, 1987.
With Makoto Ooka, Joseph Stanton, and Jean Yamasaki Toyama. *What the Kite Thinks: A Linked Poem*. Ed. Lucy Lower. Honolulu: Summer Session, University of Hawaii at Manoa. 1994.

Uncollected Work

"Kindergarten." *Bamboo Ridge* 36 (Fall 1987): 18–19.
"Poet." *Bamboo Ridge* 36 (Fall 1987): 16–17.
"And We Kept on Chatting." *Chaminade Literary Review* 1.2 (Spring 1988): 60.
"Coloring a Rainbow." *Chaminade Literary Review* 1.2 (Spring 1988): 58–59.
"This Visit." *Chaminade Literary Review* 1.2 (Spring 1988): 61.
"Filial Thoughts." *Bamboo Ridge* 44 (Fall 1989): 26.
"An Image of the Good Times." *Bamboo Ridge* 44 (Fall 1989): 24–25.
"Poetic License." *Bamboo Ridge* 45 (Winter 1989): 19.
"This Tree You Told Us Stories Of." *Zyzzyva* 6.1 (Spring 1990): 85–86.
"The Butcher." *Bamboo Ridge* 52 (Fall 1991): 83–86.
"At Middle Age." *Hawaii Review* 17.37.1 (Spring 1993): 44–45.
"I Should Have Known." *Hawaii Review* 17.37.1 (Spring 1993): 46.
"Night Blooming Cereus." *Hawaii Review* 17.37.1 (Spring 1993): 47.
"A Daughter of the Mountains." *Bamboo Ridge* 57 (Winter 1993): 56–59.
"Childhood Memories." *Bamboo Ridge* 60 (Winter 1994): 106–7.
"This Secret Charge." *Bamboo Ridge* 60 (Winter 1994): 102–3.
"The Youngest Child." *Bamboo Ridge* 60 (Winter 1994): 104–5.
"The Caretaker." *Bamboo Ridge* 63/64 (Summer/Fall 1994): 31–32.
"The Last Oldtimers." *Bamboo Ridge* 63/64 (Summer/Fall 1994): 30.
"Poems after Wang Wei" ("Empty Ridge," "Returning Home," "Leaving the Island," "Lapu-Lapu in New York," "New York"). *Bamboo Ridge* 69 (Spring 1996): 205–7.
"On a Tour Bus in Beijing." *Asian Pacific American Journal* 5.2 (Fall/Winter 1996): 17.
"Before the Fire." *Asian Pacific American Journal* 6.1 (Spring/Summer 1997): 133.
"Childhood Memories." *Bamboo Ridge* 72 (Spring 1998): 314.
"An Image of the Good Times." *Bamboo Ridge* 72 (Spring 1998): 75–76.
"Kids Do Things They Don't Mean." *Bamboo Ridge* 72 (Spring 1998): 315.

"A Wife Reminisces." *Bamboo Ridge* 72 (Spring 1998): 237–40.
"This Landscaped Home." *Bamboo Ridge* 75 (Spring 1999): 136–38.

Prose

"Matrices, Paradoxes, and Personal Passions." *Bamboo Ridge* 47 (Summer 1990): 5–16.

Studies of Wing Tek Lum

Balfantz, Gary L., and John H.Y. Wat. "Performing a Chinese-American Cultural Identity: Wing Tek Lum's 'Urban Love Songs.' " *Why Don't You Talk Right? Multicultural Communication Perspectives.* Ed. Aprele Elliott. Dubuque, IA: Kendall/Hunt, 1992. 213–29.

Fujita-Sato, Gayle K. "The Island Influence on Chinese American Writers: Wing Tek Lum, Darrell H.Y. Lum, and Eric Chock." *Amerasia* 16.2 (1990): 17–33.

Garcia, Roger. "Coming to Terms." *Asiaweek* [Hong Kong] 17 June 1988: 36.

Hai-Jew, Shalin. "Wing Tek Lum: 'It Takes a Kind of Bravery to Be Ordinary.' " *International Examiner* [Seattle] 6 January 1988: 9.

Heckathorn, John. "Deck the Shelves." *Honolulu Magazine* December 1987: 138–40.

Lum, Grande. "A Slice of Time with Poet Wing Tek Lum." *East/West News* 14 January 1988: 7.

Matsueda, Pat. "The Everyday World: Wing Tek Lum's *Expounding the Doubtful Points.* " *Literary Arts Hawaii* 85 (Summer 1987): 6–8.

Muromoto, Wayne. "Wing Tek Lum." *Hawaii Herald* 6 May 1988: 10.

Radigan, John. "Across Time and Lands." Rev. of *Expounding the Doubtful Points*, by Wing Tek Lum, *River River*, by Arthur Sze, and *Until the Morning After: Collected Poems*, by Kofi Awoonor. *Contact II* 10.59–61 (Spring 1991): 96–97.

Rodrigues, Johnette. "Probing Poetry." *New Paper* 9–16 March 1988: 8.

Shan, Te-hsing. "*Expounding the Doubtful Points*: Border-Crossings and Cultural Re-creation in Wing Tek Lum's Poems." *Remapping Chinese America: An International Conference on Chinese American Literature.* 11–12 June 1999. Taiwan: Institute of European and American Studies, Academia Sinica. 1–26.

———. "An Interview with Wing Tek Lum." *Chung-Wai Literary Monthly* 27.2 (July 1998): 139–68.

Yim, Susan. "A Window to the Past." *Honolulu Advertiser* 18 November 1987: B1+.

Yuen, Shirley Mark. "Review." *Asian American Resource Workshop Newsletter* April 1988: 9+.

PAT MATSUEDA
(1952–   )

Lavonne Leong

BIOGRAPHY

Patricia Tomoko Matsueda was born on 20 August 1952 in Fukuoka, Japan, the first of two daughters of a Japanese American serviceman and a Japanese national. Her parents divorced several years later, in part because of her father's alcoholism. At the age of seven, she immigrated to the United States with her mother and sister, settling with Matsueda's father's extended family in Honolulu, Hawaii. Matsueda has never returned to Japan.

Matsueda entered the University of Hawaii as a student of environmental studies, but changed her major to English literature with a concentration in visual arts. Her literary life began at the university under the mentorship of Frank Stewart, a nature writer and teacher whom she considers a major literary influence. From 1977 to 1980, Matsueda edited the *Hawaii Literary Arts Council Newsletter*, a position that brought her into contact with a diverse range of Hawaii writers. In 1981, she went on to found and serve as editor-in-chief of the *Paper*, one of Hawaii's early literary periodicals, which ran for six years and fourteen issues.

Matsueda's first published poem appeared in the first issue of *Bamboo Ridge*, a literary periodical founded to celebrate the controversial 1978 "Talk Story" conference in Honolulu. Matsueda began to publish in other venues, *Floating Island* and the *Hawai'i Review* among them. These and other poems were collected in 1983 in her first volume of poetry, *X*, followed two years later by *The Fish Catcher*. Her accumulating body of work won her Hawaii's Elliot Cades Award for an emerging writer in 1988. Since then, Matsueda's career has shifted in focus from creative to editorial activities. She has been a copyeditor of academic texts for Houghton Mifflin since 1990 and, since 1992, has been the managing editor of *Mānoa: A Pacific Journal for International Writing*, a literary magazine whose mission is to introduce an Asian and Pacific Rim–focused internationalism into American letters. In early 1999, Matsueda founded her second literary periodical, an online journal called *Living Waters*. After a long hiatus, she has also recently begun to write poetry again. She is currently collecting poems for another volume of poetry, *The Healing Kingdom*. Pat Matsueda lives in Honolulu with her sister, Kathy.

MAJOR WORKS AND THEMES

There is no "take-home message" in Pat Matsueda's poetry. The poems in her two published books, *X* (1983) and *The Fish Catcher* (1985), present, not a viewpoint on Asian America, but a description of its complicated, private interior. Her work illustrates the spiritual journey of the exile who is no longer sure where home is. Borders preoccupy Matsueda's work: between innocence and knowledge, dream and reality, illness and wellness, Japan and America. In her poetry, it is often hard to cross these borders more than once, but it is even more difficult to find out where it was you wanted to be in the first place.

What distinguishes Matsueda's work is her deep ambivalence. She presents dichotomies in which neither state of being is clearly preferable to the other. In "Poem for Norman," the speaker attends a children's birthday party and muses on the "grief we foresee" for the children whose innocence "blazes" on their skin. Yet in Matsueda's work, innocence can also connote the capacity for thoughtless injury. One example of this reversal is "Shika (Deer) Shrine" (*TFC* 8), in which the speaker remembers following her father, "oblivious" to the pain he was causing her mother. "Point of Recovery" (*X*; the collection is unpaginated) presents another redistribution of meaning, one in which illness is familiar, and wellness is a frightening, unexplored territory: "You had to be ill, you can't help recovering."

Matsueda depicts existence as a perilous balancing act between these kinds of dichotomies in "Heir to the High Wire" (*TFC* 12–14). She imagines herself into the lives of the tightrope-walking circus family, the Flying Wallendas. High-wire walking is dangerous, but addictive—and, as an inheritance passed down from father to son, inescapable. The speaker likens giving up the wire to asking the body "to forget love." Matsueda frequently pairs precise, intensely visual observations of light and color with disturbing descriptions of abandonment, illness, or death. A single visual image, or a single metaphor, may serve as a focus for the speaker's state of mind. In "Point of Recovery," it is the "sickly orange and brown tiles" on the floor. "The Fish Catcher" (*TFC* 29) offers an extended metaphor on the blank page as "an aquarium filled with milk." In "The Mermaid" (*TFC* 18), she pairs a dying hospital patient's shrinking consciousness with his reduced physical life; he "swallow[s] the image of the room like a pill."

Matsueda's poems about artwork are among her most intellectually subtle. "Images of Balzac Cast by Rodin" presents a complex syntax of creation: a poet writing about a photograph of a sculpture of a novelist whose final casting the sculptor never authorized. This work explores the concepts of artistic creation and "final" work and questions the stability of its own subject. Although Matsueda's subject matter is diverse, her poems pose questions to which there is no single or ideal resolution, only a range of partial answers.

CRITICAL RECEPTION

Matsueda published most of her quiet, apolitical poetry before Asian American issues became a matter for academic discussion. Apart from an article from the *Georgia Review*, which praised the relationship of the visual poems on the page of *The Fish Catcher* to their carefully written content, where "physical book and poetic text flow into each other in subtle and convincing ways" (Carter 538), her work has received little academic attention.

BIBLIOGRAPHY

Works by Pat Matsueda

Poetry

X. Honolulu: Communica Press, 1983.
The Fish Catcher. Honolulu: Petronium Press, 1985.

Uncollected Poetry

"A Return." *Hawaii Review* 8 (Fall 1978): 71.
"Discontent." *Hapa* 1 (1981): 33–34.
"Gray Promises." *Hapa* 1 (1981): 32.
"Joanie Rebel." *Hapa* 1 (1981): 31.
"Samurai." *Hapa* 2 (1982): 16–17.
"Inflamed." *Hawaii Review* 16 (Fall 1984): 27.
"The Healing Kingdom." *Kanyaku Imin: A Hundred Years of Japanese Life in Hawaii*. Ed. Leonard Lueras. Honolulu: International Savings and Loan Association, 1985. 129.
"Children." *Literary Arts Hawaii* 85 (Summer 1987): 26.
"I Have a Puzzle to Which the Answer Cannot Be Imagined." *Literary Arts Hawaii* 88/89 (Spring/Summer 1988): 12.
"Kao-Mise." *Literary Arts Hawaii* 88/89 (Spring/Summer 1988): 10.
"The Rodin Book." *Floating Island* 4 (1989): 23.
From "The People Were Stories." *Mānoa: A Pacific Journal of International Writing* 1.1–2 (Spring/Fall 1989): 176–78.
"Fiction." *Mānoa: A Pacific Journal of International Writing* 3.1 (Spring 1991): 123–24.

Autobiographical Article

"Old Neighborhoods." *Hawaii Herald* 2 January 1981: 6.

Book Reviews

Rev. of *Fierce Meadows*, by Tony Quagliano. *Hapa* 2 (1982): 122–26.
Rev. of *Expounding the Doubtful Points*, by Wing Tek Lum. *Literary Arts Hawaii* 85
    (Summer 1987): 6–8.

Studies of Pat Matsueda

Carter, Jared. "Poetry Chapbooks: Back to the Basics." *Georgia Review* 40.2 (Summer
    1986): 532–47.
Ronck, Ronn. "Farewell to the *Paper*." *Literary Arts Hawaii* 83 (New Year 1987): 4–6.

JANICE MIRIKITANI
(1941–   )

Tamiko Nimura

BIOGRAPHY

In a recent interview, Japanese American poet Janice Mirikitani acknowledged the inextricable connections between the "personal" and the "political" in her life: "I know that I cannot yet separate what has happened to me from what's happening in the world. So, if you talk about my activism not being separated from the poetry, that's true" (Interview with Hong 126–27). Indeed, her work corroborates her statement. A foundational figure of Asian American literature, Mirikitani has been recognized for her committed activism and her impassioned writings for several decades.

Janice Mirikitani was born on 5 February 1941 in Stockton, California, to Shigemi and Ted Mirikitani. While she was still an infant, the U.S. government incarcerated her family in Rohwer, Arkansas. Though she was too young at the time to remember details of camp life, the wartime incarceration haunts much of her poetry. After the war, her family moved to Chicago, where her parents divorced. She and her mother then moved back to Petaluma, California, in order to be closer to her mother's family. It was primarily on that isolated chicken farm in Petaluma, surrounded by family, that Mirikitani experienced the second major trauma that would indelibly mark her life. From age eight to age sixteen, relatives and family friends molested her sexually almost daily ("Rebirth" 67). Though she also remembers being molested in Chicago at age five, her strongest memories surround ages eight to sixteen (e-mail). Her coerced silence and her mother's complicit silence only intensified her senses of vulnerability and alienation. During these painful years, it was her grandmother's unconditional love that kept her from suicide (McManis, n.p.). Mirikitani has been courageously outspoken about these years of sexual abuse in her poetry ("Insect Collection," "Zipper," "You Turned Your Head," "Where Bodies Are Buried") and in her longest autobiographical piece ("Rebirth: Janice's Story," in Reverend Cecil Williams's book *No Hiding Place*). Many years later, dealing with her own issues of recovery, she edited an anthology of writings by incest survivors entitled *Watch Out! We're Talking* (1993). Since she saw education as "her means of escape . . . from that isolated and cruel farm" ("Rebirth" 68), she was determined to excel in school.

As Mirikitani depicts in "Rebirth" and the poem "Yea. She Knows," the 1960s began and ended in a time of political and personal tumult for her. She attended college at UCLA, where she received her bachelor of arts degree. At UCLA, she struggled with her ethnic identity; she "pursued being white and middle-class . . . a beauty queen, a cheerleader, all the things that [she] thought were part of the American dream" ("Rebirth" 68). Several of her poems (for example, "Recipe") detail the torturous extent of her struggle to be white: bleaching her face, taping her eyelids. After Mirikitani received her teaching credential in 1963 from the University of California at Berkeley, she taught English, speech, and dance for the Contra Costa School District for a year. Since she spoke about "controversial" subjects such as war, peace, abortion, and birth control, she was not asked to continue teaching ("Rebirth" 68). She then found work as an administrative assistant at Glide Memorial Church in San Francisco, an institution that would soon become the cornerstone of her activist career.

In Mirikitani's numerous biographical accounts, little information can be found about her first marriage in 1966, save that it ended in divorce. From that marriage, however, came Mirikitani's only daughter, Tianne Tsukiko Miller, who was born in 1967. She then returned to school at San Francisco State University for graduate studies in creative writing. There the Third World Liberation Front was demanding an ethnic studies department. By the time she had discontinued her graduate school classes, she and others in the Asian American Political Alliance had added their voices to the struggle. Thus inspired with coalitional energies and activities from the strike, Mirikitani and other individual artists of color formed alliances during the late 1960s and early 1970s. The alliances became a literary and arts collective, Third World Communications, with which she became the editor of the first Asian American literary magazine, *Aion* (1970–71). Editorial work kept her busy for several years; she then edited two anthologies with Third World Communications: *Third World Women* (1972) and *Time to Greez! Incantations from the Third World* (1975). In the late 1970s, Mirikitani became the project director of the landmark collection *Ayumi: A Japanese American Anthology* (1980). Edited by Mirikitani and a committee of activist artists, the collection contains prose, poetry, and artwork from four generations of Japanese Americans.

Activist work at Glide Memorial Church has now occupied Mirikitani for several decades. Glide is located in the Tenderloin district, one of San Francisco's most poverty-stricken and crime-ridden areas. In 1969, she became program director of Glide's forty-two outreach programs and president of Glide's foundation in 1982, a position she has occupied ever since. Under the leadership of Mirikitani and the Reverend Cecil Williams, it now has fifty-two outreach programs for battered women, homeless people, drug addicts, incest survivors, runaway children, and impoverished people (Zia 264). She has edited two anthologies that directly involve her work at Glide: *I Have Something to Say about This Big Trouble: Children of the Tenderloin Speak Out* (1989) (about the crack-cocaine crisis) and *Watch Out! We're Talking* (1993). Glide's "circles of recovery" (combined with the intervention of family and friends) enabled Mirikitani to come to terms with the years of sexual abuse and her close encounter with alcoholism. Several poems in her most recent collection, *We, the Dangerous* (1995), portray women from these circles ("Where Bodies Are Buried," "Jane," "Lydia"). In 1982, Mirikitani married the Reverend Cecil Williams, Glide's spiritual leader. Throughout her poetic career, she has written several poems about this challenging and nurturing partnership ("A Song for You," "Soul Food," "It Isn't Easy," "What Matters," and the moving "War of the Body"). In 1999, Glide opened the Janice Mirikitani Glide Family, Youth, and Childcare Building named in her honor.

Mirikitani has won numerous awards for her activism and poetry from Asian American community organizations, the California State Assembly, San Francisco State, and the city of San Francisco. Her legacy of activism and advocacy for the disenfranchised continues, as does her struggle against complacency. She currently lives in San Francisco, where she continues her work with Glide. In January 2000, she was named the second poet laureate of San Francisco; later that year, she was inducted as one of the first four Asian American writers into the New Asian American Literary Archives Library at the University of California at Los Angeles. She is also working on another poetry collection.

MAJOR WORKS AND THEMES

In addition to editing anthologies and publishing poems in various journals and anthologies, Mirikitani has published three collections of her writing: *Awake in the River* (1978), *Shedding Silence: Poetry and Prose* (1987), and *We, the Dangerous: New and Selected Poems* (1995). Stylistically, her work often recalls the protest literary tradition of the 1960s and the work of other women writers of color, such as Ntozake Shange, Sonia Sanchez, or Nikki Giovanni. Like Shange and Giovanni, she has written about controversial subjects. Mirikitani often breaks her poems into two columns of text in a call-and-response fashion; this technique allows her to encompass multiple voices and tonalities. Her ability to enter into others' voices indicates the profound extent of her poetic compassion.

Mirikitani's poetry insists on interconnections between her primary themes: the debilitating effects of silence; protests against stereotypes of Asian American women; the connections between generations of women; the fraught relationship between sex and violence; wars and their aftermath; and occasions for mourning. On the printed page, the echoes among these themes may sometimes appear repetitive; furthermore, lines and stanzas from certain poems reappear in other poems (for example, she includes the poem "Recipe" in a later poem, "Beauty Contest"). However, it should be emphasized that Mirikitani has billed herself as a "performance poet"; verbal repetition affects live audiences differently than readers. Many of her poems insist on an actual voice speaking them aloud. Moreover, the sheer passionate force of Mirikitani's poetry has moved audiences, both at home and abroad.

For almost forty years, many of the nisei (second-generation Japanese Americans) maintained a silence about their wartime incarceration. As a result of the "yellow power" movements in the 1960s, many sansei (third-generation Japanese Americans) sought to claim their ethnic identity. Part of this claiming included finding information and testimony about the wartime incarceration. Since the Asian American movement profoundly influenced Mirikitani's sense of ethnic identity during the 1960s, her poetry is characteristic of this quest to break silence. Several of her poems reveal a frustration with her nisei mother's reticence surrounding the Japanese Americans' wartime incarceration. In "Lullabye," a sansei daughter waits for her nisei mother to talk about the camps and is thus in limbo, "waiting for the birth of [her] mother" (*Awake* n.p.). Mirikitani repeats the word "silence" in so many poems that it becomes, peculiarly and wonderfully, a word that is no longer silent.

One of Mirikitani's most powerful portrayals of healing speech, however, is her well-known poem "Breaking Silence." As part of the Japanese American redress movement in 1981, the Wartime Relocation and Internment of Japanese American Civilians hearings evoked a flood of testimony from nisei internees. Many of the nisei had never spoken about the camp experience at all, much less to their sansei children. Incorporating her mother's testimony during these hearings into her poem, Mirikitani ends with a compassionate and triumphant blend of her mother's voice and her own. For Mirikitani, healing and wholeness necessitate examining the "cracks and fissures" of history. Rather than resting on an easily attained wholeness, she insists on embracing both pain and joy.

The 1960s movements for ethnic consciousness also kindled in Mirikitani a need to refute stereotypes of Asian American women. In "Who Is Singing This Song?" she aims to be a "saboteur of stereotypes" (*Shedding* 105). Poems such as "Salad," "Ms.," "Slaying Dragon Ladies," and "American Geisha" protest images of Asian American women as foreign ("oriental") enigmas, passive victims, geisha girls, sex slaves, or expert masseuses. She deconstructs these racist images in poems like "We, the Dangerous." Here Mirikitani subverts the Orientalist myths of "strange scents" and sensual masseuses. Instead, she substitutes images of Asian American female bodies as sites of transnational labor: prostitution ("the secret bed"), sweatshop labor, laundry women. Asian American women, the poem insists, are not purely objects of male sexual fantasy. Rather, they take care of the dirty work: relieving male sexual needs, producing cheap clothing in appalling working conditions, cleaning soiled garments. Both visions involve the co-optation of Asian American female bodies.

Almost in response to these degrading images of Asian American women, Mirikitani also writes about the compassion, strength, and survival skills of Japanese American women. Poems such as "Generations of Women," "Breaking Tradition," and "Who Is Singing This Song?" emphasize threads of memory among three generations of women in her family. Several poems address her daughter ("Sing with Your Body"). "Letter to My Daughter" is about her now-dead grandmother. Dignity was not the only skill that enabled her grandmother's survival, Mirikitani implicitly argues; love and a sense of interdependence were also necessary. By claiming her grandmother's love and her mother's silence— those who could not speak—Mirikitani secures the right for her daughter "to sing [her] own song" (*We* 138). These threads of resemblance and remembrance are a source of strength for Mirikitani's historic and poetic vision.

Though Mirikitani interconnects many of her thematic concerns, sex and violence are particularly linked in her work, especially when they are visited upon the female body. Assaults, rape, incest, and domestic violence are prominent images in her poetry. In "Spoils of War," a Vietnam veteran rapes and murders a female Asian American jogger. "Insect Collection," "Zipper," and "You Turned Your Head" include graphic descriptions of an adolescent girl being sexually molested. "Assaults and Invasions" details, excruciatingly, a battered wife's mutilation. Mirikitani specifically links these violent metaphors with her own life in "War of the Body," a poem that charts her memories of sexual abuse and their implication for healing in her marriage. In this poem, written for a literary festival in Wales on the theme of "war and peace," Mirikitani describes the "assaults and invasions" of her body and how her marriage has been a "demilitarized zone" (*We* 134). When asked about this linkage in an interview, Mirikitani noted that "the issue of sexuality and the abuse of women sexually is an unspoken, uncharted area in many ways, especially among Asian Americans; it is a taboo issue. . . . For me as an Asian American woman, sexuality has been that arena in which we have been exploited" (Interview with Hong 124). She has unapologetically chosen to break her years of coerced silence through her poetry.

Mirikitani's poetry also protests war: specifically, World War II, the Vietnam War, and the Gulf War ("Progeny"). "August 6" details her journey to Hiroshima for the 1984 Japan International Peace Conference. Other poems deal with veterans of the Vietnam War. "Jungle Rot and Open Arms," for example, is a chilling story of a soldier who fell in love with a Vietnamese woman during the war. After a violent raid, he awakens to find her killed, with only an arm left for him to bury. Here again, the racially marked Asian female body is the "spoil of war." In "We, the Dangerous," Mirikitani connects the bombing of Hiroshima with the Vietnam War and the Japanese American incarceration (*We* 27). Her transnational affinities for Asians and Asian Americans, unbound by chronological order, connect the motivations behind these wartime events. "Attack the Water" juxtaposes images of World War II with the Vietnam War. "Progeny" describes the mother of a Gulf War soldier who has called the Glide support hotline while her son is overseas. Mirikitani's insistence that all wars are linked and all wars damage women and children results in a passionate antiwar statement throughout her work.

In counterpoint to Mirikitani's war poems are her poems of mourning; for a poet-activist, these poems serve as simultaneous testament, elegy, and commentary. Some poems honor other poets, such as Pablo Neruda ("Looking for a Poem") and the Filipino American poets Serafin Syquia and Bayani Mariano ("Breathe between the Rain"). Other poems protest cultural expectations of Asian and Asian American women. The "Suicide Note" of an Asian American college student, for example, emphasizes the destructiveness of internalizing the "model-minority" myth. The young woman had left a note apologizing to her parents for not attaining a perfect grade-point average. Similarly, "Late with Lunch" describes a Korean woman's suicidal hanging for preparing her husband's lunch one hour late. In "Orchid Daughter," Mirikitani uses the voice of the immigrant mother of a murdered Vietnamese child to mourn "the war in urban America" (*We* 82). Several poems are in memory of her family members ("In Remembrance" for her uncle, "Hospitals Are to Die In" for her grandmother). Other poems express grief at the losses from war; these harbor a promise to "never forget." "Cry" was written for the ten infants who died at the Tule Lake concentration camp during World War II; "August 6" and "Shadow in Stone" speak for the victims of the Hiroshima nuclear bomb. Throughout her poetic career, Mirikitani uses her poetry to mourn for, and speak for, those who have been casualties of history.

CRITICAL RECEPTION

Mirikitani's work has elicited a fair amount of critical attention, both popular and academic. Thus far, literary critic Traise Yamamoto has done the most valuable and extensive analysis of Mirikitani's poetry. In the final chapter of *Masking Selves, Making Subjects: Japanese American Women, Identity, and the Body*, Yamamoto argues that Mirikitani's "polemical and militant politics of resistance" (221) center on the doubly vulnerable Asian American female body. This racially marked and gendered body, she insists, is subject to both "ideological and physical" intrusion ("Embodied" 222). Internment is thus a kind of rape for Japanese American women; colonization is conducted through both material force and linguistic violence. Mirikitani's work is aware of, and resists, the exoticization and hypersexualization of Asian American female bodies. Yamamoto's attentive and detailed analysis spans all three collections of Mirikitani's work, providing valuable insights into the trajectories of her poetic career.

Other literary critics have focused on individual collections or selected poems by Mirikitani. In "Notes toward a New Multicultural Criticism: Three Works by

Women of Color," John Crawford compares *Awake in the River* with the poetry of the Native American poet Joy Harjo and the Chicana poet Lorna Dee Cervantes. In his analysis of *Awake*, Crawford foregrounds Mirikitani's use of temporality and history. Mirikitani's poems negotiate between two visions of history: "diachronically ('horizontally,' in terms of temporal succession) and synchronically ('vertically,' in terms of simultaneous and systematically organized elements)"; that is, they engage history both chronologically and thematically ("Notes" 183). Deirdre Lashgari concentrates on Mirikitani's "poetics of violence . . . [and] aesthetic counterviolence" (291) in "Disrupting the Deadly Stillness: Janice Mirikitani's Poetics of Violence." *Shedding Silence*, Lashgari argues, enables border crossings through deconstruction; as a collection, it blurs the boundaries between "personal" and "political," men and women, heroes and villains, silence and speech (292, 294). Mirikitani's aesthetic allows these seeming contradictions to coexist; for example, she is able to sympathize with and recoil from a rapist's thoughts in "Spoils of War." This gives the reader space to sympathize with his violent conditioning without detracting from the horror of his assault on the jogger. In a shorter study of the poems "Lullabye" and "Breaking Silence," Stan Yogi emphasizes the ways that Mirikitani "remembers" and recovers the wartime incarceration past through her poetry. Yogi links her work with that of two other sansei poets, Lawson Fusao Inada and David Mura, as modes of "yearning for the past."

Reviews of Mirikitani's poetry have been generally positive, praising her courage in raising taboo subjects and her eloquent language. She has currently received the most attention for *Shedding Silence*. In her review of this collection, Maureen Griffin decides that "the beauty [in this book] outweighs its often somber tone and occasional full focus on ugliness" (29). Adrian Oktenberg calls Mirikitani "an unusually strong voice" (13). In his review, John Crawford notes that the tone of the harsher poems tends toward "shrillness [and thus] drown[s] out the intent of the piece[s]" (Rev. of *Shedding Silence* 166). He concludes, however, that Mirikitani is "not only a politically controversial poet, but an aesthetically dangerous one as well" (168). Similarly, Traise Yamamoto's review of *We, the Dangerous* claims that readers may find Mirikitani's work overly strident at times: "the activist orientation of these poems often seems to push out a wider range of tonalities; subtlety is sometimes sacrificed for the shock of recognition; the innocent and the oppressive are broadly and predictably drawn; and the continual insistence upon only the negative aspects of silence would seem to ignore an important dimension of the Japanese/Japanese American culture Mirikitani celebrates" (157). Yamamoto's stance treats Mirikitani's work critically and appreciatively: despite these critiques, she concludes that there is "much to appreciate in this volume" (157).

Overall, the critical and popular consensus is that Mirikitani's work must be considered an important influence in Asian American poetry. Mirikitani's own standards for "good poetry" are simple: "To me, a good poem is a good poem if it works. And it requires discipline, it requires skill, it requires a gift, it requires depth, it requires perception, it requires vision. Those, to me, are the standards of good poetry. One's commitment is one's own lonely battle, one's own determination, to make" (Interview with Hong 127). The body of Mirikitani's work is an eloquent testament to that commitment.

BIBLIOGRAPHY

Works by Janice Mirikitani

Poetry

"Sa otome (Rice-field-women)." *Third World Women*. Ed. Janice Mirikitani. San Francisco: Third World Communications, 1972. 160–62.
"Too Much to Require." Mirikitani, *Third World Women*, 163.
"Year of the Rat." Mirikitani, *Third World Women*, 162–63.
"Crazy Alice." *Time to Greez! Incantations from the Third World*. Ed. Janice Mirikitani. San Francisco: Glide Publications/Third World Communications, 1975. 10–11.
"Firepot." Mirikitani et al., *Time to Greez!* 3.
"Jungle Rot and Open Arms." Mirikitani, *Time to Greez!* 13.
"A Song for You." Mirikitani, *Time to Greez!* 12.
Awake in the River. San Francisco: Isthmus Press, 1978.
"Desert Flower." *Ayumi: A Japanese American Anthology*. Ed. Janice Mirikitani and the Japanese American Anthology Committee. San Francisco: Japanese American Anthology Committee, 1980. 215.
"For My Father." Mirikitani and the Japanese American Anthology Committee, *Ayumi*, 212.
"Loving from Vietnam to Zimbabwe." Mirikitani and the Japanese American Anthology Committee, *Ayumi*, 213–14.
"The Question Is." Mirikitani and the Japanese American Anthology Committee, *Ayumi*, 212.
"We, the Dangerous." Mirikitani and the Japanese American Anthology Committee, *Ayumi*, 211.
"The Woman and the Hawk." Mirikitani and the Japanese American Anthology Committee, *Ayumi*, 217.
"Attack the Water." *The Third Woman: Minority Women Writers of the United States*. Ed. Dexter Fisher. Boston: Houghton Mifflin, 1980. 542–43.
"Sing with Your Body." Fisher, 540–41.
"Breaking Silence." *Breaking Silence: An Anthology of Contemporary Asian American Poets*. Ed. Joseph Bruchac. Greenfield Center, NY: Greenfield Review Press, 1983. 189–91.
"Breaking Tradition." Bruchac, 192.
"Awake in the River." *The Hawk's Well: A Collection of Japanese American Art and Literature*. Vol. 1. San Jose, CA: Asian American Art Projects, 1986. 69–71.
"Japs." *The Hawk's Well*, 92–93.
"The Winner." *The Hawk's Well*, 86–90.
"Assaults and Invasions." *Bamboo Ridge* 30 (Spring 1986): 46–47.
"What's a Girl to Do?" *Bamboo Ridge* 30 (Spring 1986): 43–45.

Shedding Silence: Poetry and Prose. Berkeley, CA: Celestial Arts, 1987.

"Assaults and Invasions." *Feminist Studies* 14.3 (1988): 417–27.

"In Remembrance." *Making Waves: An Anthology of Writing by and about Asian American Women.* Ed. Asian Women United of California. Boston: Beacon Press, 1989. 349–51.

"Shadow in Stone." Asian Women United, 76–79.

"Yea. She Knows." *Amerasia Journal* 15.1 (1989): 219–28.

"Suicide Note." *Making Face, Making Soul/Haciendo Caras.* Ed. Gloria Anzaldúa. San Francisco: Aunt Lute, 1990. 75.

"The Fisherman." *The Open Boat: Poems from Asian America.* Ed. Garrett Hongo. New York: Anchor/Doubleday, 1993. 190–92.

"Shadow in Stone." Hongo, 193.

"Soul Food." Hongo, 188–89.

"Generations of Women." *The Woman That I Am: The Literature and Culture of Contemporary Women of Color.* Ed. D. Soyini Madison. New York: St. Martin's, 1994. 105–9.

We, the Dangerous: New and Selected Poems. London: Virago, 1995. Rpt. Berkeley, CA: Celestial Arts, 1995.

Autobiography

"Rebirth: Janice's Story." *No Hiding Place: Empowerment and Recovery for Our Troubled Communities.* Cecil Williams with Rebecca Laird. San Francisco: HarperSanFrancisco, 1992. 64–76.

Short Fiction

"Spoils of War." *Asian American Literature: A Brief Introduction and Anthology.* Ed. Shawn Wong. New York: HarperCollins, 1996. 186–201.

Anthologies Edited

Third World Women. San Francisco: Third World Communications, 1972.

Time to Greez! Incantations from the Third World. San Francisco: Glide Publications/ Third World Communications, 1975.

Ayumi: A Japanese American Anthology. San Francisco: Japanese American Anthology Committee, 1980.

I Have Something to Say about This Big Trouble: Children of the Tenderloin Speak Out. San Francisco: Glide Word Press, 1989.

Watch Out! We're Talking. San Francisco: Glide Word Press, 1993.

Studies of Janice Mirikitani

Articles and Reviews

Crawford, John F. "Notes toward a New Multicultural Criticism: Three Works by Women of Color." *A Gift of Tongues: Critical Challenges in Contemporary American Poetry.* Ed. Marie Harris and Kathleen Aguero. Athens: University of Georgia Press, 1987. 155–95.

———. Rev. of *Shedding Silence. Amerasia Journal* 14.1 (1988): 166–68.

Griffin, Maureen K. Rev. of *Shedding Silence. Kliatt* 22.1 (1988): 29.

Holt, Patricia. Rev. of *We, the Dangerous. San Francisco Chronicle* 25 February 1996, Sunday ed., Sunday Book Review: 1,4.

Lashgari, Deirdre. "Disrupting the Deadly Stillness: Janice Mirikitani's Poetics of Violence." *Violence, Silence, and Anger: Women's Writing as Transgression*. Ed. Deirdre Lashgarri. Charlottesville: University Press of Virginia, 1995. 291–304.

Oktenberg, Adrian. "No More Madame Butterfly." *Women's Review of Books* 5.5 (1988): 13.

Salvina, Christina Kim. "Exploring Asian American Literary Style: Janice Mirikitani and Ronyoung Kim." M.A. thesis. San Jose State University, 1994.

Usui, Masami. " 'No Hiding Place, New Speaking Space': Janice Mirikitani's Poetry of Incest and Abuse." *South Asian Literature* 32 (1996): 56–65.

Yamamoto, Traise. "Embodied Language: The Poetics of Mitsuye Yamada, Janice Mirikitani, and Kimiko Hahn." *Masking Selves, Making Subjects: Japanese American Women, Identity, and the Body*. Berkeley: University of California Press, 1999. 198–261.

———. Rev. of *We, the Dangerous. Amerasia Journal* 22.3 (1996): 155–57.

Yogi, Stan. "Yearning for the Past: The Dynamics of Memory in Sansei Internment Poetry." *Memory and Cultural Politics: New Approaches to American Ethnic Literatures*. Ed. Amritjit Singh, Joseph T. Skerrett, Jr., and Robert E. Hogan. Boston: Northeastern University Press, 1996. 245–65.

Biography

McManis, Sam. "Freeing Verse: How the City's Poet Laureate Found Her Voice and Learned to Speak Out for the Dispossessed." *San Francisco Chronicle* 21 July 2000. 26 July 2000. Available: http:www.sfgate.com/cgi-bin/article.cgi?f=/chronicle/archive/2000/07/21/wb18612.DTL+type=printable.

Mirikitani, Janice. E-mail to the author. 4 February 2001.

———. Interview with Grace Kyungwon Hong. *Words Matter: Conversations with Asian American Writers*. Ed. King-Kok Cheung. Honolulu: University of Hawai'i Press, 2000. 123–39.

———. Interview with Naomi Sodetani. *East Wind* 4.1 (1985): 61–63.

Reuman, Ann E. "Janice Mirikitani." *American Women Writers*. Vol. 5. Ed. Carol Hurd Green and Mary Grimley Mason. New York: Continuum, 1994. 307–10.

Tomaneng, Rowena. "Mirikitani, Janice." *Reference Guide to American Literature*. 4th ed. Ed. Thomas Riggs. Detroit, MI: St. James Press, 2000. 602–3.

Trudeau, Lawrence J., ed. *Asian American Literature: Reviews and Criticism of Works by American Writers of Asian Descent*. Detroit, MI: Gale Research, 1999. 333–41.

Zia, Helen. "Janice Mirikitani." *Notable Asian Americans*. Ed. Helen Zia and Susan B. Gall. Detroit: Gale Research, 1995. 263–64.

DAVID MURA
(1952–   )

Roy Osamu Kamada

BIOGRAPHY

David Alan Mura was born on 17 June 1952 at the Great Lakes Naval Training Center Hospital in Illinois while his father was stationed in Germany. Raised mostly in the suburbs of Chicago, Mura went to high school at Niles West, played basketball and football, and, according to his first memoir, *Turning Japanese*, grew up knowing "more Yiddish than Japanese" (9). Originally born David Alan Uyemura, Mura remarks that his father, who worked for the International News Service (INS) changed the family name when he was seven years old, " 'for better bylines,' [his father] said" (*Where the Body* 55). While both of his parents, Tom K. and Tesuko Mura, were in the Japanese internment camps during World War II, they, like many in the Japanese American community in the years following the war, did not speak very much of the camps. This silence, familial and historical, became one of his major themes. In 1974, Mura graduated from Grinnell College and moved to Minneapolis to attend graduate school in English literature at the University of Minnesota. In 1983, Mura married Susan Sencer, a pediatric oncologist. Mura received a U.S./Japan Creative Artist Fellowship in 1984 and spent a year living in Japan, an experience that was the basis for his award-winning 1991 memoir *Turning Japanese*. In 1991, he received his M.F.A. from Vermont College.

In 1987, Mura published *A Male Grief: Notes on Pornography and Addiction* and won the Milkweed Prize for Creative Nonfiction. His first book of poetry, *After We Lost Our Way*, won the National Poetry Series Contest in 1989, the year of its publication. In 1991, Atlantic Monthly Press published his memoir,

Turning Japanese: Memoirs of a Sansei, for which he won the 1991 Josephine Miles Book Award from the Oakland chapter of International PEN. *Turning Japanese* was also listed in the *New York Times* Notable Books of the Year. In 1995, Mura's second book of poetry, *The Colors of Desire*, won the Carl Sandburg Literary Award from the Friends of the Chicago Public Library. His second memoir, *Where the Body Meets Memory: An Odyssey of Race, Sexuality, and Identity*, was published in 1996. His book of critical essays, *Notes for a New Century*, will be published by the University of Michigan Press in its Poets on Poetry series.

Mura has also had an extensive involvement in the dramatic arts. He has created and performed a number of pieces over the years. He has worked collaboratively with Alexs Pate, Jon Jang, Kelvin Han Yee, and Esther Suzuki, among others. One piece, *Secret Colors*, was adapted to film by the Public Broadcasting System (PBS), retitled *Slowly, This*, and broadcast in the PBS series *Alive TV* in July/August 1995. Mura's other performance pieces and plays include *Relocations: Images from a Japanese American* (1990), *Silence and Desire* (1994), and *After Hours* (1995). His stage adaptation of Li-Young Lee's memoir *The Winged Seed* premiered at Pangea World Theater in October 1997.

Among his many awards, Mura has received a Lila Wallace–Reader's Digest Writers' Award (1995), two National Endowment for the Arts Literature Fellowships (1985, 1993), a Playwrights' Center McKnight Advancement Grant (1993), a Pushcart Prize (1990), two Bush Foundation Fellowships (1981, 1988), four Loft-McKnight Awards (1984, 1987, 1992, and 1998), several Minnesota State Arts Board grants (1980, 1988, 1991, and 1993), a Discovery/The Nation Award (1987), and the Fanny Fay Wood Memorial Prize from the Academy of American Poets (1977). He has served as the artistic director of the Asian American Renaissance (AAR), an Asian American arts organization in Minnesota, and as an artist associate at Pangea World Theater. He has served as board president of the Jerome Foundation, the Loft, and the Center for Arts Criticism and on the board of the AAR, Pangea, and the Minnesota Inclusiveness Program. He has been a visiting professor at the University of Minnesota and the University of Oregon. Mura has also taught at St. Olaf College, the Loft, and for COMPAS (Community Programs in the Arts), Writers and Artists in the Schools. He remains a very active poet, writer, critic, performer, and teacher, giving readings and speaking on issues of race, sexuality, and multiculturalism throughout the country. He lives in Minneapolis with his wife and their three children, Samantha, Nikko, and Tomo.

MAJOR WORKS AND THEMES

Each of David Mura's books, whether poetry or memoir, is engaged with the crucial themes of the individual's entanglements with history and how these involvements can impact a poetic, racial, national, or sexual identity. He begins his first book of poems, *After We Lost Our Way*, with a series of poems about his family that starts in the years preceding World War II. The sequence of the first four poems is indicative of Mura's larger project: to make clear the connections between the human individual, his or her identity, and the often traumatic historical events he or she lives through. Additionally, his project has been concerned with the aftereffects of trauma and the ways in which these aftereffects impact the individual psyche.

Mura opens his first collection of poems with a portrait of innocent love between his grandparents and proceeds with two epistolary poems. The first epistolary poem is written from the viewpoint of a survivor of Hiroshima writing to his sister, the other from the perspective of a husband writing to his wife from inside the Postern Internment Camp during World War II. These two epistolary poems act as a counterpoint to the first poem; while the first poem sets the stage with an idealized portrait of young love, the following two pieces indicate the traumas that await the young lovers. This short series of poems humanizes the individual within history and brings into light the adversities and atrocities that the Japanese and Japanese Americans suffered. Indeed, to further emphasize his intent to retrieve and recall what has been forgotten, Mura opens this collection of poems with Walter Benjamin's famous maxim from "Theses on the Philosophy of History": "nothing that has ever happened should be regarded as lost for history" (qtd. in *After* 3). While Benjamin was speaking specifically about his theories on material historiography, Mura's intentions mirror the sentiment; he proposes to uncover buried histories, his family's, his community's, and most of all, his own. His use of Benjamin's maxim is indicative of Mura's complex aesthetic, his willingness and desire to accommodate within his poetry a host of different discourses.

In the fourth poem of the collection, "An Argument: On 1942," the speaker's mother frets over his inability to forget about the camps: "No, no, no, she tells me. Why bring it back?" (10). Here Mura represents the denial of trauma that characterizes much of his family's reactions to internment. In his later works, Mura connects this denial of trauma to the pathology of racialization, to the internalization of shame, and to his early dysfunctional sexuality. His focus is frequently on the twin effects of trauma: the event itself coupled with the aftermath of the event. Mura's perspective is not, however, limited to the individual who suffers; he extends the effects of trauma to the community and to the descendants of those oppressed. He argues that the ultimate effects of internment and racism against Japanese Americans did not end with World War II; rather, the effects of historical trauma linger and work their way into the developing consciousness of younger generations. Mura contends in his second memoir, *Where the Body Meets Memory*, that the camps resulted in his parents feeling a profound shame, where "shame says that the very core of your being, your whole self is wrong, inferior, tainted" (243). It is this shame that results in their silence and that, according to Mura, becomes tied up with his developing sexuality.

While in this first collection of poems Mura does not explicitly link a history of racism with his own compulsive sexual behavior and the multiple affairs he had, he does introduce the topic of his early addiction to pornography. In the poem "The Bookstore," Mura narrates a descent into the underworld of the pornographic bookstore. After rummaging through the magazines, the speaker enters the video booths looking for the image of the blond that will stun him, (63). It is the desire to "possess this image" of the blond, the stereotype of white femininity, that Mura will analyze in depth in his later work. He will link his desire, as well as its pathological consequences, to his family's and his own experiences of racism. However, in this early work, Mura is not yet ready to confront the complex intersections of race and sexuality.

In his first memoir, *Turning Japanese*, Mura introduces an early section of the text with a long quote from Franz Fanon's seminal book *Black Skin, White Masks*. By invoking Fanon, Mura aligns himself with some of Fanon's views on the pathology of racism, with the psychological effects that histories of oppression have on individuals. In an interview with Bill Moyers, Mura remarks, "When Franz Fanon writes that the black school child in the French West Indies reads about *our* ancestors the Gauls and then about how the great white hunter went into Africa to civilize the savages, Fanon says the child learns self-hatred, self-alienation, and identification with the oppressor" (303, emphasis mine). In his second memoir, *Where the Body Meets Memory*, Mura recalls reading Fanon's analysis of a black man who constantly slept with white women. Mura remarks, "In an instant I understood what I'd been doing all those years I'd elevated whiteness, I'd inculcated its standards of beauty, I'd believed in the myth of white superiority. That was part of my sickness, part of the colonizing of my sexuality" (232). What Mura refers to here as "the colonizing of my sexuality," he also refers to as "the Internment of Desire"; he makes explicit the connections between sexual identity, sexual desire, and one's own racialized consciousness of one's body and self. He argues that sexuality, tied up in a consciousness of one's body and self, is dramatically impacted by a history of racism and its traumatic aftereffects. For how can one develop a healthy sexuality if the self, the thing upon which sexuality is based, is confounded by deep and traumatic anxieties?

In addition to the beginnings of these themes, his first collection of poetry also is indicative of his stylistic innovations, of his complex and postmodern aesthetic. Garrett Hongo, in a quote on the back of *After We Lost Our Way*, remarks that Mura's style has a filmic effect. Indeed, that would be the best description for the long middle section that engages the life of Pier Paolo Pasolini. But more than that, Mura's technique is truly performative; in a number of his poems, he stages dialogues, and in his second collection, *The Colors of Desire*, he provides stage directions. In this first collection, Mura makes use of a huge variety of possible forms and styles including direct address, the epistolary poem, the epigraph, the dramatic monologue, and lyric meditations interspersed with historical/biographical facts. In this fashion, Mura complicates, in profound ways, any attempts to categorize or essentialize his work under nationalized and racialized categories. Like Salman Rushdie and Maxine Hong Kingston, Mura defies simplistic categorization, either in terms of his national identity or in terms of his aesthetic inheritance. He merges genres and conflates our considerations of history with postmodern aesthetic strategies. He confounds easy categorization and requires of his readers a willingness to accommodate and appreciate multiple perspectives on historical events. Mura begins, even in this early work, to set the stage for his own transnational, postcolonial, diasporic aesthetic.

In *The Colors of Desire*, Mura extends the themes hinted at in *After We Lost Our Way* and uncovered in *Turning Japanese*. In this second collection, he begins with a lyric portrait of life before World War II; much like the opening of *After We Lost Our Way*, the opening of *The Colors of Desire* sets the stage with a portrait of tragic and doomed innocence. However, in this collection, rather than sketch out fictionalized characters caught up in internment or the aftermath of Hiroshima, Mura proceeds to turn his analytic eye upon his own self and the various legacies of history that he has inherited.

The title poem, "The Colors of Desire," is a meditation, a postmodern lyric that considers the intimate and subterranean links between various histories of racism, pornography, sexuality, and identity. The poem opens with two separate yet entangled scenes of racism: a photograph of a lynching (circa 1930) and a short scene dramatizing his teenage father, on a weekend pass from the intern- ment camp in 1942 Arkansas, choosing where to sit on a bus, with the whites or the blacks. The poem then cuts to a scene of the speaker, sitting in a porn theater, watching *Behind the Green Door* with its lurid portrayal of interracial sex. The second section of the poem connects the family members' physical violence against each other with their own status as victims of racism. Mura depicts a scene where he watches his father, a man of considerable temper, back down from a confrontation with a man yelling racist epithets. The poem then moves to a scene at night when the father beats his son, who in turn beats his brother. While he does not make an ultimately causal claim for this violence, Mura makes clear the implications that racism has in this familial milieu of violence. In an interview with Eileen Tabios regarding this scene, Mura remarks,

This is about the conditioning of the camps and the conditioning brought to bear upon Asians in America. It is also about how racial violence or insults outside the family can be internalized within the family. This passage alludes to the unreleased rage of many of the Nisei men, their sense that they had to live within a narrow spectrum of behavior or expression, that they had to watch what they said and did. ("How History" 364)

In the third section of the poem, Mura returns to his childhood and his first encounter with pornography; he ends this section with his father's voice asking why he insists on connecting the internment camps and the family violence with his obsessions with pornography. Mura concludes his title poem with a lyric meditation on the legacy that his unborn daughter will inherit. Like the structure of the whole collection, the title poem ruminates obsessively on the influence of the past upon the present and the possibilities for the future. Through the lyric image of his unborn daughter rising like a moon, Mura suggests a possibility of transcending the bounds of history even while he withholds any firm declaration to that effect. Similarly, the final three poems of this collection, "Gardens We Have Left," "In America," and "Listening," all reflect the same pattern of meditation upon the past followed by a lyric attempt to transcend the bounds of history.

Mura gestures toward a kind of redemption at the end of "The Colors of Desire," just as he attempts a similar gesture at the end of the whole collection. In the penultimate poem, "In America," Mura returns to the world before World War II that begins the collection in "Issei Strawberry," a roughly idealized moment prior to the traumas of internment. He concludes the collection with "Listening," a meditation on the powerful joy that an unborn child can bring into the lives of its parents, set in Japan and composed in a single extended sentence. He suggests a connection between himself, his wife, and his ancestors; he implies that they are all joined by the possibility of hope and joy. By prefacing this hopeful moment with a poem evoking the doomed optimism of his father before internment, Mura refrains from making a claim for complete and total redemption. In between these two poems is, of course, the trauma of history, the savagery of internment. The ghostly presence of racism haunts these two lyrics. Mura concludes his collection on a note of redemption qualified by the material effect of history, a redemption that has potential for transcendence and yet remains bound by the actual, the real effects of a history of racism, exclusion, and oppression.

In his poetry, as well as in his prose, Mura has consistently engaged the problems that a historical legacy of trauma and racism poses for the individual. He has sought to expose the impact of this legacy on the individual in its most extreme and intimate ways. His work has continually pushed the boundaries of what has been talked about in public forums on racism while pushing his own aesthetic and formal boundaries as a poet; Mura has truly succeeded in forming a postmodern, transnational, postcolonial poetics.

CRITICAL RECEPTION

David Mura's work in general has received a considerable amount of attention and praise. He has been the recipient of numerous awards and fellowships. While his prose memoirs have garnered a great deal of critical attention, his poetry has also been the subject of numerous extended studies. The reviews of his poetry collections have been very favorable and have focused largely upon Mura's investments in the legacies of histories of racism and oppression. Roger Gilbert remarks that the power of *After We Lost Our Way* "derives from Mura's unflinching attention to the psychology of pain. His commitment to the infinitely problematic task of conveying real human pain and its historical causes in a

medium dedicated to pleasure is characteristic of our moment in American poetry, but Mura's immersion in history makes him better suited to the task than
poets who merely pay lip service to what others have endured" (180). Gilbert
takes note of Mura's specific perspective, what he calls "Mura's immersion in
history."

Reviews of Mura's second collection, *The Colors of Desire*, have also been
similarly favorable, but evince some discomfort with the direct approach to
sexuality. Robert Grotjohn writes of his initial desire to dismiss this book because he finds "Mura's confessional self-absorption exasperating, especially his
recurring fascination with himself as victim of his addiction to pornography"
(183). His themes have, in other cases, provoked discomfort. In *Where the Body
Meets Memory*, Mura himself tells of a similar reaction from a sansei academic
in dialogue with Garrett Hongo: "It's an interesting book [*Turning Japanese*],"
says the academic. "But all that sexual stuff. It's kind of weird, don't you think?"
(249). Mura acknowledges that "a man of color writing about his relationship
with white women is a lightning rod, [and] runs the risk of indelibly branding
me" (249). However, despite the criticism reflecting, at times, the critic's discomfort with the material rather than any real critique of Mura's poetry, despite
the suspicion that Mura is exploiting the provocative subject of sex, critics like
Grotjohn do ultimately admit that Mura "gives us one of our most complex
literary explorations of Asian American male sexuality [and that he] shows a
more tender" boldness than past male literary treatments of the topic (183).

Mura's prose memoirs have been the subject of inquiry by critics and have
been subjected to extended critique in several dissertations. His poetry has been
discussed by Stan Yogi, George Uba, and Zhou Xiaojing. In his chapter "Yearning for the Past: The Dynamics of Memory in Sansei Internment Poetry," Stan
Yogi remarks that in contrast to poets such as Lawson Inada and Janice Mirikitani who grew up connected to the Japanese American communities and who
grew up in the midst of ethnic pride movements of the 1960s and 1970s, "David
Mura, growing up in the Midwest in the 1950s and 1960s, had little contact
with other Japanese Americans. Consequently his search for an understanding
of the internment is perhaps charged with more mystery and need" (258). Yogi
provides a detailed and salient reading of Mura's poem "An Argument: On
1942" in which he examines how Mura presents the impulse on his part to learn
about the past and the impulse on his parents' part to escape the very history
Mura so desperately wants to uncover.

In his chapter "Versions of Identity in Post-activist Asian American Poetry,"
George Uba examines a number of poets, David Mura among them, whom he
calls part of a postactivist generation of Asian American poets. He argues that
in reaction to the profound demographic changes in Asian America, the "trib-
alism" of early Asian American poetry that eschewed the traditional finesse of
Euro-American poetics is no longer an accurate method of describing the state
of Asian American poetry. He notes that postactivist poets, such as David Mura,
"hold that identity, whether tribal or otherwise, is always in doubt. Indeed, the

post-activist poem tends to recognize problematics of language and event both as a way of approaching identity and of renouncing its stability" (34). Here Uba is referring to Mura's self-conscious use of avant-garde techniques in his poetry. Such techniques and such stylistic innovations as those that Mura employs serve to destabilize traditional notions of language and meaning by pointing to the inadequacy of language in representation.

Regarding Mura in particular, Uba notes that Mura "acknowledges how activist poets serve as his literary ancestors, even as he insists upon his necessary differences from them" (39). Mura's methodology, according to Uba, is profoundly far-reaching in his endeavors. "Mura campaigns at once to recover and expand the [communalistic] impulse by embracing other marginalized lives— the oppressed, wretched, and suffering in all stations and cultures, including . . . the homosexual Italian film director and writer Pasolini. By embracing even a white male European, Mura testifies to the impossibility of containing identity along purely racial and ethnic lines" (39). Uba goes on to note that "Mura also acknowledges that all ideas about identity are in some way inadequate, partial, and contradictory, even as he asserts that it is these very properties that help us to install identity at any moment in history" (41). Thus as the poststructuralist envisions the inadequate yet necessary function of language in revealing meaning, so too does Mura, as part of his postcolonial aesthetic, understand identity to be formed by inadequate yet necessary categories. The idea of the Japanese American as a stable category is more than useless, it effaces the true and radical heterogeneity of the Asian American experience, a heterogeneity that Mura is deeply committed to. Yet, as Mura would acknowledge, the idea of racial identities as categories is essential to any and all discussions about racial, cultural, and social justice and political reformation.

In her article "David Mura's Poetics of Identity," Zhou Xiaojing takes up Uba's perspectives and extends his argument. She argues that "the significance of Mura's poetry lies in its capacity for revealing the processes and effects of racial and sexual identity formation in connection to power relations"; she examines Mura's exploration of the possibilities of established poetic forms and his experiment with new modes of signification in seeking to portray the complexity and ambivalence in the experiences of the Japanese Americans (148). Zhou makes note of how Mura employs the monologue form in order to "depict the different perspectives of three generations of Japanese Americans' responses to their internment during World War II and to their assigned racial status in the United States" (148). Zhou discusses Mura's adaptation of Aimé Césaire's techniques in his poem "Song for Uncle Tom, Tonto, & Mr. Moto." She also provides a detailed explication of Mura's series of poems on Pasolini. Using Foucault and Bakhtin as a theoretical backdrop to her discussion, Zhou argues that Mura's poetics makes use of the "dialogic relationship [inherent in the multiple subject positions of Mura's speakers] through which he reinscribes lives effaced from history and restores voices of the silenced and disempowered in his poems" (164).

While critics have rightly pointed out how Mura has complicated traditional notions of Asian American identity, a great deal of work remains to be done on this poet and memoirist. His considerations of sexuality and gender identifications make him an ideal writer for critics who would consider the intersections between postcolonial and queer identities; the complex nature of Mura's aesthetic and the moral force that drives his poetics make him truly one of the brave and necessary poets for the twenty-first century.

BIBLIOGRAPHY

Works by David Mura

Poetry

After We Lost Our Way. New York: E.P. Dutton, 1989; Pittsburgh: Carnegie Mellon University Press, 1997.
The Colors of Desire. New York: Anchor/Doubleday, 1995.

Prose

A Male Grief: Notes on Pornography and Addiction. Minneapolis, MN: Milkweed Editions, 1987.
Turning Japanese: Memoirs of a Sansei. Boston: Atlantic Monthly Press, 1991.
Where the Body Meets Memory: An Odyssey of Race, Sexuality, and Identity. New York: Anchor/Doubleday, 1996.
Notes for a New Century. Poets on Poetry series. Ann Arbor: University of Michigan Press, forthcoming.

Performance Art/Theater/Film

Relocations: Images from a Japanese American (a performance of video, slides, monologues, poetry & prose). Intermedia Arts Gallery. South Minneapolis, MN, 18 October 1990; Macalester College, January 1991; Southern Theatre, May 1991; Club Lower Links, Chicago, June 1991 (a selection). A selection of the piece filmed by filmmaker Mark Tang has appeared on KTCA Public Television in Minneapolis, and at the 1992 National Asian American Telecommunications Association Film Festival, 1992 Los Angeles Asian Pacific Film and Video Festival.
Reading of *Redress/Invasion*. Playwright's Center, Jones Commission. Minneapolis, MN, March 1992, June 1992, May 1993; East/West Players, Los Angeles, April 1992; Asian American Theater Co., San Francisco, July 1992; Pillsbury House Theater, Minneapolis, July 1994.
The Colors of Desire (a.k.a. *Secret Colors*). A performance piece created and performed by David Mura and Alexs Pate. Premiere, Walker Art Center "Out There" Series at the Southern Theater, 20–22 January 1994.
Silence and Desire. Play created, written, and performed in collaboration with Tom Rose, Kim Hines, and Maria Cheng. Premiere, Red Eye Theater, Minneapolis, MN, 14–29 October 1994.
Slowly, This. Film produced by *Alive TV* for broadcast on PBS, dir. Arthur Jafa; script and perf. by David Mura and Alexs Pate. 1994.

After Hours. Premiere at Intermedia Arts. South Minneapolis, MN, 19–21 April 1996.
Silent Children. Cowritten with Meena Natarajan for Pangea World Theater and the Minnesota Advocates for Human Rights, 1997.
Internment Voices. Cowritten with Esther Suzuki. Theater Mu at Intermedia Arts. South Minneapolis, MN, 5 June 1997.
The Winged Seed. Adaptation of Li-Young Lee's memoir. Pangea World Theater. At Guthrie Lab Theater, Minneapolis, MN, 30 October–9 November 1997.

Creative Nonfiction, Articles, and Criticism

"A Male Grief: Notes on Pornography and Addiction." *Milkweed Chronicle* Spring/Summer 1985; rpt. in *Utne Reader* (12 October/November 1985): 46–53.
"A Short Intellectual Biography of a Japanese American Sansei Writer, or, How I Learned Not to Write like James Michener or John O'Hara." *Kyoto Review* (Spring 1987): 34–47.
"The Need for Literary Criticism." *View from the Loft* 10.3 (October 1987): 2+.
"Strangers in the Village." *The Graywolf Annual Five Multi-Cultural Literacy*. Ed. Rick Simonson and Scott Walker. St. Paul, MN: Graywolf Press, 1988. 135–53.
"Caught in Contradictions: A Japanese-American in Kyoto." *Threepenny Review* 8.4 (Winter 1988): 22–23.
"A Japanese American in Tokyo." *Partisan Review* 55.1 (Winter 1988): 113–23.
"Notes for a New Poem." *Boston Review* 14.2 (April 1989): 5–6, 22–23.
"Poetry and Politics: Brecht, Rich, and C. K. Williams." *AWP Chronicle* 23.3 (November/December 1990): 1–5.
"Mirrors of the Self: Autobiography and the Japanese-American Writer." *Asian Americans: Comparative and Global Perspectives*. Ed. Shirley Hune, Hyung-chan Kim, Stephen S. Fugita, and Amy Ling. Pullman: Washington State University Press, 1991. 249–64.
"Land of the Rising Son." *Mother Jones* 16.2 (March/April 1991): 42–47.
"Muzak, Mad Av, Minimalist Fiction, Mystification, and Marx." *Colorado Review* 18.1 (Spring/Summer 1991): 1–15.
"Difficulties of the Moment: Milosz, Bakhtin, and the Cultural Hybrid." *AWP Chronicle* 24.1 (September 1991): 1+.
"Waiting for the End: Bernhard's *Concrete*." *Pequod* 33 (1992): 100–12.
"Bashed in the U.S.A." *New York Times* 28 April 1992, Op Ed section: A17 (N), A25 (L).
"Secrets and Anger." *Mother Jones* 17.5 (September/October 1992): 18–22.
"Multiculturalism: Living in the World (Whose World?)." *Green Mountains Review* 6.1 (Winter/Spring 1993): 57–77.
"No-No Boys: Re-X-amining Japanese Americans." *New England Review* 15.3 (Summer 1993): 143–65.
"Notes for the Next Century." *Conjunctions* 21 (Fall 1993): 308–17.
"The Fantasy of Miss Saigon." *Minneapolis/St. Paul Magazine* 12.12 (December 1993): 36–38.
"A Shift in Power, a Sea Change in the Arts: Asian American Constructions." *The State of Asian American Activism and Resistance in the 1990s*. Ed. Karin Aguilar-San Juan. Boston: South End Press, 1994. 183–204.
"Where We Are and Where We're Going." *Amerasia Journal* 20.3 (1994): 31–33.

"The Internment of Desire." *Under Western Eyes*. Ed. Garrett Hongo. New York: Anchor, 1995. 259–94.

"The Lover." *On a Bed of Rice: An Asian American Erotic Feast*. Ed. Geraldine Kudaka. New York: Anchor/Doubleday, 1995. 370–83.

"The Margins at the Center, the Center at the Margins: Acknowledging the Diversity of Asian American Poetry." *Reviewing Asian America: Locating Diversity*. Ed. Wendy L. Ng. Pullman: Washington State University Press, 1995. 171–84.

"Hollywood, My Children, and the New (?) Kung Fu." *Journal of the Asian American Renaissance* 2 (1996): 28–31.

"Of Racism, Sexism, and Fatherhood." *USA Weekend* 28–30 June 1996: A4+.

"How America Unsexes the Asian Male." *New York Times* 22 August 1996: C9 (L).

"Where We've Been, Where We're Going." *Green Mountains Review* 9.2/10.1 (1997): 38–55.

"Cultural Claims and Appropriation (e.g., Who Owns the Internment Camps?)." *Art Papers* 21. 2 (March–April 1997): 6–11.

"The Search for Language." *Asian Pacific American Journal* 6.2 (Fall–Winter 1997): 3–7.

"A Note from Caliban." *Boston Review* 23.3 (1998). Available: http://bostonreview.mit.edu/BR23.3/mura.html.

"Reflections on My Daughter." *Half and Half: Writers on Growing Up Biracial and Bicultural*. Ed. Claudine Chiawei O'Hearn. New York: Pantheon Books, 1998. 80–98.

"Explaining Racism to My Daughter." *Racism Explained to My Daughter*. Ed. Tahar Ben Jelloun. New York: New Press, 1999. 90–137.

"An Infinity of Traces." *Tales from the Couch: Writers on Talk Therapy*. Ed. Jason Shinder. New York: Morrow, 2000.

"In the Realm of the Sansei." *Nerve* (online magazine), 4 April 2000. Available: http://www.democracyweb.com/modelminority.com/dating/sansei.htm.   November 2000.

"Asian Americans and the Language of Home." *The Skin That We Speak: Thoughts on Language and Culture in the Classroom*. Ed. Lisa D. Delpit and Joanne Kilgour Dowdy. New York: New Press, 2002.

Interviews

Gidmark, Gill. "David Mura: Tearing Down the Door." *Asian America: Journal of Culture and the Arts* 2 (Winter 1993): 120–29.

Ikeda, Stewart David. Interview. *Yellow Light: The Flowering of Asian American Arts*. Ed. Amy Ling. Philadelphia: Temple University Press, 1999. 112–25.

Imada, Adria. Interview. *Hawaii Herald* 17 February 1995: 10.

Kane, Daniel. Interview with the Poet David Mura, October 1999. Teachers & Writers Collaborative Web page. Available: http://www.writenet.org/poetschat/poetschat_dmura.html). November 2000.

Moyers, Bill. Interview. *The Language of Life: A Festival of Poets*. Ed. James Haba. New York: Doubleday, 1995. 301–18.

Rossi, Lee. Interview. *Onthebus* 2.2 (Summer/Fall 1990): 263–73.

Tabios, Eileen. "How History Stains the Colors of Desire." *Black Lightning*. Eileen Tabios. New York: Asian American Writers' Workshop, 1998. 333–78.

Studies of David Mura

Beauregard, Guy. "*Turning Japanese: Memoirs of a Sansei.*" *Canadian Literature* 154 (Autumn 1997): 162–64.

Berger, Kenneth W. "*Turning Japanese: Memoirs of a Sansei.*" *Library Journal* 116.2 (February 1991): 84.

Bradbury, Nicholas. "*Turning Japanese: Memoirs of a Sansei.*" *Far Eastern Economic Review* 153.31 1 (August 1991): 44.

Chiang, Mark. *Trans/national Crossings of Asian America: Nationalism and Globalization in Asian American Cultural Studies.* Diss. University of California, Berkeley, 1998. Ann Arbor: UMI, 9902030.

Gilbert, Roger. "After We Lost Our Way." *Partisan Review* 61.1 (Winter 1994): 180.

Grotjohn, Robert. "The Colors of Desire." *Amerasia Journal* 23.1 (Spring 1997): 183.

Guillory, Daniel L. "The Colors of Desire." *Library Journal* (January 1995): 107.

Kan, Katharine L. "*Where the Body Meets Memory: An Odyssey of Race, Sexuality, and Identity.*" *Library Journal* 121.8. (1 May 1996): 116.

Nishime, LeiLani Linda. *Creating Race: Genre and the Cultural Construction of Asian American Identity.* Diss. University of Michigan, 1997. Ann Arbor: UMI, 9732154.

Ong, Rory. "*Where the Body Meets the Memory: An Odyssey of Race, Sexuality, and Identity.*" *Amerasia Journal* 23.3 (Winter 1997): 217.

"PEN Oakland Book Awards." *Publishers Weekly* 20 January 1992: 11.

Rossi, Lee. "David Mura." *Onthebus* 3 (1990): 20–21.

Stuttaford, Genevieve. "*Turning Japanese: Memoirs of a Sansei.*" *Publishers Weekly* 18 (January 1991): 51.

Taylor, Gordon O. " 'The Country I Had Thought Was My Home': David Mura's *Turning Japanese* and Japanese-American Narrative since World War II." *Connotations: A Journal for Critical Debate* 6.3 (1996): 283–309.

Uba, George. "Versions of Identity in Post-activist Asian American Poetry." *Reading the Literatures of Asian America.* Ed. Shirley Geok-lin Lim and Amy Ling. Philadelphia: Temple University Press, 1992. 33–48.

Yogi, Stan. "Yearning for the Past: The Dynamics of Memory in Sansei Internment Poetry." *Memory and Cultural Politics: New Approaches to American Ethnic Literatures.* Ed. Amritjit Singh, Robert E. Hogan, and Joseph T. Skerrett, Jr. Boston: Northeastern University Press, 1996. 245–65.

Yu, Timothy. "Form and Identity in Language Poetry and Asian American Poetry." *Contemporary Literature* 41.3 (Fall 2000): 422–62.

Zhou, Xiaojing. "A Poetics of Identity: David Mura's Poetry" *MELUS* 23.3 (Fall 1998): 145–66.

TRAN THI NGA
(1927–   )

Michele Janette

BIOGRAPHY

Tran Thi Nga has known many nations. Born in China, she studied in Wales, lived in Burma, and immigrated to the United States. But her country is Vietnam. "We want to swim in our own pond. Clear or stinky, still it is ours" (*Shallow Graves* 266).

Nga grew up in French colonial Vietnam, learning to speak French but also resenting the French presence. After World War II, when Chinese soldiers arrived to disarm the defeated Japanese, one of the Chinese generals fell in love with Nga. He demanded to marry her, detaining her father until she consented. He then took her to China, where she discovered that he already had a first wife. Widowed a few years later, Nga returned to Vietnam. She was again convinced to marry and again became a second wife, since her husband was already married to Nga's sister.

The sixth of nine children, and the second daughter, Nga often struggled against Confucian ideals of obedience. Her husband and her father dissuaded her from resuming schooling after her marriage and required her to go south when Vietnam was divided in 1954. There she became a social worker and midwife, doing hazardous duty for the South Vietnamese government to gain permission for study abroad. After studying at Swansea University, she spent several years as a "diplomatic wife" in Burma and then returned to social services administration in Saigon. Fed up with the corruption she encountered, however, she soon resigned, going to work instead for *Time* magazine in Saigon.

She left Vietnam in 1975 when *Time* arranged for the departure of most of its staff.

After living in refugee camps in Guam and in Fort Chaffee, Arkansas, Nga settled in Connecticut. Working in New York City, she reencountered Wendy Larsen, the wife of her former boss in Saigon. They collaborated on *Shallow Graves*, the book of poetry that pairs Larsen's experience of Vietnam with Nga's life story. In 1995, Nga retired and planned to return to Vietnam semipermanently, but finding her homeland still full of corruption, she again returned to the United States. She now divides her time among family in Florida, Connecticut, and Pennsylvania.

MAJOR WORKS AND THEMES

Tran Thi Nga is not a poet in the strict sense. The poetry that appears in *Shallow Graves* is the result of collaboration. As Larsen describes this process: "[Nga] told me her story, which I recorded on tape. . . . I transformed her memories into narrative verse trying to stay as close to her voice as possible" (foreword).

The resulting poems describe large political forces through personal detail. Nga conveys the horror of the famine during the Japanese occupation through a family story: distressed by the corpses that piled against their front door each morning, her father hired soldiers to take them away, but sometimes one would cry out, "Don't take me. I'm not dead yet" (157). She describes Confucian gender roles through lessons passed down generations of women and explores issues of imperialism and assimilation through familial disagreements over whether to learn English or to come home for holidays just to "sit around . . . and stare at each other" (264).

"Nga's Story" refers to and excerpts songs, letters, proverbs, folk poems, schoolbook poems, and classical Vietnamese epics. When Nga agrees to ransom her father by giving herself in marriage, she explicitly models her behavior after the self-sacrifice of Kieu, a national heroine and the protagonist of the nineteenth-century epic *Kim Van Kieu*. Their stories are indeed similar: both women reencounter the sweethearts of their youth; both find these sweethearts now married to their younger sisters; both agree to become second wives; both then insist that their marriages be platonic. These parallels place Nga in a Vietnamese tradition of women's strength, intelligence, and patience whose paragon is the heroine Kieu.

Nga's allusions are not just literary flourishes. They weave a fabric of cultural sophistication that often contrasts with the blithe arrogance of Americans. For example, when Nga is scolded by her son's American girlfriend for letting herself become a second wife despite being "an educated woman," the girlfriend's ungracious condescension reveals her own lack of education about the cultural traditions that shaped Nga's decisions (258). Nga's greater sophistication and sensitivity do not add up to power, however: in the end, they had to move away from the girlfriend.

Nga repeatedly casts a sharp eye on the dynamics of power. She resents and often resists her patriarchal family structure. She notices the contempt within offers of charity. Most famously, she describes her early connection with Larsen as a professional obligation: "She was my boss's wife. Of course I would do it" (220).

CRITICAL RECEPTION

Reviewers have valued *Shallow Graves* as both record and exorcism of the Vietnam War's traumas. They have particularly appreciated Nga's perspective as a Vietnamese woman, a voice not often enough heard in literature about this war. Criticism of the book has focused on the collaboration between Tran Thi Nga and Wendy Larsen. Both Vince Gotera and George Uba argue that Larsen's poems demonstrate neocolonialist attitudes toward Vietnam and the Vietnamese. They champion the subversive nature of "Nga's Story," arguing that Nga's poems "decollaborate" with Larsen's. For Terrence Des Pres, the juxtaposition of the two voices is less about subversion than about "candor" and a self-conscious, "necessary irony" in which each narrator challenges the other and both dispute the definition of Vietnam as a place of schizophrenic compartmentalization. "Not least among its virtues, *Shallow Graves* illustrates the way aesthetic resolution . . . depends on political consciousness" (193).

BIBLIOGRAPHY

Work by Tran Thi Nga

Larsen, Wendy, and Tran Thi Nga. *Shallow Graves: Two Women and Vietnam*. New York: Random House, 1986.

Studies of Tran Thi Nga

Des Pres, Terrence. "Sisters to Antigone." *Parnassus* 14.1 (1987): 187–200.
Gotera, Vince. "Reconciliation and Women's Poetry." *The United States and Viet Nam from War to Peace*. Ed. Robert M. Slabey. Jefferson, NC: McFarland, 1996. 150–60.
Uba, George. "Friend and Foe: De-collaborating Wendy Wilder Larsen and Tran Thi Nga's *Shallow Graves*." *Journal of American Culture* 16.3 (Fall 1993): 63–70.

YONE NOGUCHI
(1875–1947)

Edward Marx

BIOGRAPHY

Yonejiro Noguchi was born in Tsushima, near Nagoya, on 8 December 1875. His father was a merchant with distant samurai ancestry, while his mother's family had connections to the Buddhist priesthood. Interested in the English language from an early age, he left home at fourteen for a school in Nagoya and moved the following year to Tokyo, where he entered Keio Gijuku, a private preparatory school in the process of becoming a university, founded by Yukichi Fukuzawa, a member of the first Japanese embassy to the United States (1860) and an early advocate of Western-style modernization. With the encouragement of Fukuzawa and Shigetaka Shiga, an influential cultural nationalist with whom Noguchi lived for a time, he left for the United States in 1893.

Arriving in San Francisco, Noguchi worked for some time as a delivery boy for a Japanese-language newspaper, the *Soko Shimbun* (San Francisco news), run by a group of political exiles. Over the next two years, he also worked as a "schoolboy" or domestic servant and as a dishwasher in Palo Alto, where he journeyed to visit a friend studying at Stanford. He succeeded in improving his English sufficiently to return to the newspaper as a translator at the time of the Sino-Japanese War (1894–95).

Noguchi's decision to become a poet occurred in 1895 when he visited Joaquin Miller, the colorful and eccentric "poet of the Sierras" known for welcoming visitors to his rustic home in the Oakland hills. Miller had a fondness for Japanese houseguests and welcomed Noguchi, who was looking for a place to rest and study, and later encouraged him in his efforts to write English poetry, although he offered little in the way of practical advice. Noguchi's first published poems appeared in the *Lark*, a jocose San Francisco little magazine published by Gelett Burgess and Porter Garnett, in July 1896, and additional poems appeared later in the year in the same magazine, as well as in the *Chap-Book* (Chicago) and *Philistine* (New York).

From 1896 to 1899, Noguchi divided his time between Miller's "Heights" and San Francisco, with occasional excursions to such places as Yosemite and Los Angeles. He established connections with other California writers, including socialist poet Edwin Markham, and initiated correspondence with writers outside of California. One of these, Charles Warren Stoddard, a gay Catholic travel writer and poet, became Noguchi's intimate correspondent, assisting him with some of his early poetic productions. In 1898, Noguchi collaborated on a short-lived "magazinelet" entitled the *Twilight* with Kosen Takahashi, an illustrator for the San Francisco newspaper *Shin Sekai* (The new world), which ran for two issues. That year he also began, with the help of a young journalist, Blanche Partington, a prose narrative that would eventually evolve into *The American Diary of a Japanese Girl*.

In 1900, Noguchi traveled to the East Coast, stopping in Chicago, where he wrote his impressions of the city for the *Evening Post* and met, among others, the Asian American novelist Onoto Watanna (Winnifred Eaton). After visiting Charles Warren Stoddard in Washington, D.C., he arrived in New York, which remained his primary residence during the last four years of his American period. A reply to an advertisement he placed in the *New York Herald* for an assistant to help with his English writing brought Léonie Gilmour, a twenty-eight-year-old schoolteacher educated at Bryn Mawr and the Sorbonne, with whom Noguchi completed the pseudonymously published *American Diary of a Japanese Girl* and its sequel, *The American Letters of a Japanese Parlor-Maid*.

In 1902, Noguchi traveled to England, where he self-published and promoted a pamphlet of poems, *From the Eastern Sea*, that brought him to the attention of the English literary world and enabled him to establish contacts with such writers as William Michael Rossetti, Laurence Binyon, Arthur Symons, and Arthur Ransome. Having arrived fortuitously in the year of the Anglo-Japanese Alliance, Noguchi was widely discussed in the London press, and an expanded edition of *From the Eastern Sea* was published by the Unicorn Press in 1903.

In spite of his London success, Noguchi continued to have difficulty publishing his work after his return to New York until the advent of the Russo-Japanese War in 1904 created a sudden market for things Japanese. A secret marriage to Léonie Gilmour in 1903 ended in separation, and Noguchi took up another romantic attachment to an Alabama journalist, Ethel Armes. In the summer of 1904, he began to arrange his return to Japan, planning for Ethel to join him as his wife, and in October, after nearly eleven years, he did return. But the marriage plan ended after the revelation that Léonie, now living with her mother in Los Angeles, had given birth to a son (later the sculptor Isamu Noguchi).

Noguchi returned to Japan in 1904 a triumphant conqueror of the English and

American literary worlds, and the following year he was offered the professor-
ship in English and American literature at by now Keio University he would
hold for the next forty years. After the collapse of his engagement to Ethel
Armes, Noguchi began an ultimately successful effort to persuade Léonie to join
him with Isamu in Japan. By the time of their arrival in 1907, however, he was
involved in a relationship with his Japanese domestic assistant, Matsuko Takeda.
The reconciliation with Léonie was problematic, to say the least, and they separated permanently in 1910. Noguchi divided his time between Tokyo and Kamakura and wrote much of his best work during this period, gaining an
increasing influence as a bridge between the literary worlds of Japan and the
West, an influence that culminated in a second visit to England at the invitation
of the poet laureate, Robert Bridges, to lecture at Oxford in 1914.

Noguchi played an important role in promoting haiku and Noh drama in the
West and in promoting modern British and American literature in Japan, but
after his second visit to America, a transcontinental lecture tour of 1919–20, his
influence abroad began to wane, and he wrote increasingly in Japanese, confining his English efforts to books on Japanese art. The few English poems Noguchi published in periodicals during the 1920s and 1930s, however, show a
turn away from the fin de siècle style of his earlier poetry toward a spare, Zen-
influenced style. A trip to India in 1935–36 provided a pretext for his last volume
of English verse, *The Ganges Calls Me*. During the Pacific War, Noguchi lent
his pen to the cause of militaristic imperialism, publishing two volumes of prop-
agandistic verse in Japanese. After his house was destroyed in the American
firebombing of Tokyo in April 1945, Noguchi and his family retreated to the
village of Toyooka. Several postwar poems in English published in 1946 attest
to Noguchi's efforts to come to terms with the enormity of defeat and his determination to welcome reconstruction as an unprecedented creative opportunity.
Before his death from stomach cancer on 13 July 1947, he sought to achieve a
reconciliation with his estranged son Isamu.

MAJOR WORKS AND THEMES

Noguchi's published English poetry consists of seven collections and perhaps
another forty or fifty uncollected poems. Of the books, *Seen and Unseen, or,
Monologues of a Homeless Snail* (1897), *The Voice of the Valley* (1897), and
From the Eastern Sea (1903) may be taken as representing the main corpus of
his American work. With the addition of *The Pilgrimage* (1909), they also com-
prise most of his best English verse.

Seen and Unseen, written when Noguchi was barely twenty years old, is a
startlingly original exercise in poetic self-fashioning, a testing-out of the metaphysical machinery of English poetics. Borrowing his diction from Edgar Allan
Poe, among other influences, and his cadences from Whitman, Noguchi places
himself as the poet in nature and produces a spiritual autobiography in verse.
In poems like "What about My Songs," Noguchi shows a shrewd awareness of

problems of voice and audience, while other poems like "Seas of Loneliness" take the poet's relationship with Nature and the Universe as the field for poetic exploration. The poem may be seen as developing new poetic possibilities inherent in the marriage between Eastern meditational perspectives and the Western lyric. The poem exhibits a remarkable receptivity to natural surroundings, recording the way the subjectivity of the poet is colored by atmospheric elements and momentarily subsumed by natural events like the voice of the quail. Noguchi further deployed this sensitivity to the natural environment in his second volume of verse, *The Voice of the Valley* (1897), taking as a subject a spring trip to the Yosemite valley and adding the influence of Milton to that of Whitman and Poe.

Explicit Japanese themes do not enter into Noguchi's poetry until his third volume, *From the Eastern Sea*, where they become conspicuous elements in a number of poems. Here, however, the Japanese elements remain strongly influenced by Western Japonism, as in the opening lines of "O Hana San." Many poems in *The Pilgrimage* (1909) continue to inhabit this dreamy, fairyland Japan, but these appear alongside Zen-influenced poems such as "At the Yuigamahama Shore by Kamakura."

Noguchi began promoting haiku, or hokku, as it was then usually called, from 1904, when he wrote "A Proposal to American Poets" recommending the form as a cure for American wordiness. But his own experiments with haiku in English usually bore little resemblance to Japanese haiku, in spite of his claim in the preface to his *Japanese Hokkus* (1920) that the Japanese Hokku spirit runs through all of his poetry.

Noguchi's later style of spare realism begins to manifest itself in the mid-1920s, perhaps the best example being the poem "Keepsake," printed in *Poetry* magazine in 1926. The difference between the poem's stark objectivity and the dreaminess of Noguchi's earlier work is startling, clearly indicating in its rejection of conspicuously poetic language and subject matter an accommodation of principles of modernism he had previously eschewed. But Noguchi published only a handful of poems in the new style. His poems written in India and collected in *The Ganges Calls Me* (1938) are comparatively superficial and journalistic—a series of poetic snapshots. In contrast, the two poems printed in February 1946 in the *Japan Times* are almost painful in their intensity and, again, startling. "Life in Full Bloom" begins with images of trees and vegetables. The opening lines of the poem embody the poet summoning the forces of nature and the creative power of the will against the despair of a shattered world.

CRITICAL RECEPTION

Soon after being touted as "the latest thing in poets" in the pages of the *Critic* and *Bookman* in November 1896, Noguchi's reputation suffered a setback when he was attacked in the pages of the *San Francisco Chronicle* by an Oakland minister, Jay William Hudson, who accused him of plagiarizing from Edgar

Allan Poe. The publication of his first two books of verse the following year brought him to the attention of a small but significant coterie of readers appreciative of his innovative expressive poetic efforts in spite of his somewhat limited command of English. "While Noguchi is by no means a poet in the large, complicated modern sense of the word," wrote Willa Cather, "he has more true inspiration, more melody, from within than many a greater man" (580).

The critical response to the pamphlet and book versions of *From the Eastern Sea*, published in London in 1903, also stressed Noguchi's unusual accomplishments and limitations. Arthur Symons in an unsigned review of the *From the Eastern Sea* pamphlet conceded that "from time to time words seem to fail altogether, or to render but a treacherous service," but added that "it is through these very incoherencies that we seem to see what is most significant in this scarcely to be apprehended personality, which goes, like Eastern music, right through harmony to what lies nearest silence on the other side" (302). But in spite of the interest in Noguchi's work from a number of leading British writers, Noguchi was unable to find a publisher willing to print an American edition of the book. But Noguchi was a writer's writer, and by the time he left the United States in 1904, he could boast an enviable circle of American literary connections, including Bliss Carman, Zona Gale, Charlotte Perkins Gilman, Richard Le Gallienne, Edwin Markham, Joaquin Miller, E.C. Stedman, Charles Warren Stoddard, Edith Thomas, and Ridgely Torrence, and an equivalent list in England. Such connections, along with his four books and dozens of articles in major American periodicals, earned Noguchi considerable respect back in Japan, where he would remain an influential authority on British and American literature and culture for several decades.

The Pilgrimage, Noguchi's 1909 collection, reissued in New York in 1912, achieved most of its critical success in England. "We find in his verse, with all its modern tone," wrote Laurence Binyon, "the same attitude that we find in the old singers of his country, the same feeling of the impermanence of things, the same cherishing of elusive and transitory beauty" (41).

Poetry magazine's associate editor Eunice Tietjens was one of the few to explicitly recognize the importance of Noguchi's early volumes of poetry for the modernist movement: "Looking back on them now," she wrote in 1919, "one can see how directly they forecast the modern movement. They were in free verse—in the nineties—they were condensed, suggestive, full of rhythmical variations. In matters of technic they might have been written today, and, though few people understood them then, time has proven Mr. Noguchi a forerunner" (97).

In his earlier career, Noguchi pursued his own poetic direction under the double indulgence of a dominant art-for-art's-sake aesthetic paradigm and the Japanophilia of an audience considerably ignorant of the country and its literature. The climate after World War I was far less hospitable. In an anonymous review, Arthur Waley attacked Noguchi for his failure to be "securely intelligible" in English, his inadequate mastery of classical Japanese verse, and the excessively subjective character of his poems in Japanese. Noguchi's 1920 collection *Japanese Hokkus* was also a disappointment, Jun Fujita pointing out how Noguchi's use of the form failed to live up to Noguchi's own critical ideals. "Where is that fine and illusive mood, big enough to illuminate the infinity of the universe, which is essential to the hokku?" Fujita wondered. "I cannot find it" (164). Earl Miner, in *The Japanese Tradition in British and American Literature* (1958), attempted to explain away what he considered Noguchi's baffling popularity by arguing that Noguchi, "doing his best to reflect current English modes of the more sentimental variety, and yet a Japanese . . . assured the age that their own work was truly inspired by Japan" (186).

Since the arrival of Asian American studies in the late 1960s and early 1970s, Noguchi has gained occasional admission in anthologies like *Quiet Fire* (1996), but there has been little rush thus far to claim Noguchi as an Asian American literary ancestor. In *New Immigrant Literatures of the United States*, Alpana Sharma Knippling states that writers like Noguchi "did not express the concerns of Japanese Americans, and, therefore, they are normally called 'Americanized Japanese' rather than 'Japanese Americans' " (128). Such definitions, however, raise the contentious issue of who speaks for Japanese Americans, and I argue in " 'A Different Mode of Speech': Yone Noguchi in Meiji America" against definitions that would risk excluding nearly all first-generation Japanese American writers and would limit our understanding and appreciation of the diversity of "Japanese America." Yoshinobu Hakutani's efforts to draw attention to Noguchi as a modernist precursor and influence have not resulted thus far in widespread acknowledgment of Noguchi's importance as a modernist poet, although future research will no doubt be built on these efforts, on Hakutani's edition of Noguchi's selected prose and poetry, and on Hakutani's important interview with Isamu Noguchi about his difficult relationship with his father.

In Japan, Noguchi's reputation, tarnished by his wartime collaborations, began to revive with the work of Noguchi's son-in-law, Tokyo University English professor Usaburo Toyama, who collected and edited a three-volume collection of essays and other critical materials, titled *Shijin Yone Noguchi Kenkyu*. Toyama also encouraged the work of Ikuko Atsumi, who compiled an extensive bibliography of nearly two thousand items by and about Noguchi. Atsumi also embarked on the considerable undertaking of Noguchi's *Collected English Letters*, a work that brought to light the extraordinary breadth and sheer magnitude of Noguchi's career for the first time. The 1980s and 1990s have seen a steady trickle of Japanese articles and an occasional book on Noguchi, as well as a substantial new edition of Noguchi's Japanese essays (*Noguchi Yone Senshu*) published in 1997–98 at the fiftieth anniversary of his death. Nevertheless, Noguchi is now far less widely known in both Japan and America than his son, Isamu. It remains to be seen whether the increasingly international outlook of Asian American studies and related fields will be more accommodating to a reexamination of this first Japanese American poet and novelist in the twenty-first century.

BIBLIOGRAPHY

Works by Yone Noguchi

Poetry

Seen and Unseen; or, Monologues of a Homeless Snail. San Francisco: G. Burgess & P. Garnett, 1897.

The Voice of the Valley. Intro. Charles Warren Stoddard. San Francisco: W. Doxey, 1897.

From the Eastern Sea. London: Unicorn Press, 1903.

The Summer Cloud. Tokyo: Shunyodo, 1906.

The Pilgrimage. Kamakura: Valley Press; Yokohama: Kelly & Walsh, 1909; New York: Mitchell Kennerley, 1912.

Japanese Hokkus. Boston: Four Seas, 1920.

Niju kokusekisha no shi [Poems of a dual national]. Tokyo: Genbunsha, 1921.

Selected Poems of Yone Noguchi. Boston: Four Seas; London: E. Matthews, 1921.

"Keepsake." *Poetry* 28 (Aug. 1926): 243.

The Ganges Calls Me: Book of Poems. Tokyo: Kyobun Kwan, 1938.

"Two Poems." *Japan Times* 3 February 1946: 4.

Selected English Writings of Yone Noguchi: An East-West Literary Assimilation. Ed. Yoshinobu Hakutani. 2 vols. Rutherford: Fairleigh Dickinson University Press; London: Associated University Presses, 1990–92.

Fiction

"Miss Morning Glory" [pseud.]. *The American Diary of a Japanese Girl.* New York: Frederick A. Stokes, 1902.

The American Letters of a Japanese Parlor-Maid. Tokyo: Fuzanbo, 1905.

Essays

"A Proposal to American Poets." *Reader* 3.3 (February 1904): 248.

"Popular Songs of Japan." *Poet Lore* 15 (April 1904): 78–80.

The Spirit of Japanese Poetry. London: J. Murray; New York: E.P. Dutton, 1914.

Japan and America. Tokyo: Keio University Press; New York: Orientalia, 1921.

Through the Torii. London: E. Matthews, 1914; Boston: Four Seas, 1922.

Toyama, Usaburo, ed. *Shijin Yone Noguchi Kenkyu.* 3 vols. Tokyo: Zokei bijutsu kyokai shuppankyoku, 1963, 1965, 1975.

Noguchi Yone Senshu [Selected works of Yone Noguchi]. 3 vols. Tokyo: Kress, 1997–1998.

Autobiography

The Story of Yone Noguchi. London: Chatto & Windus, 1914; Philadelphia: G.W. Jacobs, 1915.

Letters

Collected English Letters. Ed. Ikuko Atsumi. Tokyo: Yone Noguchi Society, 1975.

Studies of Yone Noguchi

Atsumi, Ikuko. "Yone Noguchi bunken" [Yone Noguchi documents]. *Hikaku Bungaku* 12 (1969): 68–92; 15 (1972): 63–92.

[Binyon, Laurence]. "Japanese Poetry." *Times Literary Supplement* 10 February 1910: 41–42.

Cather, Willa. "The Passing Show." *Courier* 8 February 1898: 2–3. Reprinted in *The World and the Parish*. Ed. William M. Curtin. Lincoln: University of Nebraska Press, 1970. 579–80.

Coburn, Alvin Langdon. "Yone Noguchi." *Bookman* (London) 46 (April 1914): 33–36.

Fujita, Jun. "A Japanese Cosmopolite." *Poetry: A Magazine of Verse* 23 (June 1922): 162–64.

Graham, Don B. "Yone Noguchi's 'Poe Mania.' " *Markham Review* 4 (1974): 58–60.

Hakutani, Yoshinobu. "Ezra Pound, Yone Noguchi, and Imagism." *Modern Philology* 90 (August 1992): 46–69.

———. "Father and Son: A Conversation with Isamu Noguchi." *Journal of Modern Literature* 17.1 (Summer 1990): 13–33.

Hudson, Jay William. "Newest Thing in Poets, a Borrower from Poe." *San Francisco Chronicle* 22 November 1896: 16.

Kamei, Shunsuke. *Yone Noguchi, an English Poet of Japan: An Essay*. Tokyo: Yone Noguchi Society, 1965.

Knippling, Alpana Sharma, ed. *New Immigrant Literatures of the United States*. Westport, CT: Greenwood Press, 1996.

Marx, Edward. "The Cross-Cultural Poetry of Yone Noguchi." *The View from Kyoto: Essays on Twentieth-Century Poetry*. Ed. Shoichiro Sakurai. Kyoto: Rinsen, 1998. 285–302.

———. " 'A Different Mode of Speech': Yone Noguchi in Meiji America." *Re/Collecting Asian America: Readings in Cultural History*. Ed. Josephine Lee, Imogene L. Lim, and Yuko Matsukawa. Forthcoming.

Miner, Earl. *The Japanese Tradition in British and American Literature*. Westport, CT: Greenwood, 1976.

Sato, Hiroaki. "Yone Noguchi—Accomplishments and Roles." *Journal of American and Canadian Studies* 13 (1995): 105–21.

[Symons, Arthur]. "A Japanese Poet." *Saturday Review* 95 (7 March 1903): 302.

Takai, Sofu. *Eishijin Yone Noguchi no eiko: sono bei-ei ni okeru henreki kuto no hiroku* [English poet Yone Noguchi's glory: secret memoirs of an arduous pilgrimage]. Tokyo: Kioi Shobo, 1985.

Tietjens, Eunice. "Yone Noguchi." *Poetry* 15 (November 1919): 96–98.

[Waley, Arthur]. "Japanese Essays and Poems." *Times Literary Supplement* (6 April 1922): 227.

UMA PARAMESWARAN
(1938–   )

Di Gan Blackburn

BIOGRAPHY

Born in Madras and raised in Jabalpur in central India, Uma Parameswaran took her early education in India before pursuing an academic career in North America. She earned her B.A. from Jabalpur University and her M.A. in English from Nagpur University. After being granted a Fulbright Fellowship, she took an M.A. in creative writing at Indiana University and completed a Ph.D. in English at Michigan State University in 1972. She is a professor of English at the University of Winnipeg, where she has lived since 1966. Consistent with the vision and themes that run through much of her writing, Parameswaran has been an active promoter of South Asian culture in her community. Among her activities are founding PALI (Performing Arts and Literatures of India) and producing a public television program that aired weekly from 1979 to 1992 (Mittal 32). A respected literary critic, Parameswaran has played a prominent role in the development and recognition of South Asian Canadian Literature (or SACLIT, a name she coined). She is also well known within the SACLIT field for her own creative work. Her play *Rootless but Green Are the Boulevard Trees*, was the first full-length SACLIT play published ("Names Resonant and Sweet" 8), and her poetry has earned her a place as a mainstay in SACLIT anthologies (Byrdon 157).

MAJOR WORKS AND THEMES

Parameswaran's creative writings, which cut across genres and include short stories, plays, and poems, share common themes and at times even the same characters. At the most basic level, she recounts stories of the South Asian Canadian immigrant experience. Exploring the challenges of coping with ambiguous identity, she deals with assimilation and racism issues. Her works operate on a broader level as well. By writing about the sense of alienation that typifies the immigrant experience, Parameswaran also provides "resonant metaphors for the post-colonial condition" (Pandey 228).

Individual poems by Parameswaran have appeared in various anthologies, but the long narrative poem *Trishanku* is "probably her major achievement" (Kanaganayakam 1084). *Trishanku* is actually a collection of poems written in different voices. It recounts the story of an Indian Canadian family and its extended community coping with life in Winnipeg, Canada, where Parameswaran lives. The Canadian setting is deliberate. Parameswaran refuses to call SACLIT writing "Indian" and has argued strongly that it is emphatically Canadian (*Geography of Voice* xvii). In *Trishanku*, Parameswaran uses different voices representing different generations and perspectives to portray a remarkably rich immigrant experience. The poem's title is also descriptive: Trishanku is a mythical king in Hindu literature who is condemned to hang between earth and heaven, belonging to neither. As such, he is an obvious symbol of ambiguous identity.

Parameswaran's handling of the South Asian Canadian immigrant experience is nuanced. In her analysis of Parameswaran's *Rootless but Green Are the Boulevard Trees*, a play very similar to *Trishanku*, Bina Mittal notes that Parameswaran makes "no judgement ... about whether acculturation is a happy or unhappy process" (35). Parameswaran herself describes the final stage of adjustment as "a place where one can be oneself, assimilating if one is comfortable doing so, being different if one chooses to be so" ("Ganga in the Assiniboine" 85).

CRITICAL RECEPTION

Although only a few reviews of Parameswaran's poetry are available, most of them have been positive. In the introduction to *Shakti's Words*, an anthology of South Asian Canadian women writers, the editors describe her poetry with terms such as "well-crafted" and "not 'political' at the expense of craft" (xi). A later anthology in the same series calls her a "deft lyricist with a gift for political lyrical poetry" (*Geography of Voice* xii). John Oliver Perry is less impressed by the aesthetic aspect of her poetry, commenting that "rhythmic, metaphoric, or verbal delights are not to be sought in the often prosaic lines of *Trishanku*" (537). Nonetheless, he too finds her writing valuable not only for what it says about the Indo-Canadian experience, but also for what it illuminates about life in the multicultural community (537).

BIBLIOGRAPHY

Works by Uma Parameswaran

Poetry

Trishanku. Toronto: TSAR, 1988.
The Door I Shut Behind Me: Selected Fiction, Poetry, and Drama. New Delhi: Affiliated
    East West Press, 1990.
Trishanku and Other Writings. New Delhi: Prestige, 1998.

Anthologies

Shakti's Words. Ed. Diane McGifford and Judith Kearns. Toronto: TSAR, 1990.
The Geography of Voice. Ed. Diane McGifford. Toronto: TSAR, 1992.

Plays

Rootless but Green Are the Boulevard Trees. Toronto: TSAR, 1987.
Saclit Drama: Plays by South Asian Canadians. Bangalore: IBH Prakashana, 1996.
Sons Must Die and Other Plays. New Delhi: Prestige, 1998.

Short-Story Collection

What Was Always Hers. Fredericton, New Brunswick: Broken Jaw Press, 1999.

Selected Scholarship

Cyclic Hope, Cyclic Pain. Calcutta: A Writers Workshop Publication, 1973.
A Study of Representative Indo-English Novelists. New Delhi: Vikas Publishing House,
    1976.
"Ganga in the Assiniboine: Prospects for Indo-Canadian Literature." *A Meeting of
    Streams: South Asian Canadian Literature.* Ed. M.G. Vassanji. Toronto: TSAR,
    1985. 79–93.
"Salman Rushdie's Shame: An Overview of a Labyrinth." *The New Indian Novel in
    English: A Study of the 1980s.* New Delhi: Allied Publishers, 1990. 121–30.
"Names Resonant and Sweet: An Overview of South Asian Canadian Women's Writing."
    The Other Woman: Women of Colour in Contemporary Canadian Literature. Ed.
    Makeda Silvera. Toronto: Sister Vision Press, 1995. 3–17.
"I See the Glass as Half Full." *Between the Lines: South Asians and Postcoloniality.*
    Philadelphia: Temple University Press, 1996. 351–67.
Saclit: An Introduction to South-Asian Canadian Literature. Madras: EastWest Books,
    1996.
Kamala Markandaya. Jaipur: Rawat Publications, 2000.

Studies of Uma Parameswaran

Byrdon, Diana. Rev. of *Shakti's Words*, ed. Diane McGifford and Judith Kearns. *Ca-
    nadian Literature* 132 (1992): 156–57.
Kanaganayakam, Chelva. "South Asian Canadian Literature." *The Oxford Companion to*

Canadian Literature. 2nd ed. Ed. Eugene Benson and William Toye. New York: Oxford University Press, 1997. 1083–85.

McGifford, Diane. "Uma Parameswaran." *Writers of the Indian Diaspora*. Ed. Emmanuel S. Nelson. Westport, CT: Greenwood Press, 1993. 305–9.

Mittal, Bina. "Exploring the Immigrant Experience through Theatre: Uma Parameswaran's *Rootless but Green Are the Boulevard Trees*." *Canadian Theatre Review* 94 (1998): 32–35.

Pandey, M.S. "The Trishanku Motif in the Poetry of Sujata Bhatt and Uma Parameswaran." *The Literature of the Indian Diaspora: Essays in Criticism*. Ed. A.L. McLeod. New Delhi: Sterling Publishers, 2000. 225–38.

Perry, John Oliver. Rev. of *Trishanku*. *World Literature Today* 63.3 (1989): 536–37.

ALBERT SAIJO
(1926–   )

Lavonne Leong

BIOGRAPHY

Albert Saijo was born in Los Angeles on 4 February 1926, the son of a Christian preacher and a Japanese schoolteacher and writer. Saijo spent his childhood east of Los Angeles in the then-rural San Gabriel Valley. In 1942, when Saijo was sixteen, Executive Order 9066 interned Saijo's family at the Heart Mountain Relocation Center in Wyoming. After graduating from high school (while still interned), he was drafted into the U.S. Army. Saijo spent three years in the United States and Italy in an all–Japanese American unit. It was while he was in the army that Saijo found Ernest Hemingway's *A Farewell to Arms* and became interested in literature. Saijo returned to the United States, drifting from New York City to Denver and from Denver back to Los Angeles, where, in the late 1940s, he studied Zen Buddhism. During this time, he also graduated from the University of Southern California with a bachelor's degree in international politics and a minor in Chinese. He began a master's degree on the partitioning of Vietnam, but abandoned it.

In the late 1950s, Saijo moved to the Bay Area, where he met and befriended Jack Kerouac and other Beat poets in San Francisco's Chinatown. Kerouac later fictionalized Saijo in *Big Sur* as George Baso. A cross-country drive with Kerouac and Lew Welch resulted in a book of "road-trip haiku" called *Trip Trap*, a reference to Gary Snyder's 1959 poetry collection *Riprap*. In 1960, Saijo moved to Marin County, where he spent the next two decades as "YOUR BASIC MARIN COUNTY HIPPIE STONER . . . ON THE FLOOR CUZ CHAIRS SEEMED A FORM OF REPRESSION" (*Outspeaks* 196). During that time,

Saijo married and divorced and spent a great deal of time in the High Sierra, publishing one of the early West Coast primers on backpacking in the wilderness, *The Backpacker*. Saijo married a second time in the late 1970s and moved to a plot of unimproved land on California's "Lost Coast." After twelve years of building and maintaining a homestead there, Saijo moved in 1991 to Volcano, Hawaii, where he still lives with his wife, Laura, a teacher and musician.

A poem published in *Bamboo Ridge* in 1996, "Karma Lollipop," earned Saijo a Pushcart Prize. In 1997, at the age of seventy-one, he published his first solo collection of poetry, *Outspeaks: A Rhapsody*, which won the 1998 Small Press Book Award for a poetry collection.

MAJOR WORKS AND THEMES

Albert Saijo's work is a shock to the literate eye. Written all in capital letters, syntactically haphazard, and punctuated only with dashes, it looks at first like a direct transcription from a particularly energetic stream of consciousness. But if this is one long barbaric yawp, it is an outpouring grounded in the tradition of literary originality. Saijo's only collection, *Outspeaks: A Rhapsody*, is sprinkled with epigrams from the likes of Ralph Waldo Emerson, William Blake, Wallace Stevens, Emily Dickinson, and William Wordsworth. The headlong rush of Saijo's poetry brings to mind the carefully crafted, Whitmanesque diatribes of the Beat generation.

His all-capitals register reads as a shout, which can be taken as angry or exuberant. The content of his work shuttles disorientingly between erudition, scatology, spirituality, cuteness, high emotion, and a wry sense of humor that hovers somewhere between the ridiculous and the scathing: "KEPLER YOU BLEW IT" ("NATUREMART" 44). Saijo's style jars the reader out of any single political or social identity in relation to the author. As he explains in "EARTH SLANGUAGE WITH ENGLISH ON IT," his best-known poem, this is what he wants. Saijo expresses a wish for a pared-down "UNIVERSAL GRAMMAR," with "NO FORMAL-VERNACULAR OR DEMOTIC-HIERATIC OPPOSITION," a democratic "BIRTHRIGHT TONGUE" for everyone on earth: "SLANGUAGE."

With this casual, inclusive, rhapsodic "slanguage," Saijo expounds on serious subjects—racism, the environment, technology, religion, spirituality, war, politics, pain, and death—without being weighed down by their gravity. Often he approaches his topics from unexpected angles. In "KARMA LOLLIPOP," Saijo imagines a postapocalyptic world in which technologically advanced Asians colonize Caucasian territories with pious talk and colored glass beads. The title of the poem suggests that this is a gleeful imagining of Karmic retribution for several centuries of white colonization, but the uncomfortable reversal of the poem does not ignore history's complexities.

CRITICAL RECEPTION

Albert Saijo's work is difficult to classify and has received very little published critical attention to date. The significant exception is a review of *Outspeaks: A Rhapsody* in the alternative literary journal *Tinfish*, in which Juliana Spahr makes a case for Saijo as "a new Blake" (53) who "writes things other people dare not think" (52). On the back cover of *Outspeaks*, there is a quote from Lawrence Ferlinghetti: "Albert Saijo has the great vision most poets and painters never had."

BIBLIOGRAPHY

Works by Albert Saijo

Books

The Backpacker. San Francisco: 101 Productions, 1972.
With Jack Kerouac and Lew Welch. *Trip Trap: Haiku along the Road from San Francisco to New York*. Bolinas, CA: Grey Fox Press, 1973.
Outspeaks: A Rhapsody. Honolulu: Bamboo Ridge Press, 1997.

Uncollected Work

"Hunter Gatherer." *Bamboo Ridge: Journal of Hawai'i Literature and Arts* 75 (1999): 171–74.
"Writ by Hand." *Bamboo Ridge: Journal of Hawai'i Literature and Arts* 75 (1999): 175–78.
"Life Dies in Greenhouse." *Bamboo Ridge: Journal of Hawai'i Literature and Arts* 76 (2000): 21.
"Some Feng Shui." *Bamboo Ridge: Journal of Hawai'i Literature and Arts* 76 (2000): 17–18.
"Turkey Vulture." *Bamboo Ridge: Journal of Hawai'i Literature and Arts* 76 (2000): 14.
"Zoom Zone." *Bamboo Ridge: Journal of Hawai'i Literature and Arts* 76 (2000): 24.

Studies of Albert Saijo

Adams, Wanda. "An Outspoken Way with Words and Ideas." Rev. of *Outspeaks: A Rhapsody*. *Honolulu Advertiser* 28 September 1997: F5+.
Kam, Nadine. "Running on Rhapsody: Albert Saijo, the World's 'Oldest Asian Hippie' and Inspiration for Kerouac's Baso, Raps about Writing and Life in the '60s." *Honolulu Star-Bulletin* 6 June 1997: D-1.
Leong, James. "A Zen Pastry Shop." Rev. of *Outspeaks: A Rhapsody*. *Pacific Reader* Spring/Summer 1997: Poetry Section.
Spahr, Juliana. "Untitled." Rev. of *Outspeaks: A Rhapsody*. *Tinfish* 6 (March 1998): 52–54.

CATHY SONG
(1955–   )

Gayle K. Sato

BIOGRAPHY

In two interviews from the early 1980s, Cathy Song expressed uneasiness with being identified as an ethnic or regional writer. Yet her poetry has always been autobiographical, more explicitly so with each successive book, and clearly reflects the shaping—often the enabling—influences of region, ethnicity, gender, and class on her three central subjects: art, family, and women's experience. Situating Song's writing within the history of Asian American and Hawaiian literary traditions illuminates her achievement as an American poet.

Born on 20 August 1955, Song spent her early childhood in Wahiawa, a former plantation town on the island of Oahu, Hawaii. She was seven when her family moved to Waialae Kahala, a suburb of Honolulu, where she lived until she transferred from the University of Hawaii to Wellesley College. She graduated from Wellesley in 1977 with a degree in English, then earned an M.F.A. from Boston College in 1981. While living in Boston, she married Douglas McHarg Davenport, then a medical student at Tufts University. They moved to Colorado in 1984 for Davenport's residency at Denver General Hospital and returned to Hawaii in 1987. Boston, Denver, and Honolulu inform the landscapes of Song's three books, which also mark the births of her three children. *Frameless Windows, Squares of Light*, written in Colorado, where Song's daughter was born, contains the largest number of poems based on her experiences as a mother.

Song was only twenty-seven when she won the Yale Series of Younger Poets Award in 1982 for *Picture Bride*, which was nominated for the National Book

Critics Circle Award the following year. In 1993, she received the Hawaii Award for Literature—the youngest recipient in the award's history—as well as the Shelley Memorial Award from the Poetry Society of America. Since 1987, Song has taught at the University of Hawaii at Manoa and for the Poets in the Schools Program, which she passionately supports. "Through poetry they come to know their lives do matter," she has said, linking her own teaching to what Richard Hugo observed about the reason college students keep enrolling in creative-writing classes: "[H]e came to the conclusion that it was the only place on campus where the student wasn't a statistic, a Social Security number. You are an individual person and your life counts; your feelings, your thoughts, your mind is on the page. It is a very human experience. I see it when I do Poets in the Schools" (Choo 6–7).

Ella Song, the poet's mother, is a second-generation Chinese American. Her father, Andrew Song, is the son of immigrants from Korea who came to work the sugarcane fields in Waialua. Except for Song's maternal grandfather, family members provide the subjects for some frequently anthologized poems and those that occupy strategic positions in all three collections. *Picture Bride* begins with a much-discussed poem about Song's Korean grandmother, while *Frameless Windows, Squares of Light* opens with a whole section about Song's father and paternal grandfather, who are also the subjects, respectively, of "The Tower of Pisa" and "Easter, Wahiawa, 1959." *School Figures* begins with poems about Song's mother; this is the first time she is clearly identified as a second-generation Chinese American and concrete references are made to specific events from her life. In addition to parents and grandparents, Song's elder sister Andrea and younger brother Alan also appear frequently in her poems. This desire to write about family appeared early; around the age of nine, Song assumed the role of "family chronicler" (Gall 354) and began assembling her own books and magazines. She recalls: "When I was growing up an experience didn't feel complete until I wrote about it. . . . I went through so much paper that my father, who was very supportive, would buy army surplus target paper. I wrote on the backs of bull's-eyes" (Choo 6).

MAJOR WORKS AND THEMES

Song's major works are *Picture Bride* (1983), *Frameless Windows, Squares of Light* (1988), and *School Figures* (1994). When *Picture Bride* was selected as the winning manuscript for the Yale Younger Poets Competition in 1982, it was titled "From the White Place" after a painting by Georgia O'Keeffe. The publisher's decision to change the title recalls the case of Maxine Hong Kingston's *The Woman Warrior*, which was presented to the reading public as "autobiography" rather than "fiction," as the author intended. In Song's case, however, problems of interpretation have been mitigated by the fact that reviewers and critics have generally chosen to read "picture bride" as including the book's obvious concern with matters of framing, viewing, and aesthetic representation.

Although *Picture Bride* was published only ten years after Song's graduation from high school, her work had already appeared in *Hawaii Review*, *Talk Story*, *Poetry Hawaii*, and *Bridge*, magazines and anthologies showcasing Asian American and contemporary writing from and about Hawaii. Two of these early poems, "Remnants" and "Bean Sprouts," are reworked in *Picture Bride* into various poems about Song's father and the one titled "Chinatown." Two other poems published before 1983, "from A Georgia O'Keeffe Portfolio: Flower Series, No. 3., An Orchid" and "Lost Sister," were incorporated into *Picture Bride* intact, with the O'Keeffe piece retitled "An Orchid" and inserted into "Blue and White Lines after O'Keeffe." It is clear from this handful of early poems that Song had discovered her most important themes at the very beginning of her career—what it means to be part of the families one is born into or makes for oneself, to be Chinese and Korean in Hawaii, to be a daughter and mother, to discipline and release oneself through poetry and other arts.

Each of Song's three books opens with a poem and section asserting the centrality of women's experience. *Picture Bride* is initiated by an inquiry into the life of Song's Korean grandmother, imagining her journey from a tailor shop in Pusan to sugarcane fields in Waialua. The woman's feelings upon arrival or how she coped with the dislocation are only hinted at in subsequent poems, some autobiographical and some not, that present a mixed picture of the blessings and burdens of growing up female in a plantation town on rural Oahu. In "The Youngest Daughter," the girl charged with taking care of her mother longs to escape, while "Leaving" presents the endless, depressing rain of Wahiawa as another compelling reason for departure. On the other hand, in "Easter: Wahiawa, 1959," the daylong threat of rain and inevitable evening downpour are woven into a warm memory of a backyard Easter-egg hunt. Retreating to the porch with her grandfather, four-year-old Song eats the eggs he peels for her, a quiet moment resurrected years later to acknowledge the labor and perseverance behind that shared bounty. "Blue Lantern" also remembers a protective elder, the Japanese grandfather of the boy next door, who mourns his wife on the shakuhachi every night. Too young to understand his pain, Song receives the beautiful music each night like a gift, a reassurance of a world made secure by adults. None of these poems is about the woman who arrives in Waialua at the beginning of *Picture Bride*, but they depict the experiences of daughters descended from women like her. Like Kingston's "no name woman," Song's "picture bride" signifies a collective as well as individual female experience that is essential to the author's project of self-definition.

The opening section of *Frameless Windows, Squares of Light* also emphasizes the theme of women's experience, though at first glance the predominance of male subjects might suggest otherwise. "Litany" depicts Song's father as a precious last son who felt confined by his mother's fierce devotion. In "The Window and the Field," this boy has become a young man embarking on marriage, still unhappy about his predictable future in Wahiawa. Many years later, marriage is still symbolized for him by the romanticized, self-absorbed moment of carrying his bride up the steps of his father's house, a view of the past that ends conveniently at the moment everything difficult began. At this point, the poem's perspective switches to that of the bride, who remembers the same moment as one defined forever by clouds of dust and red dirt, a mangy dog, and her white-gloved hand waving at a husband who does not look back as he drives off leaving her alone. The other poems in this section include "Living near the Water," on the death of Song's paternal grandfather, and a moving portrait of Mary and Jesus called "The Binding" that laments the cruelty of extinguishing a mother's relationship to her child once she has been allowed to birth and nurture him. Collectively, these poems about actual or imagined fathers, sons, grandfathers, and husbands build a picture of the oppressions women experience through marriage. Inclusion of the poem about Mary in this section of the book implies that women like Song's grandmothers and mother, within the terms of their different social worlds, could no more opt out of marriage than the mother of Jesus. Women's suffering from the lack of freedom both within and outside of marriage is indicated in "The Window and the Field," in which Ella Song's first day of married life concludes in an image of muted pain and self-division: Sitting silently before her father-in-law, with both window and field serving as a backdrop, she removes her white gloves as if splitting apart the petals of a white gardenia.

Whereas Song's second book begins with an emphasis on father and grandfather, the opening section of *School Figures* is dominated by Song's mother. "Mother on River Street" highlights a series of misfortunes that befell Ella when she was young: adoption by Baptist Church ladies after her mother's death from cancer, crying to be held by a mother who was too sick to carry a baby in her arms, falling out of a moving car at the age of six, unnoticed by the adult passengers, and living in the basement of her half brother's home, underfed by his mean wife. These poems display greater irony, disapproval, and impatience than poems about Song's father, who is consistently represented as an aesthetically discriminating man and lover of classical music, a commercial pilot whose unused creative energies are wasted fixing broken appliances and upgrading the house. This representation of Andrew Song is probably influenced by the fact that he encouraged his daughter's creativity; his job enabled the traveling that inspired Song to write, and he brought home the paper she devoured (Gall 354; Choo 6). In contrast, the deprivations and losses sustained by Song's mother, and her personal faults, seem harder to accommodate. One is reminded of the difference between the mysterious, "extravagant" allure of the father's desk in Maxine Hong Kingston's *China Men* and the mundane, often-loathsome "necessity" signified by her mother's kitchen in *The Woman Warrior* (on the Asian American motifs of "necessity" and "extravagance," see Sau-ling Wong's *Reading Asian American Literature*). Brave Orchid's personal power and practicality are glimpsed in Song's "A Conservative View," "Shrinking the Uterus," "Eat," and "Sunworshippers," which describe a mother's penny-pinching ways, the pig's-feet soup and mustard cabbage she prepares and commands her daughter to consume, and her injunctions against self-love and self-indulgence that come to resemble self-effacement. The mother's conservative views are also linked to Song's ambivalence toward the fecundity of her female body, described in a poem about binding her breasts to stop the flow of milk after the third child's birth ("The Body's Faith"). Yet despite the range of negative feelings expressed, all of these poems are laced with humor that is both sharp and mellow, conveying the sense that Song fully accepts her mother despite everything she cannot approve of, even if with less lyricism and tenderness than is displayed in poems about her father's shortcomings.

Song's exploration of women's experience is inextricable from her representation of artistic endeavor. *Picture Bride* is centrally concerned with the difficult yet productive marriage of cultural practices and products not only quite different from each other but each defined at the core by gendered conflicts between economic and creative labor: Georgia O'Keeffe's radical departures (from men, New York City, aesthetic traditions), Utamaro's wood-block prints of the world of licensed prostitution in eighteenth-century Edo, the Japanese system of *shashin-kekkon* (literally "photograph marriage") in which marriages are negotiated long-distance through a symbolic exchange of photographs between women in the home country and men laboring abroad, and photographs from the Song family album. All of these narratives or visual texts have been assimilated, interpreted, and transformed by Song through a process that has enabled her to take her own pictures of the world. As Richard Hugo observes in his foreword to *Picture Bride*, "Cathy Song's poems do more than simply return to us a world vividly received. The world is *her* world and she alone has the artistic license to illuminate it" (xiv).

The central metaphor of *Frameless Windows, Squares of Light* calls attention to the continuing importance of "pictures" and "picturing" in Song's work. The window signifies a captured moment, a moment being captured, and a frame that necessarily limits and structures what is seen through it. Four poems explicitly elaborate on the illuminated window, and they lend their titles to the four sections of the book. The first version of the metaphor, "The Window and the Field," contains a noticeable absence of light. The window is an oppressively stable boundary reflecting the splitting of Song's mother at the moment she enters her new home as a married woman. Throughout this volume, women enter and work within houses, wave good-bye to children and husbands from porches and doors, wait indoors for them to come home, observe their family's outdoor activities from windows, sit alone in houses remembering past domiciles, and sometimes actually reenter the houses of their childhood. The second permutation of the illuminated window is "A Small Light," a dreamlike depiction of a girl who wakes at night and follows the light at her window to a dry riverbed filled with leaves. As she departs, the house containing her sleeping parents collapses, and she herself sinks into the river of leaves, the "small light" of her hair touching each leaf as she disappears. Since the light in the window becomes the light in the girl's body, and the window becomes the river, the girl's night journey perhaps symbolizes a woman/poet's need to relinquish currently lived-in structures like family and house in order to submerge herself in the currents of memory, imagination, and the unconscious.

The third version of the window metaphor is "Shadow Figures," a section of poems emphasizing recuperated and reconstructed memories. Included here are "Humble Jar" and "The Tower of Pisa," where Song speaks of her parents' unfulfilled desires, and other poems that bring to light the unspoken epiphanies of siblings, preverbal infants, and the poet herself at different points in history. The title poem "Shadow Figures" recovers a period from childhood when Song was still her brother's close companion. Looking at the house they grew up in with the eyes of an adult and seeing the actual shabbiness of a place once thought to be luxurious, Song understands life as a series of "shadow figures," still residing in the places one used to live but visible only through memory's and poetry's language. In "Frameless Windows, Squares of Light," the fourth version of the window metaphor, Song imagines her first child's loneliness, grief, and longing for the past when the birth of a younger sister changes his relationship to his mother. Song renders her son's unarticulated feelings through a series of lighted squares—blue paper windows in an Advent calendar, a foggy window on a winter day, "luminous kites" floating upward in darkness. These glowing shapes bearing witness to an impossible yet achieved attempt to separate the framing and framed sections of an illuminated window, achieved because language magically retains the emptiness of "frameless window" and the solidity of "squares of light," articulate the particular accomplishment of Song's second book—a delicate yet deft illumination of shadowed experiences.

Unlike *Picture Bride* and *Frameless Windows, Squares of Light*, the title of Song's third book, *School Figures*, does not immediately convey the author's abiding concern with memory, creation, perspective, and imagination. But the title poem itself, which concludes the volume, can be read as a summing up and affirmation of a life dedicated to artistic endeavor. "School Figures" crystallizes the figure of a young woman in college learning about beauty and design. Through overlapping images of spring orchard ramblings and ice skating in winter, anorexia and bodily adornment, remnants of paintings by Constable, Hokusai, Mondrian, Ingres, Cézanne, and Brueghel, "School Figures" remembers a girl's hunger for beauty and the sumptuous feasting possible because she was lucky enough to live in a plentiful, safe world. College life was a lesson in opulence where even anorexia, an ironic "feasting" on images and experiences of beauty, was one form of practice, study, patience, and restraint—lessons in abstinence and control without which plenitude cannot be known or savored. A similar dynamic between opulence and barrenness, indulgence and abstinence, informs the book's opening poem about a different kind of school environment and "school figure." In "The Story of Madeline," every nook and cranny of Ludwig Bemelmans's children's classic *Madeline* is brought to life in a loving, almost palpable retelling. However, Song's version also draws out the implicit loneliness and poverty of the girls' lives, seeing past spunky Madeline's antics and escapades to the unrelenting sameness of "twelve little girls in two straight lines, in rain or shine." Encountering Madeline as a girl, Song saw beauty and boldness in the pictures and narrative, but reviewing the story as an adult and mother of three, including the difficult daughter to whom *School Figures* is dedicated, Song's attention is caught by what exists in contrast to beauty and boldness. In Madeline's Paris presided over by a caring but unimaginative Miss Clavel, mothers are absent, fathers are present only through occasional gifts, and life is mainly a spartan existence of plain food and clothes. "The Story of Madeline" and "School Figures," which link the figures of two schoolgirls, suggest that knowledge of beauty is a necessity and a lifelong lesson. They also point toward the question of what the pursuit or possession of beauty means in the lives of girls and women.

CRITICAL RECEPTION

Although the past fifteen years have seen the publication of at least a dozen major critical studies by Asian American literary scholars and a proliferation of diverse, award-winning volumes of poetry, for example, by Jessica Hagedorn, Kimiko Hahn, Garrett Hongo, Lawson Inada, Juliet Kono, Alan Lau, Li-Young Lee, Janice Mirikitani, David Mura, Mitsuye Yamada, Lois-Ann Yamanaka, and Song herself, to name only a few, criticism of poetry within the field of Asian American studies has not progressed accordingly. Juliana Chang, in "Reading Asian American Poetry," notes this "critical marginalization of poetry" (84), which she sees as stemming from a view of poetry as a private activity assumed to be less socially relevant than fiction or drama and far more difficult to understand. A related perception that poetry is part of "high culture," as well as "a historical pattern of reading and marketing Asian American literature ethnographically" (86–87), further complicates and heightens this marginalization. It may even, Chang notes, have encouraged nine prominent Asian American poets to publish memoirs and prose fiction between 1990 and 1996.

But besides the general critical neglect experienced by all Asian American poets, certain aspects of Song's poetry—its lyricism, preference for tradition over experimentation in matters of style, and lack of explicit engagement with Asian American social, economic, and political issues—seem to have resulted in further critical marginalization. Scholars of Asian American literature who specialize in poetry—George Uba, Walter Lew, and Juliana Chang, for example—favor writers who foreground political or cultural critique in their texts and embrace experimental modes of expression, poets like Theresa Hak Kyung Cha, Hahn, Inada, Mura, and John Yau. While these particular critics may not, in fact, find Song's work unappealing, such is apparently the case with Elaine Kim, whose article on Korean American literature for *The Oxford Companion to Women's Writing in the United States* (1995) does not mention Song at all except to list her short story and *Frameless Windows, Squares of Light* in the attached bibliography. In a more recent article on the same topic for *An Inter-ethnic Companion to Asian American Literature*, Kim discusses Song together with Gary Pak and Willyce Kim as third-generation Korean Americans from Hawaii who share a positive attitude toward Asian American identity. However, Song's work is not shown to be inscribed with such an attitude. Emphasized instead are her resistance to being identified as an ethnic writer, Richard Hugo's Orientalist readings of her "tribal" sensibility and "centuries-old" patience, and Shirley Lim's reservations about her use of ethnic imagery. Quotations from *Picture Bride* are used to illustrate an ethnic imagery "of almost suffocating restriction" (172). The discussion concludes by implying that Song's use of ethnicity and familial experience constitutes a kind of exorcism: "To become an artist, she must leave home; she can return to her ethnicity and family only by rendering them as voiceless though aesthetically beautiful images" (173).

    Reviews of *Picture Bride* for mainstream audiences are generally appreciative of Song's themes and style, though flawed at times by ignorance of Asian American histories and by a tendency to equate "Asian" with "Asian American" or read Asian American literature ethnographically. Rosaly Roffman, in *Library Journal*, notes the theme of desired, successful escapes and Song's artistic kinship with Utamaro and O'Keeffe. Richard Jackson, writing for *American Book Review*, praises *Picture Bride* as a "poetry of adjectives" (19) whose achievement lies in description and recognition of reframed experiences, best exemplified in the conclusion of "Blue and White Lines after O'Keeffe," where the painter associates her canvas with her mother's laundry. The reviewer for *Publishers Weekly* also focuses on Song's expressive skills and strategies—the deceptive simplicity of her lines, her ability to capture transitory moments, her absorption of the influence of O'Keeffe and Utamaro, and the productive tension between a calm or reticent surface and the compressed energies that lie beneath. But this otherwise-perceptive reviewer identifies Song's Korean grandmother as a "mail order bride" (59). Lorrie Goldensohn's review for *Poetry* concentrates on the pictorial quality of the poems and especially the transmutation of shapes and substances, but she falls back on Orientalist stereotypes to explain Song's achievement as a product of "that exquisite, clarifying precision we recognize as Asian in feeling" (42). Criticism also contains biased or uninformed readings of the poems' autobiographical content. The author of the article in *Poetry Criticism* not only takes the subject of the poem "Picture Bride" to be Song's mother, but does not notice the contradiction of claiming at the same time that she is Chinese ("Cathy Song" 330).

    Reviews by Stan Yogi and Shirley Lim provide a good deal of helpful criticism and context. Yogi's review for *Amerasia Journal* identifies Song's salient themes as "ambiguities of leave-taking, ambivalence about raising children, and complexities of remembrances and familial relationships" (157). He compares the book's organization and integration of poetic themes to a "symphony developing force through counterpointed melodies and surprising variations on a theme" (157), anticipating the larger role music will play in Song's second and third books. Lim's review for *MELUS* also offers concise, insightful readings of individual poems, drawing attention to the theme of homecoming (unlike most critics and reviewers who underscore the theme of escape), to the difference between poems that are directly autobiographical and those that "fram[e] observations and emotions in an invented fiction" (96), and to the poems' characteristic "sudden eruption of metaphor which startles, teases, illuminates" (98). Lim also takes note of Song's ambivalence toward Asian American themes and contrasts what she feels is a stereotypical deployment of ethnic images to what she thinks is really the basis of Song's achievement—concentration on "the details of her world, her vision, in whose singularity we can all recognize ourselves" (99).

In addition to Lim's and Yogi's interpretive book reviews, three critical articles on *Picture Bride* discuss Song's interpretation of Utamaro, her interpretation of O'Keeffe, and her voice and vision as a writer from Hawaii. Masami Usui's "Women Disclosed: Cathy Song's Poetry and Kitagawa Utamaro's Ukiyoe" (1995) compares the details in Song's Utamaro poems to nine specific prints to which the poems probably allude. The article is accompanied by reproductions of all nine *ukiyoe* and draws upon Japanese studies of Utamaro's work. Usui's main point is that Song, viewing Utamaro as an Asian American artist who painted pictures of women, exposes his celebrated portraits of Edo prostitutes as representations of lonely, depressed women trapped within a mode of existence controlled by men and created solely for their pleasure. Gayle Fujita-Sato's " 'Third World' as Place and Paradigm in Cathy Song's *Picture Bride*" (1988) examines Song's use of O'Keeffe by comparing the special significance of blue and white in O'Keeffe's oeuvre, as well as the painter's comments on the genesis of specific paintings, to Song's use of these colors and visual texts to create her own "pictures" of the world. This productive fusion with the work of another woman artist manifests itself, for example, in the linking of O'Keeffe's *From the White Place* with Song's "The White Porch," a poem celebrating pregnancy and asserting that woman's traditional space can be the site of self-creation as well as procreation, and the subsequent linking of this recuperated space to the porch of Grandfather's house in "Easter, Wahiawa: 1959." Through analysis of such transformations, Fujita-Sato suggests that the embodiment of "Asian American" in *Picture Bride* is to be found in the process of cultural synthesis the poems embody.

Stephen Sumida's "Pictures of Art and Life" (1986) offers an extended analysis of three poems read as dramatic monologues—"The Youngest Daughter," the middle section of "Blue and White Lines after O'Keeffe," and "The Seamstress." Sumida argues that these poems are particularly significant for assessing Song's achievement as an Asian American and Hawaii-based writer because though they appear to reiterate stereotypes of exotic, essential Asianness and tropical paradise, their point is precisely the opposite. Through dramatic monologues, Song gives voice to subjects (like the daughter and seamstress) who are normally silenced or simplified through dominant discourses of race and culture. Or, in the case of "An Orchid," the central section of "Blue and White Lines" and therefore, as Sumida notes, the very center of the whole book, Song creates the voice of an outsider and tourist. Song's O'Keeffe is an artist supposedly endowed with a special talent for seeing and representing, yet she is not fully conscious of her intrusive presence and stereotyping point of view as she observes the "natives" on a Maui beach. Sumida emphasizes the danger of misreading Song's critique as a reiteration of cultural stereotypes, not only because Song's lyricism so powerfully evokes the landscape and symbolism of an erotic paradise in order to create O'Keeffe's point of view, but precisely because there are so few precedents of such a critical rendering of the tourist's perspective in literary depictions of Hawaii. (Sumida's discussion of "An Orchid" can be found, essentially unchanged, in his *And the View from the Shore: Literary Traditions of Hawai'i* [263–66].)

Compared to *Picture Bride*, mainstream reviews of *Frameless Windows, Squares of Light* and *School Figures* are more mixed. Grace Bauer, reviewing Song's second book for *Library Journal*, admires the rendering of poignant moments frozen in the flow of time but complains about lapses into prosaic, dead language. For Jessica Greenbaum, the lapses are chronic, and she attributes them to the "burden" of "responsibilities to family history" (19). Greenbaum's review consists of one example after another of Song failing to keep her language crisp, fresh, and engaging. Only the wholly exotic viewpoint expressed in "A Mehinaku Girl in Seclusion" is singled out as fully successful, which raises interesting questions about whether this poem is somehow connected to "An Orchid," which Sumida argues has a special significance in *Picture Bride*'s deployment of dramatic monologue and representation of exoticized places. Robert Shaw's review for *Poetry* is generally positive, but he thinks that many poems need trimming and a sharper thematic focus. Problems regarding reviewers' extraction of biographical data from the poems persist in these reviews of Song's second book. Greenbaum calls Song "a first-generation Asian-American whose heritage is Korean" (19), while Shaw tells us, "Her grandparents were immigrants from China" and the grandmother a "mail-order bride" (289). In contrast to these reviews for Song's second book, Pat Monaghan praises Song's witty, diverse, and precisely rendered family portraits in *School Figures*.

There is very little criticism about either the second or third book outside of Susan Schultz's article in *Dictionary of Literary Biography* and Patricia Wallace's "Divided Loyalties: Literal and Literary in the Poetry of Lorna Dee Cervantes, Cathy Song, and Rita Dove" (1993). Wallace deals only with "Picture Bride" and "Humble Jar," but her larger argument about the tug between history and art, or "literal" and "literary," makes this an extremely useful piece for reading any Asian American poet. In "Humble Jar," Wallace views the mix of practical and impractical buttons stashed in an old mayonnaise jar—all-purpose buttons that are actually used to repair items of clothing as well as fancy buttons from an old evening dress or blazer that serve only as mementos or props in a young girl's imaginative play—as emblems of the unstable boundary and complex relationship between history and art, literal and literary, necessity and extravagance. The poetics embodied by "Humble Jar" is illustrated by Song's desire to recuperate her Korean grandmother. Wallace notes how the "disappearance" of the immigrant woman in "Picture Bride"—a divergent, insightful reading of this poem—actually embodies Song's respect for the limited capacity of the literary to represent the literal: "Song doesn't claim poetry has the power to overcome . . . erasure," but "the very uncertainty of Song's poetic structures honors the degree to which the grandmother's life is not a purely literary figuration" (12).

Besides providing the best overview of Song's achievement from *Picture Bride* through *School Figures*, Susan Schultz raises a number of important issues in her article for *Dictionary of Literary Biography*, which incorporates almost all published criticism of Song's work. As a member of the English Department at the University of Hawaii at Manoa, Schultz was able to utilize information from many local sources—events, publications, and people, including the poet herself—to indicate how Song's work is firmly situated in postwar Hawaii while identifying several nonlocal influences on her writing that have not been sufficiently discussed. Poets mentioned as offering points of comparison with Song's themes and strategies include Elizabeth Bishop, Wallace Stevens, Emily Dickinson, William Butler Yeats, Robert Frost, Sylvia Plath, Lois-Ann Yamanaka, James Merrill, and Garrett Hongo. The relevance of university workshop training and painting to Song's aesthetic principles and practice is also pointed out. Like Kim, Schultz questions the effects of Song's lyricism by suggesting that it sometimes "suppress[es] the conflicts inherent in her work" (273), as in "Sunworshippers," from *Frameless Windows, Squares of Light*, which mentions an episode of anorexia but does not really explore the troubling questions raised about female identity and the body (as is true for the concluding poem of *School Figures*). Finally, Schultz places Song in a political and aesthetic "center," noting her middle-class affiliation, conservatism, and "poetry of accommodation, not protest" (273). All of these observations serve as points of departure for developing critical discussion of Song's work that moves beyond the current focus on *Picture Bride*.

BIBLIOGRAPHY

Works by Cathy Song

Poetry

"Remnants." *Hawaii Review* 5 (Spring 1975): 36–39. [Earlier version of the poem published in *Poetry Hawaii: A Contemporary Anthology*. Ed. Frank Stewart and John Unterecker. Honolulu: University of Hawaii Press, 1979. 101–3.]
"from A Georgia O'Keeffe Portfolio: Flower Series, No. 3., An Orchid." *Talk Story: An*

Anthology of Hawaii's Local Writers. Ed. Eric Chock. Foreword by Maxine Hong Kingston. Honolulu: Petronium Press/Talk Story, 1978. 82–83.

"Lost Sister." *Talk Story: An Anthology of Hawaii's Local Writers*. Ed. Eric Chock. Foreword by Maxine Hong Kingston. Honolulu: Petronium Press/Talk Story, Inc. 1978. 80–81.

"Bean Sprouts: Chinatown's Children." *Bridge* 7.3 (Spring/Summer 1980): 36–37.

"Living near the Water." *Amerasia Journal* 10.2 (1983): 105–7. *Paké: Writings by Chinese in Hawaii*. Ed. Eric Chock and Darrell H.Y. Lum. Honolulu: Bamboo Ridge Press, 1989. 200–2.

Picture Bride. Foreword by Richard Hugo. New Haven: Yale University Press, 1983.

"Easter: Wahiawa, 1959." *The Best of Bamboo Ridge: The Hawaii Writers' Quarterly*. Ed. Eric Chock and Darrell H.Y. Lum. Honolulu: Bamboo Ridge Press, 1986. 79–81.

"Tribe." *The Best of Bamboo Ridge: The Hawaii Writers' Quarterly*. Ed. Eric Chock and Darrell H.Y. Lum. Honolulu: Bamboo Ridge Press, 1986. 82–83.

"The White Porch." *The Best of Bamboo Ridge: The Hawaii Writers' Quarterly*. Ed. Eric Chock and Darrell H.Y. Lum. Honolulu: Bamboo Ridge Press, 1986. 84–85.

"The Youngest Daughter." *The Best of Bamboo Ridge: The Hawaii Writers' Quarterly*. Ed. Eric Chock and Darrell H.Y. Lum. Honolulu: Bamboo Ridge Press, 1986. 77–78.

Frameless Windows, Squares of Light: Poems. New York: Norton, 1988.

"Heaven." *Paké: Writings by Chinese in Hawaii*. Ed. Eric Chock and Darrell H.Y. Lum. Honolulu: Bamboo Ridge Press, 1989. 211–12.

"Immaculate Lives." *Paké: Writings by Chinese in Hawaii*. Ed. Eric Chock and Darrell H.Y. Lum. Honolulu: Bamboo Ridge Press, 1989. 213–14.

"A Pale Arrangement of Hands." *Paké: Writings by Chinese in Hawaii*. Ed. Eric Chock and Darrell H.Y. Lum. Honolulu: Bamboo Ridge Press, 1989. 197–99.

"Shadow Figures." *Paké: Writings by Chinese in Hawaii*. Ed. Eric Chock and Darrell H.Y. Lum. Honolulu: Bamboo Ridge Press, 1989. 203–6.

"The Tower of Pisa." *Paké: Writings by Chinese in Hawaii*. Ed. Eric Chock and Darrell H.Y. Lum. Honolulu: Bamboo Ridge Press, 1989. 207–10.

School Figures. Pittsburgh: University of Pittsburgh Press, 1994.

"Adagio." *Growing Up Local: An Anthology of Prose and Poetry from Hawai'i*. Ed. Eric Chock, James R. Harstad, Darrell Lum, and Bill Teter. Honolulu: Bamboo Ridge Press, 1998. 135–36.

"A Conservative View." *Growing Up Local: An Anthology of Prose and Poetry from Hawai'i*. Ed. Eric Chock, James R. Harstad, Darrell Lum, and Bill Teter. Honolulu: Bamboo Ridge Press, 1998. 331–33.

"The Grammar of Silk." *Growing Up Local: An Anthology of Prose and Poetry from Hawai'i*. Ed. Eric Chock, James R. Harstad, Darrell Lum, and Bill Teter. Honolulu: Bamboo Ridge Press, 1998. 137–38.

"A Conservative View." *Intersecting Circles: The Voices of Hapa Women in Poetry and Prose*. Ed. Marie Hara and Nora Okja Keller. Honolulu: Bamboo Ridge Press, 1999. 246–48.

"Shrinking the Uterus." *Intersecting Circles: The Voices of Hapa Women in Poetry and Prose*. Ed. Marie Hara and Nora Okja Keller. Honolulu: Bamboo Ridge Press, 1999. 249–50.

"The Bodhisattva Muses." *The Quietest Singing*. Ed. Darrell H.Y. Lum, Joseph Stanton, and Estelle Enoki. Honolulu: State Foundation on Culture and the Arts, 2000. 196–99.

"Caldera Illumina." *The Quietest Singing*. Ed. Darrell H.Y. Lum, Joseph Stanton, and Estelle Enoki. Honolulu: State Foundation on Culture and the Arts, 2000. 205–11.

"The Sister." *The Quietest Singing*. Ed. Darrell H.Y. Lum, Joseph Stanton, and Estelle Enoki. Honolulu: State Foundation on Culture and the Arts, 2000. 200–4.

Miscellaneous Works

"Beginnings (for Bok Pil)." *Hawaii Review* 6 (1976): 55–65.

Editor, with Juliet Kono. *Sister Stew: Fiction and Poetry by Women*. Honolulu: Bamboo Ridge Press, 1991.

Studies of Cathy Song

Bauer, Grace. Rev. of *Frameless Windows, Squares of Light*. *Library Journal* 113.11 (June 1988): 61.

"Cathy Song 1955– ." *Asian American Literature: Reviews and Criticism of Works by American Writers of Asian Descent*. Ed. Lawrence J. Trudeau. Detroit: Gale Research, 1999. 421–37.

"Cathy Song 1955– ." *Poetry Criticism*. Vol. 21. Ed. Robyn V. Young. Detroit: Gale Research, 1998. 330–51.

Chang, Juliana. "Reading Asian American Poetry." *MELUS* 21.1 (1996): 81–98.

Choo, David. "Cathy's Song: Interview with Cathy Song." *Honolulu Weekly* 15 June 1994: 6–8.

Chou, Jerome. "Cathy Song." *American Women Writers: A Critical Reference Guide from Colonial Times to the Present*. Vol. 5. Ed. Carol Hurd Green and Mary Grimley Mason. New York: Continuum, 1994. 429–30.

Fujita-Sato, Gayle K. " 'Third World' as Place and Paradigm in Cathy Song's *Picture Bride*." *MELUS* 15.1 (Spring 1988): 49–72.

Gall, Susan. "Cathy-Lynn Song." *Notable Asian Americans*. Ed. Helen Zia and Susan B. Gall. Detroit: Gale Research, 1995. 353–55.

Goldensohn, Lorrie. "Flights Home." *Poetry* 144.1 (1984): 40–47.

Green, Ann-Elizabeth. "Song, Cathy." *Contemporary Women Poets*. Ed. Pamela L. Shelton. Detroit: St. James Press, 1998. 322–24.

Greenbaum, Jessica. "Family Albums." Rev. of *Frameless Windows, Squares of Light*. *The Women's Review of Books* 6.1 (October 1988): 19.

Han, Jae-Nam. "Song, Cathy." *Feminist Writers*. Ed. Pamela Kester-Shelton. Detroit: St. James Press, 1996. 446–47.

Hugo, Richard. Foreword. *Picture Bride*. New Haven: Yale University Press, 1983. ix–xiv.

Jackson, Richard. "The Geography of Time." Rev. of *Picture Bride*. *American Book Review* 8.2 (January–February 1986): 19–20.

Kim, Elaine H. "Korean American Literature." *An Interethnic Companion to Asian American Literature*. Ed. King-Kok Cheung. New York: Cambridge University Press, 1997. 156–91.

———. "Korean-American Writing." *The Oxford Companion to Women's Writing in the*

United States. Ed. Cathy N. Davidson and Linda Wagner-Martin. New York: Oxford University Press, 1995. 463–67.

Lee, Kyhan. "Korean-American Literature: The Next Generation." *Korea Journal* 34.1 (Spring 1994): 20–35.

Lim, Shirley. Rev. of *Picture Bride*. *MELUS* 10.3 (Fall 1983): 95–99.

Monaghan, Pat. Rev. of *School Figures*. *Booklist* 91.3 (October 1994): 231.

Nomaguchi, Debbie Murakami. "I'm a Poet Who Happens to Be Asian American." *International Examiner* 2 May 1984: 9.

O'Keeffe, Georgia. *Georgia O'Keeffe*. 1976. New York: Viking, 1983.

Rev. of *Picture Bride*. *Publishers Weekly* 223.19 (1983): 59.

Roffman, Rosaly Demaios. Rev. of *Picture Bride*. *Library Journal* 108.9 (May 1983): 909–10.

Schultz, Susan M. "Cathy Song." *Dictionary of Literary Biography*. Vol. 169. *American Poets since World War II: Fifth Series*. Ed. Joseph Conte. Detroit: Gale Research, 1996. 267–74.

Shaw, Robert B. Rev. of *Frameless Windows, Squares of Light*. *Poetry* 154.5 (August 1989): 289–90.

"Song, Cathy." *The Asian American Encyclopedia*. Vol. 5. Ed. Franklin Ng. New York: Marshall Cavendish, 1995. 1361–62.

"Song, Cathy, 1955– ." *Contemporary Authors: A Bio-Bibliographical Guide to Current Writers in Fiction, General Nonfiction, Poetry, Journalism, Drama, Motion Pictures, Television, and Other Fields*. Vol. 154. Detroit: Gale Research, 1997. 392–93.

Sumida, Stephen H. *And the View from the Shore: Literary Traditions of Hawai'i*. Seattle: University of Washington Press, 1991.

———. "Pictures of Art and Life." *Contact II* 7.38–40 (1986): 52–55.

Usui, Masami. "Women Disclosed: Cathy Song's Poetry and Kitagawa Utamaro's Ukiyoe." *Ningen Bunka Kenkyu* [*Studies in Culture and the Humanities*] 4 (1995): 1–19.

Wallace, Patricia. "Divided Loyalties: Literal and Literary in the Poetry of Lorna Dee Cervantes, Cathy Song, and Rita Dove." *MELUS* 18.3 (Fall 1993): 3–19.

Yogi, Stan. Rev. of *Picture Bride*. *Amerasia Journal* 14.1 (1988): 157–60.

TOYO SUYEMOTO
(1916–   )

Robert Hayashi

BIOGRAPHY

Toyo Suyemoto was born in Oroville, California, on 14 January 1916. Her parents were Japanese immigrants who instilled in their eldest child a lifelong love of poetry. In an article "Writing of Poetry" from *Amerasia Journal* published in 1983, Suyemoto recounts the early influences and the genesis of her writing career: her mother was a poet and her father an artist, and they both taught her at an early age to observe, absorb, and appreciate the world around her. In 1935, she entered Sacramento Junior College, now Sacramento City College, where she received an A.A. in 1937. At seventeen, she began to publish her poetry in local literary journals, newspapers, and Japanese American publications. She was among a group of young second-generation Japanese American writers whose work began to appear regularly in such publications during the 1930s and 1940s. After completing her studies at Sacramento Junior College, she entered the University of California at Berkeley, where she studied Latin and English, receiving her B.A. in 1937.

Suyemoto was living in Berkeley with her family when federal authorities ordered the evacuation of Japanese Americans from their West Coast homes. Her family was eventually relocated to the Central Utah Relocation Center, commonly known as Topaz, in the fall of 1942. At Topaz, she taught English and Latin and later worked in the center's library. She continued to write at Topaz and contributed several poems to the center's English-language literary magazine, *Trek*, and its final edition, *All Aboard*. She was one of several Topaz writers whose work chronicling these days would reach, if temporarily, beyond the limited publishing realm of their prewar careers. The work by artists such as Toyo Suyemoto and her fellow Topaz writer, Mine Okubo, would come to memorialize this chapter of Japanese American life and also mark a crucial turning point in the development of Japanese American women's writing. Like many former internees, Toyo Suyemoto resettled outside of the West after her release from Topaz. She moved to Cincinnati, where she worked at the University of Cincinnati's library from 1946 to 1959.

During the late 1950s, Suyemoto participated in writing workshops at the University of Cincinnati led by the poets Randall Jarrell and Karl Shapiro. In 1964, she received an M.L.S. from the University of Michigan and soon took a position as a librarian at Ohio State University in Columbus, Ohio. She is a member of several professional library associations and served as the chairperson of both the Executive Committee and the Nominating Committee of the American Library Association. In 1975, she received an Asian American Writers Award at the Asian American Writers Conference. She retired from Ohio State University in 1985 and since then has worked on her memoirs.

MAJOR WORKS AND THEMES

Although she has continued to write poetry, as well as prose, for nearly seventy years, Toyo Suyemoto has yet to publish a book. The corpus of her published work currently includes poems that have appeared over the last several decades in an array of literary journals, newspapers, and poetry anthologies. A particularly noteworthy selection of her poems is included in Juliana Chang's ambitious collection of Asian American poetry, *Quiet Fire*. Her most widely known poems remain those that she wrote in response to her internment during World War II. In these poems, Suyemoto typically incorporates natural imagery and allusions to natural cycles that suggest the physical and spiritual challenges faced by American nikkei (an American of Japanese descent) during their forced relocation. While these poems obviously relate to a specific historical event, defining Suyemoto as only a poet of the relocation overlooks the universality of her work. These poems, due to their characteristic lack of specific geographic or historical references and their attention to spiritual concerns, resist association to simply one personal experience. Of course, the generality and indirectness of these poems do reflect the conditions of their production. Federal authorities read camp publications such as *Trek* and *All Aboard*, and overt public criticism of the government or its policies could have jeopardized the writer and her family. Therefore, many of these works are intentionally subtle and indirect. Suyemoto's entire oeuvre, however, shows her overarching concern with conditions that transcend specific historical or personal conditions, as illustrated in "Attitude." In this poem, Suyemoto characteristically focuses upon the speaker's state of mind, the spiritual progress that parallels the natural rhythms about her. In a similar fashion, her most widely known poems about the internment present general feelings of alienation, rebirth, and desire that apply to more than any one event or condition while still conveying the human tragedy of this historic injustice, as illustrated by "Gain."

CRITICAL RECEPTION

Like many nisei writers, most of the attention Suyemoto does enjoy derives from the works she produced in response to the internment. Her poems are commonly cited by scholars as particularly poignant documentations of this historical event. The suggestive simplicity and elegant formalism of her wartime poetry make it some of the finest nisei poetry of the period. Although the anti-Japanese sentiment and wartime dislocation of American nikkei greatly hampered the careers of such pioneering nisei writers, Suyemoto published a group of wartime poems in the *Yale Review* as early as 1946. However, since then, such prominent journals have mostly ignored her work.

Suyemoto's lack of critical attention is both the result of the restrictive association of Japanese American literature with the internment experience and of the formal verse structures she employs, a style that lost credence with the ascendance of free verse in American poetry over the last several decades. Her poems often incorporate quatrains that rely upon an *a b a b* rhyme scheme or on other traditional forms such as the sonnet or rondeau. Suyemoto also utilizes traditional Japanese verse forms like the tanka or haiku. Only one major critical discussion of Suyemoto's work is currently in print, a brief chapter in Susan Schweik's study of women's wartime poetry, *A Gulf So Deeply Cut*. Schweik focuses on the cultural and social forces that affected the development of nikkei women's writing, the "pre-poetics" that traditionally limited their work to only the private realm of the writer. She notes that the internment forced a conflation of the private and public realms and created an opportunity for nisei women not only to write especially evocative work, but also to have their works published. The dissolution of traditional gender roles and family constraints upon women created new opportunities for women writers such as Suyemoto. Schweik discusses the manner in which Suyemoto's career illustrates these changing conditions and, moreover, how her verse signifies the unique cultural blending that defines the work of nisei authors. Moreover, Schweik argues that this hybrid quality of her work, "a simultaneous erasure and emphasis," not only makes Suyemoto's work particularly evocative, but also explains the success Suyemoto had publishing her work outside of Topaz since it was not identifiably ethnic.

Schweik rightfully points to the poetry of issei women, who wrote in traditional Japanese forms, as an enabling influence upon their nisei daughters. However, she understates the strength and breadth of this tradition when she defines such women as atypical. Nevertheless, her comments forcefully suggest the need to recover these voices, both for their own value and to help us more fully define the development of a unique Japanese American literary tradition. Toyo Suyemoto overtly acknowledges her debt to her mother in her 1983 article from *Amerasia Journal*, in which she also includes a group of poems in tribute to all issei women. Such endeavors may help readers and critics to more fully evaluate not only the range of voices such as Suyemoto's, but the variety of influences, public and private, that shape their work.

BIBLIOGRAPHY

Works by Toyo Suyemoto

Poetry

Contributor. *American Bungaku*. Ed. Isshin H. Yamasaki. Tokyo: Keigan Sha, 1938.
"Retrospect," and "Quince." *Yale Review* 35.2 (Winter 1946): 251.
Contributor. *Japan: Theme and Variations: A Collection of Poems by Americans*. Ed. Charles E. Tuttle. Rutland: C.E. Tuttle, 1959.
Contributor. *Speaking for Ourselves: American Ethnic Writing*. Ed. Lillian Faderman and Barbara Bradshaw. Glenview, IL: Scott, Foresman, 1969.
Contributor. *Quiet Fire: A Historical Anthology of Asian American Poetry, 1892–1970*. Ed. Juliana Chang. New York: Asian American Writers' Workshop, 1996.

Articles

Contributor. *Acronyms in Education and the Behavioral Sciences*. Ed. Toyo S. Kawakami. Chicago: American Library Association, 1971.
Contributor. *Opportunities for Minorities in Librarianship*. Ed. E.J. Josey and Kenneth Peeples, Jr. Metuchen, NJ: Scarecrow Press, 1977.
"Writing of Poetry." *Amerasia Journal* 10.1 (1983): 73–79.
"Camp Memories: Rough and Broken Shards." *Japanese Americans: From Relocation to Redress*. Rev. ed. Ed. Roger Daniels, Sandra C. Taylor, and Harry H.L. Kitano. Seattle: University of Washington Press, 1991. 27–30.

Study of Toyo Suyemoto

Schweik, Susan. "Toyo Suyemoto and the 'Pre-Poetics' of Internment." *A Gulf So Deeply Cut: American Women Poets and the Second World War*. Madison: University of Wisconsin Press, 1991. 177–91.

ARTHUR SZE
(1950–   )

Zhou Xiaojing

BIOGRAPHY

Arthur Sze, a second-generation Chinese American, is the author of six books of poetry and the recipient of many awards and fellowships, including a Lila Wallace–Reader's Digest Writers' Award (1998–2000), the Asian American Literary Award in Poetry (1999), the Institute of American Indian Arts Foundation Award of Excellence (1998), a Guggenheim Fellowship (1997), the American Book Award (1996), the Lannan Literary Award for Poetry (1995), three Witter Bynner Poetry Fellowships (1980, 1983, 1994), two National Endowment for the Arts Creative Writing Fellowships (1982, 1993), and the Eisner Prize of the University of California at Berkeley (1971). Sze's poetic career began with translating Chinese poetry during his undergraduate years.

Born on 1 December 1950 in New York City, Sze grew up in Garden City on Long Island and graduated from the Lawrenceville School in 1968. Between 1968 and 1970, he attended the Massachusetts Institute of Technology, and transferred to the University of California at Berkeley in 1970 because he was truly excited to pursue poetry. At Berkeley, Sze had an individual major, studied philosophy, worked on poetry writing with Josephine Miles, and took intensive courses in Chinese language. Sze also began studying classical Chinese poetry at Berkeley, following a desire to immerse himself in the meanings and experiences embodied in Chinese characters and the prosody of the poetic forms. This desire grew out of his dissatisfaction with the opaqueness of translations, which he felt hindered his appreciation of the poetry. Chinese poetry became not only a source of inspiration for Sze's own poems, but also a heritage that

Sze seeks to reclaim by translating into English the poems of Li Bai (Li Po), Du Fu (Tu Fu), Wang Wei, Li Qingzhao (Li Ch'ing-chao), Tao Qian (T'ao Ch'ien), and Wen Yiduo (Wen I-to), among others. Sze's early translations of Chinese poems are published with his own poems in two collections, *Willow Wind* (1972; 1981; 1982; 1987) and *Two Ravens* (1976; 1984).

The influence of Chinese poetry, aesthetics, and philosophy on Sze's work is obvious, but Sze's absorption of the Chinese sources is a creative, transformative reinvention. One of the things he has drawn and transformed from the Chinese language and poetry is the principle of juxtaposition. In the West, collage juxtapositions of images emerged with modernist art and literary movements, such as Dada, cubism, and surrealism, whereas juxtaposition in Chinese language and poetry is a basic principle of organization in making meaning, expressing emotions, and producing aesthetic experience. Sze recognizes that the ideogrammatic method in the structure of a Chinese character is a mode of juxtaposition of different elements that create tension, contrast, and complement while coalescing into something new and larger than each of the disparate parts. Realizing that juxtaposition as such is a crucial formative, generative, and aesthetic principle, Sze in his poems transforms this principle into a poetics of collage composition that is at once a mode of experience and a process of cognition.

Besides his Chinese heritage, Native American cultures have a profound impact on Sze's poetry. Sze has a long and special relationship with Native Americans and their cultures. After graduating Phi Beta Kappa from Berkeley with an individual major in poetry, philosophy, and Chinese in 1972, Sze moved to New Mexico and has lived there ever since. Between 1978 and 1995, Sze was married to a Hopi weaver, Ramona Sakiestewa. Their son, Micah, is now a student at Princeton. Besides his personal life, Sze's work has been inseparable from Native Americans. Since 1984, he has been teaching at the Institute of American Indian Arts in Santa Fe, which is a federally funded two-year college where Native American students represent more than seventy tribes from across the United States. Sze served as the director of the Creative Writing Program for eight years (1989–96) and continues to teach there. He is now professor of creative writing at the institute. His close ties to Native Americans are reflected in his poems, in which Native American rituals, dances, and artifacts appear along with Chinese historical figures, events, and philosophy, as well as contemporary American culture and scenes in nature, including the Sombrero Galaxy, a supernova, and the gravitational bending of light.

Drawing from his background of science, philosophy, and multiethnic cultures, Sze's poems offer the reader a wide range of experience without sacrificing depth and subtlety. His travels around the world also contribute to the richness of his poetry. With the publication of his third and fourth books, *Dazzled* (1982) and *River River* (1987), Sze's poems became increasingly experimental. His bold experimentation shatters conventional poetic forms and pushes open the boundaries between nations and cultures. The maturation of Sze's development as a poet is particularly discernable in his fifth book, *Archipelago*

(1995), and in the new poems of his sixth, *The Redshifting Web: Poems, 1970–1998*. While seeking to create a new mode of poetry, Sze continues to translate Chinese poems. His recent translations from many centuries are collected in *The Silk Dragon*, published by Copper Canyon Press. Currently Sze lives in Santa Fe with his second wife, Carol Moldaw, who is also a poet, and their one-year-old daughter, Sarah, adopted from China.

MAJOR WORKS AND THEMES

Sze's *Archipelago*, winner of the 1995 Lannan Award and the 1996 American Book Award, marks an apex of his poetic career. It shows a new departure in form while exploring reoccurring themes and demonstrating significant development in terms of the embodiment of Sze's aesthetics and philosophy in all aspects of his poetry. Many of the poems in *Archipelago* are sequence poems, or rather serial poems, with no direct sequential narrative connections among the parts and no argumentative progression from one part to another. In fact, each part can often be read as a single poem by itself. The totality of all the parts is implied in an overarching theme, which is not easily discernable. At the same time, there is no uniformity among the parts in terms of structure or subject matter. For instance, within one sequence or serial poem, one part may be written in free verse, another in quatrains, and still another in a cluster of fragmentary single lines, each part dealing with multiple topics. Yet the disparate images and narratives separated by time and space are all parts of a whole—a web that links everything together without erasing the singularity of each component. This configuration of "the one and the many," a system of interconnected multiplicity and heterogeneity, is more than a theme in Sze's poetry; it shapes his aesthetics, particularly the structure of his poems. Thus the apparently chaotic collage juxtaposition of images, narratives, and utterances in his poems embodies Sze's worldview, which is similar to an ecological view of the world.

Although *Archipelago* illustrates his masterful treatment of major themes such as desire, passion, and cognition and demonstrates a highly accomplished idiosyncratic poetics, Sze's achievement in this book has been prefigured in his previous collections, particularly *Dazzled* and *River River*. Indeed, collage composition is a predominant poetic form in these two books, as it is in his latest poems. In the opening poem of *Dazzled*, "Viewing Photographs of China," Sze's persona uses the image of a collage that juxtaposes "facts, ideas, images" instead of searching for an essence in the world (13). Despite the seemingly unrelated, disjunctive events and phenomena described in his poems, Sze explores the bonds between people and their desperate need for one another, as well as the intricate, unexpected relations among all things in the world.

For Sze, the world is at once opaque and translucent, vast without boundaries, minute like a hole the size of a pinhead at the center of a spiderweb, and immediate like an autumn leaf falling on clear water. He often relies on surprising juxtapositions and paradoxical analogies to articulate his visions of the world and his experience of it. For instance, in "Black Lightning," his persona guesses at garlic, the sun, a desert rain, and palms while looking at the uneven lines written in braille by a blind girl and is stunned (*Dazzled* 33). In his serial poem "The Leaves of a Dream Are the Leaves of an Onion," Sze invites the reader to compare deciphering a dream to the peeling of an onion; neither will lead to the discovery of a core or an essence (*River River* 13). But the essence of life, though unnamable, Sze suggests, is always there in everything in us and around us, as he writes in "The Unnamable River": it is in the capillaries of our lungs, in the space created as we slice open a lemon, "in rain splashing on banana leaves," in the anthracite face of a coal miner, in the veins and lungs of a steelworker, and in a corpse burning on the Ganges. However, we may not find it even if we have traveled the four thousand miles of the Nile and reached its source (*River River* 59). While urging us to perceive invisible connections that will enable us to understand life better, Sze suggests that imagination is crucial in enlarging the mind for perception and revelation. This emphasis on imagination is characteristic of traditional romantic lyric poetry, and Sze's insistence on the intensity of experience is reminiscent of classical Chinese poetry. But his poem departs from both traditions in its use of bodily images and in its way of interweaving the material with the spiritual.

The body in Sze's poems is equally as important as the mind, and passion is as necessary as reason. In "Fauve," Sze suggests that imagination can be limited or liberated by bodily experience. To live deeply and passionately, Sze's persona says, is to feel blood as rivers when in rage, to experience the intertwining of love and hatred "as fibers of a rope," and to catch the scent of a wolf and turn wild (*Dazzled* 51). Human bodily functions in Sze's poems are related to the operations of the mind, to the experience of emotions, and eventually to human mortality. Rather than lamenting death and striving to transcend mortality, Sze seeks to come to terms with it. For him, recognition of one's death involves a profound understanding of one's self and life. His sequence poem "The Silk Road," collected in *Archipelago*, enacts a journey into the deepest self in order to confront death and to use it as a point of transformation. Eventually, the search for the deepest self in order to understand the meaning of death becomes an exploration of the disparity between intention and effect and of the fact that death and life are to be understood as one, coexisting in all things at various moments.

Sze's treatment of the theme in this poem is characteristic of his poetics, which incorporates elements from science, philosophy, nature, and history across cultural and national boundaries. The multicultural and inclusive aspects of his poem are reflected in the way the poem is structured. Unlike traditional romantic lyric poetry, the poem does not rely on the voice of the lyric "I" as the organizing principle. In fact, Sze situates the voices, characters, images, narratives, and observations in multiple temporal-spatial relationships rather than containing them within a single space-time. At the same time, the movement of "The Silk Road" does not rely on the progression of logical argument; rather, it depends on a succession of parallels and antitheses, which are characteristic poetic devices of classical Chinese poetry. Sze's arrangement of the lines in couplets helps foreground the similarities and contrasts between the juxtaposed images and narratives, which achieve the pleasure of shock revelation because of the unexpected leaps of recognition. The nonlinear concept of time and the nonsequential structure of Sze's poem, like those of classical Chinese poetry, also have the effect of capturing the immediacy of the experience without confining the experience to a homogeneous space-time.

Thus "The Silk Road" breaks open the lyric moment as well as the traditional lyric form. The result is a capaciousness capable of including disparate realms of knowledge and experience in search for the meaning of death. In this poem, Sze explores metaphysical questions of death not only in terms of physiology, imagination, and philosophy, but also in relation to multiple temporalities. This plurality in space-time enables his persona to understand human mortality in different forms and from varied perspectives. In section two of "The Silk Road," for instance, Sze indicates that nuclear tests on Bikini Island have produced new forms of dying and disorientation of the mind, not unlike that of the diabetic in section one, who yearns for an insulin that will make it possible for him to understand the paradox of death in life. The sense of a journey and the convergence of different histories and cultures are embedded in the title of the poem. "The Silk Road" alludes to the historical route of cross-cultural interactions and the coexistence of different realities as a result of diverse geographical locations. In connection to this historical route, and alluding to a parable in Zhuangzi's (Chuang Tsu's) writing about the uselessness of Chinese ceremonial caps for people of a remote state, who had short hair and tattooed bodies, Sze in section five of the poem suggests that values are not fixed or universal, and that realities are diverse and multiple. In the same section, Sze juxtaposes Zhuangzi's Daoist mode of thinking about time and reality with that of Plato's concept of "form" as an independent, pure essence of being (*Archipelago* 15). This juxtaposition subverts a Western philosophical tradition based on monolithic universalism and a unified, absolute concept of time. Hence the journey to understand death and the self in "The Silk Road" is a complex experience involving multilayered meanings of life, death, and knowledge. Perhaps one of Sze's most radical breaks from lyric convention is a reconceptualization of time and space in relation to all aspects of human experience, and to the production and investigation of knowledge across disciplinary and cultural boundaries.

The multiplicity of time and space and the interconnections of all things in Sze's poetry suggest an ecological view of the world as an alternative to binary, monolithic, and hierarchical systems. In *Archipelago*, Sze articulates this worldview most cogently through his poetics, which are implied in the configuration of an archipelago that consists of a cluster of apparently separate islands that are actually parts of the same submarine land mass and of the earth's crust. According to Sze, the book and its title are inspired by the Rock Garden at Royanji Temple in Kyoto, famous for its fifteen stones set in a sea of raked gravel. When he visited the garden in 1990, Sze was struck by the fact that as he walked back and forth along the walkway, he could not see all fifteen stones at the same time. The stones are positioned in such a way that the totality can never be seen at once from any particular angle. Sze realized that he could develop a book or a series of poems, each resembling a rock in the garden. Each poem or cluster of poems would have its unique configuration, but each would fit into a larger whole, like an island of an archipelago that is at once "the one and the many." This concept underlies the content and structure of *Archipelago*, which the title poem best illustrates.

"Archipelago" is a sequence poem consisting of nine sections, each of which can be read as a separate piece. Yet all the sections are linked in a way by two simultaneous but independent temporalities—the poet's persona walking in the Rock Garden at Royanji Temple, and Pueblo women dancing in New Mexico. Just as these two activities are represented as concurrent, so are the speaker's memories, reflections, and a range of phenomena from different countries and in separate time and space. Sze has developed a collage method that is similar to the cinematic technique of montage, in which varied, fragmentary images are shown in such a way that they all seem to be caught in a moment of time, thus suggesting a simultaneity that enhances the invisible connections among them. At the same time, Sze's collage juxtaposition and arrangement of multiple single lines in the poem have the effect of giving equal importance to each phenomenon. Thus human beings and their activities are shown to be only part of all things in motion in the universe.

This sense of multiple simultaneity in motion and the recognition that the world is more than we can surmise (*River River* 15) are captured in the title of Sze's sixth book, *The Redshifting Web*. The term "redshift" describes the astronomical phenomenon that when stars are moving away from us, the light they emit shifts toward the red end of the spectrum. Scientists have discovered that most galaxies appear to be "redshifted," that is, nearly all galaxies are moving away from us and from one another. This indicates that the universe is not static; it is expanding. Sze employs the term "redshift" to suggest a sense of constant motion, change, and transformation in the universe, in our everyday experience, and in reading his poetry. At the same time, all things in the universe and their constant changes, including those in the human world and in reading a poem, are intricately connected, interacting with one another, and mutually influencing one another's transformation, as the word "web" indicates. This concept of the world based on the principle of quantum mechanics parallels the basic philosophy of Daoism and Native Americans' view of the universe. Sze is familiar with all three frames of reference—natural sciences, Chinese culture, and Native American culture—and he absorbs them in his themes and poetics, which might be considered ecological. Hence one might say that an ecological view of the world is at the core of Sze's poetics and thematic concerns. But Sze's poetry resists any category or totalizing interpretations, as his persona says: "No single method can describe the world" (*River River* 6). As he continues to explore new ways of articulating his central themes in terms of a quest for passion and compassion, for self-knowledge, for a keen awareness of invisible connectedness, and for living life fully with a profound sense of the beauty and infinite mysteries in the world, Arthur Sze's poems, "though rarely overtly political, embody a politics that seeks to transform, liberate, and renew" ("Arthur Sze: The Written Word" 75).

CRITICAL RECEPTION

Sze's poetry, like that of most Asian American poets, has not received substantial critical studies. However, there have been abundant reviews of his books, especially since the publication of *Archipelago* and *The Redshifting Web*. Almost all the reviews convey perceptive, insightful praises of Sze's multiplicity, innovativeness, and exquisitely beautiful language. These reviews generally discuss the richness of cross-cultural fertilization in Sze's poetry, which shows its indebtedness to and reinvention of traditions, particularly the traditions of Chinese poetry and philosophy. Even though critical attention to Sze's translations is scant, critics unanimously regard him as a "superb," "talented" translator and recognize that the strengths of his translations lie in the fact that he not only is familiar with Chinese poetic and intellectual traditions, but also knows how the sounds and written forms of the Chinese language work in constructing meaning and organizing experience. C.L. Rawlins, a poet himself who knows the Chinese language, observes that the remarkable achievement of Sze's translations is due to his knowledge of "the way in which ideograms clash and merge and aggregate to create meaning without the grammatical scaffolding of English." Moreover, Rawlins points out that Sze does not simply borrow from these and Western poetic traditions in his own poetry; rather, he "seems to be constantly testing the fit of the two great linguistic traditions" (13). Like Rawlins, Tony Barnstone asserts that Sze turns to the great masters of "the Chinese source" in search of an alternative to the aesthetics available in the English language. Sze's poetics, Barnstone observes, is Ezra Pound's kind of "ideogrammatic method instead of Alexander Pope's rhetoric of argumentation." What Barnstone finds most interesting about Sze's early poems in *The Willow Wind* and *Two Ravens* is the fact that Sze blends Chinese and modernist techniques with "the archetypal imagery of Deep Image poetry," and the clear, familiar images in his poems edge into the surreal. Barnstone also relates Sze's early poems to the modernist modes of imagism, vorticism, and objectivism (30). Such identification of Sze's poetry in terms of European American poetic schools may "domesticate" the strange, as Barnstone himself notes, and this domestication can "discount the magic" of Sze's idiosyncratic poetry (30).

Of various comments on Sze's incorporation of his Chinese cultural heritage in his poetry, Jacqueline Osherow's are perhaps the most acute. While recognizing that Sze's "great strength and power" seem to come from his thorough absorption of "Eastern poetic traditions," Osherow contends that Sze's use of these traditions offers something different from that of other American poets. While the Eastern influence on American poetry is usually shown or understood as "imagism," in Sze's poems this influence is "present not just as a quality of perception, but of thought—made available to us in all its complexity through a precision of language so refined that it feels like marksmanship." In addition, Osherow, like most critics, notes the disparate elements in Sze's poems, but goes further to examine the implications of "all kinds of gossamer connections" and the cognitive leaps resulting from experiencing "how the minutest realities hook up to the infinite" through "meticulous and surprising conjunctions and accumulation" (123). What seems to mark the difference between Sze's poetry and the poetry of the imagists and their successors is the intellectual vigor in Sze's representation of images. Almost all critics point out that Sze's poems are difficult and demanding, showing the mind in action, probing beneath the surface of things through witty, humorous paradoxes. In this sense, Sze's poetry has a certain affinity to that of Wallace Stevens, whose work Sze admires. Much of the wit and humor in Sze's work, however, can also be identified with those in Daoist and Buddhist writings.

Although critics regard Sze's recent poems as a natural extension of his early work and of the books of his middle period, *Dazzled* and *River River*, most consider *Archipelago* the "breakthrough" book of his career. The winner of two prestigious national book prizes, *Archipelago* has brought Sze broad public recognition and critical attention even though no substantial studies have been done on his poetry so far. Rather than focusing on Sze's innovative incorporation of Chinese traditions, critics begin to emphasize the experimental aspects of his poetry. Tony Barnstone, for instance, contends that *Archipelago* represents "a full commitment to an avant-garde intellectual poetics" and shows a movement away from his early imagist poems. Barnstone perceives an affinity between Sze's experimental poetry and the fragmented juxtapositions of contemporary Chinese poets of the "Misty" school. He also discerns connections of Sze's poetry with experimental Taiwanese poet Luo Fu and with the Language poets. The similarities Sze seems to have with these poets may be the result of shared cultural and linguistic sources and common impulses to reinvent the poetic form and renew the use of language.

Critical views of Sze's poetry in general reveal a significant departure from reductive ethnocentric readings of Asian American poetry, which contain Asian American poets in an Orientalist discursive space. Even when some critics employ the terms pertaining to anthropology or ethnography in discussing Sze's poetry, their emphases are on his blending of heterogeneous, cross-cultural elements, on the disturbing strangeness of his surrealistic representation of cultures. One reviewer, for instance, calls Sze an "anthropologist" of humanity, for his poetry explores overlapping aspects of cultures, aesthetic values and spiritual experiences. Most reviewers note that Sze's poems enact a hybrid culture that synthesizes elements from both the East and the West. Eric Elshtain refers to

Sze as "an ethnographer and naturalist" who uses random combinations of images to "make some sense of 'the most mysterious of all possible worlds' " (155; *The Redshifting Web* 29). Elshtain relates Sze's uncanny juxtaposition of images to what James Clifford calls "ethnographic surrealism," which refers to the ways in which "artists and ethnographers subject their culture to the activity of fragmentation and collage rendering the familiar strange" (Elshtain 155). The significance of such a presentation of cultures, the Clifford quote suggests, is a profound subversion of cultural purity.

But not all critics perceive this subversive effect in the heterogeneous, cross-cultural juxtapositions in Sze's poetry. In his review of *River River*, Charles Alexander asserts his reservations about Sze's "notion that in recognizing the random and multiple nature of things, in abandoning attempts to move from object to meaning, we achieve a kind of dignity." From this perspective, Alexander finds that Sze's poems, "so full of marvelous heterogeneity, often resolve, perhaps too comfortably" (1). Alexander's formulation of Sze's notion and his resolution of heterogeneity in his poems does not seem to be well grounded. In fact, it contradicts his closing statement that Sze, like Susan Howe, challenges "notions of a unified authoritarian self and culture" (10). For Sze's poetry to challenge "notions of a unified authoritarian" culture, it must not resolve the heterogeneity it represents into a unity. Nevertheless, Alexander's contention here raises important larger questions about the implications and effects of multiculturalism and various claims of differences. These questions help us better understand the risks and stakes involved in Arthur Sze's experimental poetry.

BIBLIOGRAPHY

Works by Arthur Sze

Poetry and Translations of Poetry

The Willow Wind. Berkeley, CA: Rainbow Zenith Press, 1972.
Two Ravens. Guadalupita, NM: Tooth of Time Books, 1976.
The Willow Wind: Translations from the Chinese and Poems by Arthur Sze. Santa Fe: Tooth of Time Books, 1981.
Dazzled. Point Reyes, CA: Floating Island Publications, 1982.
Two Ravens: Translations from the Chinese and Poems by Arthur Sze. Santa Fe: Tooth of Time Books, 1984.
River River. Providence, RI: Lost Roads Publishers, 1987.
Archipelago. Port Townsend, WA: Copper Canyon Press, 1995.
The Redshifting Web: Poems, 1970–1998. Port Townsend, WA: Copper Canyon Press, 1998.
The Silk Dragon: Translations from the Chinese. Port Townsend, WA: Copper Canyon Press, 2001.

Interviews

"Arthur Sze: Mixing Memory and Desire." By Eileen Tabios with a draft in progress of
"Archipelago." *Black Lightning: Poetry-in-Progress.* Eileen Tabios. New York:
Asian American Writers' Workshop, 1998. 3–21.

"Arthur Sze." By Barbara Bogave. *Fresh Air.* National Public Radio. 10 September 1998.

"Arthur Sze: The Written Word." (Response to Amy Ling's questions.) *Yellow Light:
The Flowering of Asian American Arts.* Ed. Amy Ling. Philadelphia: Temple
University Press, 1999. 73–76.

"The Practice of Translating Poetry and Culture." By Doris Pai. *F Magazine.* Art Institute
of Chicago, 1999. 11.

"Revelation Waiting to Happen: A Conversation with Arthur Sze on Translating Chinese
Poetry." By Tony Barnstone. *Translation Review* 59 (August 2000): 4–19.

Essays

"Through the Empty Door: Translating Chinese Poetry." *Bloomsbury Review* 4.6 (September 1984): 15.

"The Silk Road." *Patterns/Contexts/Time/: A Symposium on Contemporary Poetry.* Ed.
Phillip Foss and Charles Bernstein. Santa Fe: Recursos de Santafe, 1990. 224–
25.

"The Wang River Sequence, a Prospectus." *First Intensity: A Magazine of New Writing*
7 (Summer 1996): 156–61.

Introduction to *Black Lightning.* Eileen Tabios. New York: Asian American Writers'
Workshop, 1998. 1.

"The Writer Reads: Arthur Sze on Josephine Miles." *Rain Taxi Review of Books* 4.1
(Spring 1999): 14–15.

"Arthur Sze Introduces Sherwin Bitsui." *American Poet: Journal of the Academy of
American Poets* (Fall 1999): 20–21.

"Translating a Poem by Li Shang-yin." *Mānoa* 11.2 (October 1999): 116–20.

Studies of Arthur Sze

Alexander, Charles. "Still and Lawless." Rev. of *River River. Poetry Flash* 192 (March
1989): 1, 10.

Alexander, Floyce. "Gifted Poet Celebrates His Chinese Heritage." Rev. of *The Willow
Wind. Albuquerque Journal* 18 July 1982: D12.

Baldinger, Jo Ann. "Arthur Sze's Creative, Spiritual Poetry." *New Mexican* 8 April 1994:
18, 35.

Barnstone, Tony. Rev. of *The Redshifting Web. Rain Taxi* 3.3 (September 1998): 30.

Bradley, John. "*The Redshifting Web: Poems 1970–1998.*" *XCP: Cross-Cultural Poetics.*
4 (April 1999): 144–46.

Elshtain, Eric P. "The Redshifting Web." *Chicago Review* 46.1 (April 2000): 155–59.

Frumkin, Gene. "Seeing the Invisible." *Mānoa* 8.2 (November 1996): 218–20.

Fujita, Gayle. "The Imagination and Contemporary Life in the Poetry of Arthur Sze: A
Review of *Dazzled.*" *Literary Arts Hawaii* 80–81 (Summer 1986): 8–11.

Gonzalez, Ray. "*Dazzled.*" *Bloomsbury Review* 3.3 (April/May 1983): 13.

———. "*The Willow Wind.*" *Bloomsbury Review* 3.2 (February/March 1983): 20–21.

Laird, W. David. Rev. of *Dazzled*. *Books of the Southwest* February 1983: 291.

Lim, Edilberto. "Arthur Sze: A New Mexican Poet Who Refuses to Be Categorized." *East West News* [San Francisco] 7 December 1983.

Lujan, James. "Chinese-American Poet Embraces Less-Than-Scientific Art." *Albuquerque Journal* 10 April 1994.

Lyon, Fern. "*Dazzled*." *New Mexico Magazine* 61.2 (February 1983).

Merrill, Christopher. "*Archipelago*." *El Palacio* 100.3 (Summer 1995): 59–62.

Milligan, Bryce. "In Praise of Poetry: 1988 Has Been a Banner Year." Rev. of *River River. San Antonio Light* 4 December 1988. K7.

Nizalowski, John. "Collaborative Journey on 'The Silk Road.'" *New Mexican* 31 Mar. 1989.

Osherow, Jacqueline. "*The Redshifting Web: Poems New and Collected*." *Antioch Review* 58.1 (Winter 2000): 123.

Penn, David. "Transcontinental Vision." Rev. of *The Redshifting Web. Tucson Weekly* 8 August 1998.

Petoskey, Barbara. "The Unmelted Pot." Rev. of *River River. High Plains Literary Review* 3.2 (September 1988): 112–14.

Rawlins, C.L. "Testing Traditions." Rev. of *Archipelago. Bloomsbury Review* 16.4 (July/August 1996): 13.

Romero, Leo. "*The Willow Wind*." *Greenfield Review* 11.1–2 (June 1983): 194.

Tritica, John. "Experimental Poet Explores Paradoxes of Life with Unpredictable, Lyrical Verses." Rev. of *Archipelago. Albuquerque Journal* 5 January 1997.

Tucker, Sara. " 'Silk Road': Imaginative Blend of Music, Poetry." *Albuquerque Journal* 4 April 1989: B6.

Woods, Phil. "*River River*." *Bloomsbury Review* 8.4 (July–August 1988).

Zhou, Xiaojing. "Intercultural Strategies in Asian American Poetry." *Re-placing America: Conversations and Contestations*. Ed. Ruth Hsu, Cynthia Franklin, and Suzanne Kosanke. Literary Studies East and West, vol. 16. Honolulu: University of Hawai'i Press and the East-West Center, 2000. 92–108.

———. " 'The Redshifting Web': Arthur's Sze's Ecopoetics." *Ecological Poetry: A Critical Introduction*. Ed. J. Scott Bryson. Salt Lake City: University of Utah Press, forthcoming.

JOSÉ GARCIA VILLA
(1908–1997)

Rocío G. Davis

BIOGRAPHY

José Garcia Villa was born on 5 August 1908 in Malate, Manila, the Philippines, one of six children of Guia Garcia and Dr. Simeon Villa. Villa began painting as a boy and published his first story in the *Manila Times* at the age of fifteen. His father enrolled him in the College of Medicine of the University of the Philippines in 1925. He received his associate in arts degree from the UP College of Liberal Arts in 1927 and transferred to the College of Law in 1928, simultaneously taking classes in fine arts. In college, he became a charter member of the university's Writers Club. In his second year of law school, his "Man-Songs" (written under the pseudonym O. Sevilla; the pseudonym he was to adopt later was Doveglion [Dove-eagle-lion]) appeared in the *Philippines Herald* and caused him to be suspended from the club for a year because of his "immoral" poems. With the prize of 1,000 pesos ($500) he won in the *Philippine Free Press* Contest for his short story "Mir-i-nisa," he immigrated to the United States in 1929, where he lived the rest of his life, except for brief visits to the Philippines.

Villa finished his B.A. at the University of New Mexico in 1933 and later enrolled at Columbia University. In New York, he worked as associate editor of New Directions (1949–51) and as Poetry Workshop director of the City College of New York and as a lecturer at the New School for Social Research (1964–73). He also held private poetry workshops at his Greenwich Village apartment. He served in the Philippine Mission to the United Nations from 1954 to 1963, becoming vice-consul in 1965. In 1946, he married Rosemary Lamb, and they had two children, Randall and Lance, before separating in 1955 and divorcing in 1960.

Villa received the Poetry Award of the American Academy of Arts and Letters (1942), the Guggenheim Fellowship in Poetry (1943), the Bollingen Foundation Fellowship (1950–51), the Shelley Memorial Award of the Poetry Society of America (1959), and Rockefeller Fellowships for poetry. He also received some of the Philippines's highest awards, including a Rizal Pro-Patria Award (1961), the Republic Cultural Heritage Award (1962), and honorary doctorates from the Far Eastern University (1959) and the University of the Philippines (1973). He was named Philippine National Artist in Literature in 1973. He died in New York City on 7 February 1997.

MAJOR WORKS AND THEMES

In the United States, impressed by Sherwood Anderson's *Winesburg, Ohio* and encouraged by his friend and mentor, Arturo B. Rotor, Villa published his only book of short stories, *Footnote to Youth: Tales of the Philippines and Others*, introduced by Edward O'Brien. Influenced by Robert Blake, e.e. cummings, Gerard Manley Hopkins, Marianne Moore, Dylan Thomas, Eleanor Wylie, Wallace Stevens, and Dame Edith Sitwell, Villa's poems, like his stories, are characterized by the theme of revolt—in content and in form. In particular, experimentation with the sounds and the appearance of words on paper would become landmarks of his poetry. His first collection of poetry published in the United States, *Have Come, Am Here*, clearly reveals the poet's personality and outlines the themes that are to be taken up repeatedly in later writing.

In these poems, we see Villa "pilgrimaging among internal rather than geographic landscapes. The questions which occupy him are characteristic of the truly romantic quester: the questions of identity, life and death, and Man and God" (Tinio 736). The theme of God is omnipresent in Villa's poetry, most often as the object of his revolt. The poet equates himself with God, as when he declares, "I am more than God's equal" (*Have Come, Am Here* Poem 32). In other poems, he challenges "Christ Oppositor" to single combat or assumes a Luciferian stance to "break God's seamless skull," in order to rebuild himself and find his "Finality" (Poem 6). In Villa's personal theology, therefore, Man is the creator of God through the human—and especially the poetic—power of thought and poetry. In Poem 95, he writes, "In the chamber of my philosophy God is instructed." Leonard Casper describes this characteristic of Villa's as "unmediated defiance, resolute aspiration, the refusal to be humiliated by anyone. In this passion for denial lies Villa's strength and, unwittingly, his weakness for self-imitation" (106).

Corollary to the poet's willful independence with which he asserts his ego, particularly in relation to God, is the obsession with love that implies the surrender of his ego to an object. In Poem 21, the poet argues that the heart that cannot love cannot be cured by death, nor sleep, "nor splendor of wound." He views romantic love as a release of the soul and repeatedly posits it as superior even to God, who "shall not be able to put out Love at all" (Poem 15). The poems also become, for the poet, a mirror in which to behold himself, and in which he may be seen by others. Villa's poetic ambition is suggested in Poem 16, where he exclaims how in his "desire to be Nude," he clothed himself in "fire." Some of these poems, nonetheless, seem to be more cavalier than metaphysical. What at first seemed sacred or profane poems clearly become manifestations of a consistent self-love; and that self is never doubted, never explored, only praised and presumed (Casper 106).

Villa also manipulates the structures of traditional poetic diction in order to discover the language of pure poetry. For Villa, "Poetry is—first of all—expertness in language and form, not in meaning; and the true meaning of a poem is its Expressive Force rather than its content—the language of poetry being a mode of action, a transmitter of energy rather than of information" (*Doveglion* flap). In his multiple definitions of poetry, he consistently privileges the power of the word: "Poetry is a struggle between a word and silence; between an eternal word and an eternal silence" ("Definitions of Poetry" 224). In his most famous poetic description of a poem (Poem 15), Villa requires that a poem be magical, musical, elusive, and even secretive, like the bride who hides what she seeks, stressing the universality of the poetic craft.

An important part of Villa's poetic endeavor was the struggle to develop an essentially poetic language that would achieve effects akin to music and painting. In this vein, Villa offered three specific experiments. First, he argues in favor of "reversed consonance," a rhyme method that required that the last consonants of the last syllable, or the last principal consonants of a word, be reversed for the corresponding rhyme, making the rhyme for *near* words like *run, rain, green, reign*. His second major innovation was his "comma poems," which he developed in his 1949 collection of poetry, *Volume Two*. He inserted commas and eliminated the spaces between all the words in the poem, contending that the commas would regulate the poem's verbal density and movement, heighten appreciation for each word, and achieve fuller tonal and sonal effects. The commas, he explained, perform a poetic rather than a prose function and "are themselves the medium as well as the technique of expression: therefore functional and valid, as medium of art and as medium of personality" (*Selected Poems* 81). In *Volume Two*, Villa reiterated many of the themes he had already developed in *Have Come, Am Here*, but the innovative poetic form required a renewed strategy for reading. Death becomes another central theme, as in Poem 20, where he sees Life "Clean,like,iodoform," between the letters of "death." The comma poems also appear to allow him a deeper introspection: "At,the,in,of,me" begins Poem 11. His third poetic experiment involved adaptations, experiments in converting prose into poems with specific line movements and shape. Villa's adaptations developed from a diversity of sources that included selections from letters, short stories, newspaper reports, book reviews, and novels.

Villa stopped writing poetry in the early 1950s; his last poem was "The Anchored Angel," written in 1953, which may be considered his poetic valedictory. After this, he devoted himself to critical and philosophical writing. Though Villa was clearly the first Filipino American poet, his writing falls more easily within the classification of modernism than within any form of ethnic writing, in spite of Werner Sollors's suggestion that it was Villa's uprooted condition that motivated "a radical formal response to the ethnic writer's need for a new poetic language" (254). Yet though his stories center on memories of the Philippines, his poetry completely ignores themes that would more naturally be associated with a Filipino writer living in the United States: exile, belonging, home. On the contrary, Villa's themes are those of his contemporary American poets, and, although he played a pivotal role in the development of Philippine letters, his own creative work largely bypasses issues of identity and transculturality.

CRITICAL RECEPTION

Although Villa lived in the United States for most of his adult life, his influence on Philippine literature in English far outweighs his influence in American letters. Yet, paradoxically, he appears to have been better appreciated as a poet in his country of adoption than in his homeland. Filipino critics did not rate his work highly, accusing him of solipsism and prophesying that the novelty of his work would quickly wear off. American poets responded enthusiastically to Villa's early poetry, which "registered the advent of a heterodox, transgressive creativity" (San Juan 191). Sitwell considers Villa "a poet with a great and perfectly original gift" and judges his poems as being "of great beauty," a poetry that "springs with a wild force, straight from the poet's being, from his blood, from his spirit, as a fire breaks from wood, or as a flower grows from its soil" (xxiii). Besides, "his somewhat curious conjunctions of subject matter are 'felt,' not forced" (qtd. in Tinio 723). With his *Volume Two*, however, and its collection of "comma poems," he met with some skepticism and considerable disapproval. Nevertheless, he is praised for his "poet's eye and the poet's ear" as well as "the sharp colors, the cunning verbal precision, and that almost Blakelike combination of innocence and outrage which his earlier poems showed so markedly" (qtd. in Kunitz 1036).

Criticism against Villa centers on his poetic experiments. Reverse consonance has been judged "altogether too esoteric to be effective" (Tinio 732) or "calisthenic only, or exhibitionist," because neither the ear nor the uninstructed eye will detect the pattern (Casper 107). The commas, for example, are challenged for their precociousness: "being invariable, it allows no subtleties of suspension, syncopation, etc.; being identical, visually, with actual commas, it hinders the exploitation of punctuation in general" (Casper 107). Although Villa has been denounced by some as a mere "aesthete," most critics now credit him with breaking the fetters of conservative literature in the Philippines and opening up new manners of expression and a new poetic diction that have made possible the development of the Philippine short story and poetry.

BIBLIOGRAPHY

Works by José Garcia Villa

Poetry

Many Voices. Manila: Philippine Book Guild, 1939.
Poems by Doveglion. Manila: Philippine Writers' League, 1941.
Have Come, Am Here. New York: Viking, 1942.
Volume Two. New York: New Directions, 1949.
Selected Poems and New. New York: McDowell, Oblensky, 1958.
A Doveglion Book of Philippine Poetry. Manila: Katha Editions, 1962.
Poems 55: The Best Poems of José García Villa as Chosen by Himself. Manila: A.S. Florentino, 1962. Tagalog translation published as *55 Poems*. Trans. Hilario S. Francia. Manila: University of the Philippines Press, 1962.
The Essential Villa. Manila: A.S. Florentino, 1965.
Makata 3: Poems in Praise of Love: The Best Love Poems of José García Villa. Manila: A.S. Florentino, 1973.
Appassionata: Poems in Praise of Love. New York: King and Cowen, 1979.
The Parlement of Giraffes: Poems for Children—Eight to Eighty. Ed. John Edwin Cowen, with original drawings by Villa. Tagalog translation by Larry Francia. Manila: Anvil, 1999.

Short Stories

Footnote to Youth: Tales of the Philippines and Others. Intro. Edward O'Brien. New York: Charles Scribner's Sons, 1933.

Selected Essays

"The Status of Philippine Poetry." *Graphic* 6 (June 1935): 10, 14, 45, 54–55.
"Definitions of Poetry." *Filipino Essays in English 1910–1954*. Ed. Leopoldo Y. Yabes. Vol. 1. *1910–1937*. Quezon City: University of the Philippines Press, 1962.

Studies of José García Villa

Abad, Gemino H., and Edna Z. Manlapaz, eds. "José García Villa." *Man of Earth*. Quezon City: Ateneo de Manila University Press, 1989. 411–15.
Alegre, Edilberto, and Doreen Fernandez. *The Writer and His Milieu*. Manila: De La Salle University Press, 1984.
Casper, Leonard. *New Writing from the Philippines: A Critique and Anthology*. Syracuse, NY: Syracuse University Press, 1966.
Chua, Jonathan. "Footnote to Villa." *Pen and Ink* 1 (1997): 16–18.
Chua, Jonathan, and Luis Cabalquinto. "Interview with the Tiger." *Pen and Ink* 1 (1997): 10–15.

Croghan, Richard V. *The Development of Philippine Literature in English since 1900.* Quezon City: Alemar-Phoenix, 1975.

Hosillos, Lucila. "Escapee to Universality (Portrait of a Filipino Poet as Escapee to the Non-existent Kingdom of Universalism)." *Diliman Review* 18 (October 1970): 329–40.

"José García Villa." *Contemporary Authors*, Vol. 25. Detroit: Gale Publishing 1962. 492–93.

Kunitz, Stanley J., ed. *Twentieth-Century American Authors* (First Supplement). New York: H.W. Wilson Co., 1955.

Quijano de Manila (Nick Joaquin). "Viva Villa!" *Doveglion and Other Cameos.* Manila: National Book Store, 1984. 288–308.

San Juan, E., Jr. "Homage to José García Villa." *The Anchored Angel: Selected Writings by José García Villa.* Ed. Eileen Tabios. Foreword by Jessica Hagedorn. New York: Kaya Press, 1999. 191–216.

Seymour-Smith, Martin. *Guide to Modern World Literature.* London: Wolfe Publishing, 1973.

Sitwell, Edith. *The American Genius.* London: John Lehmann, 1951.

Sollors, Werner. *Beyond Ethnicity.* New York: Oxford University Press, 1986.

Tabios, Eileen, ed. *The Anchored Angel: Selected Writings by José García Villa.* With a foreword by Jessica Hagedorn. New York: Kaya Press, 1999.

Tinio, Rolando S. "Villa's Values; or, The Poet You Cannot Always Make Out, or Succeed in Liking Once You Are Able To." *Brown Heritage: Essays on Philippine Cultural Tradition and Literature.* Ed. Antonio G. Manuud. Quezon City: Ateneo de Manila University Press, 1967. 722–38.

NANYING STELLA WONG
(1914–)

Shawn Holliday

BIOGRAPHY

Known more as a visual artist than as a wordsmith, Nanying Stella Wong was born on 30 March 1914 in Oakland, California, where she grew up in a fairly secure Chinese American, middle-class home. Her father owned an herbalism business, and her mother ran the family restaurant, the Peacock Inn, where Wong often featured her finest girlhood drawings. Upon dining in the restaurant, William Clapp, curator of the Oakland Art Gallery, was so impressed with Wong's early talent that he helped her earn a scholarship to the California College of Arts and Crafts. Later, she attended the University of California at Berkeley for a more liberal education. After attending graduate school at Cornell University and conducting postgraduate studies in Mexico City and Dublin, Ireland, Wong lived briefly in New York City, where she designed jewelry for Helena Rubinstein.

In 1940, Wong moved back to the Bay Area, where she has lived ever since. She taught in the Oakland public school system for several years and took to writing poetry, which has appeared in such small periodicals as *California Living* and *Sunset Magazine* and in several theme-specific anthologies of both West Coast and Asian American writers. She currently lives in Berkeley, California, where she continues to pursue her various artistic endeavors.

MAJOR WORKS AND THEMES

Nanying Stella Wong's poetry fuses two traditions. Like that of many California poets, her verse portrays the wonders of landscape and its destruction at human hands. As an Asian American poet, she is also consumed heavily with family, history, and immigration issues. Both poetic traditions appear in the second stanza of "From One Delta to Another." Together, such elements fit Wong comfortably within a blossoming Asian American poetic tradition that combines environmental concerns and Eastern culture with depictions of America's natural and human-made landscape. Largely, she considers herself a poet of protest, believing that she can effect more positive change through poetry than through visual art.

CRITICAL RECEPTION

Nanying Stella Wong has won more acclaim for her work in oils, watercolors, and sculpture than for her verse. Her early work showed such promise that Japanese American painter Chiura Obata allowed her to study at his home while she attended the University of California at Berkeley. As a mature artist, she has been a member of the Chinese Art Association and has exhibited her work at the M.H. Young Memorial Museum and at the Golden Gate International Exposition of 1939–40. Wong's work as a visual artist makes her unusually adept at painting clear, focused images with words, her strong suit in poetry. However, her written work is too lacking in originality to keep her from being eclipsed by other West Coast Asian American writers.

BIBLIOGRAPHY

Work by Nanying Stella Wong

"From One Delta to Another." *Bearing Dreams, Shaping Visions: Asian Pacific American Perspectives*. Ed. Linda A. Revilla, Gail M. Nomura, Shawn Wong, and Shirley Hune. Pullman: Washington State University Press, 1993. 127–28.

Studies of Nanying Stella Wong

Brown, Michael D. *Views from Asian California, 1920–1965*. San Francisco: Michael Brown, 1992. 63.
Hughes, Edan Milton. *Artists in California, 1786–1940*. San Francisco: Hughes Publishing Company, 1986. 512.

NELLIE WONG
(1934–   )

Ernest J. Smith

BIOGRAPHY

In an afterword to her 1997 chapbook *Stolen Moments*, Chinese American poet Nellie Wong describes herself as "a revolutionary feminist who works, writes and organizes in the movements for radical social change" (38). One of seven children, Wong was born in Oakland to Cantonese immigrant parents whose most fervent wish for their six daughters was marriage. Her father, Seow Hong Gee, first came to the United States in 1911, at the age of sixteen, to work in a granduncle's herb store in Oakland. He returned to China to marry, but his wife died shortly after giving birth to a daughter. Wong's father remarried, and the couple had two daughters before deciding to come to the United States in 1933. But the 1924 National Origins Act said that a Chinese man could not bring his wife to America, so Suey Ting Yee Gee, Wong's mother, changed her name and posed as her husband's sister, aunt to the three girls. After being imprisoned on Angel Island for four days, the girls, the youngest being but three years old, were allowed to join their parents. When Nellie was born in 1934, her mother faked a marriage certificate to a man named Sheng Wong, who posed as the girl's father. This complicated story of family history and immigration is related in Wong's poem "It's in the Blood."

Wong was raised in Oakland's Chinatown during a period when assimilation into mainstream American culture continued to be presented as the goal for immigrant families, and many of her most memorable poems recount her childhood there. Always a bright and engaged student, Wong attended Oakland High School, but her desire to go on to college was thwarted by her parents, and after graduating from high school, she spent nearly twenty years working as a secretary for Bethlehem Steel Corporation. At one point during her time there, she was demoted after mentioning to a boss that she planned on someday having children. When Wong was in her mid-thirties, her sister Florence, who admired her older sister's sense of humor, suggested that Nellie take up writing. Wong, still living with her mother following her father's death in 1961, enrolled at nearby Oakland Adult Evening School. She enrolled in the same fiction-writing class with the same instructor for several semesters before the teacher, Kathy Manoogian, convinced her to register as a freshman at San Francisco State University.

At San Francisco State during the 1970s, Wong experienced what she has termed "a discovery of myself and others that I hadn't imagined" (*Stolen Moments* 39). After initially questioning her place at the university, as an older returning student, she began to realize that she had much to offer both her professors and younger classmates. In addition to writing and English courses, Wong did work in Asian American and feminist studies. Her deepening historical, political, and ethnic consciousness led her in the direction of activism and what would become a lifelong interest in the lives of women and working people. In terms of her poetry, she has written that the work of Sylvia Plath was very important to her during this period of development.

Wong's friend Karen Brodine encouraged her to begin writing poems about her working life and, later, to begin putting together a manuscript of poems. In 1977, Kelsey St. Press published Wong's *Dreams in Harrison Railroad Park*. A small press in Berkeley, Kelsey Street was founded in 1974 in order to offer an outlet for women writers neglected by mainstream commercial publishers. Since the publication of that first volume, Wong has gone on to publish two additional collections of poems and a handful of influential essays and has touched countless lives through her work as a writer, teacher, and activist. Today Nellie Wong works as a senior affirmative action analyst at the University of California at San Francisco, is San Francisco Bay Area organizer for the Freedom Socialist Party, and is active in Radical Women, an international socialist feminist organization.

MAJOR WORKS AND THEMES

Nellie Wong's poetry revolves around the themes of cultural identity, family, work, and woman as feminist and social activist. Wong's first book, *Dreams in Harrison Railroad Park* (1977), is dedicated to her parents, and most of the poems deal with memories of growing up, struggles to come to terms with her ethnic heritage, and family and cultural pressures to assimilate. "How a Girl Got Her Chinese Name" concerns the crossing of social and cultural borders, reflected in the different names by which young Nellie was addressed by her parents and by her teachers in "Chinese school" and "American school." In "Like the Old Women Suggested," Wong offers the first of several poems re-

ferring to her sense of guilt in her youth over her dark skin and her desire to
be lighter. In this poem, she offers the image of repeated baths in mustard and
oatmeal and their failure to lighten her skin. In "When I Was Growing Up," a
poem from Wong's second volume, *The Death of a Long Steam Lady* (1986),
she begins with the line "I know now that once I longed to be white" and goes
on to discuss how magazines and blonde movie stars caused her to create an
imaginary pale skin for herself.

Other poems from each of Wong's first two volumes offer glimpses of the
poet's intense love for her family. In the title poem from *Dreams in Harrison
Railroad Park*, she shares unspoken feelings with her mother while sitting on a
park bench, and in the book's concluding poem, "Picnic," she evokes the weekly
Sunday picnics she shared on an Oakland hillside with her parents. "Song for
My Father: In Four Photographs," from *The Death of Long Steam Lady*, uses
four photographs from various stages in her father's life to reconstruct his biography and to summon memories of his personality and behavior. A more
ominous tone pervades several poems from the first volume, such as "Under
Cover," where Wong's mother works to protect her daughters from public scru-
tiny, or "Drums, Gongs," which implicitly critiques the commodification of ethnicity in the crowning of "Miss Chinatown U.S.A." One of the book's most
haunting poems is "Can't Tell," which chronicles the family's effort to distinguish themselves from their Japanese neighbors at the outbreak of World War
II.

Several poems from *Dreams in Harrison Railroad Park* confront racism and
sexism. "We Can Always" catalogues insensitive racist stereotypes of the Chinese propagated by various forms of the media. Another poem, "Loose Women,
You Say?" offers another catalogue, a list of women performing activities ranging from the everyday to the more extreme or self-protective, such as killing a
rapist. The poem is something of a social history of women in the modern era,
some working in jobs stereotypically associated with men, others forced to sell
their bodies for profit, and still others merely asserting their selfhood. However,
each line is presented as a question, suggesting that a patriarchal worldview will
find a way to label all women "loose women." In "Relining Shelves," the poet,
while working in her kitchen, ruminates on examples of the physical subjugation
of women. This is one of several Wong poems in which she identifies with the
oppressed, the homeless, the laborer, or the lonely figure of innocent youth about
to confront the harsh realities of the adult world. "On Plaza Garibaldi" takes
place during a Mexican street festival, and following the catalogue of the sounds
and smells of the festival, Wong ends the poem with an image of a young girl
being watched by older men, and her own struggle of conscience in attempting
not to identify with the girl. "Woman in Print" explores the poet's feelings
toward a nameless woman who frequents a coffee shop, while "Poem for a
Trolley Boy" is one of Wong's paeans to the solitary, accomplished, and un-
regarded efforts of the working class.

Wong's collection *The Death of a Long Steam Lady*, published by West End

Press in 1986, is divided into four sections of poems, grouped under the titles "Song from Dark," "When I Was Growing Up," "It's in the Blood," and "Red Journeys." The opening section concludes with two memorable poems on the poet's mother, recently dead, that serve as a transition into the sequence of memory poems in the middle of the volume. Some of these poems are lighter in tone and feel, such as a flashback to the Chinese restaurant where the poet worked as a girl, while other poems like "It's in the Blood" trace Wong's cultural identity through the struggles and triumphs of her family. In "Of Necessity," she returns to the theme of lost opportunities and the abnegation of self in light of her parents' expectations.

The text that lends the volume its title, "The Death of a Long Steam Lady," is actually a very short story, one concerning an unspoken sense of community among Asian Americans. In the story, a younger woman reflects on a relationship with an older woman with whom she regularly lunched in an outdoor square. The woman has died without the younger woman ever learning her name, and the reflections take place as Paisley Chan prepares to attend the funeral of the woman she knows only as Long Steam Lady. The book's final group of poems, titled "Red Journeys," suggests some of the intersections and conflicts between a poet's actions as both a member of the working class and a social activist. "Under Our Own Wings," the poem that concludes the volume, is especially powerful in its panoramic sweep of the Asian American community's effort to resist "our invisibility, our supposed assimilation" in a culture driven by forces of "white supremacy."

Wong's most recent collection of poems is from another independent publisher, Chicory Blue Press. The tenth in a series of chapbooks established to publish the work of women artists over sixty years of age, *Stolen Moments* offers a leaner, more pared-down type of lyric. The title poem deals with a theme common to the volume as a whole: a working woman's tenacity for "bartering my labor for moments," the moments necessary to be a creative, reflective artist. The sense of poet as witness and voice of social resistance is consistently strong throughout *Stolen Moments*, even in small poems like the five-line "A Secretary's Song" or the more disturbing "When You Think of a Spa," concerning a group of unseen "illegal immigrants," Asian women sold into prostitution. Wong concludes the volume with "Launching 62," a poem written on the occasion of her sixty-second birthday. Set in the poet's favorite restaurant, the poem moves through a sequence of vignettes, an internal "ancient song" comprised of a catalogue of activities embodying the spirit of resistance, even as the United States wages air strikes against Iraq in the Gulf War.

CRITICAL RECEPTION

Nellie Wong's poetry has not received extensive critical attention or been reviewed in major literary magazines or journals, yet it stands as a pioneering effort in the area of emergent Asian American literature. In recent years, a great deal of critical attention has been focused on contemporary Asian American writers and their connections to an earlier generation of artists, including Wong. As George Uba writes, "The raw energy of Asian-Pacific American 'activist' poets of the late 1960s and early 1970s gave impetus to a literature in the process of self-discovery" (33). Wong broke new ground for poets seeking to explore cultural identity as subject, and her role as activist and spokesperson has touched many artists working in different media.

The inclusion of some of Wong's essays in collections of writings by women activists and writers of color testifies to her ongoing significance in literary, social, and political circles devoted to giving voice to traditionally marginalized voices. An influential book both within and outside academic circles, *This Bridge Called My Back: Writings by Radical Women of Color* (1981), includes Wong's autobiographical essay "In Search of the Self as Hero: Confetti of Voices on New Year's Night." Wong, addressing herself as "you," assumes the role of a woman representing a generation of Asian American women, and by extension other women, emerging into a recognition of cultural and gendered identity. She discusses Chinese American women writers important to her own artistic and personal growth, and how language can enable a woman to cross unspoken boundaries and overcome "spiritual malaise" (180). During the same year that this essay was published, a film collective called Women Make Movies issued a film devoted to the work of Wong and Mitsuye Yamada titled *Mitsuye and Nellie: Asian American Poets*. In the film, Wong reads from her poetry and discusses her family's immigration from China and her relationship with both her parents and siblings, the importance of community, and the difficulty of attaining recognition from "white majority presses."

In "Socialist Feminism: Our Bridge to Freedom," a 1991 essay, Wong begins with a song of factory women to demonstrate the "multi-issue oppression" common to women and all people of color. Her larger argument is that feminism is inseparable from socialism, and that true socialism cannot exist in a patriarchal society. Drawing upon her own experience as a Chinese American working woman, Wong explores the connections between racism, sexism, colonialism, homophobia, and the oppression of workers in a capitalist economy. Only after marrying and then enrolling in college as a woman in her thirties, Wong reflects, was she able to understand that "[w]hat I had thought was personal and private was truly political, social, and public" (291). Her poetry, prose, and personal example have enabled a younger generation of writers to more easily grasp and explore this connection.

BIBLIOGRAPHY

Works by Nellie Wong

Poetry

Dreams in Harrison Railroad Park. San Francisco: Kelsey St. Press, 1977.
The Death of a Long Steam Lady. Los Angeles: West End Press, 1986.
Stolen Moments. A Crimson Edge Chapbook. Goshen, CT: Chicory Blue Press, 1997.

Essays

"In Search of the Self as Hero: Confetti of Voices on New Year's Night (A Letter to
    Myself)." *This Bridge Called My Back: Writings by Radical Women of Color.*
    Ed. Cherríe Moraga and Gloria Anzaldúa. Watertown, MA: Persephone Press,
    1981.
"Socialist Feminism: Our Bridge to Freedom." *Third World Women and the Politics of
    Feminism.* Ed. Chandra Talpade Mohanty, Ann Russo, and Lourdes Torres. Bloo-
    mington: Indiana University Press, 1991. 288–96.

Short Story

"Broad Shoulders." *Making Waves: An Anthology of Writings by and about Asian Amer-
    ican Women.* Ed. Asian Women United of California. Boston: Beacon, 1989. 260–
    65.

Studies of Nellie Wong

Leong, Russell. "Poetry within Earshot." *Amerasia Journal* 15.1 (1989): 165–93.
Mitsuye and Nellie: Asian American Poets. San Francisco: Light-Saraf Films, 1981.
Uba, George. "Versions of Identity in Post-activist Asian American Poetry." *Reading the
    Literatures of Asian America.* Ed. Shirley Geok-lin Lim and Amy Ling. Phila-
    delphia: Temple University Press, 1992. 33–48.
Yee, Marian. Rev. of *Dreams in Harrison Railroad Park. Calyx* 11 (1988): 243–47.

RITA WONG
(1968–   )

Gaik Cheng Khoo

BIOGRAPHY

Born in the year of the monkey, Calgary-bred Rita Wong is a first-generation Chinese Canadian whose southern Chinese parents immigrated from Hong Kong. Wong spent her formative years as the daughter of a corner-grocery-store owner. "Occupied with small details, sunset grocery can be duller than counting the 20,000 times I breathe each day," she claims ("sunset grocery," *monkey-puzzle* 11). After graduating with a B.A. Honors in English and a minor in East Asian studies at the University of Calgary in 1990, she spent some time teaching in Japan before returning to pursue an M.A. in English at the University of Alberta in 1991–92. Wong traveled next to China to teach English, and her experience there inspired some interesting poems that deal with her position as a diasporic Chinese in her imagined ethnic homeland. After her time in China, she returned to Calgary and worked part-time at a bookstore and also for the Alberta Network of Immigrant Women before moving to Vancouver to get a master's in archival studies at the University of British Columbia. Wong then worked as an archivist with the U'mista Cultural Centre in Alert Bay helping to organize Kwakwaka'wakw archives.

Although her book of poetry *monkeypuzzle* was only published in 1998, Wong had already submitted and published poetry in various magazines and journals in the early 1990s. Slightly different versions of the *monkeypuzzle* poems appear in *Contemporary Verse 2, West Coast Line, absinthe, ARIEL*, and later in *Swallowing Clouds: An Anthology of Chinese-Canadian Poetry. monkeypuzzle* was nominated for the Lambda Literary Award for lesbian poetry in 1999 despite

Wong's self-definition as bisexual. While simultaneously struggling to resist compartmentalization, Wong acknowledges the importance of owning categories such as "Asian Canadian bisexual feminist" as long as they are not reductive. Rejecting them, she realizes, has serious political consequences too.

During the summer of 1999, when four rusty smugglers' boats arrived from Fujian Province on the British Columbia shores, Wong became one of the founding members of a women's ad hoc group, Direct Action against Refugee Exploitation (DAARE), in response to a predominant racist media discourse that hearkened back to notions of "the yellow peril." At present, she is busy completing a doctoral degree in English at Simon Fraser University. Her thesis topic revolves around class and sexuality in Asian North American literature and what it means in terms of solidarity with First Nations peoples. As for her next book, she explains that she first has to find a line in *monkeypuzzle* that will be the connective thread. Very engaged with critiquing the world and fueled by her strong belief that activism is part and process of daily living, Wong attempts ways of writing around rather than about what puzzles her to create what she hopes is a productive tension.

MAJOR WORKS AND THEMES

A young writer and activist, Rita Wong combines a true poet's sensual and (com)passionate sensitivity with an intellectual sociopolitical consciousness that is sincere and heartfelt, as is reflected in her collection *monkeypuzzle*. In "down south peachwomen: minimum wage pickers" from *monkeypuzzle*, Wong's imagery and rhythmic lyricism sing loud and clear without sounding didactic. She is drawn to the economy of poetry and the need to challenge the limits of language whose syntax contains embedded power relations: between English and Cantonese, gender and imperialism. She plays with sounds and meanings, fragmenting syllables, hybridizing words, wondering how sounds of one change and flow into meanings of others, for example, in "chaos feary" (*Swallowing Clouds* 22). Her love of language and poetic deftness shines through even in the love poems: "let me dive into this winedark sea, be the vessel of your allusions" ("warn the town, the beast is loose," *monkeypuzzle* 86).

CRITICAL RECEPTION

monkeypuzzle won the Asian Canadian Writers' Workshop Emerging Writer Award in 1997. After its U.S. release, the book was nominated for an American literary award, the Lambda, a promising and respectable beginning for this poet. Rita Wong's work has been described as "salt and tongue poetry, with the intensity and taste of a lover . . . pungent in its insistence on the body marked and still breathing" (Fred Wah on the back cover). What seems like a clear consensus is the recognition of her lyrical power and her ability to blend individual desire and social love, passion and social compassion into an organic poetic vision. Finally, Rita Wong, like other Asian Canadian poets in their early thirties such as Louise Bak and Jen Lam, is still a relatively marginalized name in mainstream Canadian literary publications and academic circles despite their stage performances, their prolific submissions, and their activism in the localized communities of Vancouver or Toronto.

BIBLIOGRAPHY

Works by Rita Wong

Poetry

"in memory of the Chipko movement." *Secrets from the Orange Couch* 3.1 (April 1990): 30.
"Liberation Day." *Secrets from the Orange Couch* 3.1 (April 1990): 29.
"Beware the tigers in the mountains." *Fireweed* 36 (Summer 1992): 41–46.
"hard as a church pew to spew out stained milk." *Contemporary Verse 2* 14.3 (Winter 1992): 59.
"kwong, try wong, try chan." *Contemporary Verse 2* 14.3 (Winter 1992): 57.
Another Way to Dance: Contemporary Asian Poetry from Canada and the United States. Ed. Cyril Dabydeen. Toronto: TSAR, 1996. 225–31.
"memory palace." *Tessera* 22 (1997): 101–3.
"Down the Hall." *Prairie Fire* 18.4 (December 1997): 10.
"a Chinese grocery store is the safest place in the world." *absinthe* 10.1 (1998): 34.
monkeypuzzle. Vancouver: Press Gang, 1998.
"chaos feary." *Swallowing Clouds: An Anthology of Chinese-Canadian Poetry.* Ed. Andy Quan and Jim Wong-Chu. Vancouver: Arsenal Pulp Press, 1999. 22.
"let me dive." *ARIEL: A Review of International English Literature* 30.2 (April 1999): 202.
"The 'I' in Migrant." *West Coast Line* 33.3 (December 1999/February 2000): 105–8.

Prose, Essays

"Jumping on Hyphens." *The Other Woman: Women of Colour in Contemporary Canadian Literature.* Ed. Makeda Silvera. Toronto: Sister Vision Press, 1995.
"Touch: A Natural History." *Hot and Bothered: Short Short Fiction on Lesbian Desire.* Ed. Karen Tulchinsky. Vancouver: Arsenal Pulp Press, 1998. 155.
"An Intelligent and Humane Response: Direct Action against Refugee Exploitation Forum on Immigration and Refugee Rights." *Kinesis* October/November 1999: 12, 17.

Studies of Rita Wong

Bassnett, Madeline. Rev. of *monkeypuzzle. Books in Canada* 28.4 (May 1999): 37–38.
Clarke, George Elliott. "April Is the Most Poetic Month." *Halifax Sunday Herald,* Nova Scotia 25 April 1999: C9.
Harris, Jennifer. Rev. of *monkeypuzzle. Fireweed* 66 (October 1999): 79–81.
Kong, Sook C. Rev. of *monkeypuzzle. Herizons* 13.1 (Spring 1999): 34–35.

Lai, Larissa. "Interview with Rita Wong." *West Coast Line* 33.3 (December 1999/February 2000): 72–82.

Libin, M. "Open the Brutal." *Canadian Literature* 163 (Winter 1999): 16, 204–6.

Liu, Timothy. "Review Essay: Asian-American Poets Face Multiple Minority Status." *Lambda Book Report: A Review of Contemporary Gay and Lesbian Literature* 7.10 (May 1999): 15–16.

Ng, Taien Chan. Rev. of *monkeypuzzle*. *Matrix Magazine* 55 (2000): 64.

Rev. of *monkeypuzzle*. *National Post* 1.297 (9 October 1999): 8.

Tang, Denise. Rev. of *monkeypuzzle*. *Kinesis* March 1999: 16.

Thien, Madeleine. "Poetry and Politics in Rita Wong's *monkeypuzzle*." *Rice Paper* 5.1 (1999): 19.

MERLE WOO
(1941–   )

Su-ching Huang

BIOGRAPHY

Merle Woo was born on 24 October 1941 to a Chinese father, Richard Woo, and a Korean mother, Helene Chang Woo. Helene Chang was born in Los Angeles, where her father worked as a ginseng salesman and traveling Methodist minister. The Changs immigrated to Shanghai, China, when Helene was little, but at ten she was sent back alone to the United States to live in an orphanage run by white missionary women. She ran away from the orphanage at sixteen to start her own life. After an abusive first husband, she married Richard Woo. A paper son (entering the United States on false documents), Richard Woo emigrated from southern China. He worked two full-time jobs most of his life.

To give their daughter a better education, Richard and Helene Woo sent Merle to Catholic schools, which they thought were better than public schools, although neither of them was Catholic. Merle Woo earned her B.A. in English from San Francisco State University (SFSU) in 1965. She married while in college and later had two children (Emily and Paul). Pursuing an M.A. in English literature at SFSU, Woo witnessed firsthand the 1968–69 Third World Student Strikes at SFSU and was radicalized. She admits to being a beneficiary of such campus activism, for the establishment of ethnic studies, the Educational Opportunity Program (EOP), and affirmative action helped her get jobs. After finishing her M.A. in 1969, she started to teach in the Educational Opportunity Program at SFSU. During her years in the EOP, Woo attempted to make English learning more relevant to her students of color and began to incorporate Third World literature into her teaching. In 1977, Woo was offered a part-time lectureship in women's studies at SFSU and was a pioneer in introducing Third World women's literature into the curriculum. In the meantime, she also taught part-time in the Subject A Department at the University of California at Berkeley to support herself and two children. In 1978, she became a full-time lecturer in ethnic/Asian American studies at the University of California at Berkeley. She came out around 1979 as a lesbian and started organizing Berkeley Radical Activists for Change in Education and the Freedom Socialist Party, based on Trotskyism and socialist feminism.

Woo was also involved in theater. She was among the cast, including Frank Chin, in the performance of Lonny Kaneko's play *Lady Is Dying* in San Francisco in 1977. Together with two other Asian American poets, Nellie Wong and Kitty Tsui, Woo formed Unbound Feet Three, a performance group addressing political issues and uniting art and politics. Although the group split in 1981, they continued to speak out and engage themselves in social activism.

In 1982, Woo was suddenly terminated by Berkeley under a newly implemented four-year rule, which prescribes the nonrenewal of untenured lecturers after they have taught for four years. Woo claimed that the rule was used arbitrarily against women, lesbians, gay men, people of color—they made up a large part of the lecturer population—and those critical of university policies. Woo believed that she was fired for her political views, her unionism, and her activism. With widespread support from students, feminists, lesbians, gay men, people of color, the American Federation of Teachers, and others, Woo filed a number of lawsuits against the University of California for infringement of free speech and contract. After a California Public Employment Relations Board (PERB) ruling in favor of Woo and some stalling, the University of California Regents settled the case out of court in 1984, and Woo was reinstated, but only for another two years. In 1986, despite sweeping support from students, Woo's contract was not renewed. Returning to teach in women's studies at SFSU, Woo filed a union grievance against the University of California for discrimination on the basis of her race, gender, sexual orientation, and political ideology. The ruling was in favor of Woo, but the university continued stalling. While considering a lawsuit, Woo was diagnosed with breast cancer and decided to drop her case to better spend her potentially few remaining years. While striving for cancer survival, she has carried on unswervingly her activism, including fighting against the predominantly all-white-male medical establishment.

Woo is actively involved in local, national, and international activism against all forms of oppression. She identifies herself as a socialist feminist, an Asian American lesbian educator and writer, a unionist, and a cancer survivor, and she stresses that no aspect of her struggle is "expendable." She is a leader in the Freedom Socialist Party as well in Radical Women and advocates a multi-issue coalition of the oppressed—students, the aged, women, people of color, lesbians and gays, immigrants, the working class, and other economic underclasses. Uniting art and politics, she frequently reads at local gatherings and takes initiative roles in promoting civil rights. She has constantly appeared at celebrations such as laborfests, gay pride parades, immigrant pride days, and women's rights days, among others.

MAJOR WORKS AND THEMES

Autobiographical references abound in Woo's poems, as they are all concerned with how the poet experiences the world and identifies herself. Her poems demonstrate the importance of a multi-issue feminism. Struggles against racism, sexism, class exploitation, and other forms of oppression are recurrent themes in Woo's poems, in which she draws on her experiences as a woman of color, a lesbian, a lecturer, and a daughter of immigrants, among others, to elucidate the intersection of the personal and the political. Woo emphasizes the connection between art and politics, and her poems in that sense all carry strong political messages. She believes in using words as a tool against oppression.

Woo's conviction in the power of words can be found in "Poem for the Creative Writing Class, Spring 1982," in which the speaker sees classrooms as "cages with beautiful birds in them" and words as wings that enable flights from incarceration. Growing up Asian American, Woo learned early about racism. A woman of color, she is also acutely aware of sexism and its collusion with racism and class exploitation. Many of her poems depict the aforementioned oppressions and show how the oppressed adopt various strategies of resistance to triumph eventually. Several poems in the collection *Yellow Woman Speaks* use portraits of friends and family to advance that theme. The poem "The Subversive: For Nellie Wong" paints a picture of Wong, another Asian American socialist feminist poet and activist, as a comrade who fights fiercely by the poet's side. The poem "For Dick Woo (Woo Nay)" is a portrait of the poet's father, who emigrated from China at thirteen, was detained on Angel Island for one and a half years, and led the life of a typical Chinese immigrant father—working two jobs in Chinatown, gambling after work, distant from his daughter despite some tender moments. Looking back at those childhood memories, the poet cherishes the moments she now shares with her father, who has just had an open-heart surgery, and though she feels pain seeing him suffer, she is at least content to be close to him again and tending to his needs.

The poem "Korea" is also a portrait of an immigrant—the poet's aunt. A trickster figure, the aunt changes her name from Korea Chang to Cora Chandler to pass as white. Unlike the stereotypical Asian woman, she is far from reticent and submissive. She is outspoken and sexually expressive and flirts with sailors; her kind of people are gamblers, prostitutes, and lesbians. Instead of mulling over the aunt's difficult life as an immigrant woman, the poet focuses on the aunt's image as a fighter, who "taught [the poet] to fight with whatever tools [she] had." Overwhelmed by dominating white privileges and aesthetics, Auntie Cora appropriates white looks and values for survival, and the poet admires her. A contrast to the poet's own mother—a more traditional Asian woman, resilient, self-effacing, and passively toiling in the hope of better lives—Auntie Cora is unruly and full of life. She also initiates the poet's exploration of sexuality.

Another trickster figure can be found in "Class Szechuan-Style," a poem set in a Chinese restaurant. The poet overhears a white couple entertaining a Hong Kong businessman, who appears "obsequious" and "totally accommodating" as the white man shows off his knowledge of Chinese languages. While the poet's son Paul comments on the white man's stereotyping of Asians as ignorant, the poet observes how the Hong Kong businessman is actually the one who strategically succumbs to that stereotyping to be in control. Like the poet's Auntie Cora, he uses the white man's prejudice to get back at him. The title of "Class Szechuan-Style" yields interpretations at various levels. If the Chinese restaurant is a classroom, the teacher could be the Hong Kong businessman who demonstrates his premeditated resistance; or the poet herself, who is a lecturer at the University of California at Berkeley and is using the happenings at the restaurant to teach her son life lessons; or the two ex-students who approach the poet during the meal and show their gratitude for her teaching. Woo has always believed in students' participation in decision making, and her dedication to students touches them. The Filipino, Vince, a student from her EOP class at SFSU, tells the poet how he had to quit to work full-time. After learning of her transfer to Berkeley, he considers it a "moving up." However, the poet anticipates hard times. The reader can see how Woo always sides with the oppressed but does not patronize them. When Vince says, "It must be harder for you!" she thinks, "It's all the same," realizing that whether lecturer at Berkeley or baggage mover at United Airlines, they are both exploited by the same patriarchal capitalist system. Later in the poem, Woo recounts her development from an "accommodating, non-confrontive, academic Asian woman" to an unrelenting activist. When lecturers in Asian American studies at Berkeley were being fired and democratic decision making was being compromised, she knew to fight back. On the ride home from the restaurant, she affirms her determination to follow the principles of "integrity, visibility, and revolutionary possibility" to guide her battle against the establishment. In a fiery and passionate voice, the poem "Yellow Woman Speaks" compares the revolutionary yellow woman to a beast with teeth like "unsheathed swords." Exposing the stereotyping and exploitation of Asian women, the poet puts forward a completely new and feisty image of them and vows vengeance against those who "abuse and exploit" them.

As anticipated by "Class Szechuan-Style," the poem "Currents" relates Woo's combat against unfair termination at Berkeley and the support from the Chinese American community. Walking in the rain on the streets of Chinatown, the poet is made aware of the poverty and the language barrier there. However, her coalition with the working class does not stop in the ethnic enclave. Ending the poem with a news item about a conscientious, hardworking old white woman, the poet aligns herself also with working-class women of other races, testifying to Woo's multi-issue agenda.

Woo's coalition also does not stop within the borders of the United States.

In the poem "Whenever You're Cornered, the Only Way Out Is to Fight," she cites a news article about a woman catching a leopard in northern China to show the strength of women and of the oppressed all over the world. Showing the "fighting-back images in the face of great adversity," the poet cheers all her comrades and sisters on. In a similar vein, "A Linwistek: Song for My Comrades" reads like a manifesto for all oppressed people "from the Atlantic to the Pacific" to unite and strive for freedom.

Woo is one of the first few Asian American lesbian poets who unequivocally deal with lesbian sexuality. Lesbianism allows women existence outside patriarchy and its economic system. It provides women the opportunity to cease being men's accessories and to be liberated from the confining role of housewife and mother. The poem "The Right to Choose," written on the occasion of a rally to protect reproductive rights, attacks "The Private Property Tradition" that relegates women to subservient roles and asserts women's rights to choose, be it abortion or loving other women. "Untitled" is so far the only poem by Woo that explicitly deals with lesbian sexuality. With the image of "riding the flying mare . . . through mist and above mountains," the poem touches on the forbidden subject of lesbian sex and oral pleasure. The sensual imagery in the poem not only celebrates women's love for each other but also promotes active female desire.

In the prose "Letter to Ma," Woo recounts her experience growing up Asian American in San Francisco's Chinatown and how she became an activist. By comparing her own life with her Ma's, Woo tries to convince the latter how their life is more connected than the latter thinks. At sixteen, Woo's mother escaped the missionary "Home" and its grueling menial labor to lead her own life as maid, waitress, salesclerk, office worker, and so on. Woo describes her mother as "strong, courageous, and persevering" (141); however, her perception of her father was not always positive. She recalls thinking her father "womanly" when she was little because he was humiliated by two white cops but did not dare to protest. Later Woo realized that he had spent a year and a half on Angel Island and that as a paper son, he was in constant fear of being deported. Woo brings up the father's hardships to show the importance of Asian men fighting together with Third World women against sexism and racism. In "Letter to Ma," Woo delineates her growth as a Chinese/Korean American woman and shows how she has found strength in her mother's example and the Asian heritage. Advocating the alliance of all the oppressed, she envisions a larger framework that "will not support repression, hatred, exploitation and isolation" and that is "bonded not by color, sex or class, but by love and the common goal for the liberation of mind, heart, and spirit" (147).

CRITICAL RECEPTION

Woo's works have been widely anthologized. Her personal narrative, "Letter to Ma," has appeared in several multicultural anthologies and has been included in many women's studies or ethnic studies course syllabi. Her poems are anthologized in several collections of Asian American poetry, such as *Breaking Silence* (1983). However, like numerous other Asian American poets, Woo has received scant critical attention. Spanish scholar Eulalia C. Piñero Gil in her article "The Anxiety of Origins: Asian American Poets as Cultural Warriors" cites Woo to comment on Asian American poetics in general. Gil rightly notes Woo's view of language as a weapon for sociopolitical changes and her appeal to the collective experience of the disenfranchised. Gil, nevertheless, does not mention specific poems by Woo in her criticism.

In her article "Landmarks in Literature by Asian American Lesbians," Asian American scholar Karin Aguilar–San Juan cites Woo's poem "Untitled" as an example of an Asian American erotic lesbian sex poem, which "not only breaks the silence about lesbians but also breaks a silence about sex that has traditionally existed in Asian American culture" (939). Aguilar–San Juan ends her article by pointing out the issues she thinks Asian American lesbian and gay writers should concern themselves with: "teaching lesbian/gay writing in heterosexual academic environments; race and problems of representation; the role of writers in shaping the lesbian/gay movement; the moral dimensions of writing about sex; the politics of book reviewing" (942). Although Aguilar–San Juan's declaration is not a direct comment on Woo's poems, Woo, a multi-issue socialist feminist, has certainly been dedicating herself to achieving these goals.

BIBLIOGRAPHY

Works by Merle Woo

Poetry

Yellow Woman Speaks: Selected Poems. Seattle: Radical Women Publications, 1986.
"Untitled." *The Forbidden Stitch: An Asian American Women's Anthology.* Ed. Shirley Geok-lin Lim, Mayumi Tsutakawa, and Margarita Donnelly. Corvallis, OR: Calyx Books, 1989. 131.

Drama

"Home Movies: A Dramatic Monologue." *3 Asian American Writers Speak Out on Feminism.* Nellie Wong, Merle Woo, Mitsuye Yamada. Ed. Karen Brodine. San Francisco: SF Radical Women, 1979.

Video Production

Monterey's Boat People. Prod. Vincent DiGirolamo and Spencer Nakasako. Narrated by Merle Woo. San Francisco: National Asian American Telecommunication Association (NAATA), 1982.

Articles

"Some Basic Ingredients for Home Movies: A Work in Progress." *3 Asian American Writers Speak Out on Feminism*. Nellie Wong, Merle Woo, Mitsuye Yamada. Ed. Karen Brodine. San Francisco: SF Radical Women, 1979.

"Campus Politics: Bootcamp for Revolutionary Feminism." *Off Our Backs: A Women's News Journal* 12.5 (1982): 25+.

"Letter to Ma." *This Bridge Called My Back: Writings by Radical Women of Color*. 2nd ed. Ed. Cherríe Moraga and Gloria Anzaldúa. Latham, NY: Kitchen Table/Women of Color Press, 1983. 140–47.

"Our Common Enemy, Our Common Cause: Freedom Organizing in the Eighties." *Apartheid U.S.A.* Ed. Audre Lorde. Latham, NY: Kitchen Table/Women of Color Press, 1986. 13–23.

"What Have We Accomplished from the Third-World Strike through the Conservative 80s?" *Amerasia Journal* 15.1 (1989): 81–89.

Introduction. *Woman Sitting at the Machine, Thinking: Poems*. By Karen Brodine. Pref. Meridel Le Sueur. Seattle: Red Letter Press, 1990.

"Forging the Future, Remembering Our Roots: Building Multicultural, Feminist Lesbian, and Gay Studies." *Tilting the Tower: Lesbians, Teaching, Queer Subjects*. Ed. Linda Garber. New York: Routledge, 1994. 163–67.

"The Politics of Breast Cancer." *The Very Inside: An Anthology of Writing by Asian and Pacific Islander Lesbian and Bisexual Women*. Ed. Sharon Lim-Hing. Toronto: Sister Vision Press, 1994. 416–25.

"Soul Food for Rabble-Rousers." Rev. of *Revolution, She Wrote*, by Clara Fraser. *Freedom Socialist* 19.1 (1998). Available: http://www.socialism.com/fsarticles/Vol19no1/191_CF_book review.html. Nov. 2000.

Studies of Merle Woo

Aguilar–San Juan, Karin. "Landmarks in Literature by Asian American Lesbians." *Signs* 18.4 (1993): 936–43.

Gil, Eulalia C. Piñero. "The Anxiety of Origins: Asian American Poets as Cultural Warriors." *Hitting Critical Mass: A Journal of Asian American Cultural Criticism* 4.1 (1996): 121–34.

Hayes, Loie. "Merle Woo." *Outstanding Lives: Profiles of Lesbians and Gay Men*. Ed. Christa Brelin and Michael J. Tyrkus. Detroit: Visible Ink Press, 1997. 389–92.

MITSUYE (MAY) YAMADA
(1923–   )

Di Gan Blackburn

BIOGRAPHY

Mitsuye Yamada's childhood was marked by a stronger Japanese influence than that of most Japanese Americans. Though her parents were U.S. residents, Yamada herself was born on 5 July 1923 in Fukuoka, Japan, and moved to Seattle, Washington, three and a half years later. As a child, in addition to attending local public schools, Yamada took daily classes in the Japanese language, as well as lessons in Japanese dance, calligraphy, flower arrangement, and the tea ceremony, without which, her mother would tell to her, "you won't know who you are" ("Unbecoming American" 201). In an interview with Helen Jaskoski, Yamada recalls that her mother often emphasized that she was Japanese—unlike her American-born brothers—and consequently should act differently (99). At eleven, she went to Japan for schooling, only to find that her American experience left her an outsider there also. The ambivalent identity reflected in these childhood experiences becomes a consistent theme in Yamada's later poetry, most obviously in "Here," a poem about being a Japanese outsider in America, and "There," a poem about being an American outsider in Japan. Returning to the United States, Yamada threw herself into the normal American high-school routine. With the exception of her daily language class, she dropped the other Japanese courses and devoted her energies to participating in the high school magazine and debate clubs. This fairly uneventful period ended with the U.S. entry into World War II.

The ordeal that followed was to be the locus of much of her poetry: the relocation and internment of Japanese Americans. Yamada saw her own family separated. Her father, Jack Kaichiro Yasutake, an interpreter for the U.S. Immigration Service, was arrested for alleged spying. The rest of the family was sent to the Minidoka Relocation Center in the Idaho desert in 1942. On renouncing loyalty to the emperor of Japan, Yamada was able to leave for the University of Cincinnati in 1944. Though they would not be published for another thirty years, many pieces in her first volume of poetry, *Camp Notes*, were written during this time. Her second volume of poetry, *Desert Run*, published in 1988, also recalls the internment experience.

Yamada had shown an inclination toward writing as a young girl, but her path to the status of "published poet" was not direct. Her father founded the Senryu Poetry Society in Seattle, and Yamada remembers serving the group of about twenty when they met at her home. She showed an early inclination toward academics, performing better in school than her brothers did (to her father's disappointment) and participating in the creative-writing magazine at her high school. Subsequent to earning a B.A. from New York University in 1947 and an M.A. from the University of Chicago in 1953, Yamada embarked on an active academic career. She was an instructor at Cypress College in Cypress, California from 1960 to 1976 and at Fullerton College in Fullerton, California, from 1966 to 1969. Since 1976, she has been an associate professor of English at Cypress. Her other academic activities include helping many universities establish Asian studies programs and serving on the boards of Amnesty International and *MELUS*. She holds memberships in the American Civil Liberties Union (ACLU), the Pacific Asian American Center, the National Women's Political Caucus, and the International Women's Writing Guild. In addition, she works to establish local multicultural feminist writing groups and participates in a number of workshops. She is married to Yoshikazu Yamada and has four children, Jeni, Stephan, Douglas, and Hedi, and lives in Orange County, California.

MAJOR WORKS AND THEMES

Yamada's poetry gives voice to her experience as a woman and as a Japanese American. In her own words, "Poetry simply tells what is happening. I can express what is happening to me in poetry better than in any other genre" (*Contemporary Authors Online*). Ethnicity, gender, language, identity, and community—all issues of considerable personal relevance—provide the focus for much of her writing.

At first glance, it is Yamada's role as a nisei poet that stands out. The titles of her two volumes of poetry, *Camp Notes* and *Desert Run*, both refer directly to the Japanese American internment experience. Her first volume reads like a personal documentation in poetry of the event: there are poems dealing with the departure from Seattle, with life in the camp, and finally, with life in the "free world" outside. *Camp Notes and Other Poems* is composed around a core of poems that Yamada wrote in the years between 1942 and 1944, with additional pieces and some revision being added later, perhaps shortly before they were published in 1976.

Yamada's second volume of poems, published in 1988 as *Desert Run: Poems and Stories*, returns to the scene of the internment. Like the first volume, *Desert Run* deals with the Japanese American experience. What makes it different from *Camp Notes* is that in *Desert Run* the reader notes an expansion in scope: besides telling the ethnic story, the poems are increasingly concerned with the female experience. Several of these poems deal with domestic and sexual violence. While Yamada indicates that her writing "generally express[es] [her] ethnic experiences" (qtd. in Jaskoski 97), there is an apparent shift in this volume, and in her later works generally, to a greater emphasis on feminist concerns.

Yamada's early writings are more formally structured in the traditional style of her (mainly male) contemporaries. Later, influenced by the work of 1960s women poets and writers such as Carolyn Kizer and Tillie Olsen, Yamada gradually abandoned the masculine, objective tone for more direct and feeling lines. Her poetry appears to be more open and free in expressing emotions (Jaskoski 101). Some of this development can also be traced to the difference between the two collections. As Yamamoto points out, while *Camp Notes* "reveal[s] how language buffets and muffles" intense human emotions, *Desert Run* "more or less leaves this tactic behind, no longer attempting to mask anger with tonal irony" (215).

More recently, Yamada has moved toward an even more direct style of writing, at times forgoing poetry. Yamada realizes the need for taking "a more political stance" and has changed the subjects of her writing from personal poetry to essays dealing with social and political issues. Feeling that her ethnic identity as a Japanese American and her gender identity as a woman have finally joined as a "singular identity," Yamada sees it her obligation to tell the world about such a complex mergence. Some of the evolution in Yamada's style can be ascribed to the struggle to seek and clarify this "singular identity," and just as importantly, to assert that identity through language. The capacity of language to silence people is a special concern for Yamada. Believing that the principal survival concern of Asian American women has been to "redefine oneself" from the misrepresentations of others, Yamada reacts sharply against culturally imposed silence ("Unbecoming American" 209). For the same reason, the experience and thoughts of marginalized immigrant women have motivated her to argue passionately against the "English-only" standard that effectively silences some of these women (Mortimer 189).

In addition to ethnic, gender, and linguistic concerns, Yamada has also recognized geography, especially that of the desert, as a part of her writing and identity. Her first prolonged experience with the desert, at the relocation center in Idaho, did not lend itself to appreciating the apparently barren land's qualities. When she moved to southern California along with her husband and family in 1960, she continued to feel out of place in a strange land. Gradually, however, she has come to "feel a strong kinship with this land that struggles to retain its essential character" and finds parallels between the misunderstood desert and herself ("Unbecoming American" 209).

CRITICAL RECEPTION

Surprisingly, Yamada's significant ethnic experience during the World War II Japanese American internment is not the primary concern of critical studies. Instead, it is the specifically female experience of that event that catches most critics' attention. Taking the feminist approach, several articles find in Yamada's writing much value for understanding not only Yamada's personal experience, but also that of other women. A few critics also address the effect of internment on Asian American political identity.

One of the major studies is Susan Schweik's "A Needle with Mama's Voice: Mitsuye Yamada's *Camp Notes* and the American Canon of War Poetry," which appears in the book *Arms and the Woman: War, Gender, and Literary Representation*. Schweik draws attention to the long period between the initial writing of many of the pieces in *Camp Notes* and their publication thirty years later. Like Yamada, Schweik is concerned with the silencing of female perspectives, specifically, female perspectives in the canon of war writings. She explores the "two perils"—"the danger of invisibility and the danger of visibility"—and brings attention to the constraints imposed on Yamada as well as to the danger of visibility in a racist and sexist society (228).

Sharing Schweik's and Yamada's concern with voice and language, Traise Yamamoto in her "Embodied Language: The Poetics of Mitsuye Yamada, Janice Mirikitani, and Kimiko Hahn" further explores Yamada's poetics in the context of the book's overall concern with identity and representation. Redefining her identity as a Japanese American woman—in the words of Yamamoto's book's title, "making subjects"—in the face of opposing constructions is identified as one of the major themes of Yamada's work. The authorities' use of language in the internment camps provides further examples of the power of language in representation (209). Masami Usui in her article "A Language of Her Own in Mitsuye Yamada's Poetry and Stories" discusses Yamada's relation to language not simply in terms of giving voice to marginalized experience but also in terms of the problematic use of either Japanese or English. Referring to titles such as "Drowning in My Own Language" for examples, Usui points out that although Yamada is fluent in both English and Japanese, she is not completely at home with either language because of the cultural values attendant in both. Commenting on a *MELUS* interview of Yamada, Usui views Yamada's rejection of form in her poetry as a part of the process of finding "a language of her own" (8).

Anita Patterson takes a rather different tack in "Resistance to Images of the Internment: Mitsuye Yamada's *Camp Notes*." Patterson sees in Yamada's ethnic writing a concern with the concept of political obligation (103). Through an extended discussion of photographic images of the internment, Patterson relates the power of creative imagery to political representation. Interestingly, she also suggests that Yamada's later distrust of orderly arrangement is a result of her exposure to the "relationship between obligation and the creation of images" (120).

One of the few reviews of Yamada's work is of an anthology edited by Yamada and Sarie Sachie Hylkema, *Sowing Ti Leaves: Writings by Multi-cultural Women*. The reviewer, Lisa Mortimer, primarily comments on Yamada's role in bringing together and giving voice to multicultural women in her community. In defense of Yamada's work, Mortimer asserts that "though many see the experiences of women of color as illegitimate, they are, in fact, valid, productive, energizing and worth sharing with others" (187).

Overall, Yamada has received a certain amount of attention as a minority female writer both for her poetry on intense personal experiences and for her essays addressing racial, social, and political issues. Partly because of the soon-to-be-rigid formula of minority-literature scholarship, which usually confines the critic's attention to race and gender issues, and partly due to Yamada's own decision to reject the restraint of form in favor of more open and direct communication, very few critical responses have been given to the stylistic or aesthetic values of Yamada's poetry.

BIBLIOGRAPHY

Works by Mitsuye Yamada

Poetry

Camp Notes and Other Poems. San Lorenzo, CA: Shameless Hussy Press, 1976.
Desert Run: Poems and Stories. Latham, NY: Kitchen Table/Women of Color Press, 1988.

Anthologies

The Webs We Weave: Orange County Poetry Anthology. Ed. John Brander and Mitsuye Yamada. Laguna Beach, CA: Literary Arts Press, 1986.
Sowing Ti Leaves: Writings by Multi-cultural Women. Ed. Mitsuye Yamada and Sarie Sachie Hylkema. Irvine, CA: MCWW, 1990.
No More Masks! An Anthology of Twentieth-Century American Women Poets. Ed. Florence Howe. New York: HarperPerennial, 1993.

Essays

"I Still Carry It Around." *Rikka* 3–4 (1976): 11–19.
"Experiential Approaches to Teaching Joy Kogawa's *Obasan*." *Teaching American Ethnic Literatures: Nineteen Essays*. Ed. John R. Maitino and David R. Peck. Albuquerque: University of New Mexico Press, 1996. 293–311.
"Unbecoming American." *Becoming American: Personal Essays by First Generation Immigrant Women*. New York: Hyperion, 2000. 198–209.

Studies of Mitsuye Yamada

Contemporary Authors Online. 1999. Gale Literary Database. Available: http://www.galenet.com/servlet/GLD (10 January 2001).

Jaskoski, Helen. "A *MELUS* Interview." *MELUS* 15.1 (1988): 97–108.

Mitsuye and Nellie: Asian American Poets. San Francisco: Light-Saraf Films, 1981.

"Mitsuye Yamada." *Voices from the Gaps: Women Writers of Color.* Ed. Sakiko Matsuda. Available: http://voices.cla.umn.edu/authors/MitsuyeYamada.html (10 January 2001).

Mortimer, Lisa. Rev. of *Sowing Ti Leaves: Writings by Multi-cultural Women*, ed. Mitsuye Yamada and Sarie Sachie Hylkema. *Amerasia* 17.1 (1991): 187–89.

Patterson, Anita Haya. "Resistance to Images of the Internment: Mitsuye Yamada's *Camp Notes*." *MELUS* 23.3 (1998): 103–27.

Schweik, Susan. "A Needle with Mama's Voice: Mitsuye Yamada's *Camp Notes* and the American Canon of War Poetry." *Arms and the Woman: War, Gender, and Literary Representation.* Ed. Helen M. Cooper, Adrienne Auslander Munich, and Susan Merrill Squier. Chapel Hill: University of North Carolina Press, 1989. 225–43.

Usui, Masami. "A Language of Her Own in Mitsuye Yamada's Poetry and Stories." *Studies in Culture and the Humanities: Bulletin of the Faculty of Integrated Arts and Sciences* [Hiroshima University] 5.3 (1996): 1–17.

Yamada, Mitsuye. "A Woman Is Talking to Death." Interview with Stan Yogi. *KPFA.* Berkeley, CA. 13 May and 10 June 1990.

Yamamoto, Traise. "Embodied Language: The Poetics of Mitsuye Yamada, Janice Mirikitani, and Kimiko Hahn." *Masking Selves, Making Subjects: Japanese American Women, Identity, and the Body.* Berkeley: University of California Press, 1999. 198–261.

LOIS-ANN YAMANAKA
(1961–)

Peter E. Morgan

BIOGRAPHY

Lois-Ann Yamanaka, a third-generation descendant of Japanese immigrants to Hawaii, was born on 7 September 1961 in Ho'olchua, Molokai, Hawaii, to Harry (a school principal, now retired and pursuing his lifetime hobby and part-time business, taxidermy) and Jean (an elementary school teacher). Yamanaka and her three sisters grew up in the plantation town of Pahala on the Big Island, earned her B.Ed. (1983) and M.Ed. (1987) from the University of Hawaii at Manoa, and now lives in Kalihi, Oahu. Set against a "green but cruel" (James 91) background that has often been represented by outsiders as simply idyllic, her work explores the raw cultural dynamics of the working-class, island communities in which she has lived.

Writing against the myths nurtured by mainland economic, cultural, and artistic domination of Hawaii, Yamanaka, who describes herself as a "funky loud-mouthed thing" (Nguyen 41), embraces Pidgin (though she was taught as a child to look down upon the Creole language) in an effort to promote the decolonization of the Hawaiian experience: "with language rests culture. . . . It is *impossible* to ban the sound of one's memory" (qtd. in Fernandez 85), she says. "I write in the pidgin of the contract workers to the sugar plantations. . . . Our language has been labeled the language of ignorant people, substandard, and inappropriate in any form of expression—written or oral. . . . I met poet/teacher Faye Kicknosway in 1987 . . . and I was encouraged to write in the voice of my place without shame or fear" ("Empty Heart" 544).

While her language and perspective are shaped by memory, she is quick to point out that she is "like all writers, a vampire, a bloodsucker" (Shea 32), constantly assimilating stories and images from her environment and weaving them into her own tapestry of experience. Delving into the racial and sometimes religious blends produced by Hawaii's unique history (Yamanaka herself is a third-generation Southern Baptist, if not one who would be at home in the South), she explores with sensitivity the hardships and joys of motherhood, the struggles and rewards of planned and unplanned pregnancy, and the shock of giving birth to a special-needs child (she and husband John Infererra have one son, John). Similarly, after ten years as a public school teacher, much of it spent teaching and advocating for at-risk youth, she writes (and speaks) passionately of the personal and social problems facing adolescents in today's Hawaii.

Following the separate publication of a number of poems, Yamanaka published her first and only book of poetry to date, *Saturday Night at the Pahala Theatre* (1993), a collection of "verse novelas" for which she won the Pushcart Prize XVIII in 1993 and the 1994 Asian American Studies National Book Award. Her subsequent prose, tuned with the ear of a poet, is alternately economical, brutal, beautiful, lyrical, and razor sharp, while her ability to represent subtly different Pidgin dialects speaks to a sensitivity and skill with language that have earned her a reputation as one of the foremost poetic voices of the Hawaiian renaissance of the last two decades and brought her recognition in the form of a National Endowment for the Humanities grant (1990), the Elliot Cades Award for Literature (1993), a Carnegie Foundation grant (1994), a National Endowment for the Arts creative-writing fellowship (1994), the Pushcart Prize XIX (1994, for "Yarn Wig"), the Rona Jaffe Award for Women Writers (1996), the Lannan Literary Award (1998), the American Book Award (2000, for *Heads by Harry*), and many others. Yamanaka continues to find support and nourishment in the monthly meetings of the Bamboo Ridge Writers Group, which formed out of the 1978 "Talk Story" conference organized by Darrell Lum and Eric Chock and has now become an influential publishing collective.

MAJOR WORKS AND THEMES

Following *Saturday Night at the Pahala Theatre* in 1993, Yamanaka's next book, *Wild Meat and the Bully Burgers* (1996)—like Sandra Cisneros's *The House on Mango Street*, a major creative influence on Yamanaka—presents a series of short narratives, prose poems in which novel and poetic form negotiate to animate the voices, sensations, humor, and heartache of Hawaii's Asian immigrant underclass. *Blu's Hanging* (1997), the first of her more sustained novels, continues to explore the awful vulnerability of children—and at the same time their ability to survive—while *Heads by Harry* (1999) examines the struggles of teens growing up local in Hilo and trying to establish a sense of identity as well as map out a future against the racism and plantation legacy that pervade the Hawaiian melting pot. Life is rich but hard for her characters, pulled in different directions in the blending of the traditional and immigrant cultures of the island and the individual, deeply personal struggles with sexuality, drugs, and self-image that so many experience but so few discuss. *Name Me Nobody* (1999), Yamanaka's first novel written specifically for young adults, treats similar issues from a teen perspective: acceptance (of self and others), how to define oneself in relationship to race, body type, and sexuality, and how to understand (or at least survive) the various kinds of love that crowd the teen heart and compete with one another for emotional space. Finally, in the raw and unforgettable *Father of the Four Passages* (2001)—a novel that reads once again more like poetry than prose—Yamanaka continues her exploration of love, motherhood, and faith as a young, drug-taking protagonist comes to terms with her son's autism and her own guilt. An extremely productive writer, she is currently engaged in several book projects, among them a book of ghost stories for youth and a book about a father who abandons his children.

CRITICAL RECEPTION

Critics and reviewers praise Yamanaka's poetry for both its language and its cut-to-the-quick content: "Yamanaka is blessed with a poet's ear," Jessica Hagedorn says in *Harper's Bazaar*, and *Saturday Night* has been widely acclaimed as "witty" and "street-smart": her "characters speak in dramatic monologues as tight and fierce as anything Browning might have dreamed of, but their voices hold true to the idiomatic language of tough, vulnerable preteen girls holding private talks" (Kallet 11). Her poetry, "precise and lethal as a drive-by," "is enabled by its elegant structure as much as its indolent diction . . . not a lonely specimen of street life but a bold push at the borders of meaning and memory. Yamanaka's lyrics explode from an imagination familiar and feral as the stench of Spam and rice floating out of a housing project. Slow kine" (Chua 7–10). Sandra Cisneros says of Yamanaka's work, "You laugh, then you think about it, and it breaks your heart" (qtd. in Shea 32).

Lisa Steinman explores Yamanaka's astute presentation of issues of voice and local culture using Pidgin to locate the reader firmly in place and time while presenting much broader adolescent themes. Pidgin, she says, "is implicitly a language of the 'true self.' This seems to be the point of the book as a whole . . . a mirror of Hawaiian diversity and of the selves it is possible to imagine in such a culture." Steinman, however, questions what it means to celebrate a language that reflects the fragmentation of cultures under colonial rule and wonders whether *haole* readers can read it in a position other than that of voyeur (399–402). Rosalee Shim, in a close reading of *Saturday Night*, explores the symbolism of eyes in Yamanaka's poetry and traces evidence of an "ocular power" she claims marks, brands, and constructs the female ethnic subject in the eyes of others.

Wendy Motooka discusses the controversy that has arisen over what some readers, ignoring the broad context of Yamanaka's sophisticated representation of local cultures and unstinting multicultural activism and advocacy, have seen as racist stereotypes in *Saturday Night* (particularly in the poem "Kala Gave Me Anykine Advice Especially about Filipinos When I Moved to Pahala") and later in *Blu's Hanging*. Motooka correctly suggests that such readings lie essentially in methodological differences between the disciplines of sociology/ethnic studies (from which the most vocal objectors came) and literature. She demonstrates how sociologists like Candace Kujikane "[labor] hard to get outside the disconcerting ambiguity and multiplicity of re-circulated tales, and into the rigid, authoritative 'reality' of 'actual' sociological truth," even going so far as to suggest that poems like "Kala" should come with a footnote saying that the speaker's voice does not necessarily represent the views of the poet (Motooka 24–27). Of course, most readers take this as a given and read what Kala is told about looking out for "the Filipino man" in the same vein as the subsequent advice she is given, "no use somebody's deodorant."

In the poetry and prose of Lois-Ann Yamanaka (as in that of the many fine "local" Hawaiian writers of her generation), the "concrete fantasy" (Wilson 95) of James Michener's *South Pacific* is caricatured and finally deconstructed: "Tapping into deeper memories and ties to place as appropriated and enriched by layers of indigenous and settler cultures, Yamanaka is no cultural purist but rifely postmodern in her Asian/Pacific/American identity tactics . . . [and] vanquishes Michener's slobbering Bloody Mary with a grounded vision of compassionate interiority" (Wilson 105–6).

BIBLIOGRAPHY

Works by Lois-Ann Yamanaka

Poetry

Saturday Night at the Pahala Theatre. Honolulu: Bamboo Ridge Press, 1993.
Many individual poems published separately in anthologies, reviews, and journals.

Novels

Wild Meat and the Bully Burgers. New York: Farrar, Straus and Giroux, 1996.
Blu's Hanging. New York: Farrar, Straus and Giroux, 1997.
Heads by Harry. New York: Farrar, Straus and Giroux, 1999.
Name Me Nobody. New York: Hyperion, 1999.
Father of the Four Passages. New York: Farrar, Straus and Giroux, 2001.

Selected Short Works

"Empty Heart." *Charlie Chan Is Dead: An Anthology of Contemporary Asian American Fiction*. Ed. Jessica Hagedorn. New York: Penguin, 1993. 544–50.
"Ten Thousand in the Round." *The Beacon Best of 2000: Great Writing by Women and Men of All Colors and Cultures*. Ed. Edwidge Danticat. Boston: Beacon, 2000.
"Wake." *Conjunctions* 34 (Spring 2000): 282–89.

Studies of Lois-Ann Yamanaka

Chua, Lawrence. Rev. of *Saturday Night at the Pahala Theater*. *Village Voice* 38.49 (7 December 1993): 7–10.

Fernandez, Sandy. "Lois-Ann Yamanaka: Pidgin's Revenge." *Ms.* 7 (July/August 1996): 85.

Hagedorn, Jessica. "Under the Rainbow." *Harper's Bazaar* (April 1997): 164.

James, Jamie. "This Hawaii Is Not for Tourists." *Atlantic Monthly* 238.2 (February 1999): 90–94.

Joyce, Alice. "Adult Books: Fiction" section. *Booklist* 92.7 (1 December 1995): 611.

Kallet, Marilyn. "This Is Who We Are." *American Book Review* 17.1 (11 September–October 1995): 11.

Motooka, Wendy. "Sentimentalism, Authenticity, and Hawai'i Literature." *Bamboo Ridge: A Hawai'i Writers Journal* 73 (Spring 1998): 22–32.

Nguyen, Lan N. *People* 26 May 1997: 41.

Shea, Renee H. "Pidgin Politics and Paradise Revised." *Poets and Writers* 26.5 (September/October 1998): 32–39.

Shim, Rosalee. "Power in the Eye of the Beholder: A Close Reading of Lois-Ann Yamanaka's *Saturday Night at the Pahala Theater*." *Hitting Critical Mass: A Journal of Asian American Cultural Criticism* 3.1 (Winter 1995): 85–91.

Soong, Micheline M. "*Yosegire Buton*, the 'Crazy' Patchwork Quilt: An Alternative Narrative Strategy of Three Local Japanese Women Writers of Hawai'i." Diss. UCLA, 1999.

Steinman, Lisa M. "Likely Stories of Likely Selves." *Michigan Quarterly Review* 35.2 (Spring 1996): 399–419.

Wilson, Rob. "Bloody Mary Meets Lois-Ann Yamanaka: Imagining Asia/Pacific—from *South Pacific* to Bamboo Ridge." *Transnational Asia Pacific: Gender, Culture, and the Public Sphere*. Ed. Shirley Geok-lin Lim, Larry E. Smith, and Wimal Dissanayake. Urbana: University of Illinois Press, 1999. 92–110.

JOHN YAU
(1950–   )

Zhou Xiaojing

BIOGRAPHY

John Yau, poet, critic, teacher, curator, and fiction writer, was born in Lynn, Massachusetts, in 1950, shortly after his parents left Shanghai. He received a B.A. from Bard College and an M.F.A. from Brooklyn College. He has taught at various colleges and universities, most recently at Brown University, the University of California at Berkeley, and Hofstra University. He is the recipient of a National Endowment for the Arts fellowship (1977–78) and two Ingram-Merrill Foundation fellowships (1979–80, 1985–86). In 1988, he received a New York Foundation for the Arts Award, a Lavan award (Academy of American Poets), and a General Electric Foundation award. He is also the recipient of the 1992 Brendan Gill Award for *Big City Primer: Reading New York at the End of the Twentieth Century* (1991), his collaborative book with photographer Bill Barrette. Yau's 1992 volume *Edificio Sayonara* won the Jerome Shestack Prize (*American Poetry Review*) in 1993. He has also curated art exhibitions. As Ahmanson curatorial fellow (1993–96), he organized a retrospective of paintings and drawings by Ed Moses, which opened at the Museum of Contemporary Art in Los Angeles in the spring of 1996. Among Yau's other honors is the inclusion of his poem "Predella" in *The Best American Poetry* for 1988. His recent sequence poem, "Borrowed Love Poems," the title poem of his next book of poetry, is included in *The Best American Poetry* for 2000. Yau considers writing sequence lyric poems on love in the late 1990s as rebellious a gesture as the marriage between his Chinese grandfather and English grandmother, and as necessary as the birth of his Eurasian father at a time when in many parts of the world antimiscegenation laws were in effect.

Yau lives in Manhattan. His current projects include a memoir, fiction, and research for a book on the Chinese American film actress Anna May Wong. A book of his essays on poetry and art is forthcoming from the University of Michigan Press.

MAJOR WORKS AND THEMES

Yau is a versatile and prolific writer whose themes and styles are challenging and wide ranging. While problematizing the means for the production of knowledge, his poetry engages with contemporary debates over relations between language and subjectivity, between representation and identity construction. As an art critic who has written extensively on contemporary art, Yau, like Gertrude Stein and John Ashbery, shares with modernist and postmodernist artists their explorations of materials as subject matter and their challenges to the stability of meaning and authenticity of representation. However, Yau's work differs significantly from that by both modernist and postmodernist poets, with whom he is often identified. One of the most distinct differences of Yau's writing from that of contemporary mainstream American poets is his investigation of racial and cultural identities. However, Yau's poetry is by no means confined to what might be considered characteristic of Asian American themes such as issues of exile, assimilation, cultural dislocation, and identity politics. Yau's major thematic concerns, including his negotiations with various subject positions and the complexity of identity construction and formation, are nonetheless intricately related to his mixed-race background and to his "borderlands" experience as a Eurasian. Although Yau is closely linked to the mainstream American art world, he, like many other Asian American poets, seeks to incorporate Asian histories, cultures, and literary traditions into his poems not simply to resist Eurocentrism, but also to explore new modes of poetry. At the same time, he draws from contemporary arts and cinema in expanding the possibilities of image, narrative, and composition in his poetry and prose.

In his first volume of poetry, *Crossing Canal Street*, Yau already shows a remarkable innovativeness in his employment of image and form that allude sometimes to classical Chinese poetic traditions and sometimes to Ezra Pound's and William Carlos Williams's imagist poems. But Yau's poems depart from all these traditions even as they resonate with them. In poems such as "Crossing Canal Street: Five Photographs of a Bird Calling to Her Invisible Lover in a Subway Station," "Suggested by a Chinese Woman Eating Alone on Mott Street," and "Suggested by a Waitress in YEE's," Yau is able to capture a moment's perception through fluid, evocative, and unforgettable images that render everyday sights, including those in Chinatown, startlingly new, forcing the reader to experience them as if for the first time. As Robert Kelly writes in his preface to *Crossing Canal Street*, Yau's poems enchant the reader to "move with his ears and hear with his eyes." In "An Old Chinese Gentleman Drops In to See His Cronies In a Coffeeshop," Yau's description of five old men seamlessly transports them from a coffeeshop in Chinatown, New York, to a half-imagined and all-reinvented terrain in China where ancient poets gather together before being banished again from their home provinces. In contrast to such wonderfully warm and lyrical imagery and atmosphere, Yau portrays a different scene of Chinese diaspora in "A Recent Saturday Night," in which images of Chinese immigrants' dislocation and recent Chinese history are brought into sharp focus. Juxtaposing phrases such as "New Land" and "Old Land," "Middle Kingdom" and "The China Pearl" with signs of "Coca Cola," "Kim Toy Luncheon," and "Chinese National Party," as well as lined-up empty chairs in a room, Yau offers an intimate glimpse of a Chinese immigrant community.

In Yau's later poems, Chinese American experience and images become increasingly contextualized within the construction of identities of race and gender in mainstream American popular culture. At the same time, Yau has begun to write some autobiographical poems that are different from the so-called confessional and anecdotal lyric poems that have become the predominant mode of American poetry since the late 1950s. Rather than indulging in self-expression and self-examination, as most of the confessional poets do, Yau's autobiographical poems situate the self beyond familial circles and personal relationships to deal with the social and historical conditions for the information of individual and collective identities, as well as the conditions that motivate individuals' renegotiations with their identities. But for Yau, individual identities are not entirely social constructs, and the private, elusive self is not completely accessible. Moreover, the self, the lyric "I," is constructed in language, which is not a transparent medium. These themes in Yau's poems develop with his increasingly bold experimentations with language and poetic forms. His explorations of new possibilities for the syntax, sound, and structure of language in the early stage of his poetic career are similar to Gertrude Stein's manipulation of language, but are soon replaced by his own invention of Cantonese-sounding words and words with double meanings that are related to Chinese Americans and the stereotypes of them produced by mainstream America. These developments in Yau's poems are discernible in *Radiant Silhouette: New and Selected Work, 1974–1988* (1989), which contains poems and short prose pieces selected from his earlier books, *The Reading of an Ever-changing Tale* (1977), *Sometimes* (1979), *The Sleepless Night of Eugene Delacroix* (1980), *Broken Off by the Music* (1981), *Corpse and Mirror* (1983), and *Dragon's Blood* (1989).

Yau's major themes and technical strategies converge in the serial poems of "Genghis Chan: Private Eye," which first appeared in his eighth volume, *Dragon's Blood*, reprinted in *Radiant Silhouette*, and the series continues to expand in two later volumes, *Edificio Sayonara* (1992) and *Forbidden Entries* (1996). In his earlier poems such as "Ten Songs" and "Shanghai Shenanigans" reprinted in *Radiant Silhouette*, Yau foregrounds the structure of language and the poetic form, illustrating how the sounds and syntax of the language can be manipulated in such a way as to resist making sense, articulating emotions, and constructing identity. "Ten Songs" begins with a dangling participle sentence, "Trying to find a way to say something that would make it make its sense" (*Radiant Silhouette* 18), and continues with four similar dangling sentences that interlock. These become five complex predicative sentences in the second half of the poem, without making any sense or revealing any emotions or thoughts. In fact, the lyric "I" is absent from the poem, which develops with strictly linguistic elements and structure. Thus both the language and the poem become performative rather than expressive or referential. "Shanghai Shenanigans" enacts a similar linguistic performance, but does something more. The reference in the title to a particular place and social behaviors enhances the nonreferentiality of the language that Yau uses in the poem, which consists of five couplets. Beginning with the second, each couplet starts with the ending word or phrase of the preceding couplet. This restrictive structure resonates with traditional poetic structures such as those of the sestina, the Pindaric ode, and the Shakespearean sonnet, but is radically different from them all. The structure of Yau's poem neither corresponds to a theme nor is governed by any logic of argument or sequence of narrative. The connections between the couplets are purely linguistic. The images such as the breeze and the perfume (*Radiant Silhouette* 106) are fragmentary and surreal. Both the language and imagery of "Shanghai Shenanigans" refuse to reveal any recognizable markers of either the location of Shanghai or the behaviors comprising the shenanigans. The title, then, is a linguistic sound unit without a definitive referent. Paradoxically, by repressing the referential aspects of language, Yau enhances the importance of the referentiality of language in constructing meaning while exposing the radically destabilized connections between meaning constructed through language and the "real" that exists outside of language. As a result, language as a seemingly transparent means for expression and representation is significantly undermined.

In his "Genghis Chan: Private Eye" serial poems, Yau combines investigation of language with interrogation of identity construction to subvert the representations of Asian Americans in mainstream American popular culture. At the same time, he breaks away from traditional lyric poetry by rejecting the transcendence of the lyric "I." Moreover, Yau also challenges some postmodernist notions of the self that reduce the individual to a mere social construct. He explores these complex themes mostly through Genghis Chan's monologues. The name "Genghis Chan" simultaneously evokes two opposing stereotypes of Asian Americans, the "yellow peril" and the "model minority." The first is connected to the historical figure Genghis Khan, associated with the fictional character Fu Manchu, the "yellow peril" incarnate in Hollywood films and Sax Rohmer's novels; the second refers to "Charlie Chan," a Chinese American detective from Hawaii, played by three white men (Warner Oland, Sidney Toler, and Roland Winters) in forty-eight Hollywood films, adapted from five Charlie Chan novels by Earl Derr Biggers. In collapsing the two names and stereotypes together, Yau suggests containment of the threatening "yellow peril" by transforming it into a subordinate "model-minority" image through representational tactics. In contrast to such stereotypical public figures as those in the title, the subtitle, "Private Eye," though echoing Charlie Chan's occupation as a detective, also puns on the lyric "I" whose utterance is supposed to be private, overheard by the reader, and whose transcendence is supposed to be the virtue of traditional lyric and confessional poetry. Yau's use of this racially marked name rejects the transcendence of the lyric "I" and situates the speaker's private speech in specific social, historical, and cultural contexts. These multiple resonances in the serial title point to the intersections between the public and the private, between the collective and the personal, while enhancing the tension between a stable social construct of identity and the shifting, elusive identity of the speaking "I."

For Yau, the possibilities and limits of representing or knowing the "I" are conditioned by the structure of language and by the poet's identity and subject positions. "Where the I begins is in a sentence," Yau writes in his essay "Between the Forest and Its Trees." In articulating the self and representing the world, "I am obeying the rules of language, the illusions of order it casts upon the swiftly metamorphosizing world" (38). Yau contends that if the "I" continues to write in conventional structures of language and established modes of narrative, this "I" might reproduce "a false mirror" of the self and the world (38). In addition to linguistic and narrative construction and constraints, Yau suggests in the same essay that the identity of "I," the speaking subject, has a history in terms of the social and discursive constructs of the "I" within social power relations and generic conventions (37). He then asks, among other questions, "How does the I emerge from the sentences imposed on it by others?" (38). Yau's "Genghis Chan: Private Eye" series enacts his attempt to parody, to rearticulate, and to move beyond the discursively and socially constructed Chinese American "I" in order to emerge as a new subject who resists the social construct of his identity.

In the first piece of the Genghis Chan series, for instance, the speaker shows no immediate resemblance to the stereotypes the title alludes to. Although the "I" reveals a self whose detective identity alludes to Charlie Chan, it refuses to be identical with him, thus remaining elusive and open to alternative identities. The "I" in this poem is unsettling because the speaker cannot be identified according to any of the definitive racial and gender codes that we expect to find—codes that are implied in the name in the title. In other words, the "I" in this poem breaks down the correspondence between the name and its identity, and between the bodily appearance and interior attributes. The speaker identifies himself with those who are parasites looking for a body "to cling to" (*Radiant Silhouette* 189), thus pointing to the fictive representation of a Chinese American that naturalizes his "Chineseness" and otherness through his "Chinese" appearance, which ironically is performed by white men. By exposing the split between the body and the mind, between appearance and essence, Yau raises questions about Hollywood's representation of Chinese Americans that assumes a stable relationship between the body and racial and gender "essence." Thus in his "Genghis Chan: Private Eye" series, Yau disrupts the production of stereotypical Asian American identity even as he parodies the stereotypes by refusing to give any familiar racial codes for the reader to simultaneously decode and encode the speaker's identity and words. Indeed, Yau subverts identity construction by disturbing its means of production—image, narrative, and language, especially the relationship between the signifier and its referent.

The identity of the "I" in "Genghis Chan: Private Eye," however, is constantly shifting, speaking in multiple voices. Sometimes the "I" speaks in a voice of a white man playing the role of Charlie Chan, sometimes in the voice of the Hawaiian Chinese American detective himself, and still other times in the collective voice of Chinese Americans. In "Genghis Chan: Private Eye IV," the speaker alludes to a night scene in which the Chinese American detective encounters a white woman, evoking the style and theme of film noir, particularly its characteristic romantic narration. But being a Chinese American male, Genghis Chan has little chance of a romantic relationship with his white female client because of socially policed racial boundaries. Yau uses surreal images to convey the sense of the racial boundaries, referring to the white woman forbidden to men of color as "a form of concrete . . . cleanly poured," and Genghis Chan himself as "the quarantined flash," alluding to both his racially marked body and the cinematic representation of his racial image (*Radiant Silhouette* 192). In his later "Genghis Chan: Private Eye" poems collected in *Edificio Sayonara* (1992), Yau continues to explore various possibilities of using surreal images and unconventional language to draw the reader's attention to the fictitiousness of Genghis/Charlie Chan's racial image as a cultural production and commodity. In "Genghis Chan: Private Eye VIII," for example, the speaker refers to himself as someone who is "plugged in the new image fertilizer" and who speaks to his inaudible copy (*Edificio Sayonara* 73). In "Genghis Chan: Private Eye XIV," the "I" speaks of his new yellow name being "ladled over" like a blue dollar special offered at a diner (*Edificio Sayonara* 79).

But Genghis Chan is more than a parody of the Hollywood Charlie Chan who is subservient to the social order based on racial hierarchy. He is part of the unsettling presence of immigrants who challenge the claims of the American democracy. In "Genghis Chan: Private Eye XIX," Yau displaces several words in Genghis Chan's speech to disrupt the meaning of familiar English phrases and sayings, thus articulating immigrants' resistance to assimilation through language. The seemingly misplaced words actually satirize Chinese immigrants' status and reveal the racism against them. Yau's play with words has absorbed some of the Language poets' beliefs and ways of using words that are intended to show that writing can be an act that critiques society and that writing must involve the reader in repossessing the language through active participation in its process of producing utterances. Yau's linguistic manipulation and the speaker's insistence on his connection to his "stamped mother"—marked officially and symbolically as immigrant and alien Other—and their connection to "the junk" create a disturbing effect that undermines Charlie Chan's image as the epitome of the assimilated, submissive "model minority" (*Edificio Sayonara* 85–86). Yau's autobiographical reference in the poem at once mimics and departs from the solipsistic autobiographical "poet-I" in confessional poetry. The "I" in this poem, as in many others of the "Genghis Chan: Private Eye" series, speaks in a voice that is at once individual and collective.

Even though Yau sometimes seems to be playing with words in his "Genghis Chan" series, using "words as physical things in some way, literally cut[ting] them up and play[ing] around with them," as he says in an interview with Edward Foster (44), the materiality of the words he is exploring is still related to issues of racial identity. Take, for example, "Genghis Chan: Private Eye XXIV" from Yau's volume *Forbidden Entries* (1996). This poem breaks away from grammatical rules, syntactic order, and traditional poetic form, relying on sound as the organizing principle. With the exception of one word, "machine," all the words in the poem are monosyllabic, evoking the Chinese language, Cantonese accent, and American slang. At the same time, these monosyllabic words make it impossible for the rhythm to vary. Hence the dominant number of consonants together with short spondaic couplets creates a mechanical, menacing sound, mimicking Chinese American dialect, parodying the persistent and sometimes-insidious repetitive pattern of Chinese American stereotypes of the "yellow-peril" threat and the almost mechanical, hardworking "model-minority" overachiever. However, considered individually, the phrases or couplets, such as "dim sum" (Sunday-brunch delicacies) and "chow mein" (stir-fried noodles with vegetables and meat), cannot themselves stand for Chinese American stereotypes (*Forbidden Entries* 102). Hence Yau seems to be using these words that signify cultural difference to show how ethnic difference is naturalized and fixed as racial/ethnic essence by mainstream America for racial discrimination. On the other hand, by using these words to assert Chinese American cultural difference, even as it parodies and subverts Chinese American stereotypes, Yau's mimicry of a Chinese American dialect resists assimilation.

This double-edged, multivoiced parody is characteristic of Yau's "Genghis Chan: Private Eye" series and other poems. The subversive capacity of these poems results in part from Yau's use of the serial form, which is a postmodern mode of long poems that departs from the traditional sequence mode. Without the strictures of a unified theme, a sequential narrative, or an externally imposed organization, the serial form is open to multiple, disparate combinations and numerous variations on the same theme. Yau begins to explore the possibilities of the serial form in his early serial poems collected in *Broken Off by the Music, Corpse and Mirror*, and *Dragon's Blood* and continues to expand and test the limits of the form in his later serial poems collected in *Radiant Silhouette, Edificio Sayonara*, and *Forbidden Entries*. The multiplicity of voices, identities, and perspectives and their incompleteness and openness in these serial poems are embedded in Yau's collage composition of his early prose poems such as "Postcards from Nebraska" and "The Discovery of Honey" collected in *The*

Sleepless Night of Eugene Delacroix, later reprinted in *Radiant Silhouette*. For instance, "Postcards from Nebraska" consists of twenty-one "postcards," each written in a distinct style and vocabulary and in a highly individualized voice. But it is ambivalent whether all of these postcards are written by one person or by a number of people from Nebraska. The ambivalence foregrounds the fact that the identity of the "I" who writes these words is in part constructed by the language and in part hidden behind the linguistic surface. Thus Yau problematizes a fixed relation between language and identity. He extends this investigation of the relation between language and identity in "Genghis Chan: Private Eye" to destabilize the fixity of linguistic characteristics such as pidgin English on racial identity. Yau also develops the possibilities of collage organization in serial poems, including "Postcards from Trakl," which consists of twenty-two poems/postcards, collected in *Edificio Sayonara*. In fact, most of the poems in *Radiant Silhouette, Edificio Sayonara*, and *Forbidden Entries* are serial poems and prose poems.

Along with serial poems, the prose poem is another predominant form that characterizes postmodern poetry and Yau's work. Like other American poets such as William Carlos Williams, Robert Creeley, and John Ashbery, Yau expands the relation between prose and poetry, first explored by French poets such as Baudelaire, Rimbaud, and Mallarmé during the nineteenth century. Continuing to use the prose poem as a less restrictive form for the exploration of complex, varied subjectivity, Yau foregrounds the linguistic materiality and stylistic devices in prose, participating in postmodern investigation of the relations between language and subjectivity. As in "Genghis Chan: Private Eye," Yau's prose poems, such as Peter Lorre's monologue series in *Forbidden Entries*, also engage with Asian Americans' identities of race and gender. Yau employs similar collage juxtaposition of voices and perspectives in his prose pieces collected in *Hawaiian Cowboys* (1994).

In several of the stories in this collection, Yau reveals the contradictions and ambiguities of living on the borders of race and ethnicity and examines the various ways in which racial and ethnic stereotypes have affected people's lives and shaped their relationships. But Yau's prose writings show a wider range of narrative possibilities for dealing with identity issues than his poems. *Hawaiian Cowboys* consists of thirteen short stories that question the assumptions that one can freely invent an ethnic identity for oneself or a community without situating that identity in a socially and historically bounded context. Indeed, his stories illustrate the pervasiveness of racial ideology in a society where people's preferences and applications of "common sense" in everyday life are often racially coded. While dramatizing the operations of racial ideology in these stories, Yau tests the limits of narrative and refashions the short story into a mode of cultural criticism. Yau's collage narrative in "A New Set of Rules Every Other Day" is a good example of his major themes and techniques. It consists of twenty-four subtitled fragmentary sections—a collage that serves multiple functions. The flexible structure of collage enables Yau to locate his narrator's experience in multiple places and to include numerous incidents, characters, and voices, thus simultaneously condensing the time-space of single narratives and expanding the space of the short story. For instance, the opening section, entitled "Social Studies," immediately but indirectly reveals the narrator's racial identity and its impact on the narrator and others in a social context where people's behavior is regulated by racial categories: "Some girls said they wouldn't kiss me because I wasn't black. Others said it was because I wasn't white. And still others kissed me because they were sure I was an exotic plant in need of constant tending" (*Hawaiian Cowboys* 23).

The following two sections provide two kinds of seemingly unrelated information, but both suggest a significant connection to the first in terms of exposing naturalized racial characteristics. Such collage juxtaposition of voices and narratives serves to reveal and subvert racial prejudice among people of a small-town community, including Chinese Americans themselves. As in his poems, Yau also challenges racial and ethnic authenticity in stories such as "How to Become Chinese" and "Family Album." At the same time, issues concerning mixed-race identity also emerge in the stories and are explored in depth in "A Little Memento from the Boys," a story about the experience of three Eurasian boys. The "borderland" identity of mixed-race children challenges the racial ideology from another perspective, raising questions about the boundaries of identity categories. In its totality, Yau's work demonstrates an uncompromising confrontation with current debates on language, subjectivity, and identity construction and reinvention.

CRITICAL RECEPTION

From the beginning of his writing career, Yau's work has received significant critical attention. Critics recognize the innovativeness of Yau's poetics, including his exploration of the structure of language and his incorporation of cinematic elements, such as those of film noir, in his poems. Kris Hemensley finds Yau's poems not only "enigmatic and playful," but also transgressive and philosophical (Campbell et al. 117). While praising Yau's poetry for its "immaculate craftsmanship" and "fluid grace," some critics, however, overlook Yau's challenge to realism and authenticity. David Chaloner, for instance, regards the resistance of Yau's poetry to realist representations as an attribute of "the curiously timeless presence of an ancient sensibility" (114), an "inheritance from the more ancient culture of China" (113). Among the early criticism on Yau's poetry, Priscilla Wald's work seems to be the most perceptive and significant. In her article, "Guilty by Dissociation: John Yau's Poetics of Possibility," Wald offers sensitive readings of Yau's prose poems "Cenotaph" and "Cenotaph of Snow" in *Radiant Silhouette*, relating problems of Chinese immigrants' assimilation to racist Orientalism while situating the Chinese boy narrator's identity within a complex web of personal and social relationships. Summarizing Yau's thematic concerns, Wald notes that Yau's work is intended to "confront us with . . . our identification," and that "it is a task that resonates with the full force of the experience of United States racism as the exoticized (and colonized) other" ("Guilty" 121). Wald further contends that for Yau, identity "is an intricately political question, and the way we know ourselves stands in direct opposition to the way we are known" ("Guilty" 121). But Yau's numerous poems indicate that we do not always know ourselves with clarity and certainty. More important, his poems and prose pieces suggest that our ideas of who we are, like our perceptions of others, are often mediated by dominant ideologies of race and gender, by historical circumstances, and by the limits of language. Thus a dichotomized view of the self as perceived by the self and others forecloses a more complete understanding of Yau's exploration of the relations between language and subjectivity, between representation and identity construction, and between dominant racial ideology and individual identity formation.

Critical reception of Yau's work, especially from European Americans, has not always been positive. Interestingly, negative criticism on Yau is related to racial stereotypes and to Yau's own racial identity. Marjorie Perloff in her review of *Forbidden Entries* singles out the poems of the "Genghis Chan: Private Eye" series as examples of "the more overt representations of racial oppression" that are "the volume's least successful poems." The failure of these poems, Perloff contends, results from the fact that Yau's version of the stereotyping of Chinese Americans in American mainstream culture "is itself guilty of reductionism." Perloff finds that in poems such as "Bar Orient," "the image of 'China' seems as out of date as it is one-dimensional" (40). What is intriguing about Perloff's critique of Yau's "least successful poems" is that it seems to have collapsed parody with "truthful" representation while judging the poems on the basis of an authenticity that Yau's parody does not presume. Overlooking the effects and limits of parody in Yau's poems, Perloff finds additional faults with them. Adding that even though Yau's version of the stereotyping can arguably be seen as "intentional," Perloff still feels "unease" with the images in "Bar Orient," which "don't quite grapple with the poet's own conflicted identity" (40). Perloff's question about the authenticity of Yau's representation of Chinese American culture overlooks the subversive intent of Yau's parody and assumes an authentic ethnic culture that Yau's poems undermine. As Juliana Chang points out in her review of *Forbidden Entries*, "To use criteria of cultural, ethnic, or racial authenticity in evaluating the writing of John Yau . . . is to miss the point of his writing, which calls into question the notion of a wholly knowable self that one can thus evaluate" (226).

Other Asian American critics offer insightful readings of Yau's poetry. Juliana Chang examines Yau's use of strategies such as parody and mystery-fiction genres to destabilize notions of language and subjectivity. Dorothy Wang focuses on the functions and effects of parody in Yau's poems. Timothy Yu analyzes Yau's integration of history, ethnicity, and the poetics of Language poetry. George Uba is perhaps the first Asian American critic who recognizes the significance of Yau's exploration of the structure of language in relation to identity construction. In his chapter, "Versions of Identity in Post-activist Asian American Poetry," Uba observes, "Behind the problematics of identity lies Yau's skepticism regarding the organizing properties of myth and other forms of narrative" (44). Uba considers Yau's poetry part of a new departure in Asian American poetic traditions developed during the late 1960s and early 1970s. The critical attention Yau's poetry receives reflects the complexity, richness, and challenges of his poetics, which resists complete identification with any poetic traditions.

BIBLIOGRAPHY

Works by John Yau

Poetry

Crossing Canal Street. Binghamton, NY: Bellevue Press, 1976.
The Reading of an Ever-changing Tale. Clinton, NY: Nobodaddy Press, 1977.
Sometimes. New York: Sheep Meadow Press, 1979.
The Sleepless Night of Eugene Delacroix. Brooklyn, NY: Released Press, 1980.
Broken Off by the Music. Providence, RI: Burning Deck, 1981.
Notarikon. With drawings by Jake Berthot. New York: Jordan Davies, 1981.
Corpse and Mirror. New York: Holt, Rinehart, and Winston, 1983.
Dragon's Blood. Colombes, France: Collectif Généraion, 1989.
Radiant Silhouette: New and Selected Work, 1974–1988. Santa Rosa, CA: Black Sparrow
       Press, 1989.
Big City Primer: Reading New York at the End of the Twentieth Century. With Bill
       Barrette. New York: Timken, 1991.
Edificio Sayonara. Santa Rosa, CA: Black Sparrow Press, 1992.
Postcards from Trakl. New York: ULAE, 1994.
Forbidden Entries. Santa Rosa, CA: Black Sparrow Press, 1996.
I Was a Poet in the House of Frankenstein. Brooklyn, NY: Poetry New York, 1999.
"Three Peter Lorre Poems." *Conjunctions* 32 (1999): 154–62.

Short Stories

Hawaiian Cowboys. Santa Rosa, CA: Black Sparrow Press, 1994.
My Symptoms. Santa Rosa, CA: Black Sparrow Press, 1998.

Critical Studies

A.R. Penck. New York: Abrams, 1993.
In the Realm of Appearances: The Art of Andy Warhol. Hopewell, NJ: Ecco Press, 1993.
Ed Moses: A Retrospective of the Paintings and Drawings, 1951–1996. Los Angeles:
       Museum of Contemporary Art and University of California Press, 1996.

Monographs

Maurice Golubov: Paintings, 1925–1980. Charlotte, NC: Mint Museum of Art, 1980.
Bodies and Souls. New York: Artists' Choice Museum, 1983.

In Honor of the Brooklyn Bridge. New York: David Findlay Gallery, 1983.

Jim Nutt: Recent Work. London: Mayor Gallery, 1983.

John Moore. New York: Hirschl and Adler Modern, 1983.

The New Response: Contemporary Painters of the Hudson River. Albany, NY: Albany
    Institute of History and Art, 1985.

Four Painters: Michael Kessler, Archie Rand, Mark Schlesinger, Lynton Wells. Flint,
    MI: Flint Institute of Arts, 1989.

Chuck Close: Recent Paintings. New York: Pace Wildenstein, 1995.

Beware the Lady: New Paintings and Works on Paper. By Susan Bee. New York: A.I.R.
    Gallery, 2000.

Essays on Art and Poetry (Selected Listing)

"David True's Pendulum." *Artforum* 21 (February 1983): 40–43.

"How We Live: The Paintings of Robert Birmelin, Eric Fischl, and Ed Paschke." *Art-
    forum* 21 (April 1983): 60–67.

"Malcolm Morley's Baedeker." *Arts Magazine* 57 (May 1983): 97–99.

"Joan Thorpe's Visionary Universe." *Arts Magazine* 58 (September 1983): 118–19.

"Disrupted Narratives: Recent Paintings of Robert Birmelin." *Arts Magazine* 58 (March
    1984): 114–15.

"Hiroshi Sugimoto: No Such Thing as Time." *Artforum* 22 (April 1984): 48–52.

"Howard Buchwald's Recent Paintings: Tying and Untying a Gordian Knot." *Arts Mag-
    azine* 59 (May 1984): 118–19.

"Poets and Art." *Artforum* 23 (November 1984): 84–89.

"Richard Artschwager's Linear Investigations." *Drawing* 6 (January/February 1985): 97–
    100.

"O'Keeffe's Misfocus." *Art News* 87 (February 1988): 114–19.

"Nathan Farb: A World of Stillness and Light." *Art News* 87 (April 1988): 85–86.

"Biennale: Jasper Johns." *Contemporanea* 1 (July/August 1988): 65–69.

"Brice Marden." *Flash Art* 142 (October 1988): 92–95.

"Please Wait by the Coatroom" (Wifredo Lam in the Museum of Modern Art). *Arts
    Magazine* 63 (December 1988): 56–59.

"Alone in a Landscape." *Contemporanea* 2 (June 1989): 81–83.

"Making His Mark" (on Brice Marden). *Vogue* (July 1989): 190–95.

"Archie Rand: The Figure of the Artist." *Sulfur* 25 (Fall 1989): 186–91.

"Some Notes on Clark Coolidge's 'Shied Witnesses.' " *Talisman: A Journal of Contem-
    porary Poetry and Poetics* 4 (Spring 1990): 88–91.

"Between the Forest and Its Trees." *Amerasia Journal* 20.3 (1994): 37–43.

"Neither Us nor Them." *American Poetry Review* 23.2 (March/April 1994): 45–54.

Introduction. *New Generation: Poems from China Today*. Ed. Wang Ping. Trans. Wang
    Ping with Elizabeth Fox. Brooklyn, NY: Hanging Loose Press, 1999. 12–20.

Anthologies Edited

Fairfield Porter: The Collected Poems with Selected Drawings. Ed. with David Kermani.
    New York: Tibor de Nagy, 1985.

*In Pursuit of the Invisible: Selections from the Collection of Janice and Mickey Cartin:
    An Exhibition at the Loomis Chaffee School*. West Stockbridge, MA: Hard Press,
    1996.

An Anthology of Fetish Fiction. New York: Four Walls Eight Windows, 1998.
The Footprints of One Who Has Not Stepped Forth. By Richard Anders. Trans. Andrew Joron. New York: Black Square Editions, 2000.

Interviews

"An Interview with John Yau." By Edward Foster. *Talisman* 5 (Fall 1990): 31–50.
"A Bughouse Interaction with John Yau and Jenny Scobel at the La Placita Dining Room in Albuquerque, New Mexico, on Saturday, March 26, 1994." *Bughouse* 2 (Summer 1994): 47–60.
"Approximating Midnight: Her Conversation with John Yau And." By Eileen Tabios. *Black Lightning: Poetry-in-Progress*. New York: Asian American Writers' Workshop, 1998. 381–402.

Review

Rev. of *The Little Door Slides Back*, by Jeff Clark, *Madonna Anno Domini*, by Joshua Clover, and *Imagination Verses*, by Jennifer Moxley. *Boston Review* 22.6 (December/January 1997–1998): 51–53.

Studies of John Yau

Ashbery, John. Rev. of *The Reading of an Ever-changing Tale*. *Nation* 11 November 1978: 518.
Barone, Dennis. Rev. of *My Symptoms*. *Review of Contemporary Fiction* (Fall 1998): 253.
Bloom, Harold. Rev. of *The Reading of an Ever-changing Tale*. *New Republic* 26 November 1977: 26.
Campell, Bruce, David Chaloner, William Corbett, Joseph Donahue, Peter Gizzi, Kris Hemensley, Albert Mobilio, and Priscilla Wald. "A Symposium on John Yau: Commentary and Criticism." *Talisman* 5 (Fall 1990): 113–34.
Chaloner, David. "On John Yau." *Talisman* 5 (Fall 1990): 113–14.
Chang, Juliana. Rev. of *Forbidden Entries*. *MELUS* 23.3 (Fall 1998): 226–28.
———. "Word and Flesh: Materiality, Violence, and Asian American Poetics." Diss. University of California, Berkeley, 1995.
Elman, Richard. Rev. of *Corpse and Mirror*. *New York Times Book Review* 18 September 1983: 36.
Eshleman, Clayton. Rev. of *Corpse and Mirror*. *Los Angeles Times Book Review* 7 August 1983: 3.
Evenson, Brian. Rev. of *Hawaiian Cowboys*. *Review of Contemporary Fiction* 16.1 (Spring 1996): 171–72.
Friedman, B.H. Rev. of *Broken Off by the Music, Crossing Canal Street, Notarikon, The Reading of an Ever-changing Tale, The Sleepless Night of Eugene Delacroix*, and *Sometimes*. *American Book Review* 4.2 (1982): 19.
Hales, Peter B. Rev. of *Big City Primer: Reading New York City at the End of the Twentieth Century*. *New York Times Book Review* 1 December 1991: 22.
Kelly, Robert. Preface. *Crossing Canal Street*. Binghamton, NY: Bellevue Press, 1976. n.p.
Lim, Shirley. "Reconstructing Asian-American Poetry: A Case for Ethnopoetics." Rev. of *Corpse and Mirror*. *MELUS* 14.2 (Summer 1987): 51–63.

McDowell, Robert. Rev. of *Corpse and Mirror*. *Hudson Review* 36.1 (Spring 1983): 126–27.

Mobilio, Albert. Rev. of *Big City Primer: Reading New York City at the End of the Twentieth Century*. *Arts Magazine* 66.7 (March 1992): 25–26.

Perloff, Marjorie. Rev. of *Forbidden Entries*. *Boston Review* 22.3–4 (Summer 1997): 39–41.

Racks, George. Rev. of *Sometimes*. *Library Journal* 105 (15 March 1980): 728.

Rev. of *A.R. Penck*. *Publishers Weekly* 240.46 (15 November 1993): 66.

Rev. of *Corpse and Mirror*. *Publishers Weekly* 223 (8 April 1983): 54.

Rev. of *Corpse and Mirror*. *Virginia Quarterly Review* 60 (Winter 1984): 23.

Rev. of *Forbidden Entries*. *Publishers Weekly* 243.48 (25 November 1996): 71–72.

Rev. of *My Symptoms*. *Publishers Weekly* 245.29 (20 July 1998): 207.

Shafarzek, Susan. Rev. of *The Sleepless Night of Eugene Delacroix*. *Library Journal* (15 December 1980): 1545.

Sihjeldahl, Peter. Rev. of *The Sleepless Night of Eugene Delacroix*. *Parnassus* (Spring/Summer 1981): 294–95.

Tucker, Ken. Rev. of *Corpse and Mirror*. *Village Voice Literary Supplement* 17 (May 1983): 5.

Uba, George. "Versions of Identity in Post-activist Asian American Poetry." *Reading the Literatures of Asian America*. Ed. Shirley Geok-lin Lim and Amy Ling. Philadelphia: Temple University Press, 1992. 33–48.

Wakoski, Diane. "John Yau." *Contemporary Poets*. 4th ed. Ed. James Vinson and D.L. Kirkpatrick. New York: St. Martin's Press, 1985. 954–55.

Wald, Priscilla. " 'Chaos Goes Uncourted': John Yau's Dis(-)orienting Poetics." *Cohesion and Dissent in America*. Ed. Carol Colatrella and Joseph Alkana. Albany: State University of New York Press, 1994. 133–58.

Wang, Dorothy Joan. "Necessary Figures: Metaphor, Irony, and Parody in the Poetry of Li-Young Lee, Marilyn Chin, and John Yau." Diss. University of California, Berkeley, 1998.

Yu, Timothy. "Form and Identity in Language Poetry and Asian American Poetry." *Contemporary Literature* 41.3 (Fall 2000): 422–62.

SELECTED BIBLIOGRAPHY

POETRY ANTHOLOGIES

Bay Area Philipino American Writers. *Without Names: A Collection of Poems*. San Francisco: Kearny Street Workshop Press, 1995.

Bruchac, Joseph, ed. *Breaking Silence: An Anthology of Contemporary Asian American Poets*. Greenfield Center, NY: Greenfield Review Press, 1983.

Cachapero, Emily, ed. *Liwanag: Literary and Graphic Expressions by Filipinos in America*. San Francisco: Liwanag Press, 1975.

Carbo, Nick, ed. *Returning a Borrowed Tongue: An Anthology of Filipino and Filipino American Poetry*. Minneapolis: Coffee House Press, 1995.

Chang, Juliana, ed. *Quiet Fire: A Historical Anthology of Asian American Poetry, 1892–1970*. New York: Asian American Writers' Workshop, 1996.

Chiang, Fay, ed. *American Born and Foreign: An Anthology of Asian American Poetry*. Spec. issue of *Sunbury: A Poetry Magazine* 7–8 (1979): 1–152.

Chock, Eric, James R. Harstad, Darrell Lum, and Bill Teter, eds. *Growing Up Local: An Anthology of Poetry and Prose from Hawai'i*. Honolulu: Bamboo Ridge Press, 1998.

Chock, Eric, and Darrell H.Y. Lum, eds. *Paké: Writings by Chinese in Hawaii*. Honolulu: Bamboo Ridge Press, 1989.

Coss, Clare, ed. *The Arc of Love: An Anthology of Lesbian Love Poems*. New York: Scribner, 1996.

Dabydeen, Cyril, ed. *Another Way to Dance: Asian-Canadian Poetry*. Stratford, Ontario: Williams-Wallace, 1990.

———, ed. *Another Way to Dance: Contemporary Asian Poetry from Canada and the United States*. Toronto: TSAR, 1996.

Gill, Stephen, ed. *Green Snow: Anthology of Canadian Poets of Asian Origin*. Cornwall, Ontario: Vesta, 1976.

Hongo, Garrett, ed. *The Open Boat: Poems from Asian America*. New York: Anchor Books, 1993.

Hongo, Garrett, Alan Chong Lau, and Lawson Fusao Inada. *The Buddha Bandits down Highway 99*. Mountain View, CA: Buddhahead, 1978.

Lai, Him Mark, Genny Lim, and Judy Yung, eds. *Island: Poetry and History of Chinese Immigrants on Angel Island, 1910–1940*. San Francisco: San Francisco Study Center, 1980.

Lew, Walter K., ed. *Premonitions: The Kaya Anthology of New Asian North American Poetry*. New York: Kaya Productions, 1995.

Lim, Shirley, Mayumi Tsutakawa, and Margarita Donnelly, eds. *The Forbidden Stitch: An Asian American Women's Anthology*. Corvallis, OR: Calyx Books, 1989.

Lim-Hing, Sharon, ed. *The Very Inside: An Anthology of Writing by Asian and Pacific Islander Lesbian and Bisexual Women*. Toronto: Sister Vision Press, 1994.

McGifford, Diane, and Judith Kearns, eds. *Shakti's Words: An Anthology of South Asian Canadian Women's Poetry*. Toronto: TSAR, 1990.

Mirikitani, Janice, ed. *Ayumi: A Japanese American Anthology*. San Francisco: Japanese American Anthology Committee, 1980.

Mirikitani, Janice, ed. *Time to Greez! Incantations from the Third World*. San Francisco: Glide Publications/Third World Communications, 1975.

Quan, Andy, and Jim Wong-Chu, eds. *Swallowing Clouds: An Anthology of Chinese-Canadian Poetry*. Vancouver: Arsenal Pulp Press, 1999.

Rustomji-Kerns, Roshni, ed. *Living in America: Poetry and Fiction by South Asian American Writers*. Boulder, CO: Westview Press, 1995.

Shikatani, Gerry, and David Aylward, eds. *Paper Doors: An Anthology of Japanese-Canadian Poetry*. Toronto: Coach House, 1981.

Tran, Barbara, Monique T.D. Tru'o'ng, and Luu Truong Khoi, eds. *Watermark: Vietnamese American Poetry and Prose*. New York: Asian American Writers' Workshop, 1998.

Wand, David Hsin-Fu, ed. *Asian-American Heritage*. New York: Washington Square Press, 1974.

Wang, L. Ling-chi, and Henry Yiheng Zhao, eds. *Chinese American Poetry: An Anthology*. Santa Barbara, CA: Asian American Voices, 1991.

SECONDARY SOURCES

Baker, Houston A., ed. *Three American Literatures: Essays in Chicano, Native American, and Asian-American Literature for Teachers of American Literature*. New York: MLA, 1982.

Brogan, Jacqueline Vaught, and Cordelia Chavez Candelaria, eds. *Women Poets of the Americas: Toward a Pan-American Gathering*. Notre Dame: University of Notre Dame Press, 1999.

Chang, Juliana. "Reading Asian American Poetry." *MELUS* 21.1 (Spring 1996): 81–98.

Cheung, King-Kok, ed. *An Interethnic Companion to Asian American Literature*. New York: Cambridge University Press, 1997.

———, ed. *Words Matter: Conversations with Asian American Writers*. Honolulu: University of Hawai'i Press, 2000.

Fujita-Sato, Gayle K. " 'Third World' as Place and Paradigm in Cathy Song's *Picture Bride.*" *MELUS* 15.1 (Spring 1988): 49–72.

Gee, Emma, ed. *Counterpoint: Perspectives on Asian America.* Los Angeles: UCLA Asian American Studies Center, 1976.

Ghymn, Esther Mikyung, ed. *Asian American Studies: Identities, Images, Issues Past and Present.* New York: Peter Lang, 2000.

Gregson, Ian. *Contemporary Poetry and Postmodernism: Dialogue and Estrangement.* New York: St. Martin's Press, 1996.

Hirabayashi, Lane Ryo, ed. *Teaching Asian America: Diversity and the Problem of Community.* Lanham, MD: Rowman, 1998.

Hsu, Ruth, Cynthia Franklin, and Suzanne Kosanke, eds. *Re-placing America: Conversations and Contestations: Selected Essays.* Honolulu: University of Hawai'i and the East-West Center, 2000.

Huang, Guiyou, ed. *Asian American Autobiographers: A Bio-Bibliographical Critical Sourcebook.* Westport, CT: Greenwood Press, 2001.

Kamboureli, Smaro, ed. *Making a Difference: Canadian Multicultural Literature.* Toronto: Oxford University Press, 1996.

Kanaganayakam, Chelva. *Dark Antonyms and Paradise: The Poetry of Rienzi Crusz.* Toronto: TSAR, 1997.

Lim, Shirley Geok-lin, and Amy Ling, eds. *Reading the Literatures of Asian America.* Philadelphia: Temple University Press, 1992.

Ling, Amy, ed. *Yellow Light: The Flowering of Asian American Arts.* Philadelphia: Temple University Press, 1999.

Moyers, Bill D. *The Language of Life: A Festival of Poets.* New York: Doubleday, 1995.

Mukherjee, Arun. *Towards an Aesthetic of Opposition: Essays on Literature Criticism and Cultural Imperialism.* Stratford, Ontario: Williams-Wallace, 1988.

Nelson, Emmanuel S., ed. *Asian American Novelists: A Bio-Bibliographical Critical Sourcebook.* Westport, CT: Greenwood Press, 2000.

———, ed. *Reworlding: The Literature of the Indian Diaspora.* Westport, CT: Greenwood Press, 1992.

———, ed. *Writers of the Indian Diaspora: A Bio-Bibliographical Critical Sourcebook.* Westport, CT: Greenwood Press, 1993.

Simpson, Megan. *Poetic Epistemologies: Gender and Knowing in Women's Language-oriented Writing.* Albany: State University of New York Press, 2000.

Singh, Amritjit, Joseph T. Skerrett, Jr., and Robert E. Hogan, eds. *Memory and Cultural Politics: New Approaches to American Ethnic Literatures.* Boston: Northeastern University Press, 1996.

Tabios, Eileen. *Black Lightning: Poetry-in-Progress.* New York: Asian American Writers' Workshop, 1998.

Trudeau, Lawrence J., ed. *Asian American Literature: Reviews and Criticism of Works by American Writers of Asian Descent.* Detroit, MI: Gale Research, 1999.

Uba, George. "Coordinates of Asian American Poetry: A Survey of the History and a Guide to Teaching." *A Resource Guide to Asian American Literature.* Ed. Sau-ling Cynthia Wong and Stephen H. Sumida. New York: MLA, 2001. 309–31.

———. "Versions of Identity in Post-activist Asian American Poetry." *Reading the Literatures of Asian America.* Ed. Shirley Geok-lin Lim and Amy Ling. Philadelphia: Temple University Press, 1992. 33–48.

Women of South Asian Descent Collective, ed. *Our Feet Walk the Sky: Women of the South Asian Diaspora*. San Francisco: Aunt Lute, 1993.

Wong, Sau-ling Cynthia, and Stephen H. Sumida, eds. *A Resource Guide to Asian American Literature*. New York: MLA, 2001.

Wong, Sunn Shelley. "Sizing Up Asian American Poetry." *A Resource Guide to Asian American Literature*. Ed. Sau-ling Cynthia Wong and Stephen H. Sumida. New York: MLA, 2001. 285–308.

Yamamoto, Traise. *Masking Selves, Making Subjects: Japanese American Women, Identity, and the Body*. Berkeley: University of California Press, 1999.

Zhou, Xiaojing. "Inheritance and Invention in Li-Young Lee's Poetry." *MELUS* 21.1 (Spring 1996): 113–32.

INDEX

Aguilar-San Juan, Karin, 328
Ahmed Faiz, Faiz, 31
Ai (Ogawa, Florence), 15–20
  bibliography, 19–20
  biography of, 15–16
  critical reception, 18–19
  major works and themes, 16–18
Ai Qing, 71
Alexander, Charles, 301
Alexander, Meena, 21–29
  bibliography, 27–29
  biography of, 21–22
  critical reception, 26–27
  major works and themes, 22–26
Ali, Agha Shahid, 31–35
  bibliography, 34–35
  biography of, 31
  critical reception, 33–34
  major works and themes, 32–33
Altieri, Charles, 80
Ancheta, Shirley, 107
Armes, Ethel, 260–261
Ashbery, John, 344, 350
Asian America(n), definition of term, 1–2
Asian American poetry
  critical work of 1980s-present, 3–4

lack of popularization/critical attention
  of, 1
overview of, 3
reading and teaching practice of, 2–3
Asian American poets
  gender representation of, 10
  internment theme, 2, 8, 133, 145, 148,
    233, 236, 243
  mainstream acceptance of, 5–6
  racial/ethnic/national and cultural heri-
    tages of, 10
Asian Canadian writing, 2, 8
Atsumi, Ikuko, 264

Bahri, Deepika, 59
Bai Jüyi (Po Chü-yi), 73
Bak, Louise, 321
Bakhtin, Mikhail, 209, 250
Balfantz, Gary, 225
Bamboo Ridge (literary journal), 8, 84,
  173, 229
Bannerji, Himani, 8, 37–44
  bibliography, 40–44
  biography of, 37
  critical reception, 39
  major works and themes, 37–39

Baraka, Amiri, 102
Barnstone, Tony, 299–300
Barrette, Bill, 343
Barthes, Roland, 116
Baudelaire, Charles, 79, 130, 350
Bauer, Grace, 284
Bay Area Philipino American Writers
     (BAYPAW), 53, 55
Baym, Nina, 5
Benjamin, Walter, 245
Berling, Judith A., 190
Berryman, John, 79
Berssenbrugge, Mei-Mei, 10, 45–51
   bibliography, 51
   biography of, 45
   critical reception, 49–51
   major works and themes, 45–48
Bhabha, Homi, 77
Binyon, Laurence, 260, 263
Bishop, Elizabeth, 285
Blackburn, Di Gan, 89, 267, 331
Blake, Robert, 306
Blake, William, 272
Bose, Brinda, 216
Bowering, Marilyn, 198
Bowers, Neil, 62
Brainard, Dulcy, 95
Brand, Bill, 117
Brand, Dionne, 181
Bridges, Robert, 261
Brodine, Karen, 314
Browne, Michael Dennis, 79–80
Bulosan, Carlos, 102
Burgess, Gelett, 260

Campomanes, Oscar V., 55, 108
Cardenal, Ernesto, 117
Carlos, Laurie, 102
Carman, Bliss, 263
Casper, Leonard, 306
Cather, Willa, 263
Cerenio, Virginia R., 53–57
   bibliography, 56–57
   biography of, 53
   critical reception, 55–56
   major works and themes, 53–55
Cervantes, Lorna Dee, 239
Cha, Theresa Hak Kyung, 168, 281

Chakraborty, Chandrima, 37
Chaloner, David, 351
Chan, Jeffery Paul, 147, 154
Chandra, G. S. Sharat, 59–63
   bibliography, 62–63
   biography of, 59–60
   critical reception, 62
   major works and themes, 60–61
Chang, Diana, 10, 65–67
   bibliography, 67–70
   biography of, 65
   critical reception, 66–67
   major works and themes, 65–66
Chang, Juliana, 4, 108–109, 117–118,
     151–152, 281, 290, 352
Chao, Pao, 151
Cheung, King-Kok, 77, 130
Chin, Frank, 66, 83–84, 134, 147, 154,
     223–224, 324
Chin, Marilyn Mei Ling, 5, 71–82
   bibliography, 81–82
   biography of, 71–72
   critical reception, 78–81
   major works and themes, 72–78
Chock, Eric, 8–9, 83–87, 153, 225
   bibliography, 86–87
   biography of, 83–84
   critical reception, 85–86
   major works and themes, 84–85
Chow, Balance, 4
Cimon, Anne, 198
Cisneros, Sandra, 338–339
Cixous, Hélène, 77, 114
Clem, Bill, 219
Clément, Catherine, 114
Clifford, James, 301
Confucianism, 189–190, 256
Crawford, John, 239
Creeley, Robert, 350
Crusz, Rienzi, 8, 89–91
   bibliography, 91
   biography of, 89
   critical reception, 90–91
   major works and themes, 89–90
Cruz, Isagani R., 222
Cruz, Victor Hernandez, 102
cummings, e. e., 306

Dabydeen, Cyril, 5
Davies, Ioan, 39
Davis, Rocío G., 305
Davis, Thulani, 102
de Almeida, Eduardo, 65
de Jesús, Melinda L., 53, 201
de Régnier, Henri, 128
Dempster, Brian Komei, 185
Derrida, Jacques, 216
Des Pres, Terrence, 257
Dickinson, Emily, 32, 206, 272, 285
Divakaruni, Chitra Banerjee, 93–99
  bibliography, 98–99
  biography of, 93–94
  critical reception, 97–98
  major works and themes, 94–97
Donne, John, 206
Dorn, Edward, 102
Du Fu (Tu Fu), 79, 294
Duncan, Erika, 22
Duranceau, Ellen Finnie, 107

Eaton, Allen, 148
Eberhart, John, 60
Eliot, T. S., 33, 79, 114, 206
Elshtain, Eric, 300
Emanuel, Lynn, 176
Emerson, Ralph Waldo, 272
Emi, Frank, 150
Eng, David, 161
Eoyang, Eugene, 71
Evans, Alice, 133, 136

Fanon, Frantz, 246
Fawcett, Brian, 198
Filipelli, Laurie, 140
Fink, Thomas, 50, 67
Flaubert, Gustave, 116
Foster, Edward, 349
Foucault, Jean, 250
Fowler, Gene, 127, 130
Francis, Janet, 146
Fraser, Kathleen, 49, 165, 169
Frost, Robert, 11, 33, 79, 285
Fujikane, Candace, 86, 340
Fujita-Sato, Gayle, 3–4, 145, 151, 225,
  275, 283
Fukuzawa, Yukichi, 259

Gadamer, Hans-Georg, 209
Gadd, Bernard, 216
Gale, Zona, 263
Gangster Choir, 102
Garnett, Porter, 260
Garvey, Hugh, 203
Gates, Henry Louis, Jr., 169
Gier, Jean Vengua, 55
Gil, Eulalia C. Piñero, 328
Gilbert, Roger, 248–249
Gilbert, Sandra, 114
Gilman, Charlotte Perkins, 263
Gilmour, Léonie, 260–261
Giovanni, Nikki, 235
Godard, Barbara, 39
Goldensohn, Lorrie, 282
Goldman, Emma, 126, 129
Gonzalez, N. V. M., 54, 102, 108
Gotera, Vince, 257
Greenbaum, Jessica, 284
Greene, Susan, 121
Gregson, Ian, 25
Griffin, Maureen, 239
Grotjohn, Robert, 249
Guest, Paul, 222

Hagedorn, Jessica, 5, 11, 101–111, 281,
  339
  bibliography, 109–111
  biography of, 101–103
  critical reception, 107–109
  major works and themes, 103–107
Hahn, Kimiko, 10, 113–119, 281
  bibliography, 118–119
  biography of, 113–114
  critical reception, 117–118
  major works and themes, 114–117
haiku, 129, 262
Hakutani, Yoshinobu, 264
Hall, Dana Naone, 84
Hamill, Sam, 186
Harjo, Joy, 239
Harper, Michael, 154
Hartman, Yukihide Maeshima, 121–124
  bibliography, 124
  biography of, 121–122
  critical reception, 123–124
  major works and themes, 122–123

Hartmann, Sadakichi, 3, 10, 125–132
  bibliography, 130–132
  biography of, 125–127
  critical reception, 129–130
  major works and themes, 127–129
Hawaiian poets, 2, 8–9
  Creole English of, 8–9, 84–85, 175,
    337
  critical reception of, 9
Hayashi, Robert, 289
Hemensley, Kris, 351
Hemingway, Ernest, 271
Hesford, Walter, 208–209
Holliday, Shawn, 311
Hongo, Garrett, 5, 8–9, 46, 133–144, 152–
    154, 185, 246, 249, 281, 285
  bibliography, 141–144
  biography of, 133–135
  critical reception, 139–140
  major works and themes, 136–139
Hoover, Paul, 45, 47
Hopkins, Gerard Manley, 306
Horiuchi, Miles, 154
Howe, Susan, 169
Hsu, Kai-yu, 147
Huang, Guiyou, 1
Huang, Su-ching, 323
Huang, Yibing, 210
Hudson, Jay William, 262
Hudspith, Vicky, 122
Hughes, Langston, 11
Hugo, Richard, 279, 282
Huot, Nikolas, 15, 173, 195
Hwang, Jason, 47
Hylkem, Sarie Sachie, 335

Inada, Fusaji, 154
Inada, Lawson Fusao, 4–5, 134, 145–157,
    160, 185, 239, 249, 281
  bibliography, 154–157
  biography of, 145–146
  critical reception, 150–154
  major works and themes, 146–150
Inada, Lowell, 154
Inada, Miles, 154
Irigaray, Luce, 114

Jacinto, Jaime, 55
Jackson, Gale, 114

Jackson, Richard, 282
Jailall, Sabi M., 39
James, Caryn, 108
Jamison, Laura, 97
Janette, Michele, 255
Jang, Jon, 244
Jarman, Mark, 140
Jarrell, Randall, 290
Jayo, Norman, 102
Johnson, Jackie Pualani, 173

Kamada, Roy Osamu, 133, 243
Kanaganayakam, Chelva, 90
Kaneko, Lonny, 153, 159–163, 186, 324
  bibliography, 162–163
  biography of, 159
  critical reception, 161
  major works and themes, 159–161
Kang, Hyun Yi, 168
Kaplan, Caren, 152
Katrak, Ketu, 23–24, 26, 32, 34
Kawabata, Yasunari, 116
Keats, John, 79, 206
Keckler, W. B., 49–50
Keller, Nora Okja, 84
Kelly, Robert, 344
Kerouac, Jack, 271
Khoo, Gaik Cheng, 179, 319
Kicknosway, Faye, 337
Kim, Elaine, 107, 130, 147, 150, 161,
    168, 281–282
Kim, Myung Mi, 80, 165–171
  bibliography, 169–171
  biography of, 165–166
  critical reception, 168–169
  major works and themes, 166–168
Kim, Willyce, 282
King, Bruce, 26–27, 33–34
Kingston, Maxine Hong, 74, 152, 247,
    276–278
Kinnell, Galway, 15, 139
Kitchen, Judith, 210
Kizer, Carolyn, 333
Klein, Melanie, 116
Knippling, Alpana Sharma, 264
Knowlton, Edgar, 168
Knox, George, 130
Koh, Karlyn, 181

Kono, Juliet Sanae, 8–9, 153, 173–177, 281
  bibliography, 176–177
  biography of, 173
  critical reception, 175–176
  major works and themes, 174–175
Kraus, Joe, 121
Kubo, Mari, 84
Kuromiya, Yosh, 150
Kwa, Lydia, 8, 10, 179–183
  bibliography, 181–183
  biography of, 179–180
  critical reception, 180–181
  major works and themes, 180

Lai, Larissa, 180
Lam, Jen, 321
Laozi (Lao Tzu), 190
Larkin, Philip, 151
Larsen, Wendy, 10, 257
Lashgari, Deirdre, 239
Lau, Alan Chong, 8, 134, 154, 185–187, 281
  bibliography, 187
  biography of, 185
  critical reception, 186–187
  major works and themes, 185–186
Lau, Carolyn, 189–193
  bibliography, 192–193
  biography of, 189
  critical reception, 192
  major works and themes, 189–192
Lau, Evelyn, 8, 195–200
  bibliography, 198–200
  biography of, 195–196
  critical reception, 197–198
  major works and themes, 196–197
Lawrence, Keith, 59
Lawton, Harry, 130
Le Gallienne, Richard, 263
Lê Thi Diem, Thúy, 8, 10, 201–204
  bibliography, 203–204
  biography of, 201
  critical reception, 203
  major works and themes, 201–203
Lee, Bennett, 181
Lee, James Kyung-Jin, 165, 209
Lee, Li-Young, 5–7, 205–211, 244, 281

  bibliography, 210–211
  biography of, 205–206
  critical reception, 208–210
  major works and themes, 206–208
Leong, Lavonne, 223, 229, 271
Levertov, Denise, 139
Levine, Philip, 146, 154
Lew, Walter, 281
Li Bai (Li Po), 77, 294
Li Qingzhao (Li Ch'ing-chao), 294
Li, Xilao, 130
Lim, Genny, 186
Lim, Shirley Geok-Lin, 3, 66, 152, 213–218, 282–283
  bibliography, 217–218
  biography of, 213–215
  critical reception, 216
  major works and themes, 215–216
Lim-Wilson, Fatima, 219–222
  bibliography, 222
  biography of, 219–220
  critical reception, 222
  major works and themes, 220–222
Ling, Amy, 66, 77
Lipman, Joel, 50
Liu, Miles X., 12
Liu, Timothy, 5
Lorca, Federico García, 139
Lowe, Lisa, 77
Lu, James, 152–153
Lum, Darrell H. Y., 5, 8–9, 84, 175, 225–226
Lum, Wing Tek, 8–9, 84, 153, 223–227
  bibliography, 226–227
  biography of, 223–224
  critical reception, 225–226
  major works and themes, 224–225

McCauley, Robbie, 102
McPherson, Michael, 84
Maitri, 94
Mallarmé, Stéphanie, 126, 128, 350
Manoa: A Pacific Journal for International Writing, 230
Mapapatra, Jayanta, 26
Mariano, Bayani, 238
Markham, Edwin, 260, 263
Marlatt, Daphne, 181

Marlowe, Christopher, 93
Márquez, Robert, 117
Marshall, Tod, 209
Marx, Edward, 3, 259
Matsueda, Pat, 8–9, 225–226, 229–232
    bibliography, 231–232
    biography of, 229–230
    critical reception, 231
    major works and themes, 230–231
Matsunari, Rowena Tomaneng, 189
Mazumdar, Sucheta, 94
Means, Laurel, 216
Mencius, 190
Menon, Vikas, 169
Merill, James, 285
Merrill, Stuart, 128
Meyers, Burt, 134
Miles, Josephine, 293
Millard, Elizabeth, 118
Miller, Joaquin, 259, 263
Miller, Philip, 62
Miner, Earl, 264
Mirikitani, Janice, 5, 10, 102, 151, 160,
        233–242, 249, 281
    bibliography, 240–242
    biography of, 233–235
    critical reception, 238–240
    major works and themes, 235–238
Mitchell, Roger, 209–210
Mittal, Bina, 268
Monaghan, Pat, 94, 284
Moore, Marianne, 306
Morales, Rodney, 84
Morgan, Nina, 213, 216
Morgan, Peter E., 337
Mori, Toshio, 153–154
Mortimer, Lisa, 335
Moser, Linda Trinh, 125
Moses, Ed, 343
Mother Earth, 126
Motooka, Wendy, 339–340
Mukherjee, Arun, 39
Mullen, Harryette, 169
Mura, David, 4–5, 8, 11, 151, 153, 239,
        243–254, 281
    bibliography, 251–254
    biography of, 243–244
    critical reception, 248–251

    major works and themes, 244–248
Murayama, Milton, 175

Nair, Hema, 21–22, 26
Nandy, Pritish, 33
Nash, Susan Smith, 50
Native Americans, 11, 16, 294
Needham, Lawrence, 33
Nelson, Emmanuel, 7, 12
Neruda, Pablo, 206, 238
Newman, Denise, 49
Nga, Tran Thi, 10, 255–257
    bibliography, 257
    biography of, 255–256
    critical reception, 257
    major works and themes, 256–257
Nimura, Tamiko, 159, 233
Noguchi, Isamu, 260, 264
Noguchi, Yone, 3, 259–266
    bibliography, 265–266
    biography of, 259–261
    critical reception, 262–264
    major works and themes, 261–262
North, Charles, 121
Nouveau, Germain, 130
Nunes, Susan, 9

Obata, Chiura, 312
O'Brien, Edward, 306
Okada, John, 154
Oktenberg, Adrian, 239
Okubo, Mine, 290
Olsen, Tillie, 333
Ong, Han, 103
Oppen, George, 169
Osherow, Jacqueline, 299–300

Pak, Gary, 84, 282
Palubinskas, Helen, 147
Palumbo-Liu, David, 161
Parameswaran, Uma, 8, 90, 267–270
    bibliography, 269–270
    biography of, 267
    critical reception, 268
    major works and themes, 267–268
Park, Jane Chi Yun, 169
Partington, Blanche, 260
Pasolini, Pier Paolo, 246, 250

Pate, Alexs, 244
Patterson, Anita, 334
Peng, Wenlan, 71
Perloff, Marjorie, 352
Perry, John Oliver, 33, 268
Pettingell, Phoebe, 140
Philip, Marlene, 39
Phillips, Robert, 50
Plath, Sylvia, 79, 285, 314
Poe, Edgar Allan, 261–263
Pound, Erza, 79, 129, 299, 344

Ransome, Arthur, 260
Rasiah, Dharini, 94
Rasula, Jed, 49
Rawlins, C. L., 299
Ray, Richard, 123
Redmond, Eugene, 18
Reed, Ishmael, 102, 154
Rexroth, Kenneth, 102, 107, 130
Rich, Adrienne, 77, 114
Rilke, Rainer Maria, 206
Rimbaud, Arthur, 128, 350
Robles, Al, 102
Roche, Judith, 186
Roethke, Theodore, 159
Roffman, Rosaly, 282
Ronnerman, Jane, 60
Rossetti, William Michael, 260
Roth, Marissa, 103
Rotor, Arturo B., 306
Rushdie, Salman, 247
Rustomji-Kearns, Roshni, 96
Rutsala, Vern, 151

Saguisag, Rene, 219
Said, Edward, 7, 77, 116
Saijo, Albert, 8–9, 271–273
    bibliography, 273
    biography of, 271–272
    critical reception, 273
    major works and themes, 272
Saito, Busuke, 154
Sakamoto, Edward, 175
San Juan, Epifanio, Jr., 109
Sanchez, Sonia, 102, 235
Santos, Bienvenido, 102
Scalapino, Leslie, 50

Schultz, Robert, 140
Schultz, Susan, 284–285
Schweik, Susan, 3, 291, 334
Seaman, Donna, 107
Shah, Purvi, 21, 31, 93
Shahani, Roshan G., 39
Shange, Ntozake, 102, 235
Shapiro, Karl, 290
Sharma, Kavita A., 39
Shaw, Robert, 284
Sherman, Susan, 114
Shiga, Shigetaka, 259
Shikatani, Gerry, 197
Shikibu, Murasaki, 115
Shim, Rosalee, 339
Shonagon, Sei, 117
Simpson, Megan, 49
Singh, Kirpal, 215
Sitwell, Edith, 306, 308
Slater, Michael, 121, 123
Smith, E. Russell, 198
Smith, Ernest J., 313
Snyder, Gary, 271
Song, Cathy, 5, 8–10, 84, 176, 275–288
    bibliography, 285–288
    biography of, 275–276
    critical reception, 281–285
    major works and themes, 276–281
Sorby, Angela, 222
South Asian Canadian Literature (SA-
    CLIT), 8, 90, 267–268
Spahr, Juliana, 273
Speirs, Logan, 62
Spivak, Gayatri Chakravorty, 77
Srikanth, Rajini, 95
Stedman, E. C., 263
Stein, Gertrude, 129, 344–345
Steinman, Lisa, 339
Stern, Gerald, 206, 209
Stevens, Wallace, 272, 285, 300, 306
Stewart, Frank, 229
Stieglitz, Alfred, 126
Stoddard, Charles Warren, 260, 263
Struthers, Ann, 61–62
Sugunasiri, Suwanda, 91
Sumida, Stephen, 9, 83, 283–284
Suyemoto, Toyo, 289–292
    bibliography, 292

biography of, 289–290
  critical reception, 291–292
  major works and themes, 290–291
Suzuki, Esther, 244
Swinburne, A. C., 126
Symons, Arthur, 260, 263
Syquia, Lou, 102
Syquia, Serafin, 102, 238
Sze, Arthur, 5, 11, 293–303
  bibliography, 301–303
  biography of, 293–295
  critical reception, 299–301
  major works and themes, 295–299

Tabios, Eileen, 48, 50, 77, 247
Tagami, Jeff, 55
Takahashi, Kosen, 260
Takeda, Matsuko, 261
The Tale of Genji (Shikibu), 115–116
Talk Story writers conference, 83
T'ao Ch'ien (Tao Yuanming), 224, 294
Taoism, 190–191
Tay, Eddie, 216
Thomas, Dylan, 306
Thomas, Edith, 263
Thorpe, Michael, 39, 91
Throop, Anne, 128
Tietjens, Eunice, 263
Tompkins, Phyllis, 83
Torrence, Ridgely, 263
Toyama, Usaburo, 264
Tsui, Kitty, 324
Turning Japanese (Mura), 11
Tuttle, Richard, 45, 47

Uba, George, 2–4, 11, 79, 101, 108, 139,
  147, 249–250, 257, 281, 317, 352–
  353
Usui, Masami, 283, 334

Van Deusen, Marshall, 128–130
Vasudeva, Mary, 59
Verlaine, Paul, 128, 130
Vevaina, Coomi S., 39
Vietnamese Americans, 10–11, 202
Villa, José Garcia, 5, 121, 305–310
  bibliography, 309–310
  biography of, 305–306

critical reception, 308–309
  major works and themes, 306–308
Villon, François, 151
Vivien, Renée, 130

Wah, Fred, 5, 181
Wakoski, Diane, 139
Wald, Priscilla, 3, 351–352
Waley, Arthur, 263
Walker, Alice, 148
Wallace, Patricia, 3, 284–285
Wallenstein, Barry, 186
Wang, Dorothy Joan, 79
Wang, L. Ling-chi, 209
Wang Wei, 294
Warren, Robert Penn, 151
Warsh, Lewis, 121
Wat, John, 225
Watanna, Onoto (Winnifred Eaton), 260
Welch, Lew, 271
Wen Yiduo (Wen I-to), 294
Whitman, Walt, 3, 126–128, 130, 206,
  261–262
Williams, C. K., 135
Williams, Cecil, 235
Williams, William Carlos, 62, 79, 114,
  344, 350
Wojahn, David, 18
Wong, Anna May, 344
Wong, Chu, 181
Wong, Nanying Stella, 5, 311–312
  bibliography, 312
  biography of, 311
  critical reception, 312
  major works and themes, 311–312
Wong, Nellie, 313–318, 324
  bibliography, 317–318
  biography of, 313–314
  critical reception, 316–317
  major works and themes, 314–316
Wong, Rita, 8, 10, 319–322
  bibliography, 321–322
  biography of, 319–320
  critical reception, 320–321
  major works and themes, 320
Wong, Sau-ling, 151, 161, 278
Wong, Shawn, 147, 154
Wong, Sunn Shelley, 2–3, 5, 109

Woo, Merle, 8, 10, 323–329
  bibliography, 328–329
  biography of, 323–325
  critical reception, 327–328
  major works and themes, 325–327
Woodcock, George, 181
Woolf, Virginia, 32, 115
Wordsworth, William, 24, 151, 272
Wright, Charles, 135
Wylie, Eleanor, 306

Xu, Wenying, 6, 205
Xunzi (Hsun-tzu), 190

Yamada, Mitsuye (May), 281, 317, 331–
  336
  bibliography of, 335–336
  biography of, 331–332, 335–336
  critical reception, 334–335
  major works and themes, 332–334
Yamamoto, Traise, 238–239, 334
Yamanaka, Lois-Ann, 8, 84, 175, 281,
  285, 337–341
  bibliography, 340–341
  biography of, 337–338

critical reception, 339–340
  major works and themes, 338–339
Yamauchi, Wakako, 134
Yau, John, 3, 5, 10, 80, 281, 343–356
  bibliography, 353–356
  biography of, 343–344
  critical reception, 351–353
  major works and themes, 344–351
Yeats, William Butler, 285
Yee, Kelvin Han, 244
Yeh, Tzu, 225
Yen, Rhoda J., 83
Yen, Xiaoping, 45–51
Yogi, Stan, 4, 130, 151, 176, 239, 249,
  282–283
Yoshikami, Theodora, 47
Yoshimasu, Gozo, 71
Young, Jeffrey R., 21
Yu, Timothy, 352

Zhang, Benzi, 152
Zhao, Henry Yiheng, 209
Zheng, Da, 79
Zhou, Xiaojing, 4–5, 71, 113, 209, 216,
  249–250, 293, 343
Zhuangzi (Chuang Tsu), 80, 190, 297

ABOUT THE EDITOR AND CONTRIBUTORS

DI GAN BLACKBURN, a Ph.D. candidate in English at Baylor University in Waco, Texas, is writing her dissertation on "Christianity in 'Post-colonial' Fiction by Women Writers of East Asian Cultural Heritage." Her fields of interest include literature and Christianity, ethnic women's fiction, and modern and contemporary American literature; her major publications include a book article, "Trapped Daughters," in *Captive and Free* (2001), as well as poetry and dictionary entries.

CHANDRIMA CHAKRABORTY is a Ph.D. student in the English faculty at York University, Toronto, Canada. She completed her M.A. and an M.Phil. in English at Jawaharlal Nehru University in New Delhi, India, and came to Canada in 1999.

BILL CLEM is a doctoral student with emphases in American multicultural literatures and women's studies at Northern Illinois University. An instructor in English at Waubonsee Community College, Clem teaches first-year composition and American literatures.

ROCÍO G. DAVIS has degrees from the Ateneo de Manila University and the University of Navarre (Spain), where she is currently Associate Professor of American and Postcolonial Literature. Her most recent publications include *Tricks with a Glass: Writing Ethnicity in Canada* (ed. with Rosalia Baena, 2000), *Small Worlds: Transcultural Visions of Childhood* (ed. with Rosalia

Baena 2001), and *Asian American and Asian Canadian Short Story Cycles: Paradigms of a Transcultural Genre* (2001).

EDUARDO DE ALMEIDA is a doctoral student in English at the University of Chicago. He specializes in Asian American literature and critical theory. His other research interests include twentieth-century American literature, Victorian literature and culture, modernism, cinema studies, postcolonial literature and theory, and ethnic studies.

MELINDA L. DE JESÚS is Assistant Professor of Asian Pacific American Studies at Arizona State University. She teaches and writes about Asian American literature and culture, U.S. Third World feminist theory and literature, and new media pedagogy. Her work has appeared in *LIT: Literature, Interpretation, Theory, Asian American Playwrights, Sisters of Color International (SOCI) Online Journal, Works and Days, Delinquents and Debutantes*, and *Women Artists of Color: A Biocritical Sourcebook*. She is currently editing a volume of oral histories of Filipino Americans from her hometown of Bethlehem, Pennsylvania.

BRIAN KOMEI DEMPSTER is the editor of *From Our Side of the Fence: Growing Up in America's Concentration Camps* (2001). His poems have appeared in *Asian Pacific American Journal, Crab Orchard Review, Green Mountains Review, Ploughshares*, and *Quarterly West*.

ROBERT HAYASHI is writing a dissertation combining environmental and racial history with a particular focus on nikkei in Idaho and is expected to receive his Ph.D. in American Studies from the University of Massachusetts at Amherst in 2002. He has published poems in *Kansas Quarterly, Poem*, and *Allegheny Review* and has contributed to *Literature, Race, and Ethnicity: Contesting American Identities*, as well as to a forthcoming collection of chapters on early Asian American authors.

SHAWN HOLLIDAY is Assistant Professor of English at Alice Lloyd College, a small, private, liberal arts school located in Pippa Passes in southeastern Kentucky. His first book, *Thomas Wolfe and the Politics of Modernism*, is forthcoming. He is currently editing an anthology entitled *"My Back Pages": American Writers on Popular Culture*.

GUIYOU HUANG, Associate Professor and Chair of the English Department and Director of the University Honors Program, teaches American and ethnic American literatures at Kutztown University of Pennsylvania. A biographee in *Marquis Who's Who in America* (56th ed., 2001) and in *2000 Outstanding Scholars of the Twenty-First Century* (2001), he is the author of *Whitmanism, Imagism, and Modernism in China and America* (1997), *Asian, Asian American, American: Texts in Between* (forthcoming), and *The Columbia Guide to Asian American Literature* (forthcoming) and the editor of *Asian American Autobi-*

ographers: A Bio-Bibliographical Critical Sourcebook (2001). He has also published numerous articles on Walt Whitman, Ezra Pound, Charlotte Perkins Gilman, Maxine Hong Kingston, Frank Chin, Confucius, and Lao Tzu in English, as well as articles, reviews, and translations in Chinese, including articles on Mao Zedong's poetry.

SU-CHING HUANG is a Ph.D. candidate in English at the University of Rochester. She has taught at the University of Rochester and the Rochester Institute of Technology. She is completing her dissertation on the politics of mobility in Asian American and Asian diaspora literatures. Her article on Chinese American writer/artist Chiang Yee was published in *Crossings: Travel, Art, Literature, Politics*, edited by Rudolphus Teeuwen and Shu-li Chang (2001).

NIKOLAS HUOT is a doctoral candidate in English at Georgia State University. His research interests include Asian American and African American literatures.

MICHELE JANETTE received her Ph.D. from Yale University in 1997. She is currently an Assistant Professor of English at Kansas State University. She has published articles on Maxine Hong Kingston and Velina Hasu Houston and is working on a volume of Vietnamese immigrant narratives.

ROY OSAMU KAMADA is a Ph.D. candidate in English at the University of California at Davis. He has taught at Davis, the University of Virginia, and for Kearny Street Workshop. His work has appeared in *The Diasporic Imagination: Identifying Asian-American Representations in America* and *Ecological Poetry: A Critical Introduction*. He has received grants from the James Irvine Foundation and the Vermont Studio Center, awards from the Academy of American Poets, and a Henry Hoyns Fellowship at the University of Virginia. He is currently completing work on his dissertation, "Postcolonial Romanticisms: Landscape and the Possibilities of Inheritance."

GAIK CHENG KHOO received her Ph.D. from the University of British Columbia, Canada, in interdisciplinary studies. Her areas of interest include Southeast Asia, postcolonial theory and literature, gender studies, and film. Her articles on Malaysian film and literature appear in *West Coast Line* and upcoming anthologies such as *Risking Malaysia, Refocusing: Women Filmmakers*. Aside from teaching in these fields, she is also a creative writer and is currently working on a would-be novel.

JOE KRAUS received his Ph.D. in American literature from Northwestern University in 2000 and is Assistant Professor of English at King's College in Wilkes-Barre, Pennsylvania. He is coauthor of *An Accidental Anarchist* (1998), and his work has appeared in *American Scholar, MELUS*, and *Centennial Review*.

KEITH LAWRENCE is Associate Professor of English at Brigham Young University. He received his Ph.D. in English from the University of Southern California (1987) and teaches courses in Asian American, early American, and world literatures. He is completing a book on early American narratives and coediting a collection of articles on Asian American authors before 1960. In 1999, the General Education Program at Brigham Young awarded him a three-year Alcuin Fellowship for excellence in teaching.

JAMES KYUNG-JIN LEE is Assistant Professor of English and Asian American Studies at the University of Texas at Austin and serves as an associate editor of *The Heath Anthology of American Literature* (4th edition) and book-review editor of *Amerasia Journal*. He has published articles in *Literary Studies: East and West*, *Korean Culture*, and other critical collections. He is currently at work on a book-length project on race, redevelopment, and contemporary urban U.S. narratives.

LAVONNE LEONG is completing her doctorate in English literature at Oxford University. She has been awarded the United Kingdom's Overseas Research Scholarship and is a Worcester College Senior Scholar. Her teaching and research interests include British modernism and Victorian literature, Asian American literature, postcolonial literature, and contemporary American literature.

EDWARD MARX received his Ph.D. from the City University of New York and has taught at the City College of New York, the University of Minnesota, and Kyoto University. He is currently working on a biography of Yone Noguchi.

ROWENA TOMANENG MATSUNARI received her B.A. in English at the University of California at Irvine and her M.A. in English at the University of California at Santa Barbara. She currently teaches English and women's studies at De Anza College in Cupertino, California. Her teaching and research focus on ethnic American literature and cultural studies.

NINA MORGAN is Assistant Professor of English at Kennesaw State University in Kennesaw, Georgia, where she teaches critical theory and ethnic American literature. She has been an editor of the *Review of Japanese Culture and Society* and the review editor of *Asian America*. Her recent publications include interviews with Shirley Geok-lin Lim and with Frank Chin (in *The Diasporic Imagination: Identifying Asian-American Representations in America*, 2000).

PETER E. MORGAN teaches literature and cultural studies at the University of West Georgia.

LINDA TRINH MOSER received a Ph.D. in English from the University of California at Davis and is currently Assistant Professor of English at Southwest

Missouri State University. She teaches undergraduate and graduate courses in ethnic American literature and non-European world literature. Her research focuses on the writers Sui Sin Far and Onoto Watanna as well as on issues related to those of mixed race. She is currently editing a collection entitled " 'The Love of Sakuro Jiro and the Three-headed Maiden' and Other Short Works by Onoto Watanna."

TAMIKO NIMURA is currently pursuing her doctoral degree at the University of Washington. Her work has been published in the *San Francisco Chronicle* and *Rafu Shimpo*.

GAYLE K. SATO, a sansei from Hawaii, is Professor of English at Meiji University in Tokyo. She has been living and teaching in Japan since 1987. Her articles have appeared in various journals and collections of criticism, including *MELUS, Amerasia Journal, Japanese Journal of American Studies, Reading the Literatures of Asian America*, and *The Oxford Companion to Women's Writing in the United States*.

PURVI SHAH is finishing her dissertation at Rutgers University, where she has taught courses on American literature, women writers, and composition. Her research interests include anthologies and canonization, Asian American literature, and contemporary poetry. Among other places, she has had articles published in *Dragon Ladies: Asian American Feminists Breathe Fire* and *Asian Pacific American Journal*.

ERNEST J. SMITH received his doctorate from New York University and is Associate Professor of English at the University of Central Florida, where he teaches courses in modern American literature. His publications include a book on Hart Crane, *"The Imaged Word": The Infrastructure of Hart Crane's White Buildings*, as well as articles on Crane, John Berryman, Edna St. Vincent Millay, Marianne Moore, Adrienne Rich, and other poets.

GEORGE UBA is Professor of English and former chair of the Department of Asian American Studies, California State University at Northridge. He has published widely on Asian American poetry and on such contemporary writers as Marilyn Chin, Jessica Hagedorn, Garrett Hongo, David Mura, and John Yau. His most recent publication is the chapter "Coordinates of Asian American Poetry: A Survey of the History and a Guide to Teaching" in *A Resource Guide to Asian American Literature*, edited by Sau-ling Cynthia Wong and Stephen H. Sumida (2001).

WENYING XU is Associate Professor of English at Florida Atlantic University. She teaches and researches U.S. ethnic literatures and late-nineteenth-century American fiction. Her scholarly and creative works have appeared in *Prairie*

Schooner, Victorian Literature and Culture, Modern Language Studies, Paintbrush, Philosophy and Social Action, Asian American Novelists, Asian American Autobiographers, Room of One's Own, and *MELUS.*

RHODA J. YEN, a 1999 graduate of Georgetown University Law Center, is an attorney and free-lance writer living in West Palm Beach, Florida, whose primary research interests include race and gender issues and the law. Her scholarly articles have appeared in *Computer Law Review and Technology Journal, Asian Law Journal,* and *Bulletin of Law and Technology.*

XIAOPING YEN is Associate Professor of English at LaGuardia Community College in New York. He teaches writing, literature, and journalism and is the author of *The Peony Pavilion,* a novel based on the sixteenth-century Chinese opera.

ZHOU XIAOJING received her Ph.D. in English from the Memorial University of Newfoundland, Canada, and teaches at the State University of New York at Buffalo. Her publications include *Elizabeth Bishop: Rebel "in Shades and Shadows"* (1999) and numerous articles in anthologies and journals. Her major teaching and research interests are Asian American media arts and Asian American literature, particularly poetry, fiction, and autobiography.